KEKKAISHI

結界師(けっかいし)

19

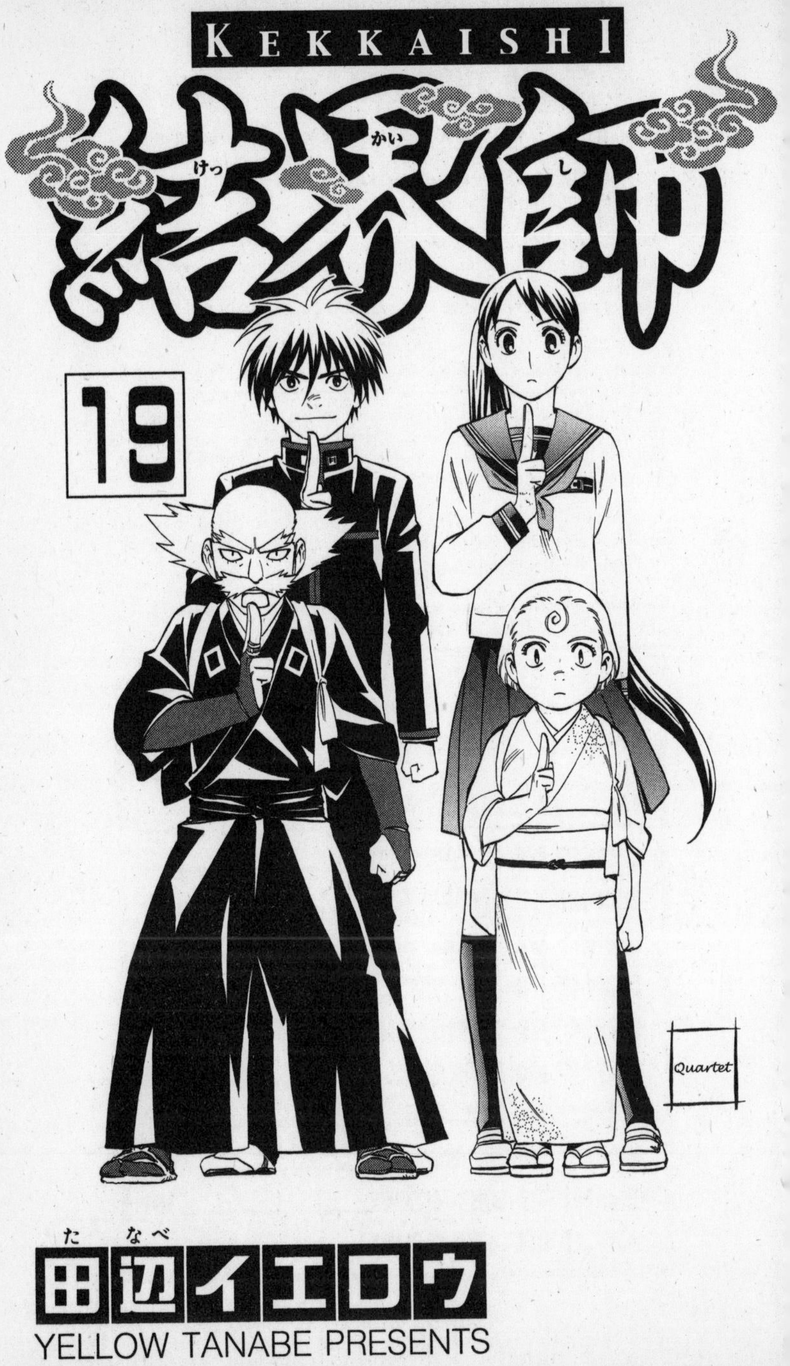
Quartet

田辺(たなべ)イエロウ

YELLOW TANABE PRESENTS

The Story Thus Far

Yoshimori Sumimura and Tokine Yukimura have an ancestral duty to protect the Karasumori Forest from supernatural beings called ayakashi. People with their gift for terminating ayakashi are called kekkaishi, or "barrier masters."

When Yoshimori starts the ninth grade, the Shadow Organization enrolls Night Troopers Shu and Sen in the Karasumori school system to monitor the kekkaishi guardians. Secretly, Shu is studying to develop his telepathic powers and possibly abandon the Night Troops.

One day, an ayakashi in the form of a tiny black butterfly enters the Karasumori School grounds... The mysterious creature multiplies exponentially despite Yoshimori and his colleagues' desperate efforts to terminate it and its "offspring." Soon the school is engulfed in a cloud of talking butterflies who warn of impending doom! Then they begin to attack the students...

Yoshimori's grandfather Shigemori and Tokine's grandmother Tokiko rush to their grandchildren's aid. For the first time, all four kekkaishi heirs will stand and fight together!

The quartet pitches a huge cubic kekkai to envelop the mass of butterflies. Will they be able to maintain their formation and coordinate their energies in time to save hundreds of innocent students...?

KEKKAISHI VOL. 19

TABLE OF CONTENTS

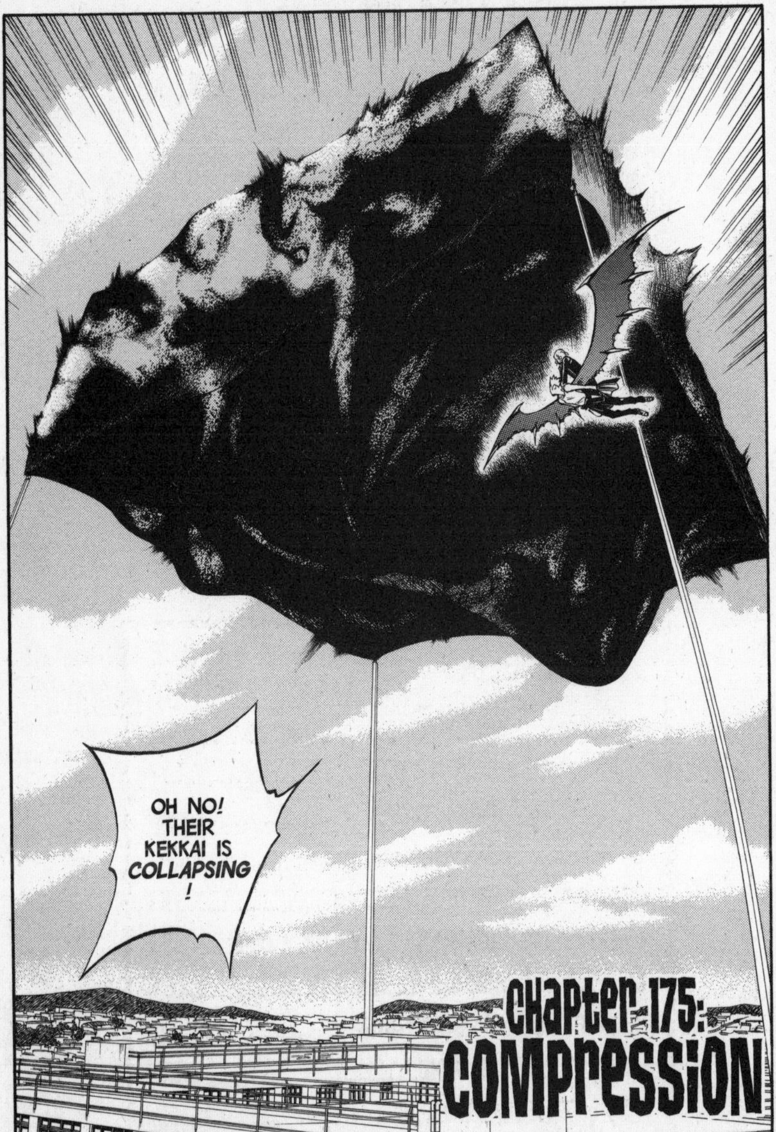
OH NO! THEIR KEKKAI IS COLLAPSING!
Chapter 175: Compression

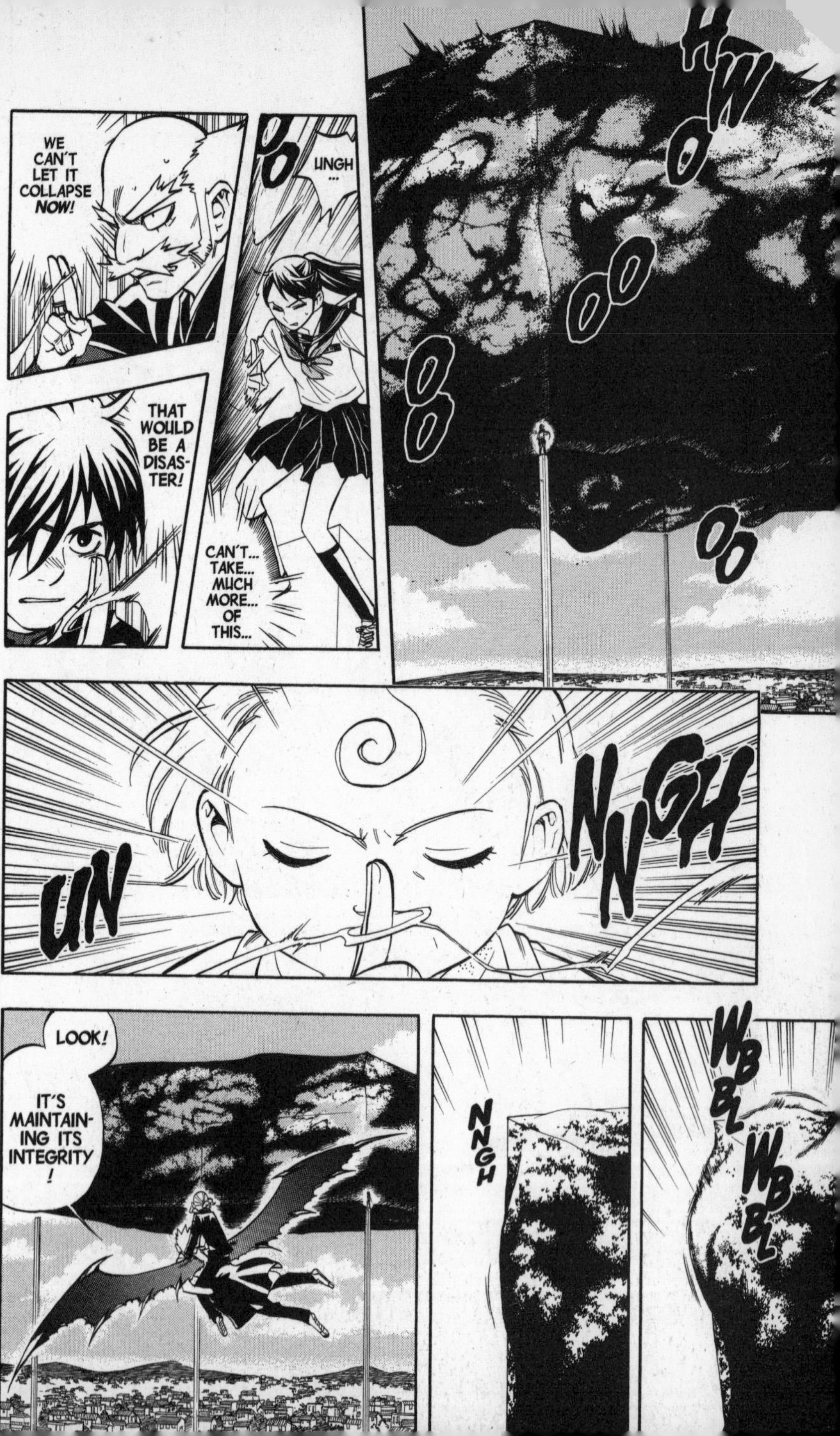
HWOOOOOOOOO
UNGH...
CAN'T... TAKE... MUCH MORE... OF THIS...
WE CAN'T LET IT COLLAPSE NOW!
THAT WOULD BE A DISASTER!
UNNNGH
WBBL WBBL
NNGH
LOOK!
IT'S MAINTAINING ITS INTEGRITY!

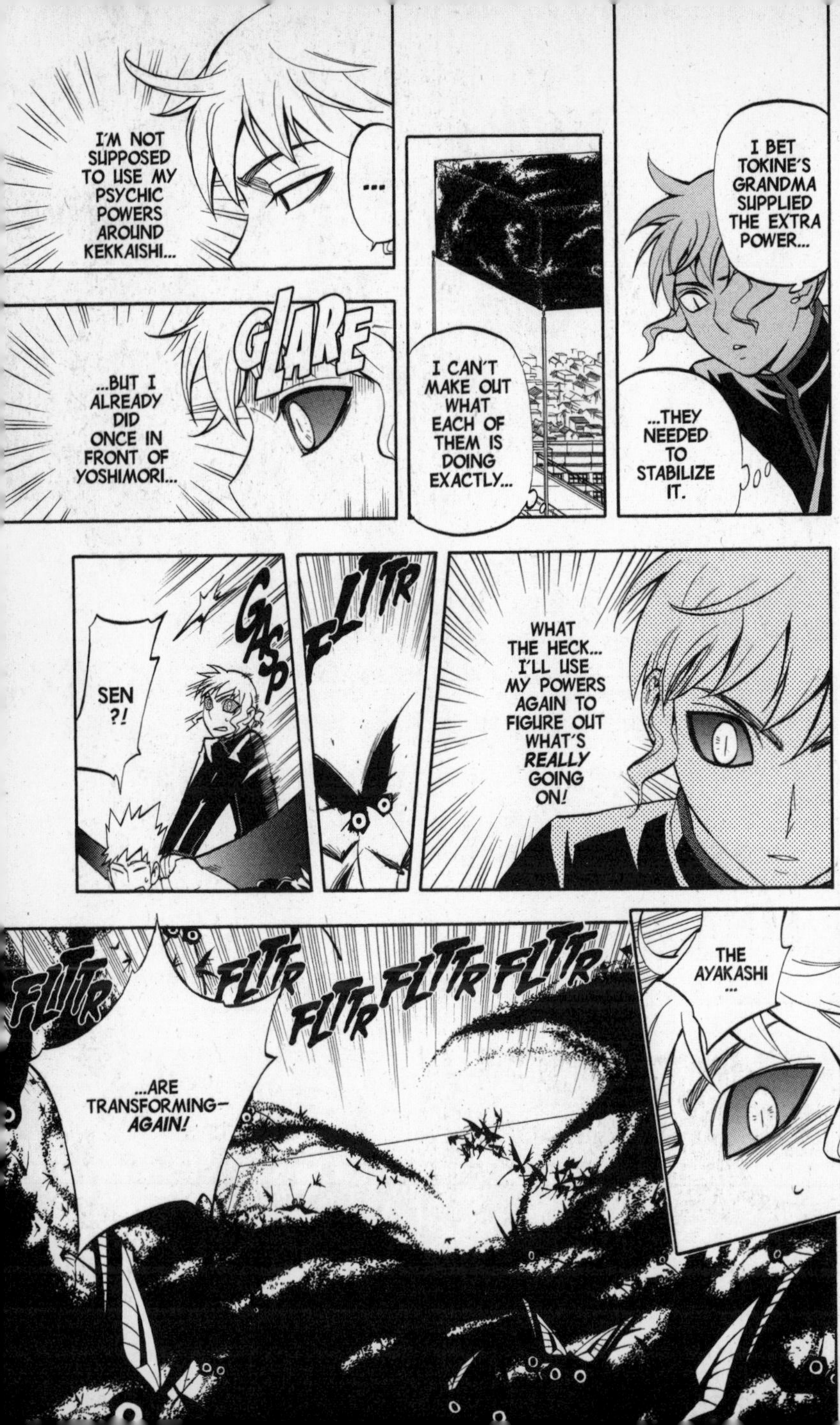
I BET TOKINE'S GRANDMA SUPPLIED THE EXTRA POWER...
...THEY NEEDED TO STABILIZE IT.
I CAN'T MAKE OUT WHAT EACH OF THEM IS DOING EXACTLY...
...
I'M NOT SUPPOSED TO USE MY PSYCHIC POWERS AROUND KEKKAISHI...
GLARE
...BUT I ALREADY DID ONCE IN FRONT OF YOSHIMORI...
WHAT THE HECK... I'LL USE MY POWERS AGAIN TO FIGURE OUT WHAT'S *REALLY* GOING ON!
FLITTR
GASP
SEN ?!
THE AYAKASHI ...
FLITTR FLITTR FLITTR FLITTR
FLITTR
FLITTR
...ARE TRANSFORMING— *AGAIN!*

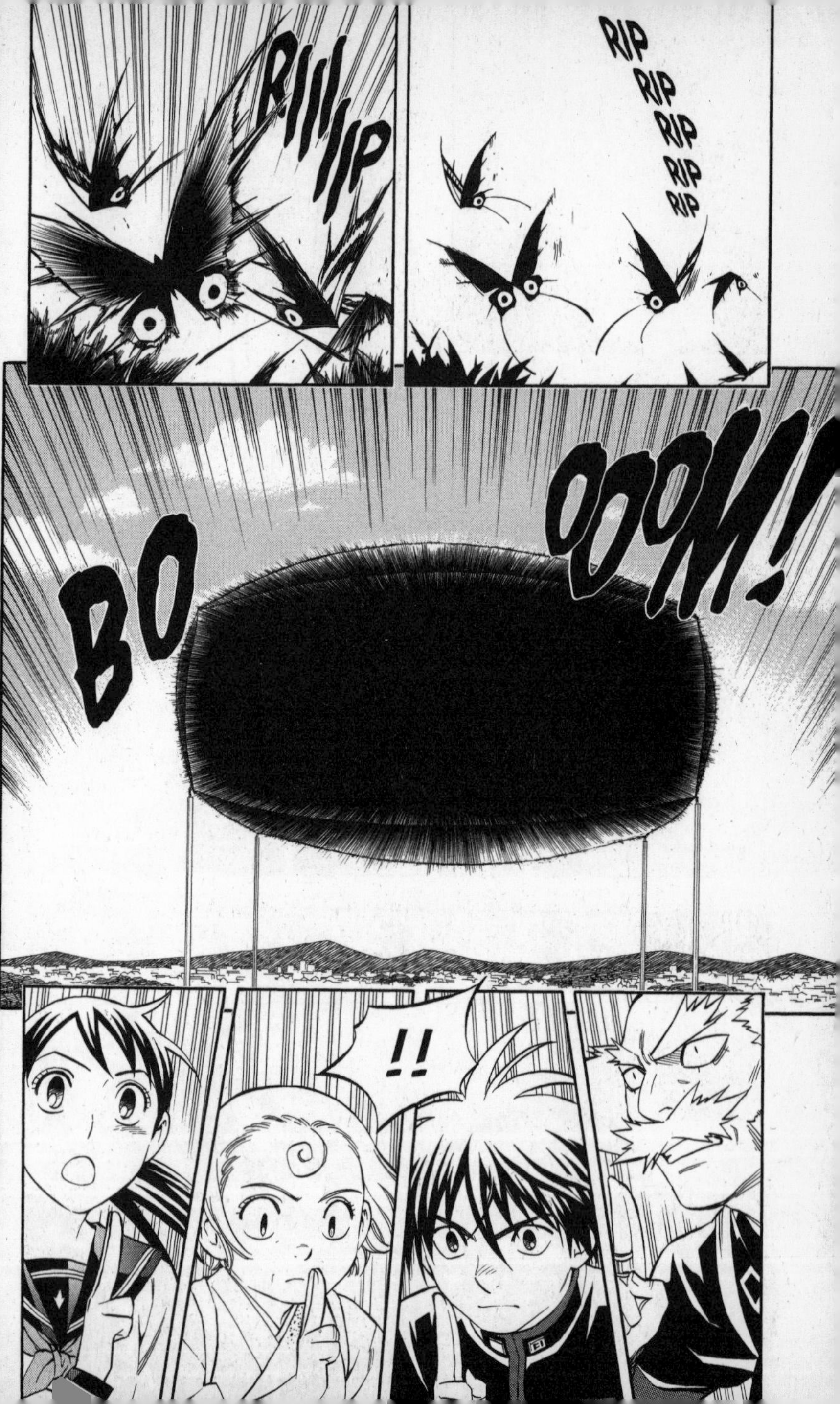
RIP
RIP
RIP
RIP
RIP
RIIIIIP
BOOOOM!!
!!

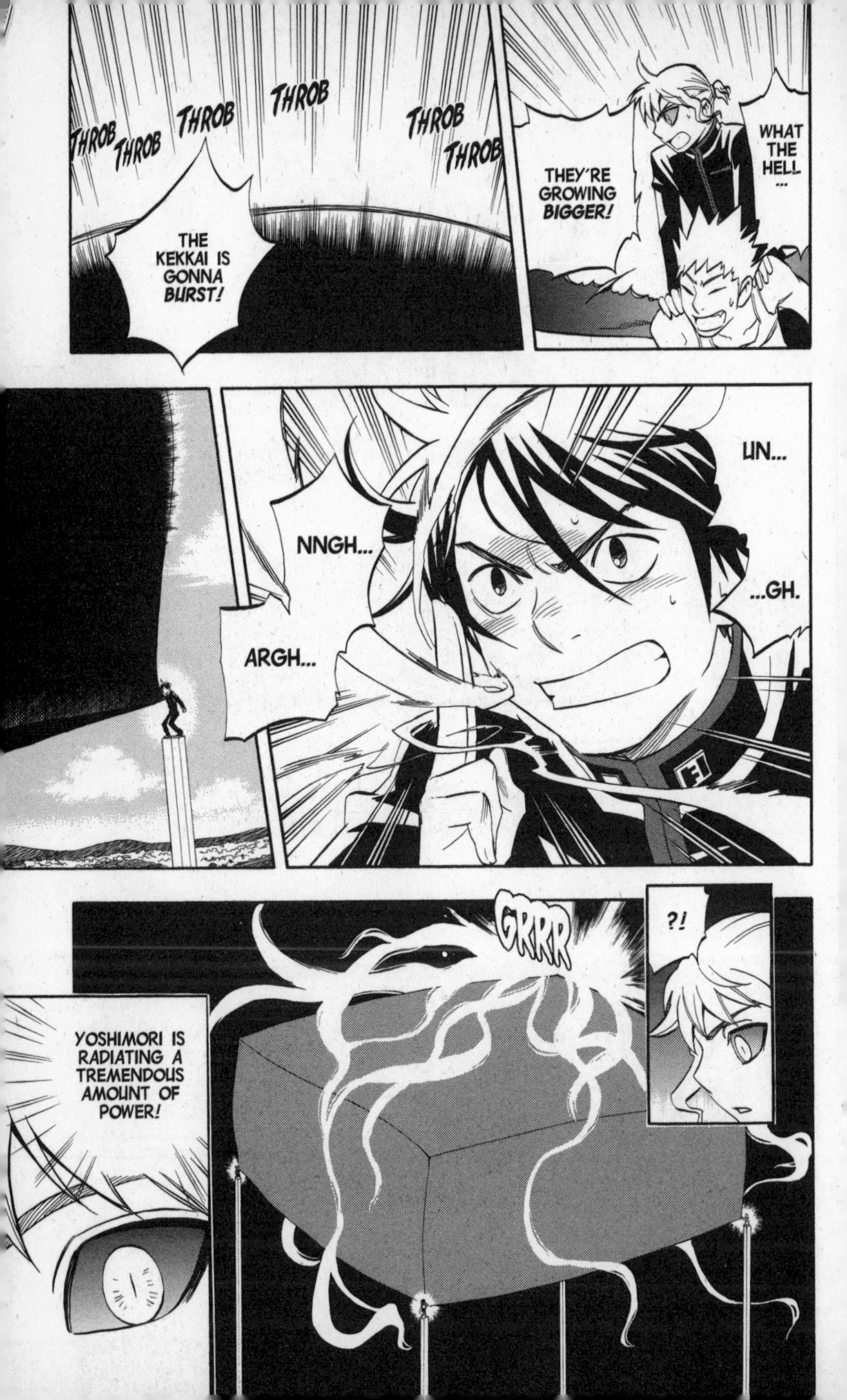
WHAT THE HELL...
THEY'RE GROWING BIGGER!
THROB THROB THROB THROB THROB THROB
THE KEKKAI IS GONNA BURST!
UN...
...GH.
NNGH...
ARGH...
?!
GRRR
YOSHIMORI IS RADIATING A TREMENDOUS AMOUNT OF POWER!

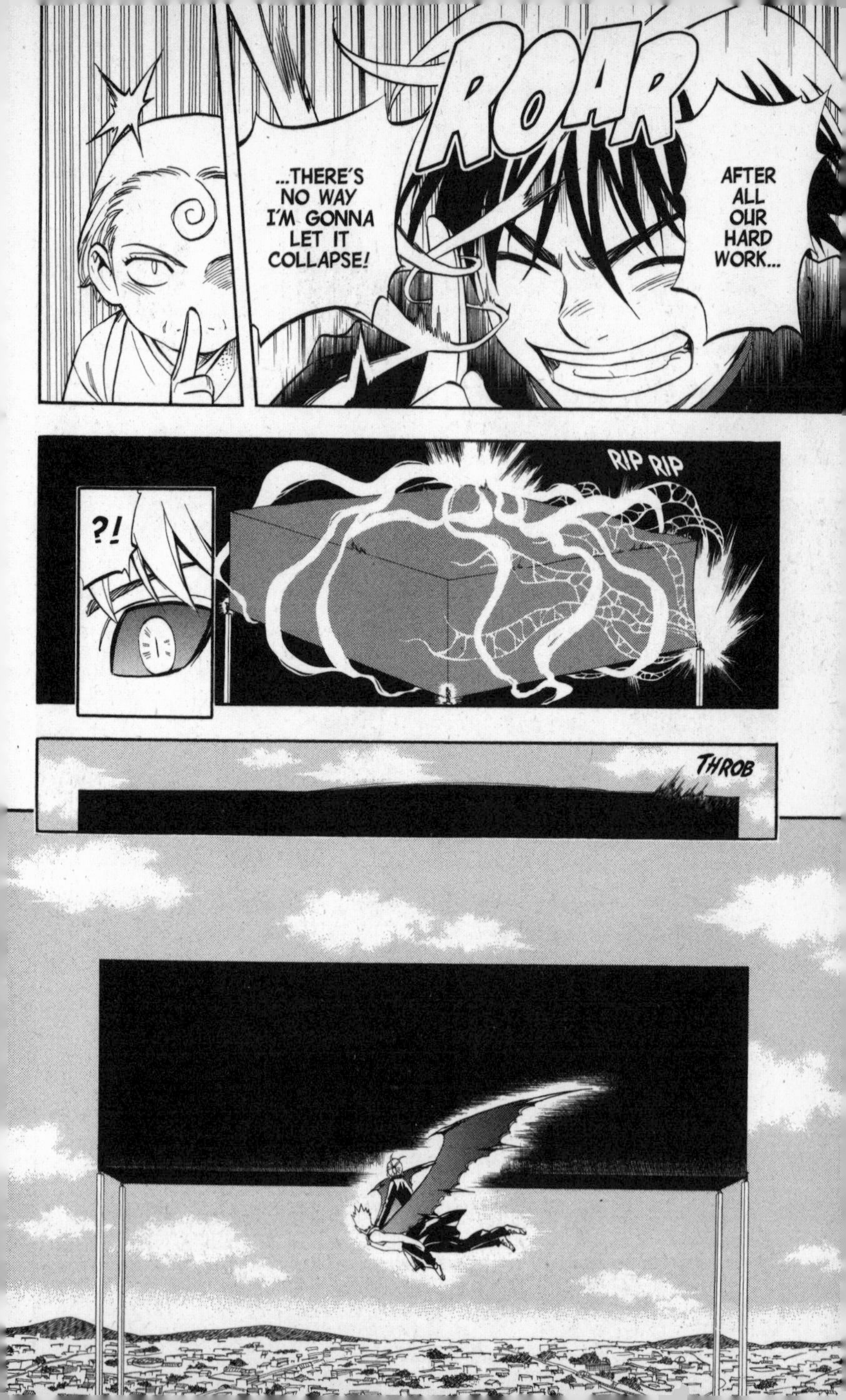
ROAR
AFTER ALL OUR HARD WORK...
...THERE'S NO WAY I'M GONNA LET IT COLLAPSE!
RIP RIP
?!
THROB

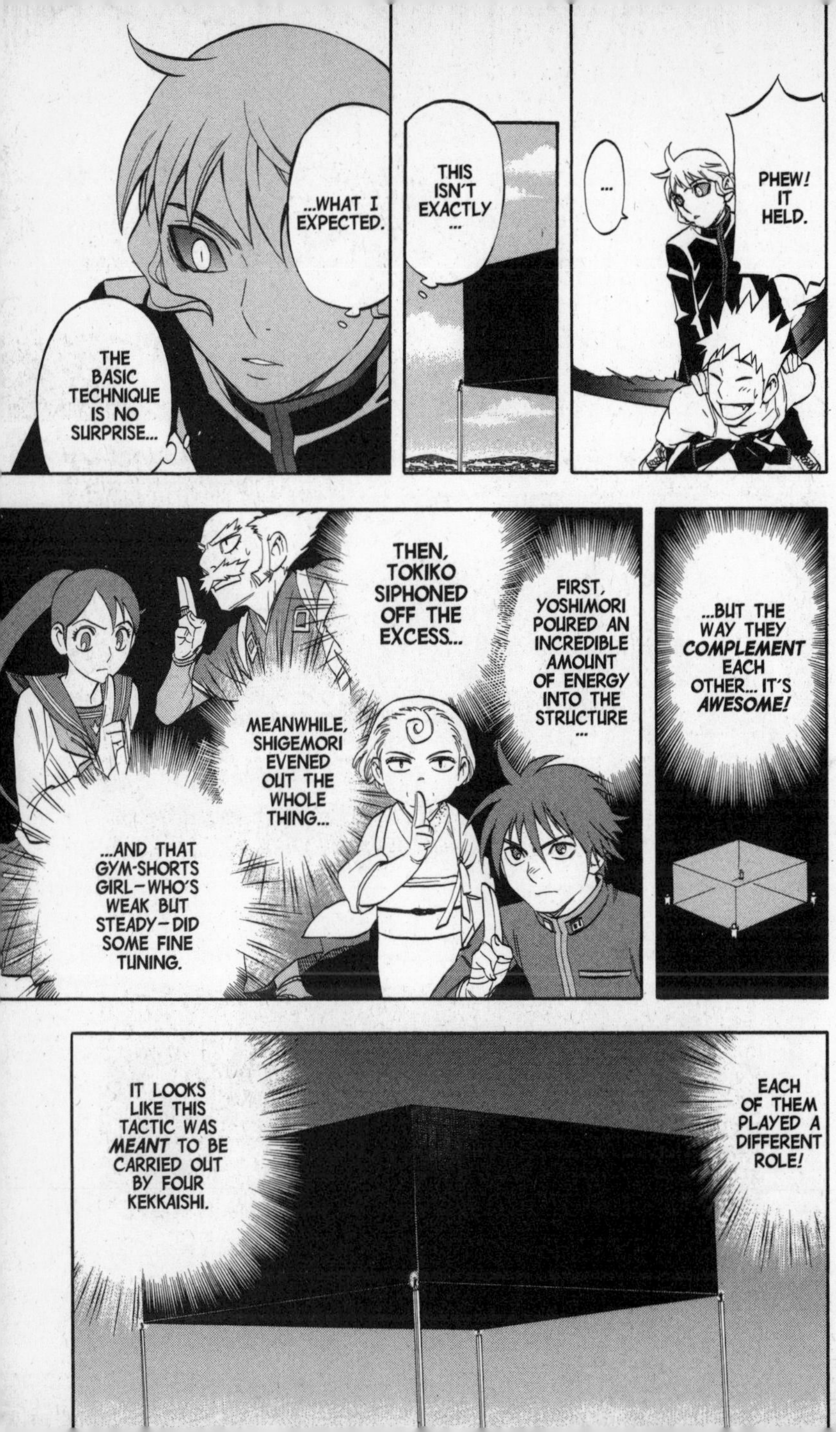
PHEW! IT HELD.
...
THIS ISN'T EXACTLY ...
...WHAT I EXPECTED.
THE BASIC TECHNIQUE IS NO SURPRISE...
...BUT THE WAY THEY *COMPLEMENT* EACH OTHER... IT'S *AWESOME!*
FIRST, YOSHIMORI POURED AN INCREDIBLE AMOUNT OF ENERGY INTO THE STRUCTURE ...
THEN, TOKIKO SIPHONED OFF THE EXCESS...
MEANWHILE, SHIGEMORI EVENED OUT THE WHOLE THING...
...AND THAT GYM-SHORTS GIRL—WHO'S WEAK BUT STEADY—DID SOME FINE TUNING.
EACH OF THEM PLAYED A DIFFERENT ROLE!
IT LOOKS LIKE THIS TACTIC WAS *MEANT* TO BE CARRIED OUT BY FOUR KEKKAISHI.

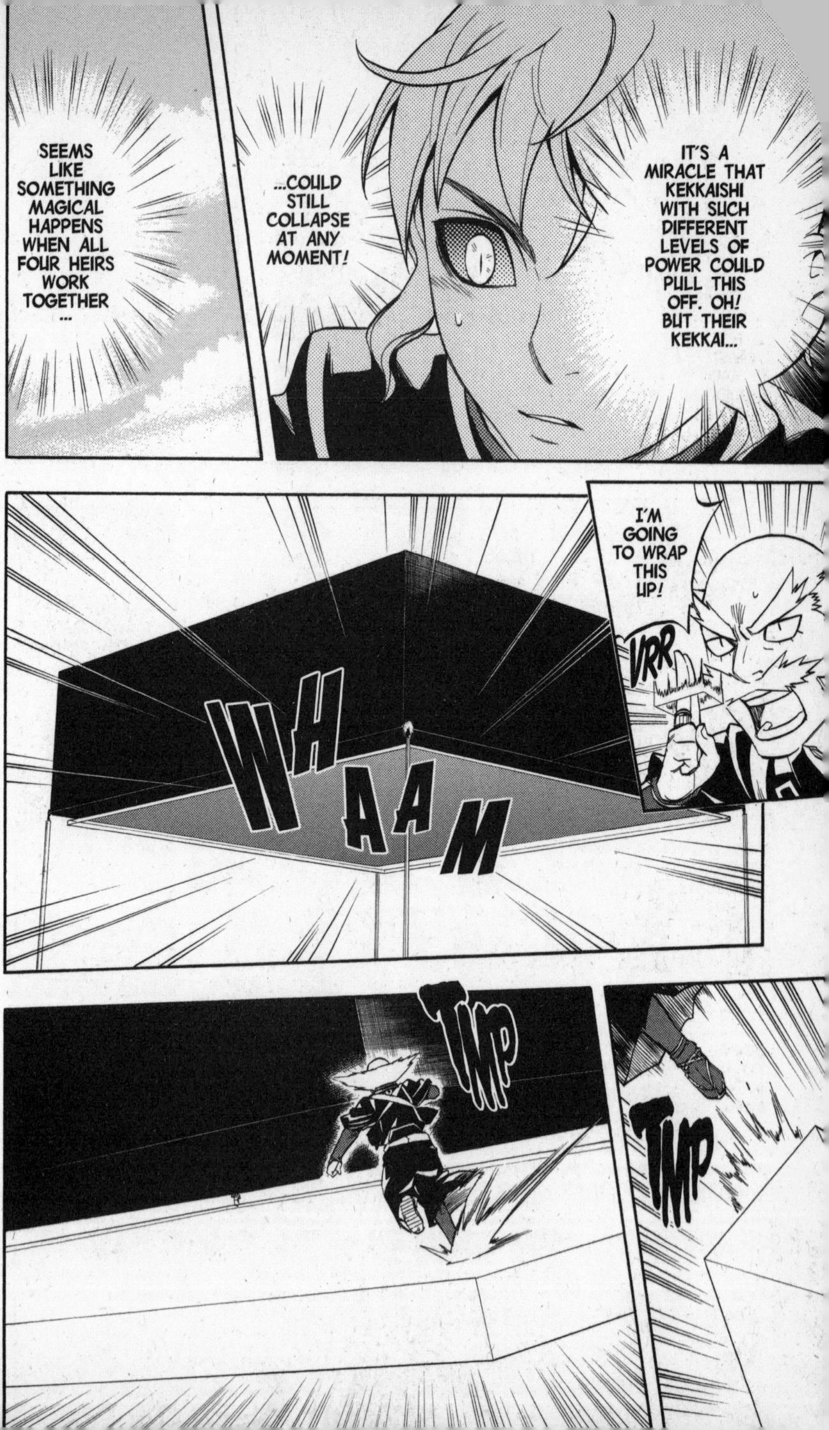
IT'S A MIRACLE THAT KEKKAISHI WITH SUCH DIFFERENT LEVELS OF POWER COULD PULL THIS OFF. OH! BUT THEIR KEKKAI...
...COULD STILL COLLAPSE AT ANY MOMENT!
SEEMS LIKE SOMETHING MAGICAL HAPPENS WHEN ALL FOUR HEIRS WORK TOGETHER ...
I'M GOING TO WRAP THIS UP!
VRR
WHAAM
TMP
TMP

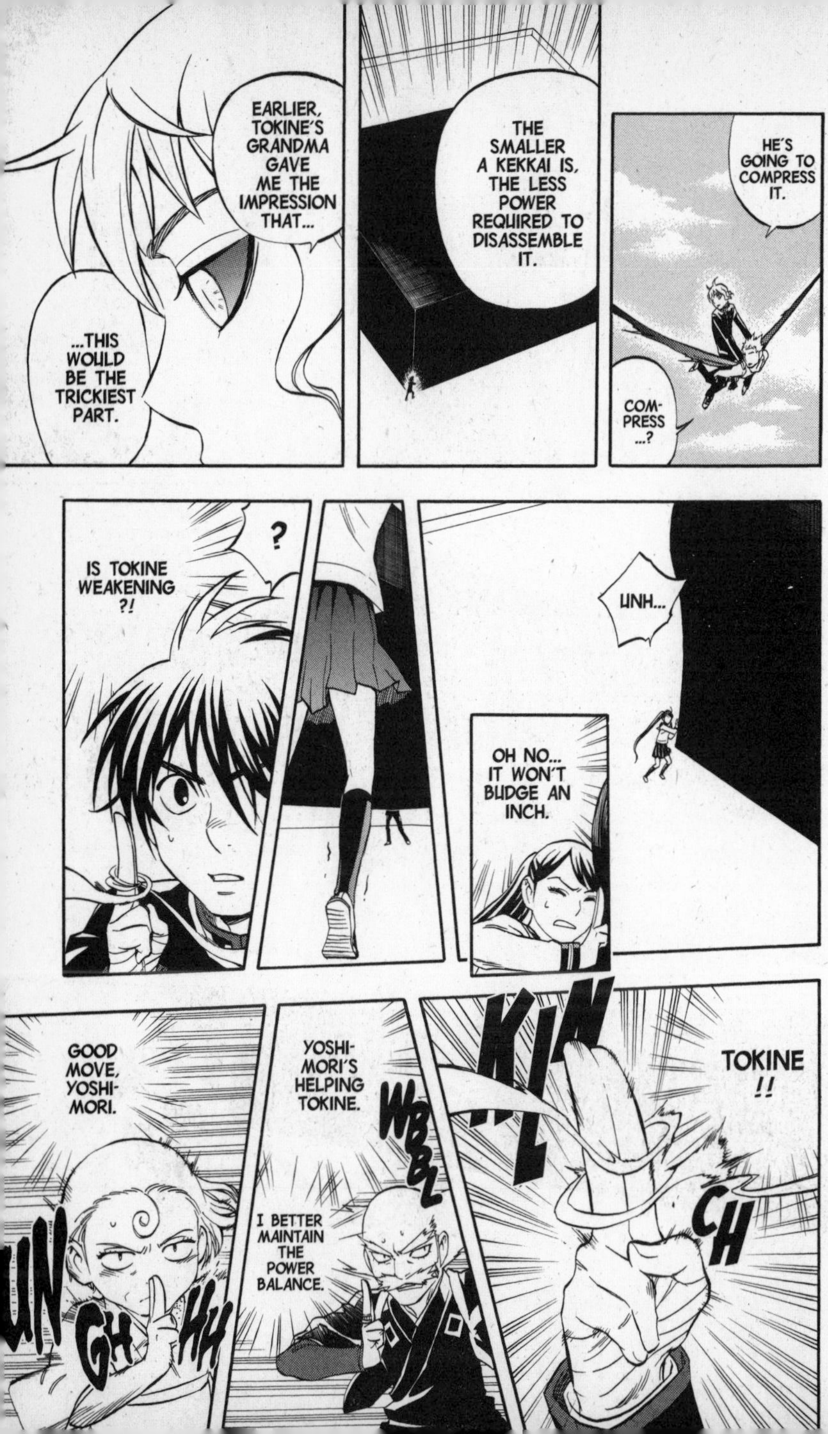
HE'S GOING TO COMPRESS IT.
COMPRESS ...?
THE SMALLER A KEKKAI IS, THE LESS POWER REQUIRED TO DISASSEMBLE IT.
EARLIER, TOKINE'S GRANDMA GAVE ME THE IMPRESSION THAT...
...THIS WOULD BE THE TRICKIEST PART.
UNH...
OH NO... IT WON'T BUDGE AN INCH.
?
IS TOKINE WEAKENING ?!
KLIN
TOKINE !!
CH
YOSHI-MORI'S HELPING TOKINE.
WBBL
I BETTER MAINTAIN THE POWER BALANCE.
GOOD MOVE, YOSHI-MORI.
UNGHHH

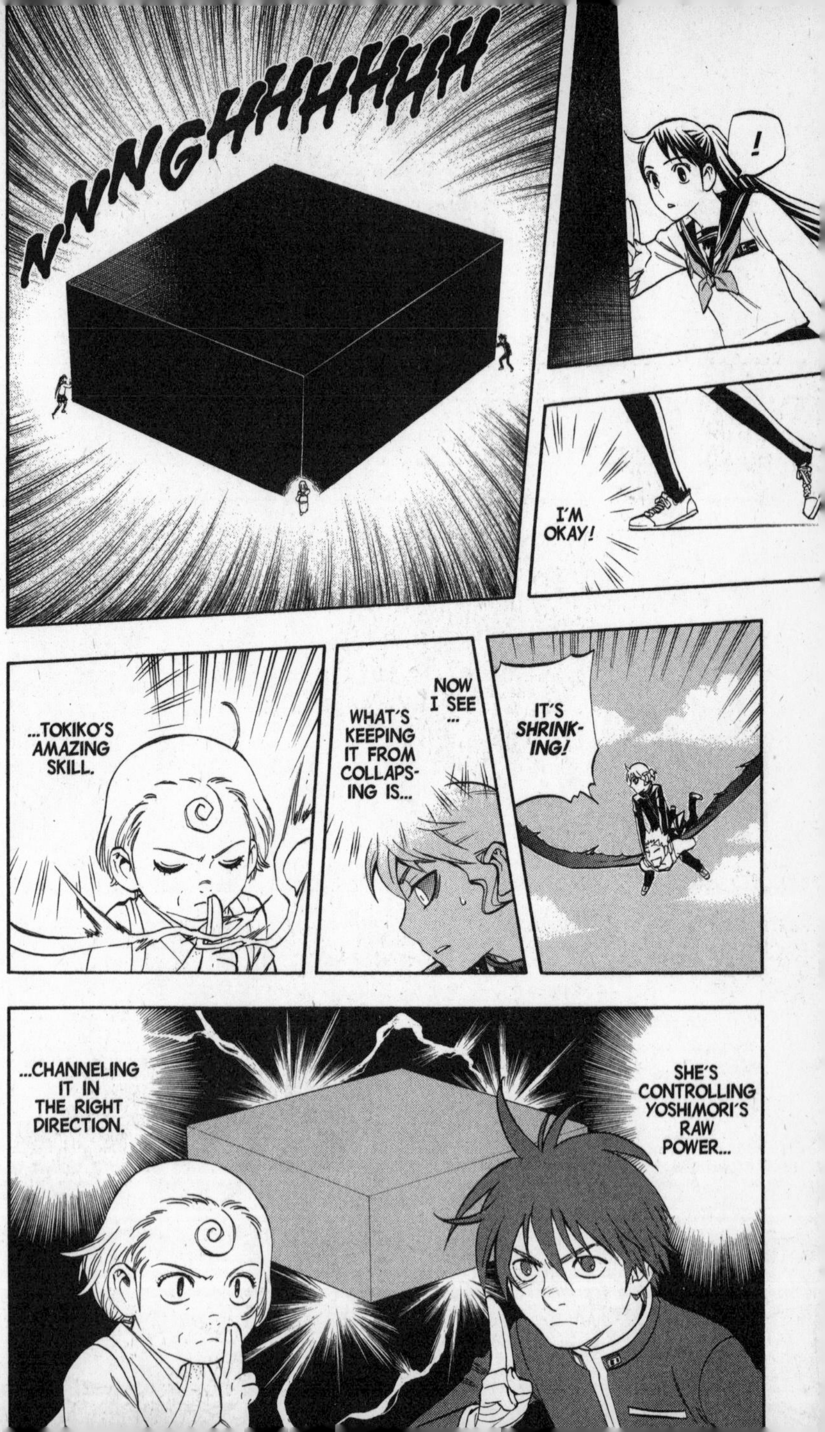
!
I'M OKAY!
N-NNGHHHHHHH
IT'S SHRINKING!
NOW I SEE...
WHAT'S KEEPING IT FROM COLLAPSING IS...
...TOKIKO'S AMAZING SKILL.
SHE'S CONTROLLING YOSHIMORI'S RAW POWER...
...CHANNELING IT IN THE RIGHT DIRECTION.

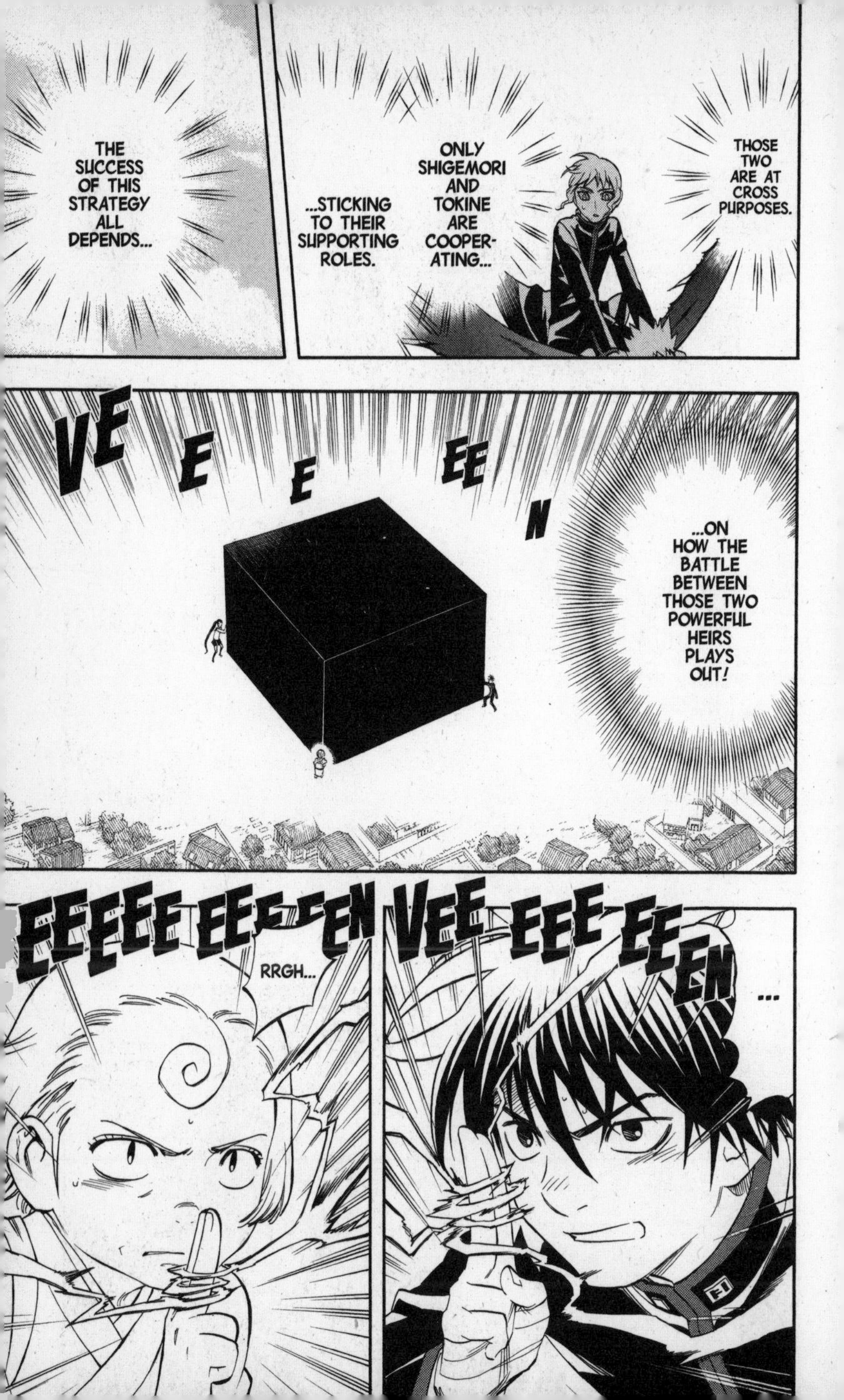
THOSE TWO ARE AT CROSS PURPOSES.
ONLY SHIGEMORI AND TOKINE ARE COOPERATING...
...STICKING TO THEIR SUPPORTING ROLES.
THE SUCCESS OF THIS STRATEGY ALL DEPENDS...
VEEEEEN
...ON HOW THE BATTLE BETWEEN THOSE TWO POWERFUL HEIRS PLAYS OUT!
VEEEEEEEEEN...
EEEEEEEEEEEN
RRGH...

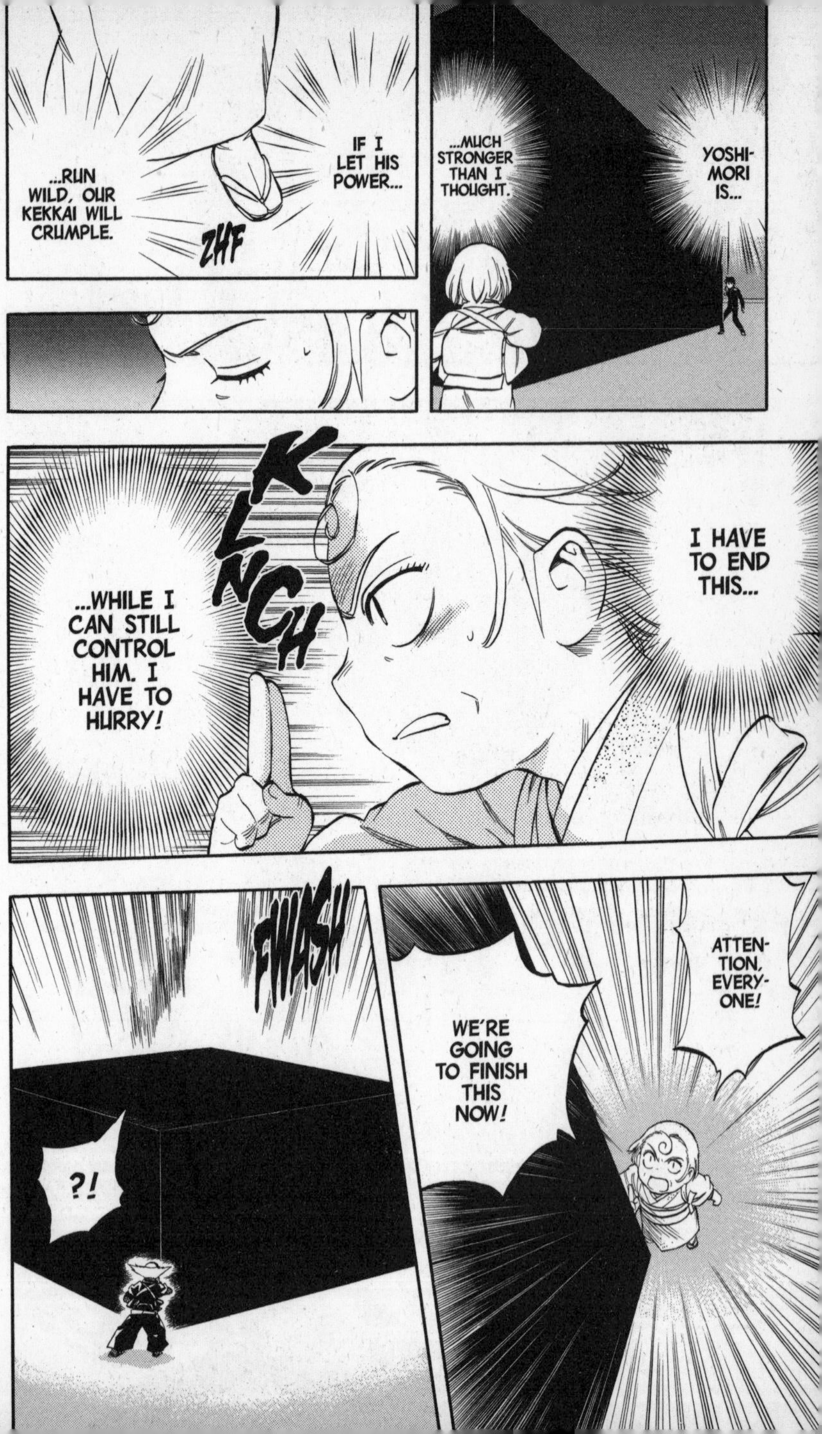
YOSHI-MORI IS...
...MUCH STRONGER THAN I THOUGHT.
IF I LET HIS POWER...
...RUN WILD, OUR KEKKAI WILL CRUMPLE.
ZHF
KLNCH
I HAVE TO END THIS...
...WHILE I CAN STILL CONTROL HIM. I HAVE TO HURRY!
ATTEN-TION, EVERY-ONE!
WE'RE GOING TO FINISH THIS NOW!
FWASH
?!

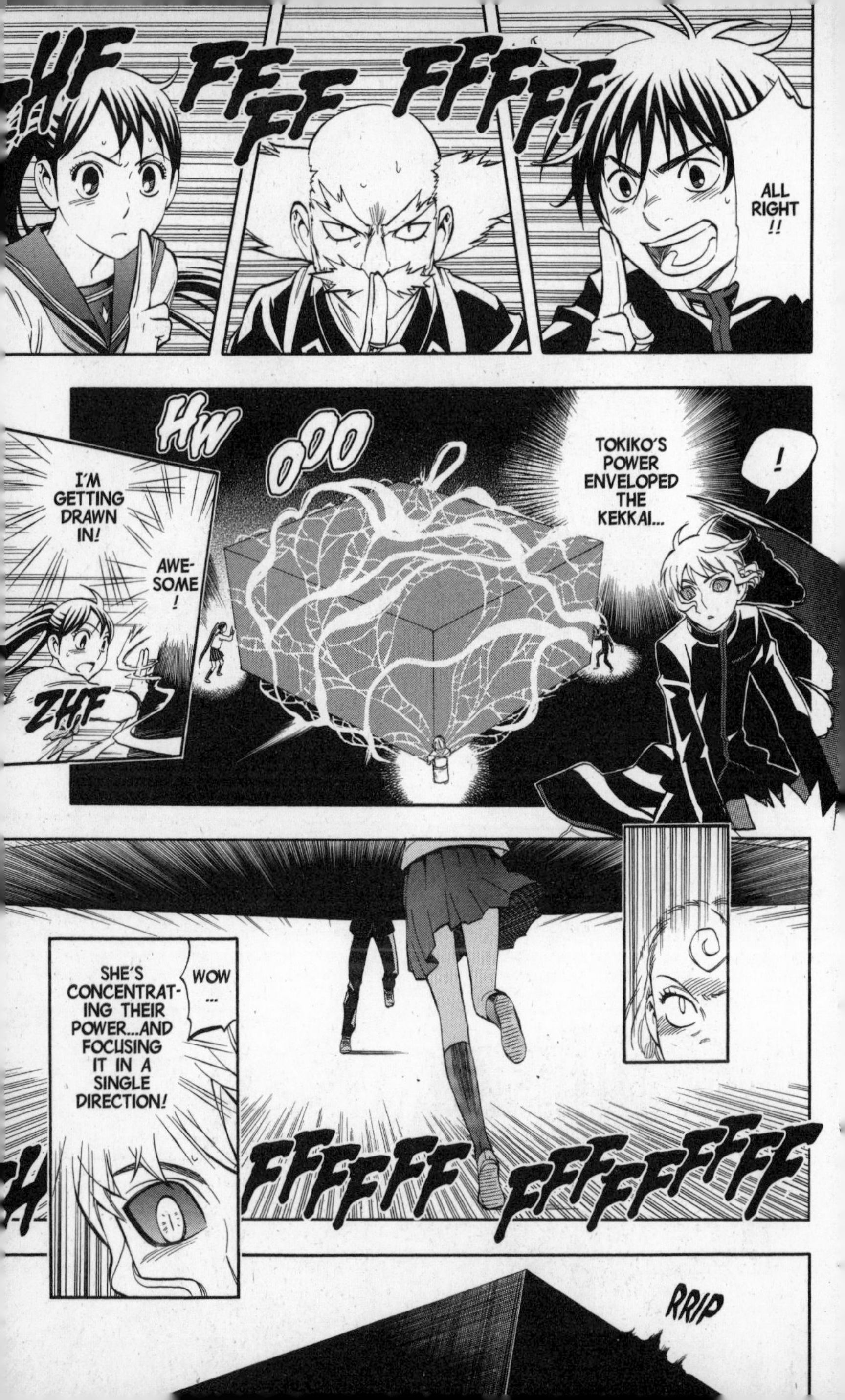
HF FFFF FFFFFF
ALL RIGHT !!
TOKIKO'S POWER ENVELOPED THE KEKKAI...
!
HW OOO
I'M GETTING DRAWN IN!
AWE-SOME!
ZHF
WOW ...
SHE'S CONCENTRAT-ING THEIR POWER...AND FOCUSING IT IN A SINGLE DIRECTION!
H FFFFFF FFFFFFFFF
RRIP

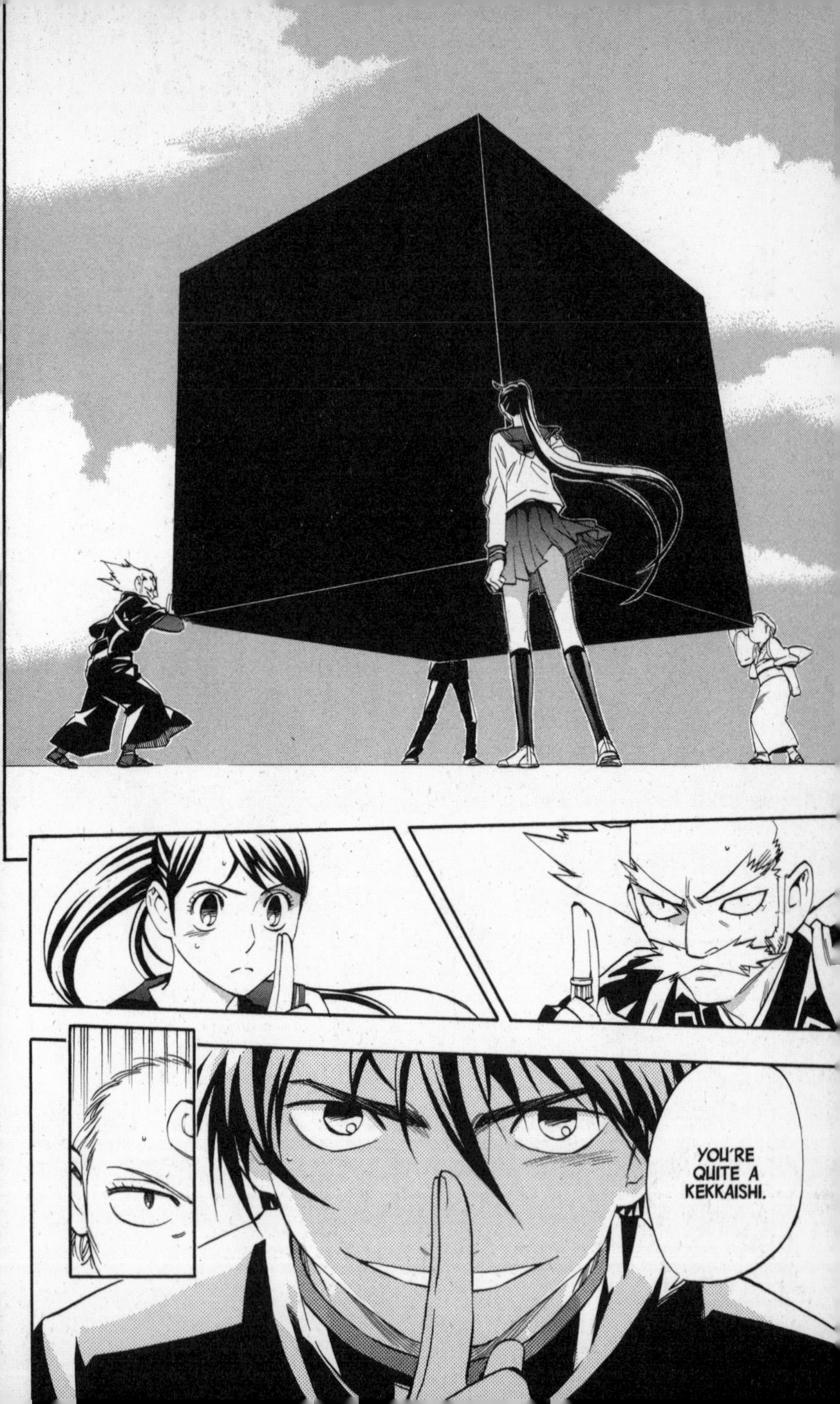
YOU'RE QUITE A KEKKAISHI.

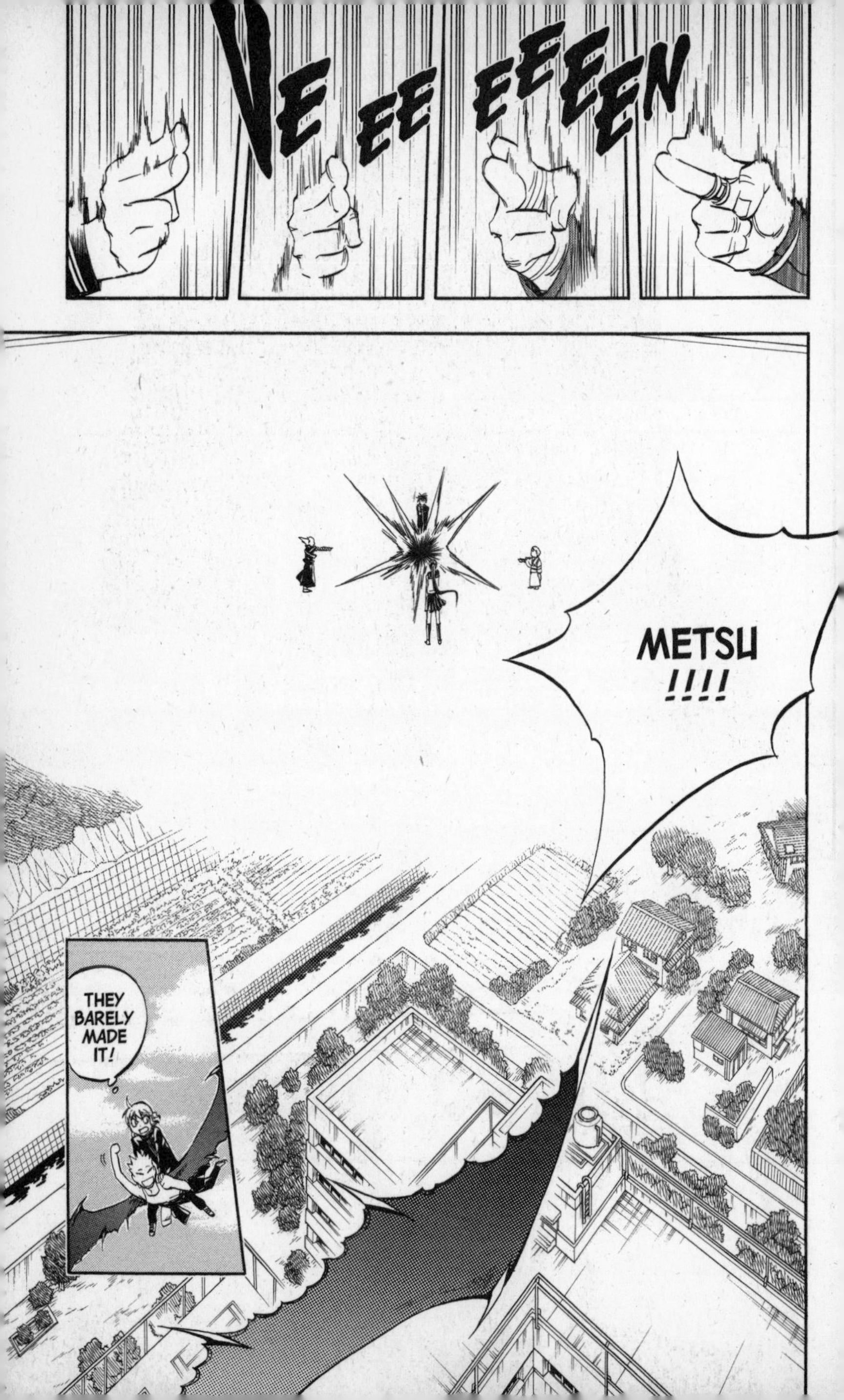
VEEEEEEEN
METSU!!!!
THEY BARELY MADE IT!

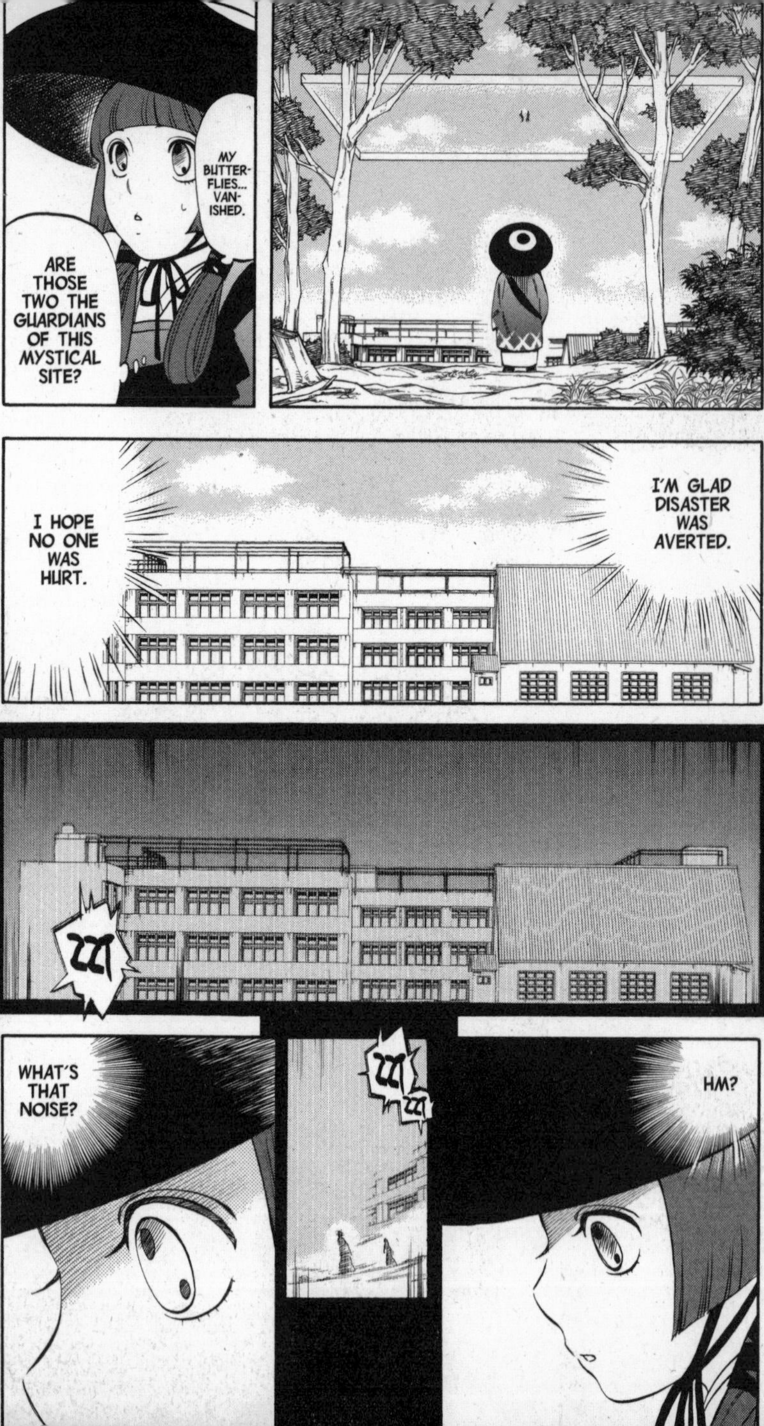
MY BUTTER-FLIES... VAN-ISHED.
ARE THOSE TWO THE GUARDIANS OF THIS MYSTICAL SITE?
I'M GLAD DISASTER WAS AVERTED.
I HOPE NO ONE WAS HURT.
HM?
WHAT'S THAT NOISE?

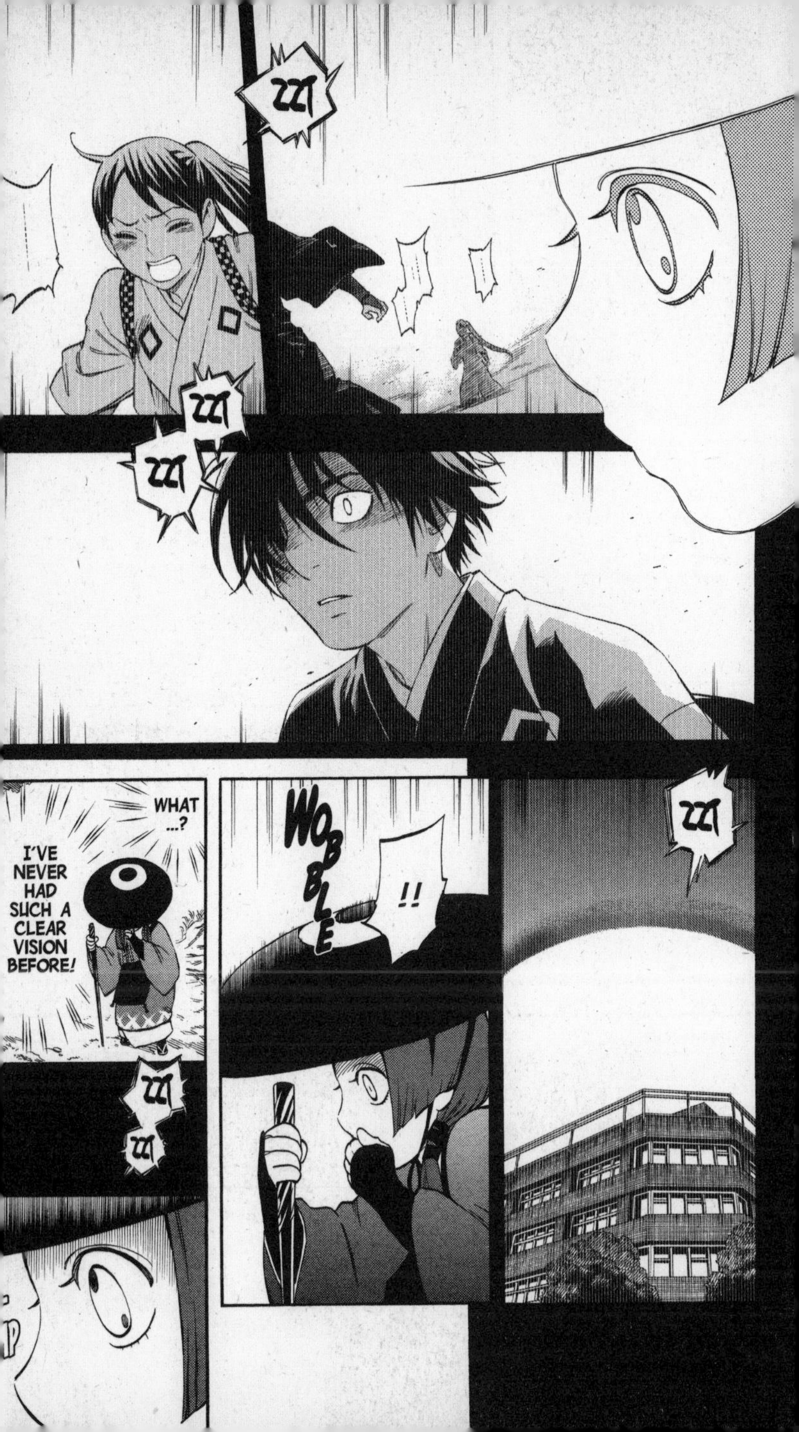
ZZT
ZZT
ZZT
ZZT
WOBBLE
!!
WHAT ...?
I'VE NEVER HAD SUCH A CLEAR VISION BEFORE!
ZZT
ZZT

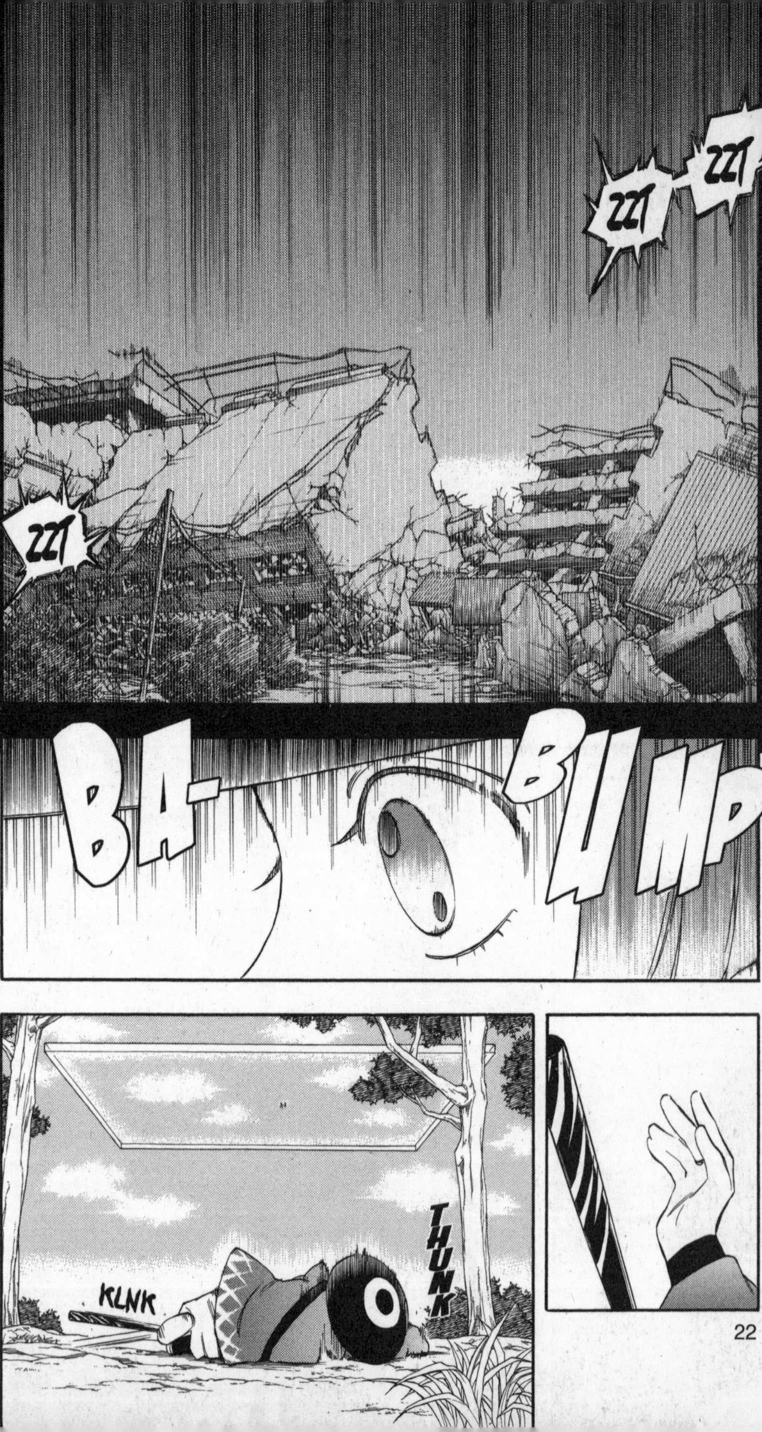
ZZT
ZZT
ZZT
BA-BUMP
THUNK
KLNK

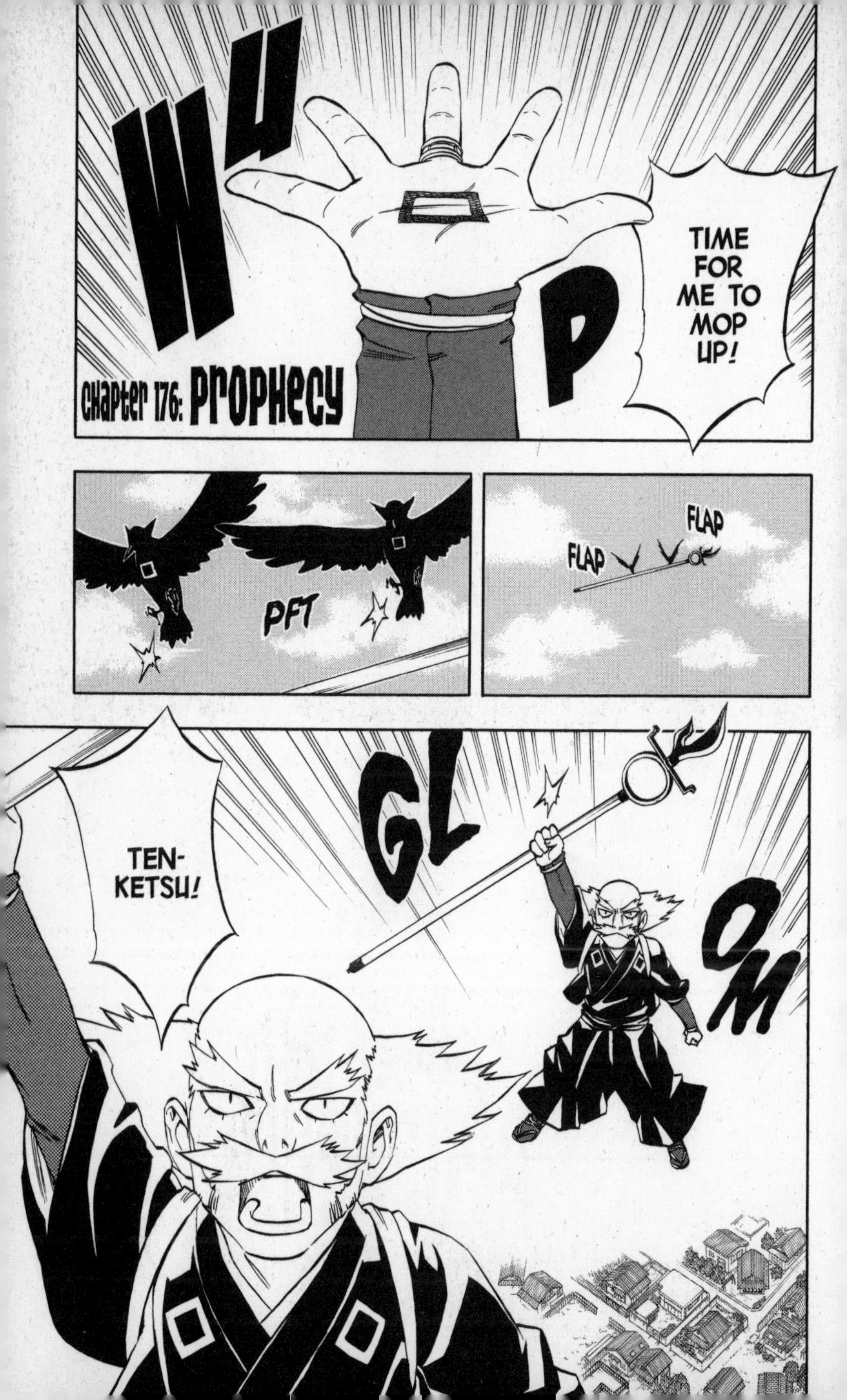
TIME FOR ME TO MOP UP!
Chapter 176: Prophecy
FLAP
FLAP
PFT
GLOM
TEN-KETSU!

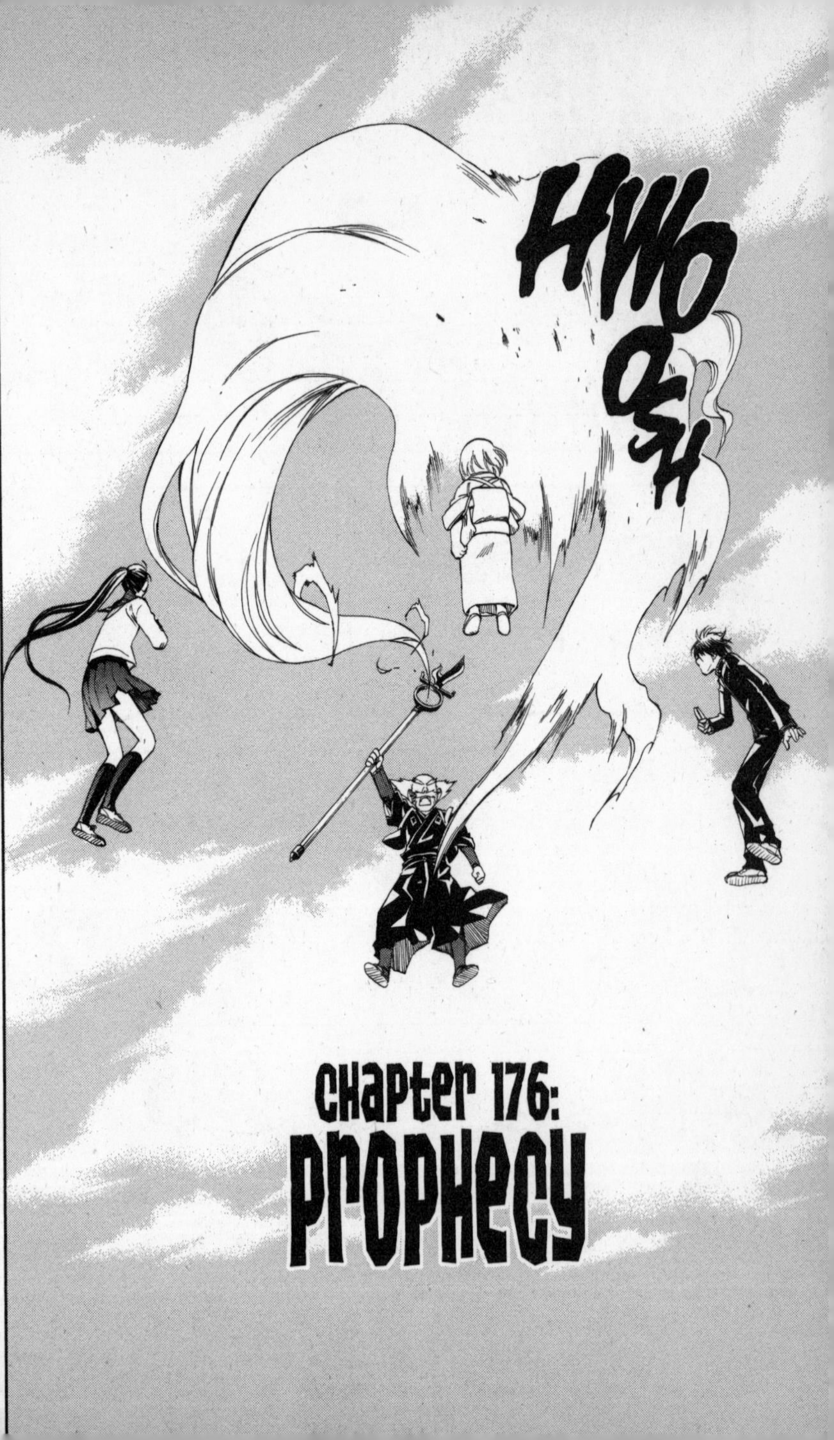
HWOOSH

Chapter 176:
Prophecy

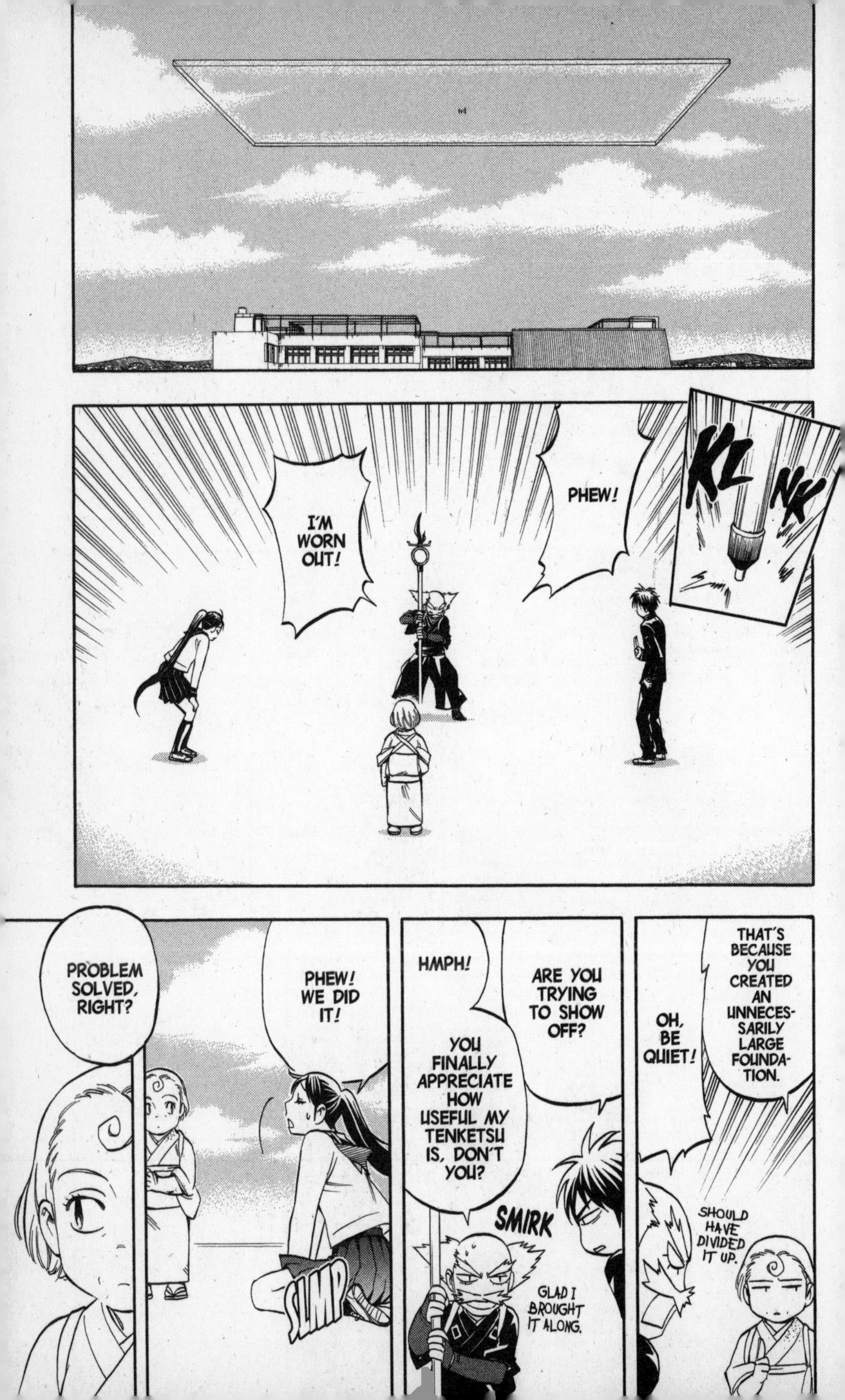
KLINK
PHEW!
I'M WORN OUT!
THAT'S BECAUSE YOU CREATED AN UNNECES-SARILY LARGE FOUNDA-TION.
OH, BE QUIET!
SHOULD HAVE DIVIDED IT UP.
ARE YOU TRYING TO SHOW OFF?
HMPH!
YOU FINALLY APPRECIATE HOW USEFUL MY TENKETSU IS, DON'T YOU?
SMIRK
GLAD I BROUGHT IT ALONG.
PHEW! WE DID IT!
SLUMP
PROBLEM SOLVED, RIGHT?

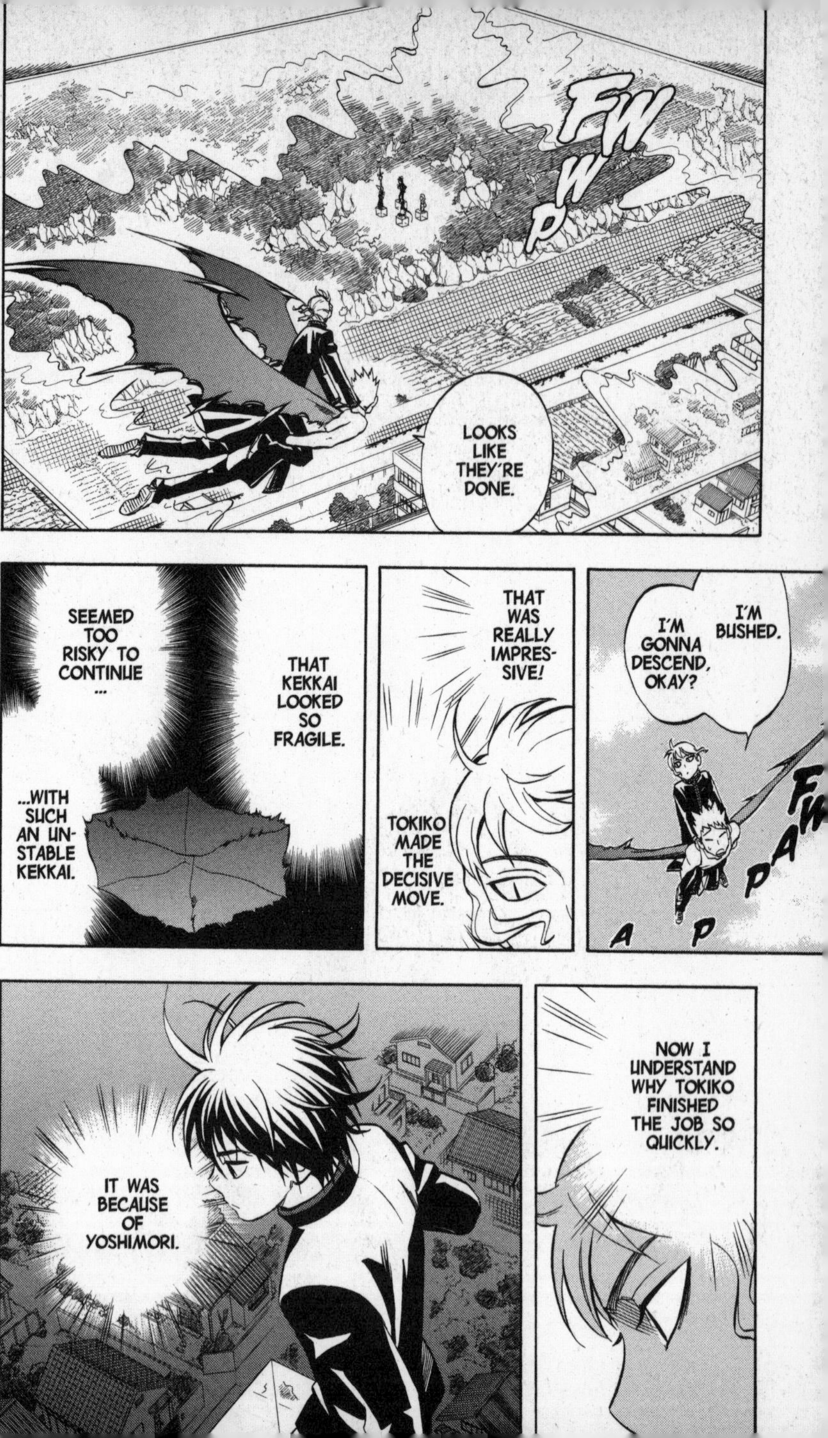
FWWP
LOOKS LIKE THEY'RE DONE.
I'M BUSHED.
I'M GONNA DESCEND, OKAY?
FWAP
AP
THAT WAS REALLY IMPRESSIVE!
TOKIKO MADE THE DECISIVE MOVE.
THAT KEKKAI LOOKED SO FRAGILE.
SEEMED TOO RISKY TO CONTINUE...
...WITH SUCH AN UNSTABLE KEKKAI.
NOW I UNDERSTAND WHY TOKIKO FINISHED THE JOB SO QUICKLY.
IT WAS BECAUSE OF YOSHIMORI.

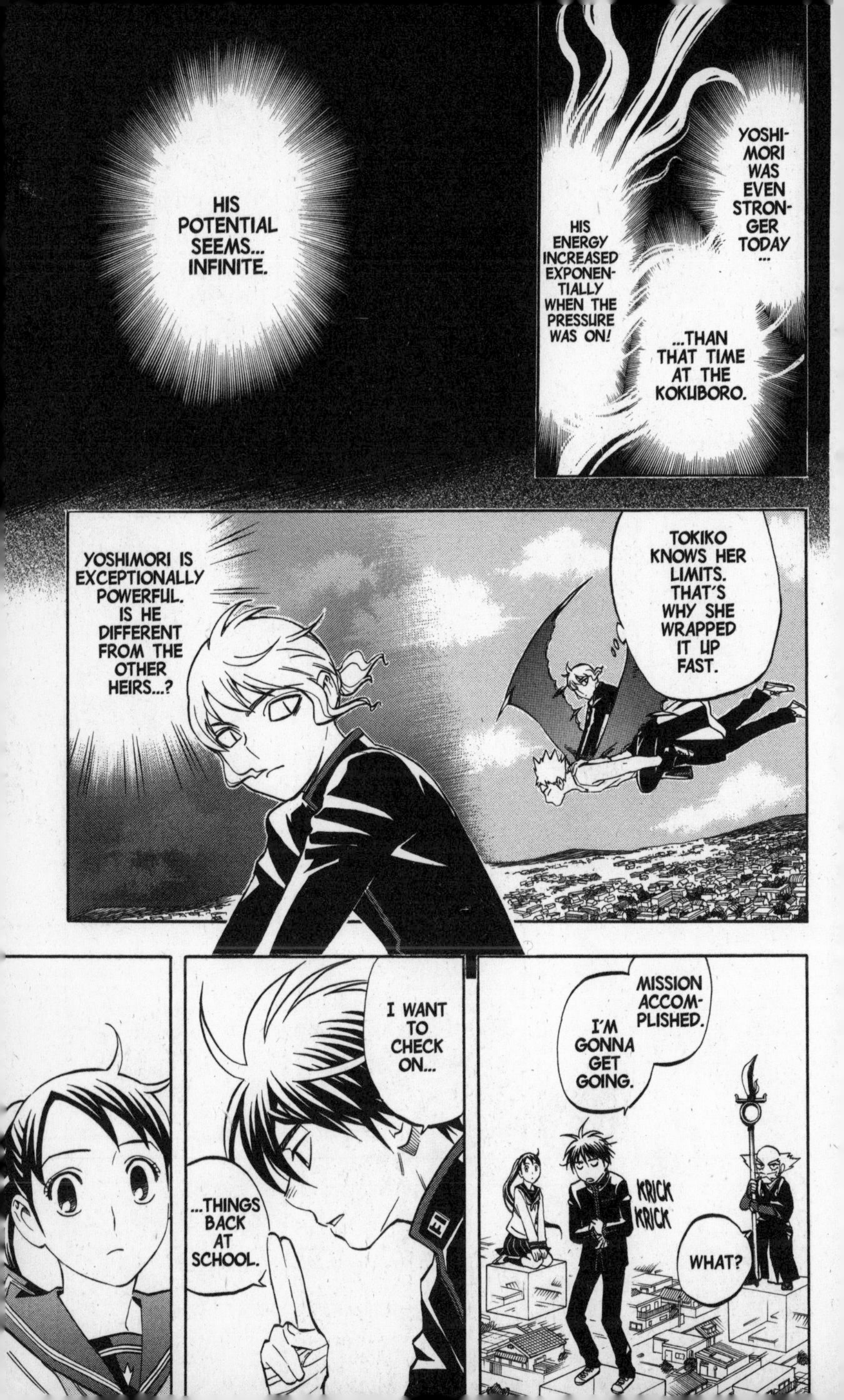
YOSHIMORI WAS EVEN STRONGER TODAY...
...THAN THAT TIME AT THE KOKUBORO.
HIS ENERGY INCREASED EXPONENTIALLY WHEN THE PRESSURE WAS ON!
HIS POTENTIAL SEEMS... INFINITE.
TOKIKO KNOWS HER LIMITS. THAT'S WHY SHE WRAPPED IT UP FAST.
YOSHIMORI IS EXCEPTIONALLY POWERFUL. IS HE DIFFERENT FROM THE OTHER HEIRS...?
MISSION ACCOMPLISHED.
I'M GONNA GET GOING.
KRICK KRICK
WHAT?
I WANT TO CHECK ON...
...THINGS BACK AT SCHOOL.

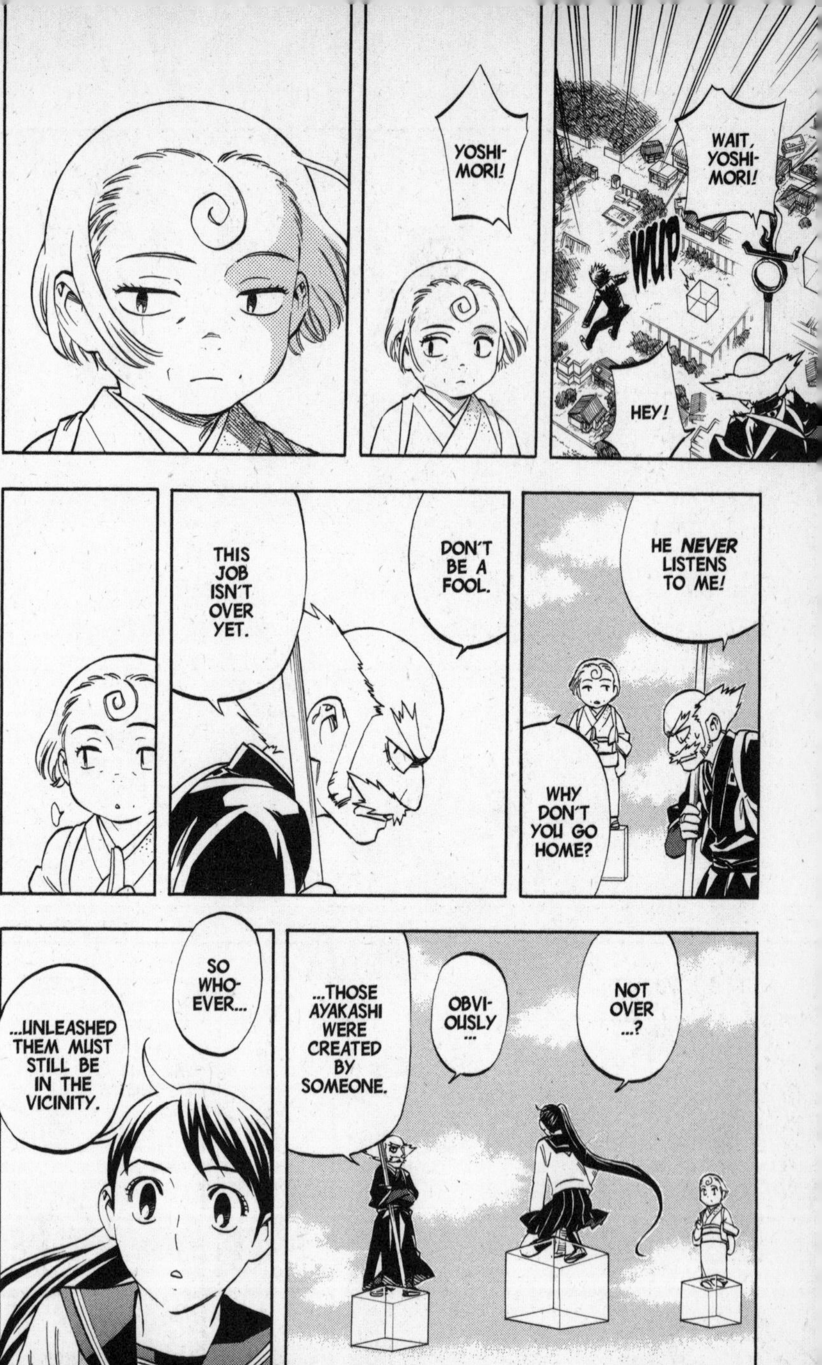
WAIT, YOSHI-MORI!
WUP
HEY!
YOSHI-MORI!
HE *NEVER* LISTENS TO ME!
WHY DON'T YOU GO HOME?
DON'T BE A FOOL.
THIS JOB ISN'T OVER YET.
NOT OVER ...?
OBVI-OUSLY ...
...THOSE AYAKASHI WERE CREATED BY SOMEONE.
SO WHO-EVER...
...UNLEASHED THEM MUST STILL BE IN THE VICINITY.

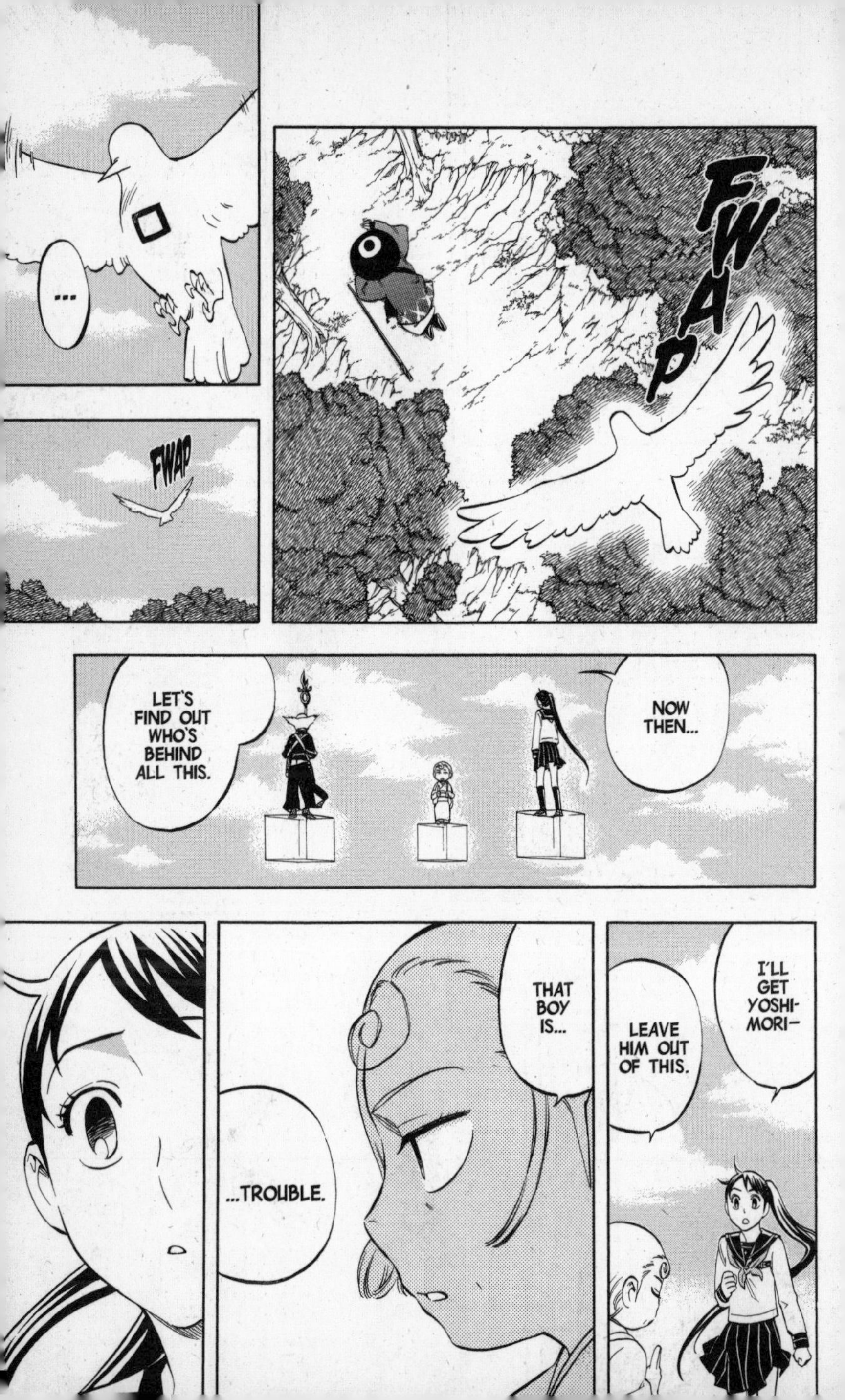
FWAP
...
FWAP
NOW THEN...
LET'S FIND OUT WHO'S BEHIND ALL THIS.
I'LL GET YOSHI-MORI—
LEAVE HIM OUT OF THIS.
THAT BOY IS...
...TROUBLE.

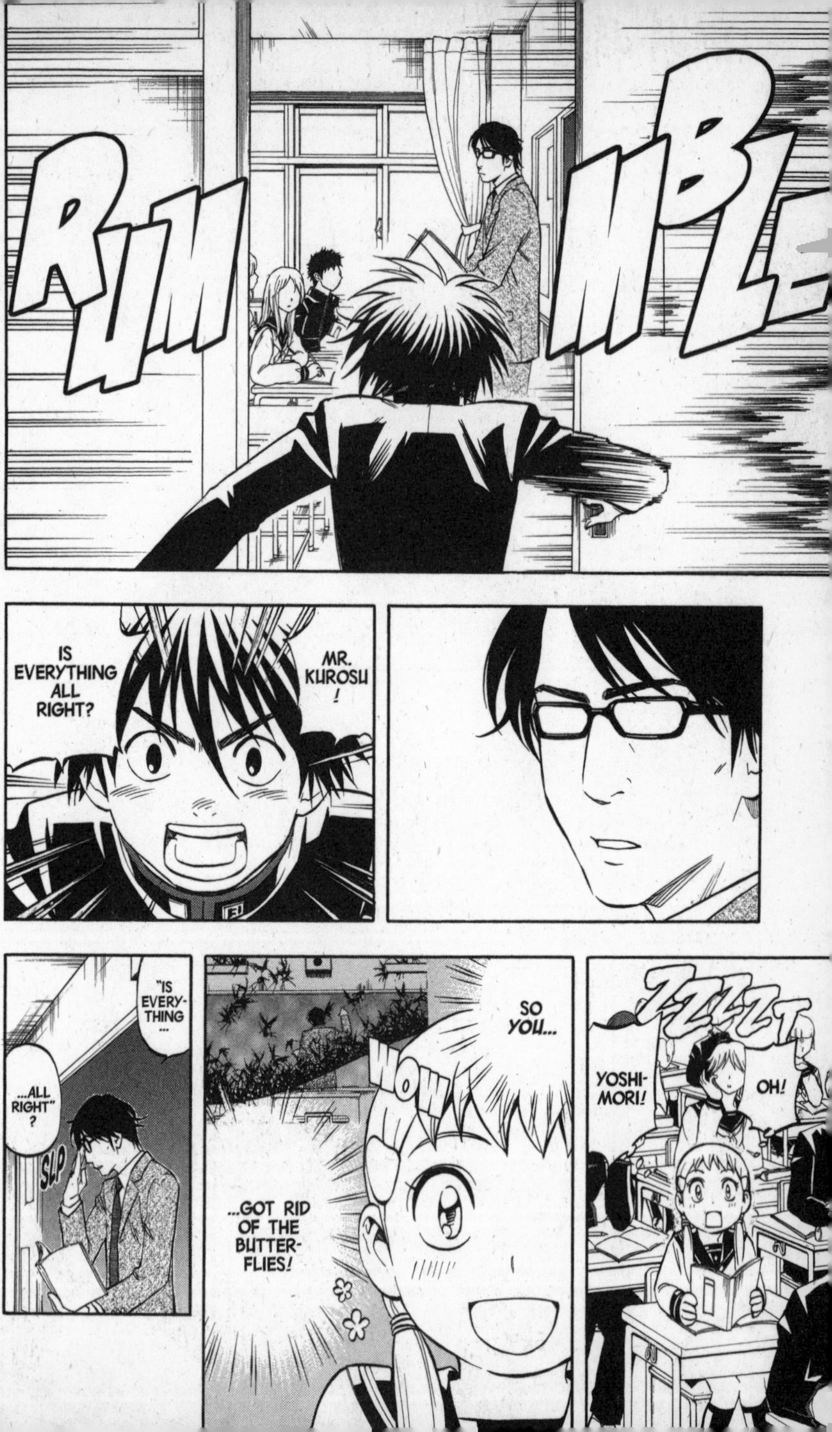
RUM
MBLE
MR. KUROSU!
IS EVERYTHING ALL RIGHT?
ZZZZT
OH!
YOSHI-MORI!
SO YOU...
WOW
...GOT RID OF THE BUTTER-FLIES!
"IS EVERY-THING...
...ALL RIGHT"?
SLP

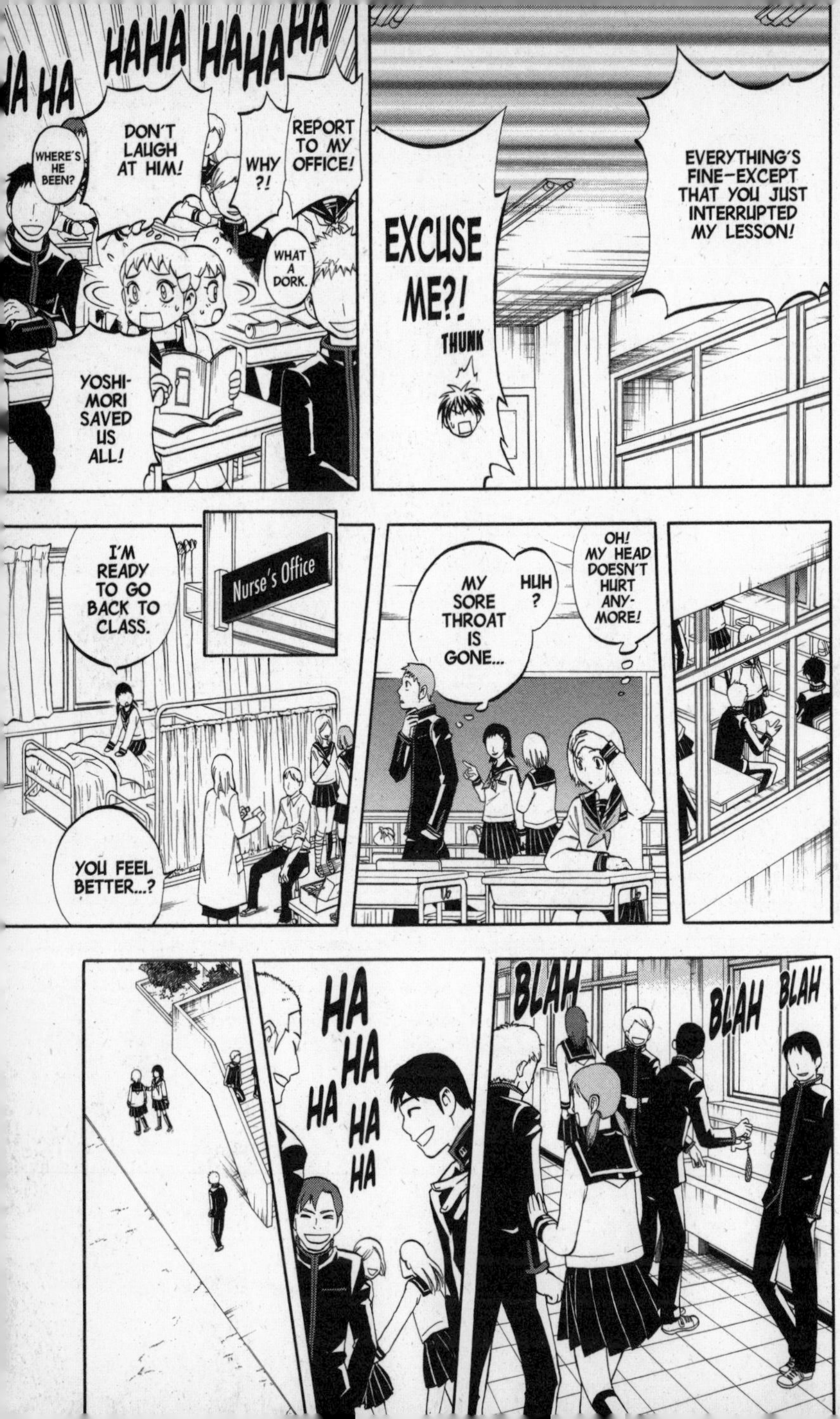
EVERYTHING'S FINE—EXCEPT THAT YOU JUST INTERRUPTED MY LESSON!
EXCUSE ME?!
THUNK
HA HA HAHA HAHAHA
REPORT TO MY OFFICE!
WHY?!
DON'T LAUGH AT HIM!
WHERE'S HE BEEN?
WHAT A DORK.
YOSHIMORI SAVED US ALL!
OH! MY HEAD DOESN'T HURT ANYMORE!
HUH?
MY SORE THROAT IS GONE...
Nurse's Office
I'M READY TO GO BACK TO CLASS.
YOU FEEL BETTER...?
BLAH BLAH BLAH
HA HA HA HA HA HA

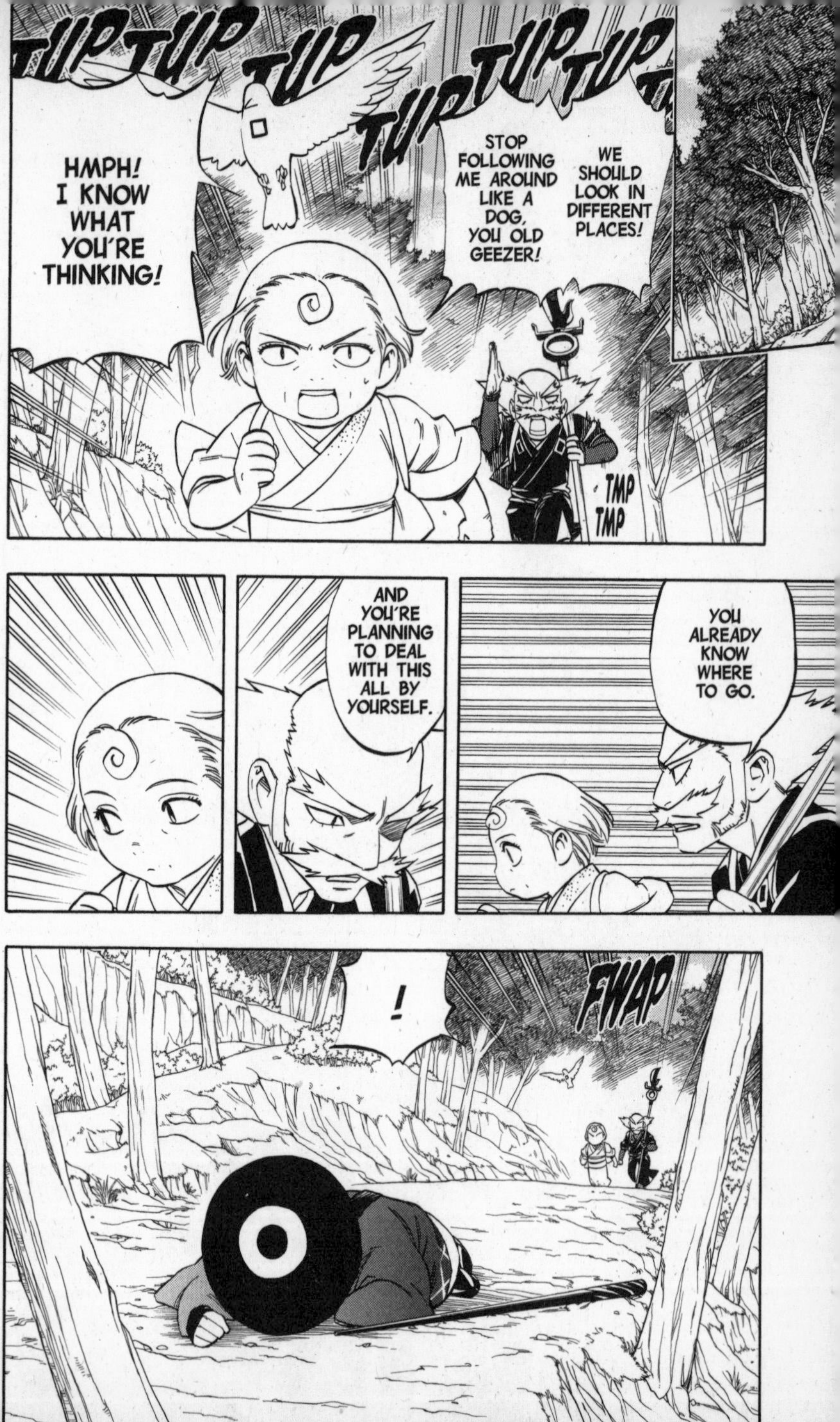
TUP TUP TUP TUP TUP TUP
WE SHOULD LOOK IN DIFFERENT PLACES!
STOP FOLLOWING ME AROUND LIKE A DOG, YOU OLD GEEZER!
HMPH! I KNOW WHAT YOU'RE THINKING!
TMP TMP
YOU ALREADY KNOW WHERE TO GO.
AND YOU'RE PLANNING TO DEAL WITH THIS ALL BY YOURSELF.
FWAP
!

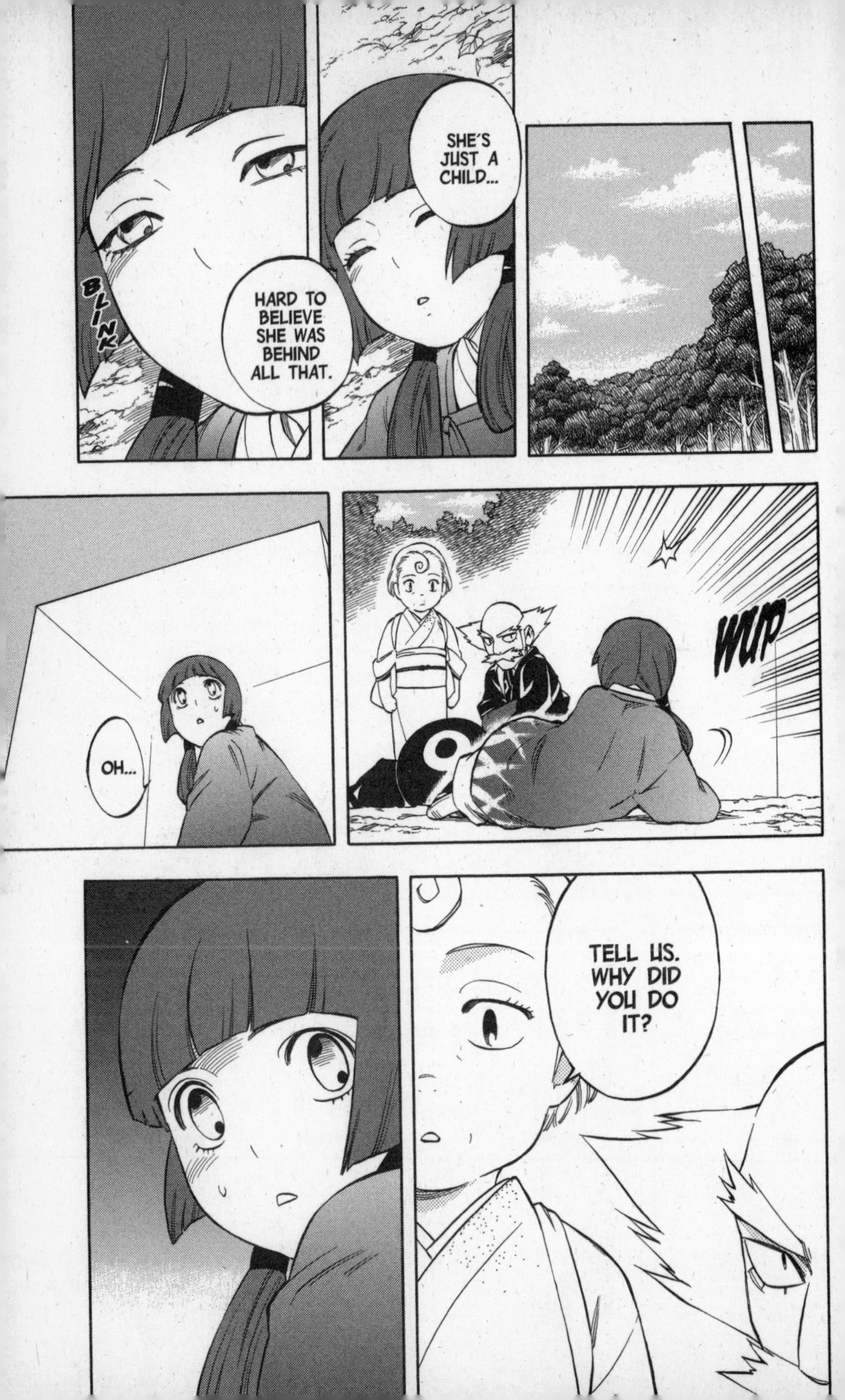
SHE'S JUST A CHILD...
HARD TO BELIEVE SHE WAS BEHIND ALL THAT.
BLINK
WUP
OH...
TELL US. WHY DID YOU DO IT?

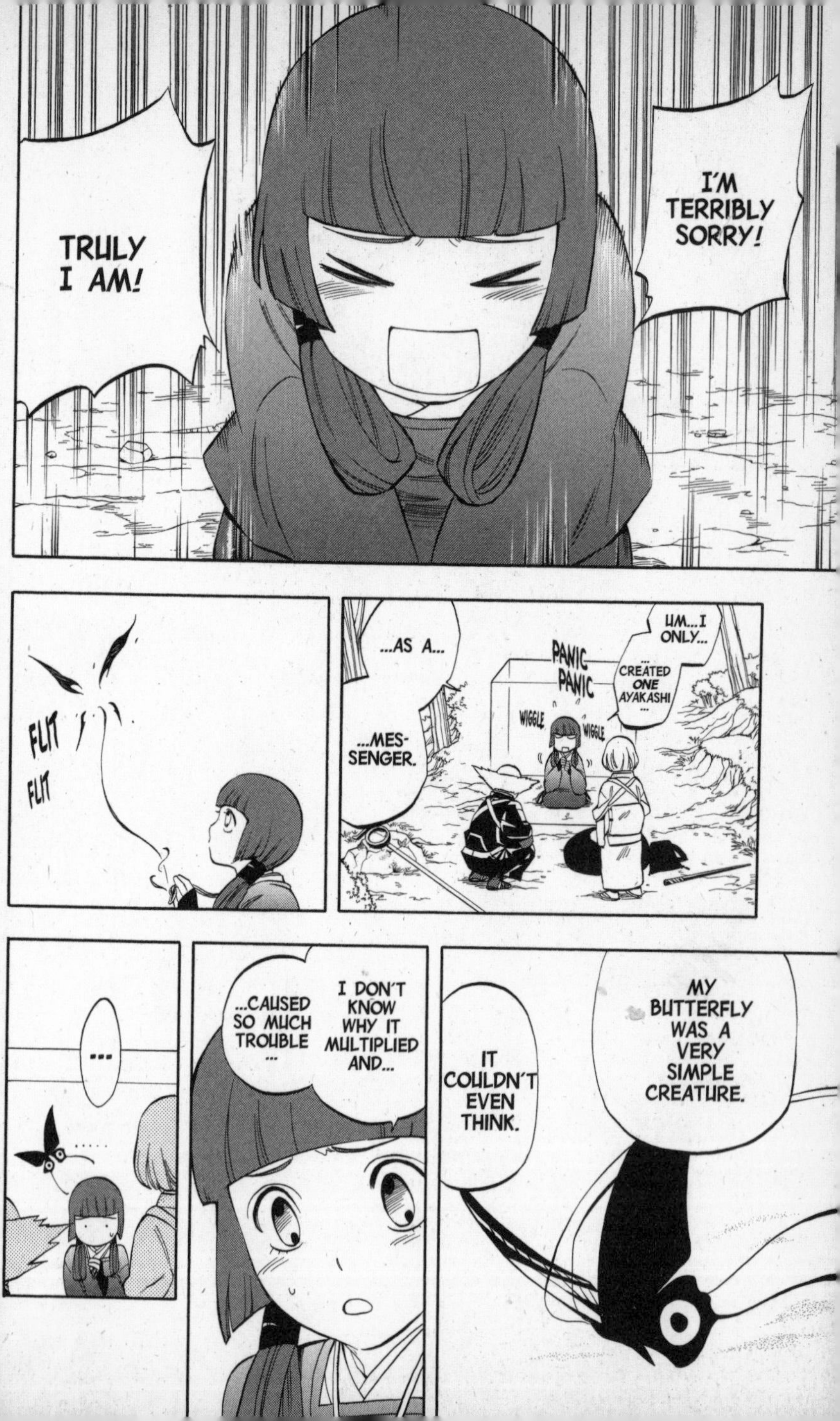
I'M TERRIBLY SORRY!
TRULY I AM!
UM...I ONLY...
...CREATED ONE AYAKASHI...
PANIC PANIC
WIGGLE WIGGLE
...AS A...
...MES-SENGER.
FLIT FLIT
MY BUTTERFLY WAS A VERY SIMPLE CREATURE.
IT COULDN'T EVEN THINK.
I DON'T KNOW WHY IT MULTIPLIED AND...
...CAUSED SO MUCH TROUBLE...
...
.....

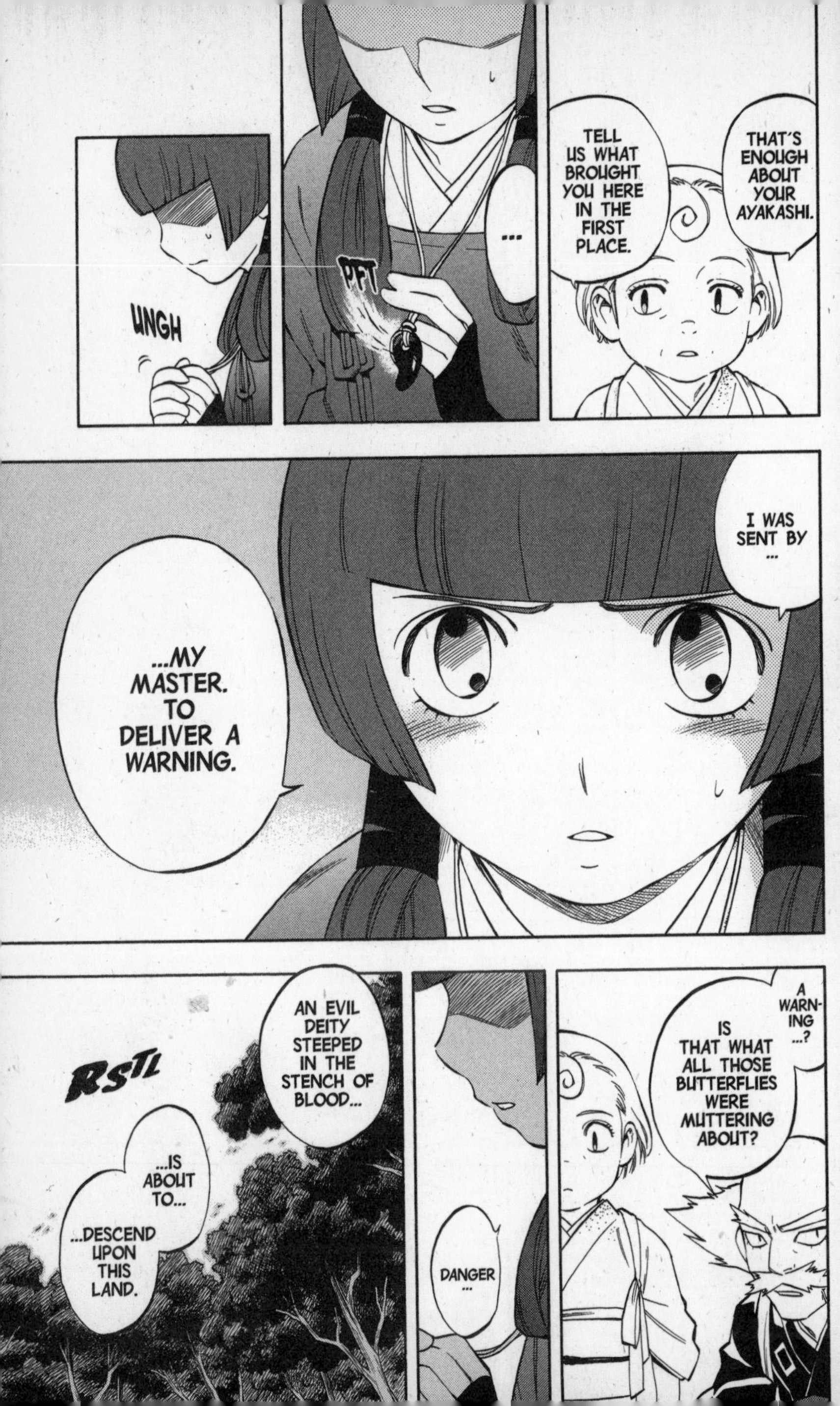
THAT'S ENOUGH ABOUT YOUR AYAKASHI.
TELL US WHAT BROUGHT YOU HERE IN THE FIRST PLACE.
...
PFT
UNGH
I WAS SENT BY ...
...MY MASTER. TO DELIVER A WARNING.
A WARN-ING ...?
IS THAT WHAT ALL THOSE BUTTERFLIES WERE MUTTERING ABOUT?
DANGER ...
AN EVIL DEITY STEEPED IN THE STENCH OF BLOOD...
RSTL
...IS ABOUT TO...
...DESCEND UPON THIS LAND.

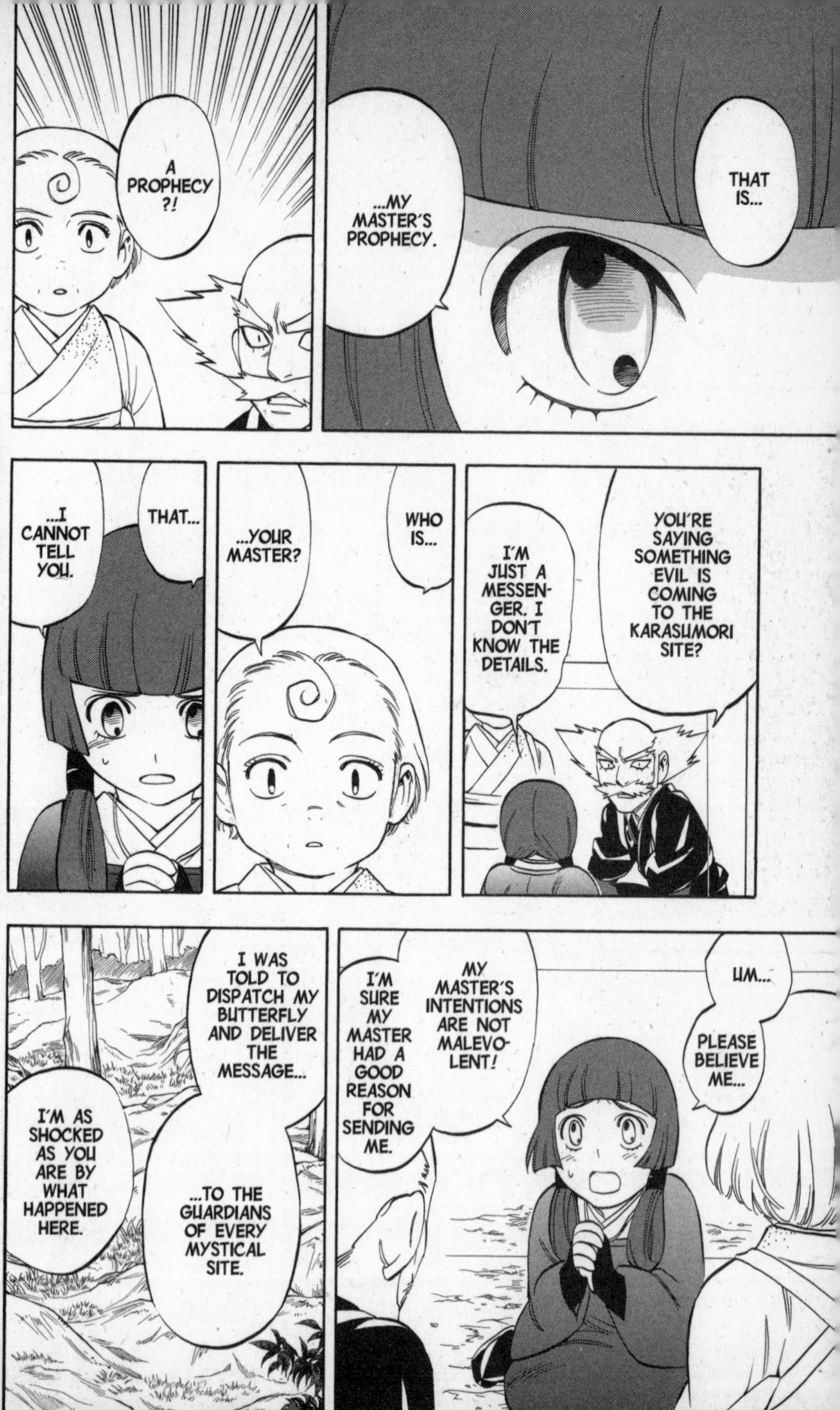
THAT IS...
...MY MASTER'S PROPHECY.
A PROPHECY ?!
YOU'RE SAYING SOMETHING EVIL IS COMING TO THE KARASUMORI SITE?
I'M JUST A MESSENGER. I DON'T KNOW THE DETAILS.
WHO IS...
...YOUR MASTER?
THAT...
...I CANNOT TELL YOU.
UM...
PLEASE BELIEVE ME...
MY MASTER'S INTENTIONS ARE NOT MALEVOLENT!
I'M SURE MY MASTER HAD A GOOD REASON FOR SENDING ME.
I WAS TOLD TO DISPATCH MY BUTTERFLY AND DELIVER THE MESSAGE...
...TO THE GUARDIANS OF EVERY MYSTICAL SITE.
I'M AS SHOCKED AS YOU ARE BY WHAT HAPPENED HERE.

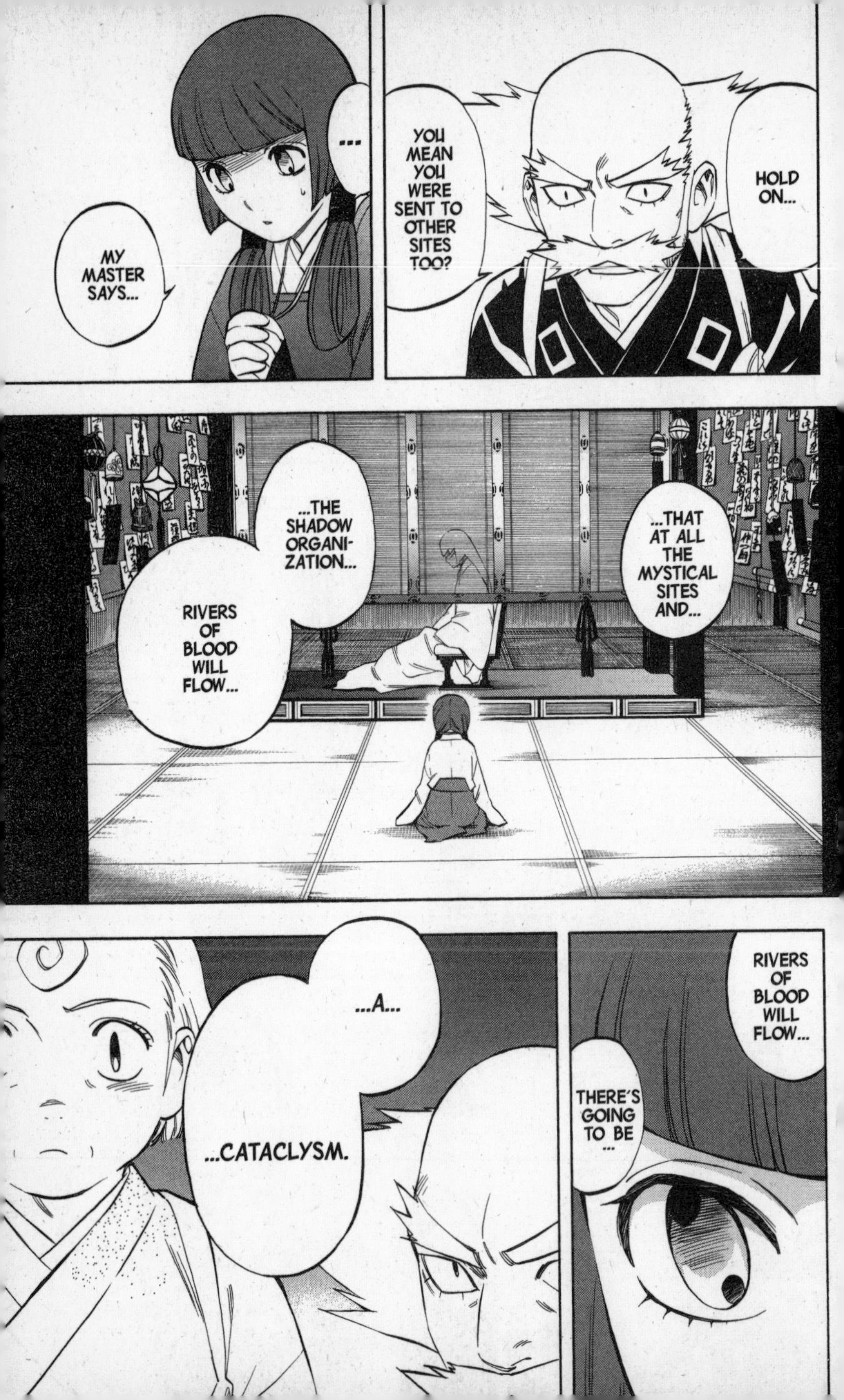
HOLD ON...
YOU MEAN YOU WERE SENT TO OTHER SITES TOO?
...
MY MASTER SAYS...
...THAT AT ALL THE MYSTICAL SITES AND...
...THE SHADOW ORGANIZATION...
RIVERS OF BLOOD WILL FLOW...
RIVERS OF BLOOD WILL FLOW...
THERE'S GOING TO BE ...
...A...
...CATACLYSM.

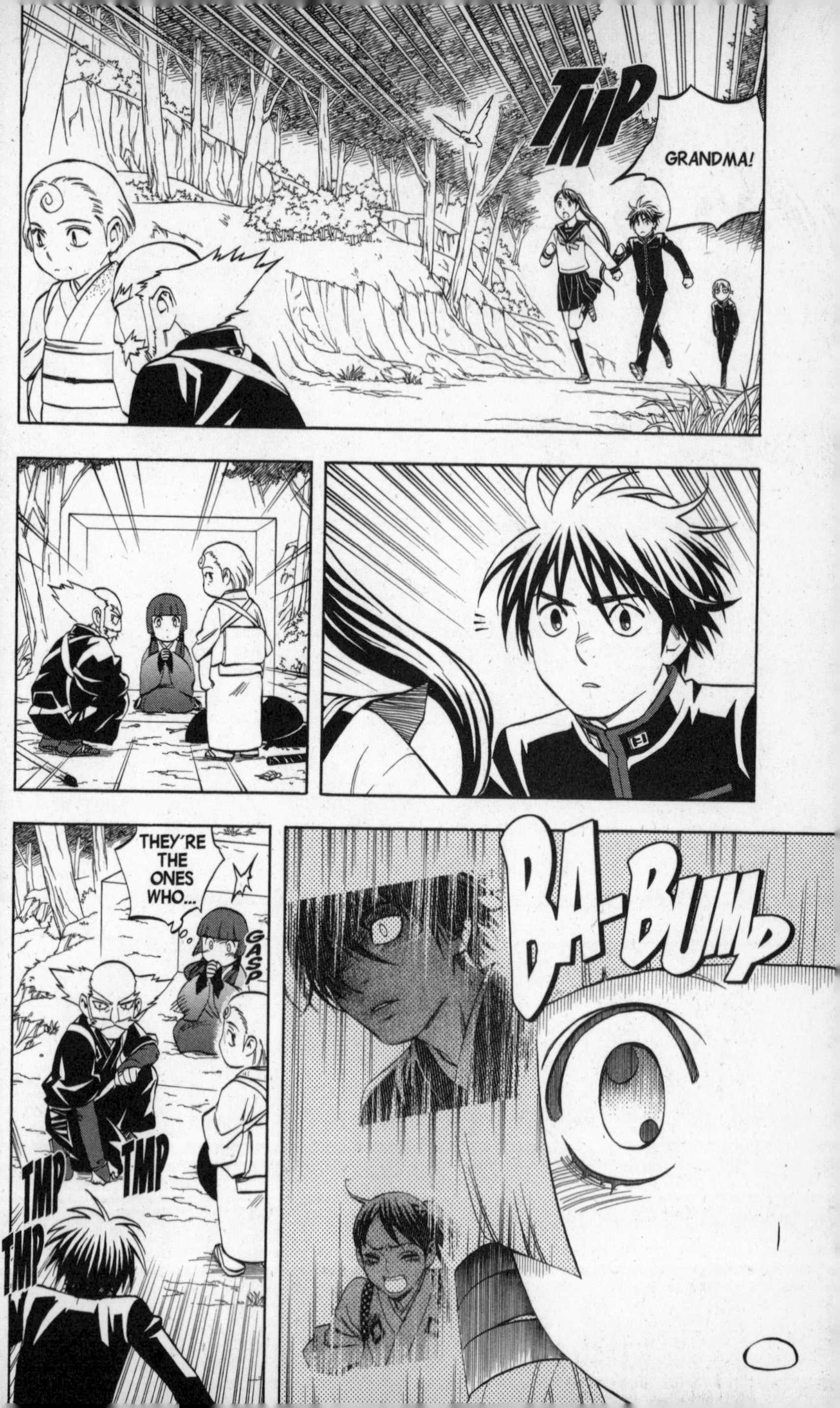
TMP
GRANDMA!
BA-BUMP
THEY'RE THE ONES WHO...
GASP
TMP
TMP
TMP

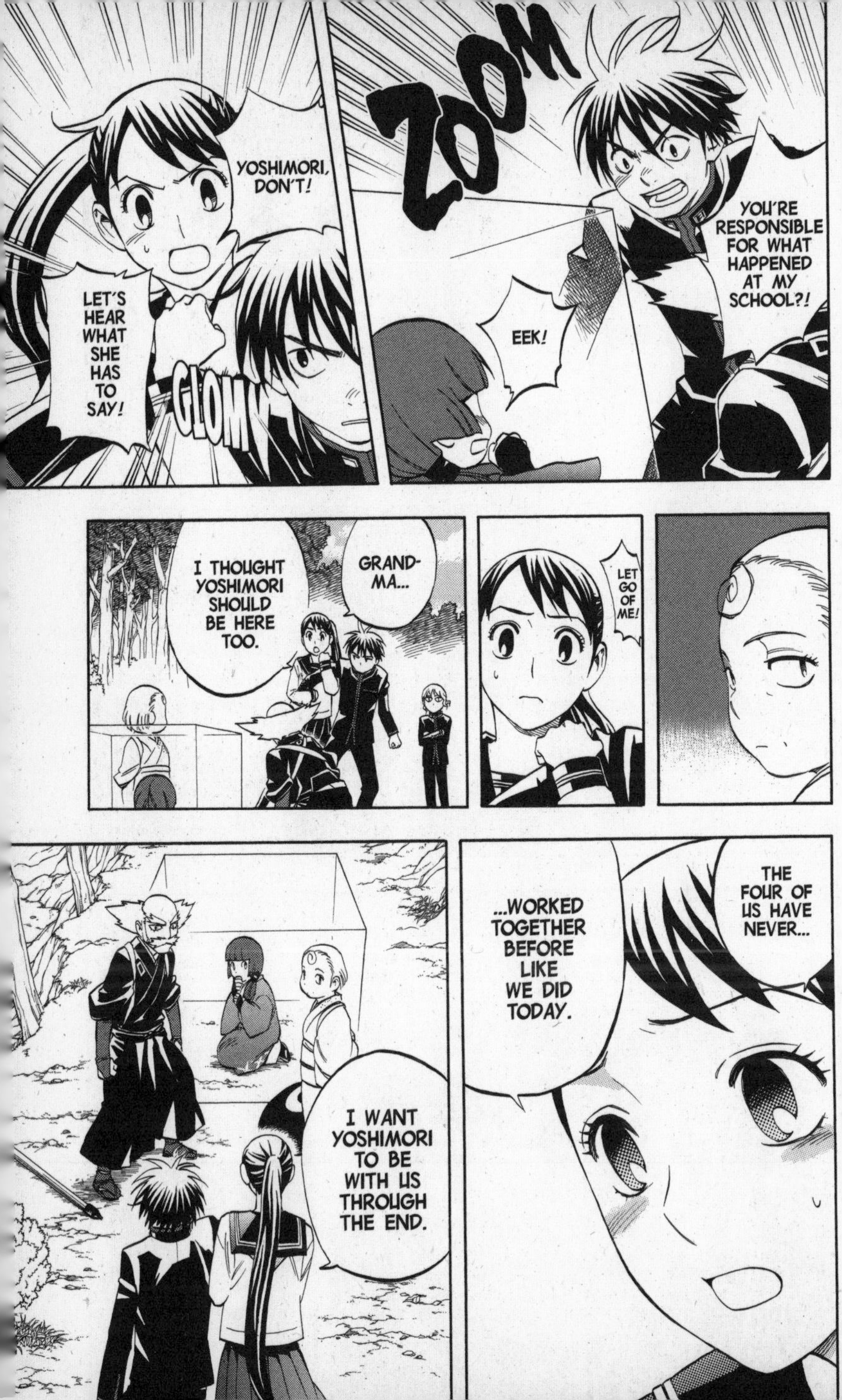
ZOOM
YOU'RE RESPONSIBLE FOR WHAT HAPPENED AT MY SCHOOL?!
EEK!
YOSHIMORI, DON'T!
LET'S HEAR WHAT SHE HAS TO SAY!
GLOM
LET GO OF ME!
GRAND-MA...
I THOUGHT YOSHIMORI SHOULD BE HERE TOO.
THE FOUR OF US HAVE NEVER...
...WORKED TOGETHER BEFORE LIKE WE DID TODAY.
I WANT YOSHIMORI TO BE WITH US THROUGH THE END.

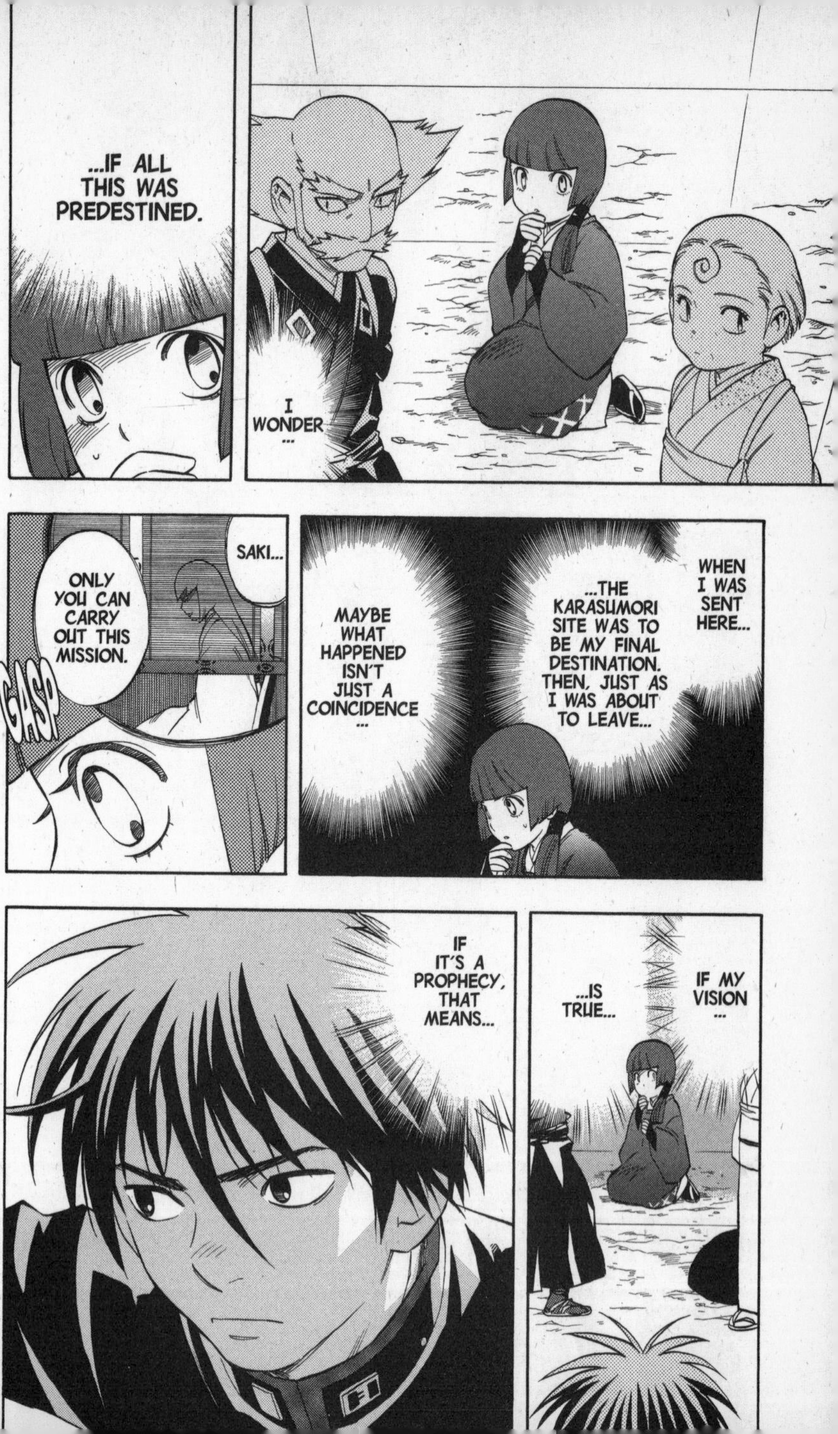
I WONDER...
...IF ALL THIS WAS PREDESTINED.
WHEN I WAS SENT HERE...
...THE KARASUMORI SITE WAS TO BE MY FINAL DESTINATION. THEN, JUST AS I WAS ABOUT TO LEAVE...
MAYBE WHAT HAPPENED ISN'T JUST A COINCIDENCE...
SAKI...
ONLY YOU CAN CARRY OUT THIS MISSION.
GASP
IF MY VISION...
...IS TRUE...
IF IT'S A PROPHECY, THAT MEANS...

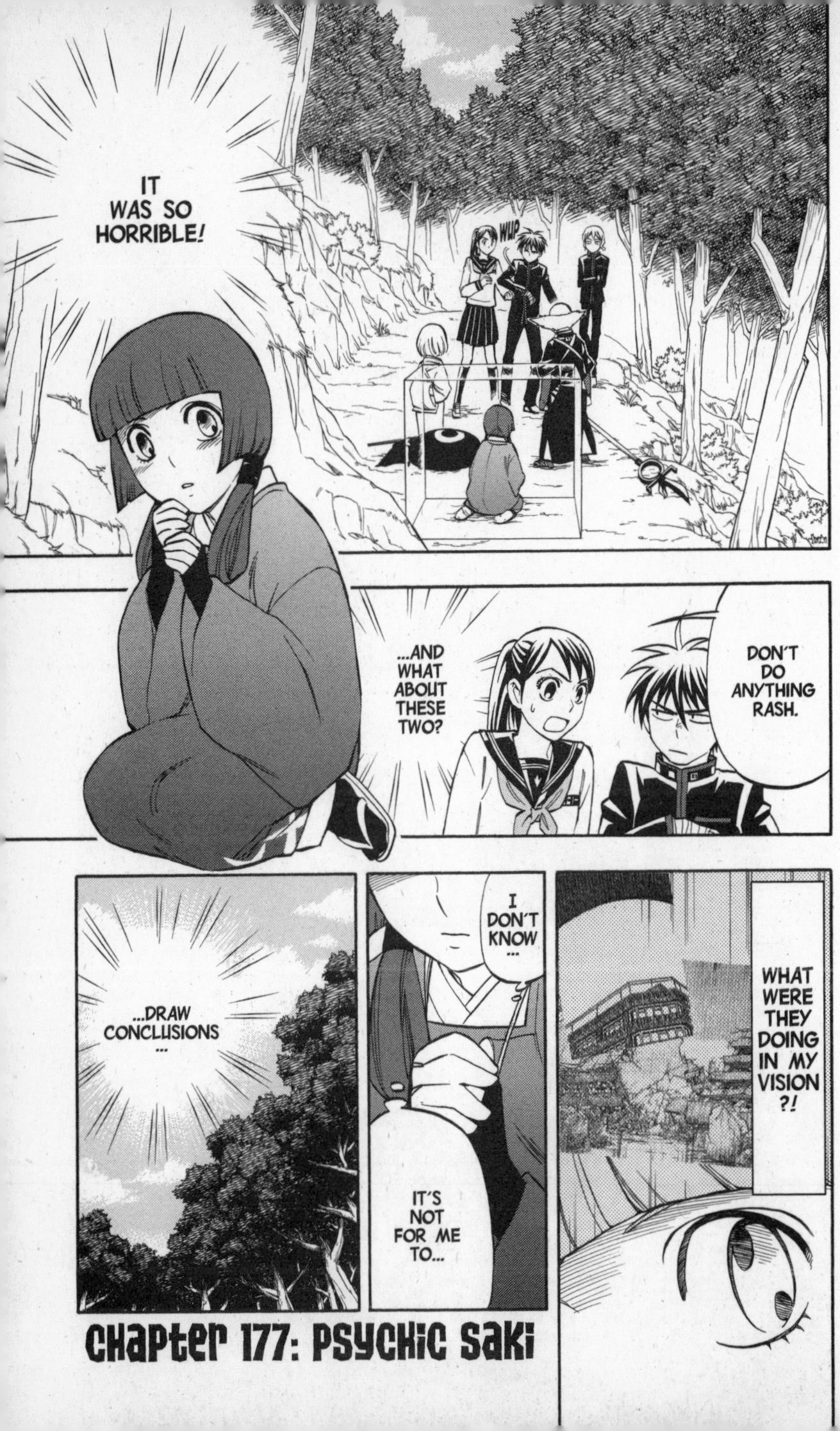
WUP
IT WAS SO HORRIBLE!
DON'T DO ANYTHING RASH.
...AND WHAT ABOUT THESE TWO?
WHAT WERE THEY DOING IN MY VISION?!
I DON'T KNOW...
IT'S NOT FOR ME TO...
...DRAW CONCLUSIONS...

Chapter 177: Psychic Saki

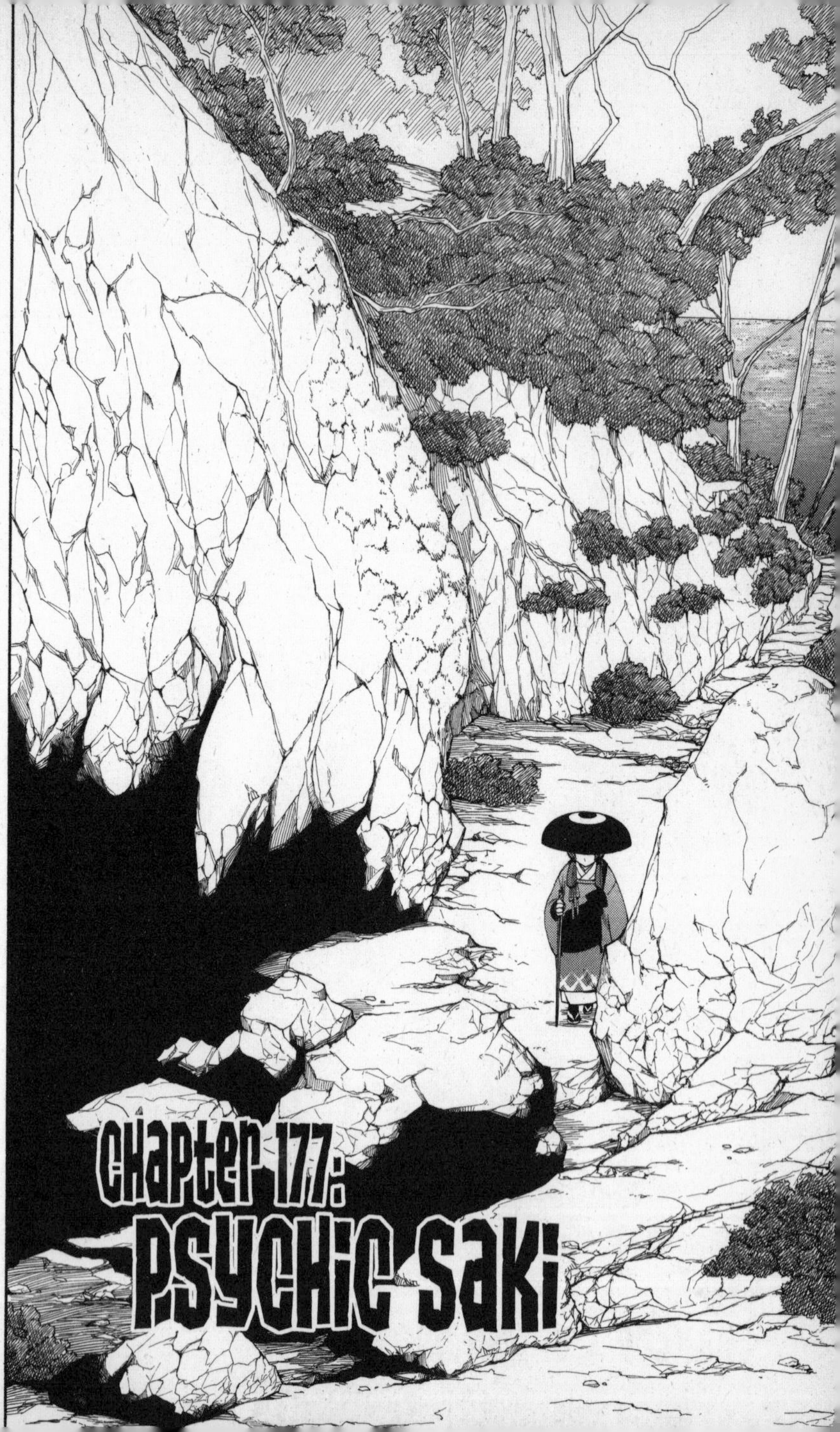
Chapter 177:
Psychic Saki

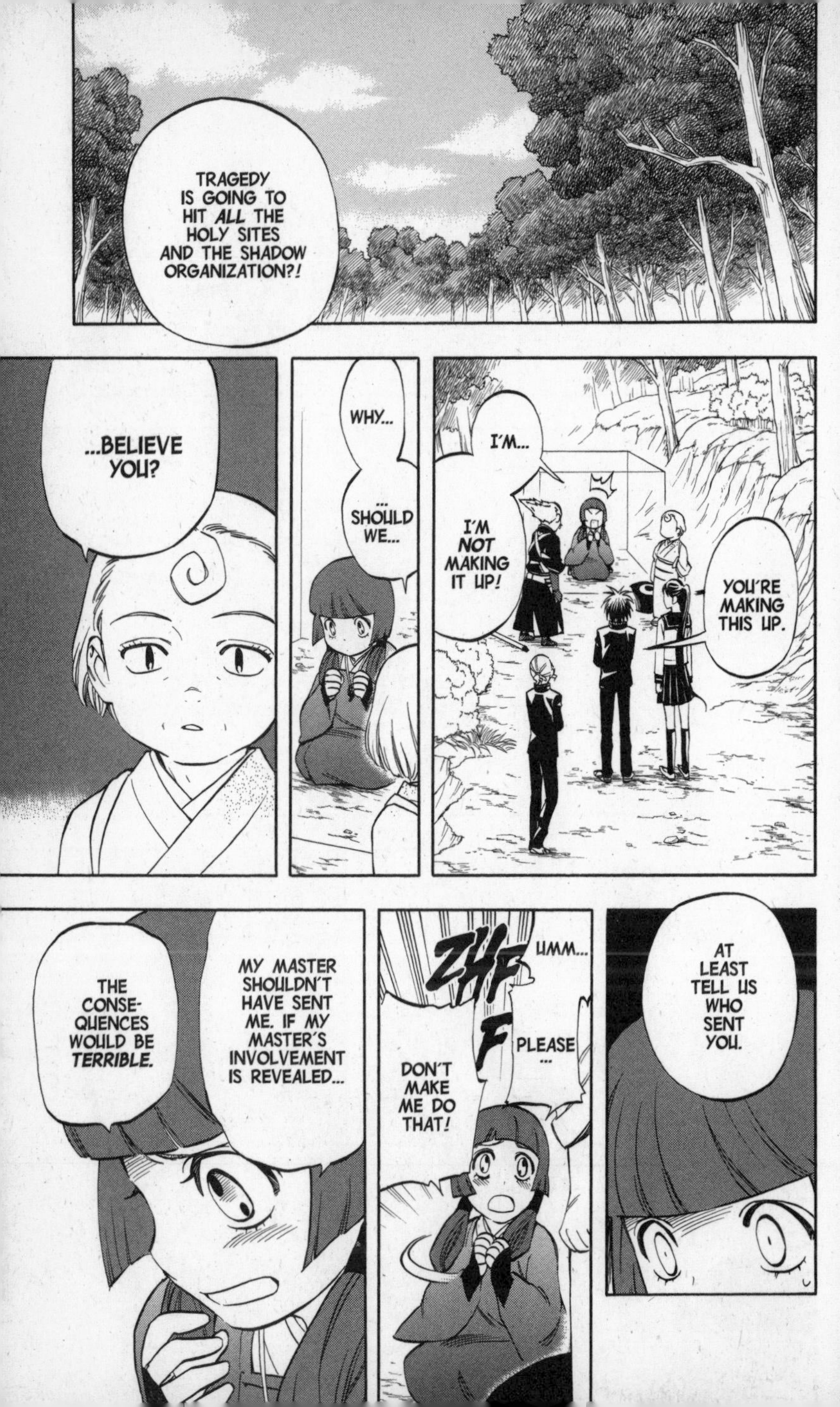
TRAGEDY IS GOING TO HIT *ALL* THE HOLY SITES AND THE SHADOW ORGANIZATION?!
YOU'RE MAKING THIS UP.
I'M...
I'M *NOT* MAKING IT UP!
WHY...
...SHOULD WE...
...BELIEVE *YOU*?
AT LEAST TELL US WHO SENT YOU.
UMM...
PLEASE...
DON'T MAKE ME DO THAT!
ZHFF
MY MASTER SHOULDN'T HAVE SENT ME. IF MY MASTER'S INVOLVEMENT IS REVEALED...
THE CONSEQUENCES WOULD BE *TERRIBLE.*

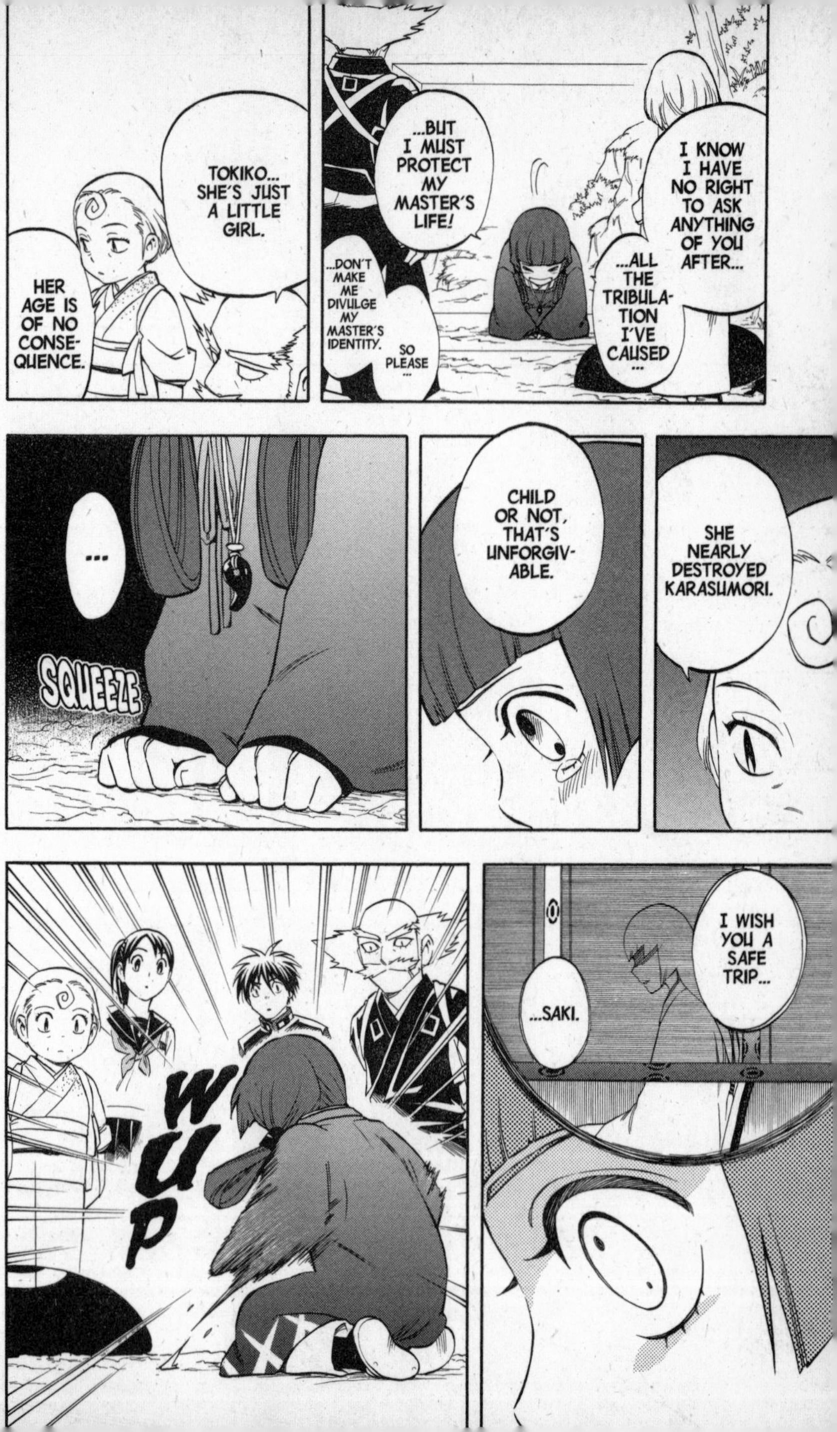

I KNOW I HAVE NO RIGHT TO ASK ANYTHING OF YOU AFTER...
...ALL THE TRIBULATION I'VE CAUSED...
...BUT I MUST PROTECT MY MASTER'S LIFE!
...DON'T MAKE ME DIVULGE MY MASTER'S IDENTITY.
SO PLEASE...
TOKIKO... SHE'S JUST A LITTLE GIRL.
HER AGE IS OF NO CONSEQUENCE.
SHE NEARLY DESTROYED KARASUMORI.
CHILD OR NOT, THAT'S UNFORGIVABLE.
...
SQUEEZE
I WISH YOU A SAFE TRIP...
...SAKI.
WUP

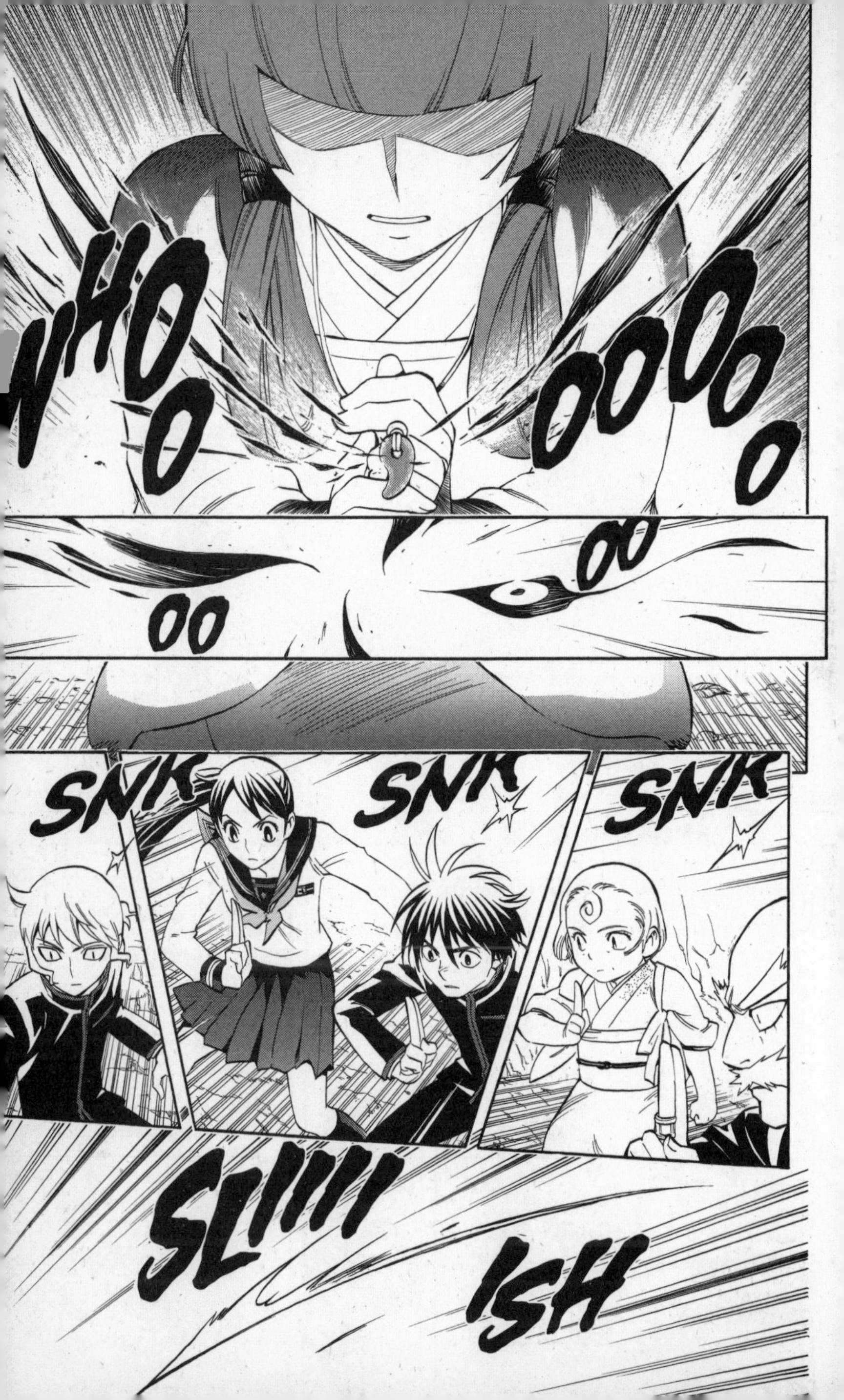
WHOOOOOOOO
OOOO
SNK
SNK
SNK
SLIIIIISH

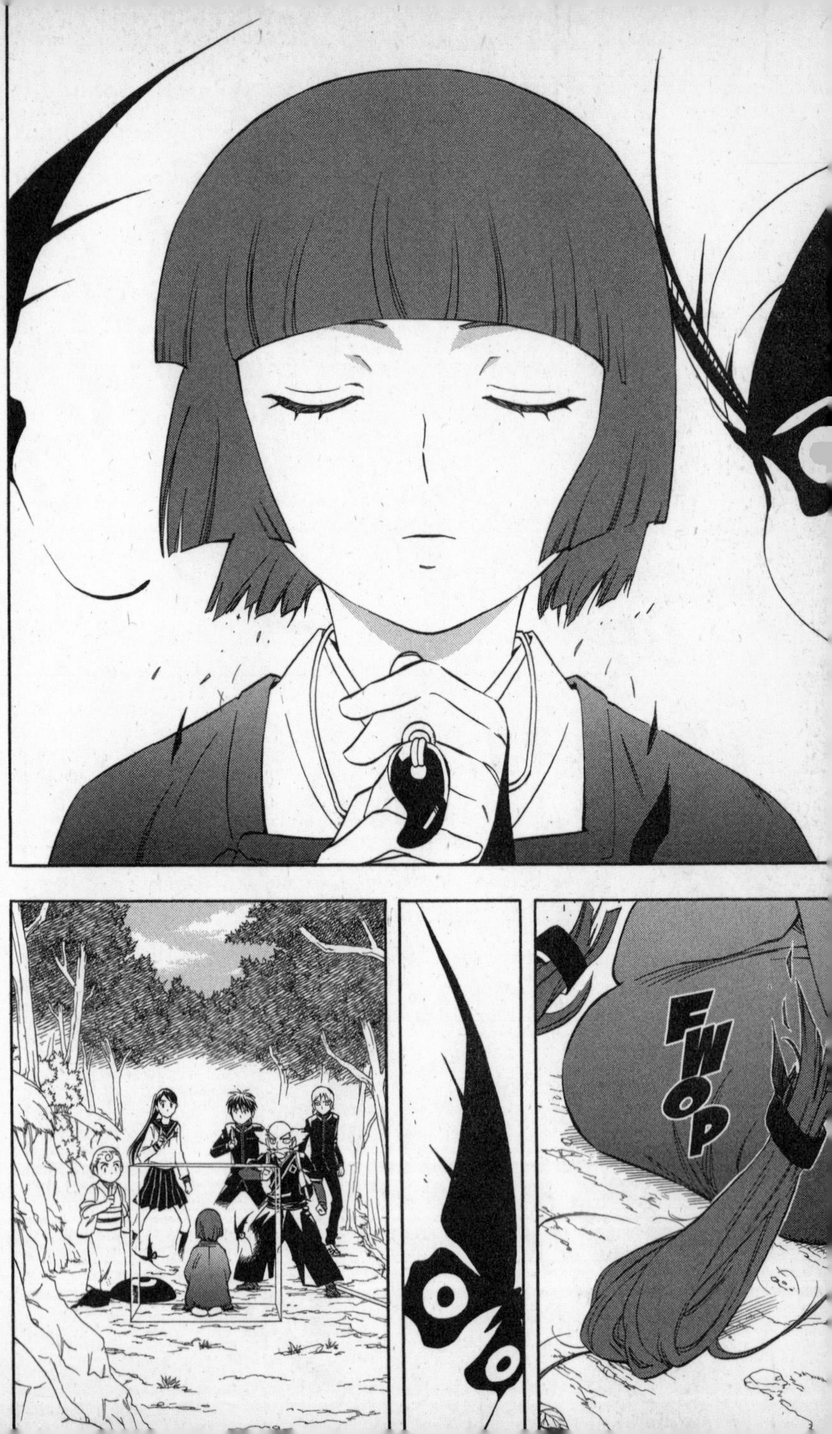
FWOP

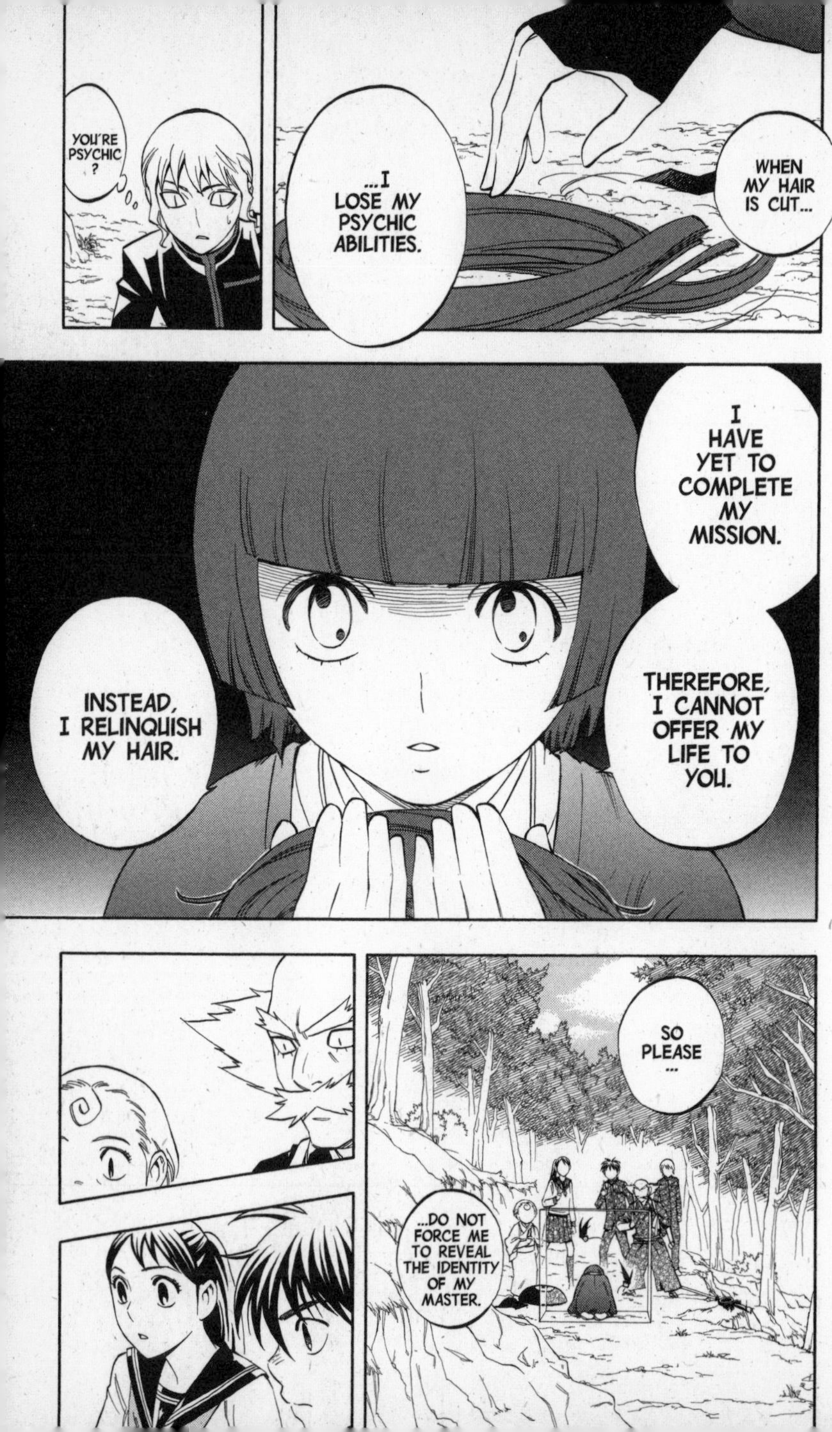
WHEN MY HAIR IS CUT...
...I LOSE MY PSYCHIC ABILITIES.
YOU'RE PSYCHIC?
I HAVE YET TO COMPLETE MY MISSION.
THEREFORE, I CANNOT OFFER MY LIFE TO YOU.
INSTEAD, I RELINQUISH MY HAIR.
SO PLEASE...
...DO NOT FORCE ME TO REVEAL THE IDENTITY OF MY MASTER.

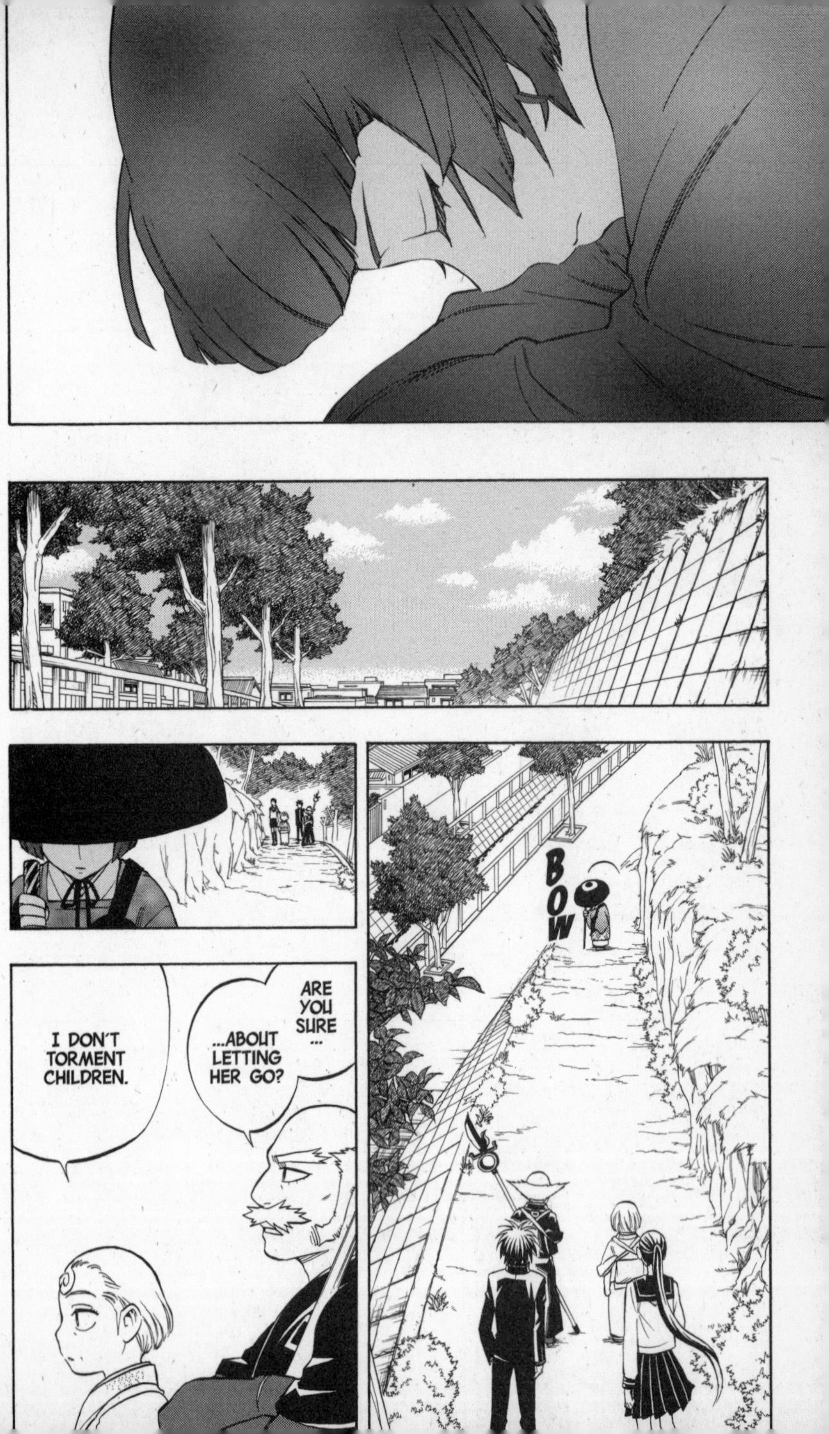
BOW
ARE YOU SURE ...
...ABOUT LETTING HER GO?
I DON'T TORMENT CHILDREN.

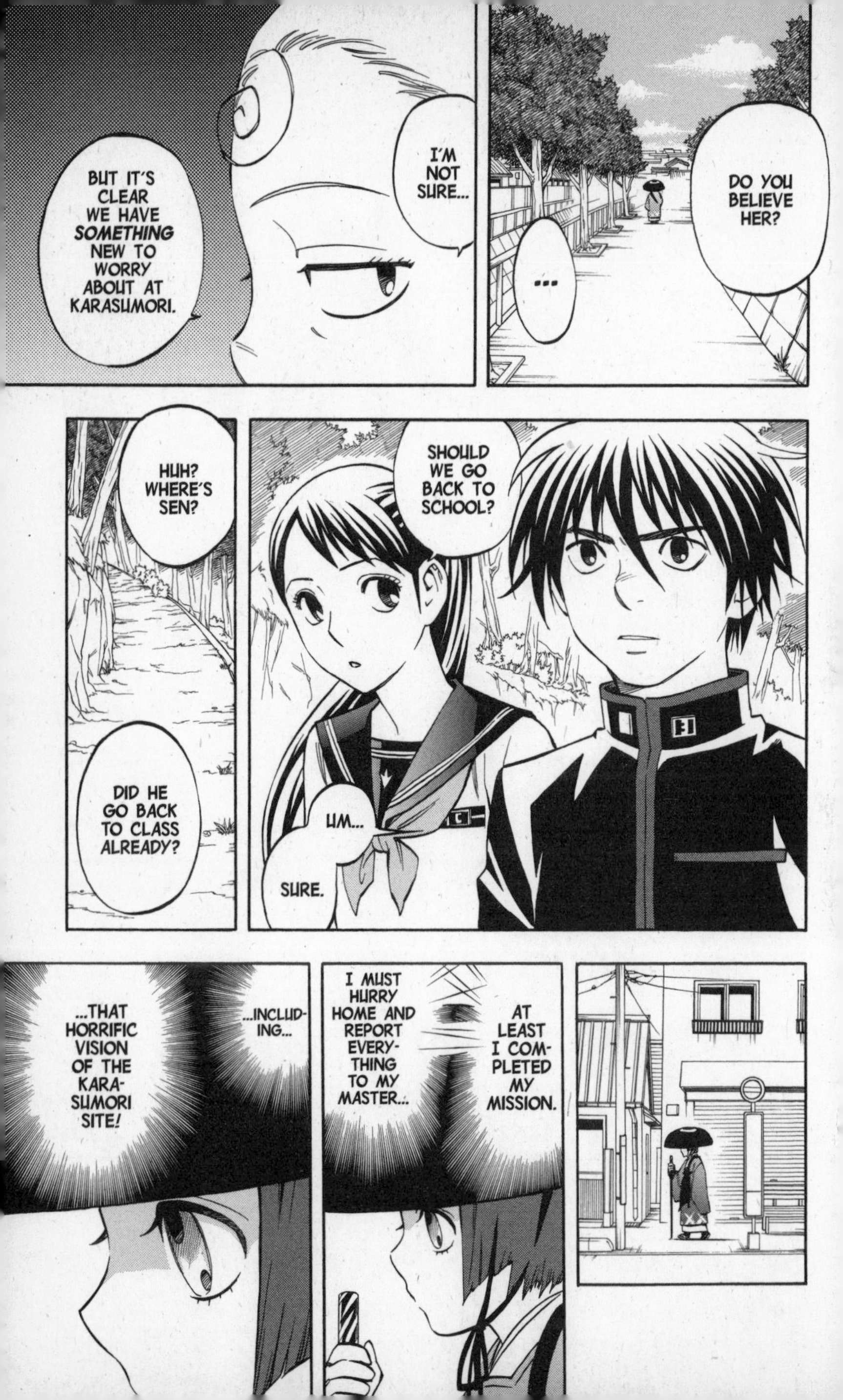
DO YOU BELIEVE HER?
...
I'M NOT SURE...
BUT IT'S CLEAR WE HAVE *SOMETHING* NEW TO WORRY ABOUT AT KARASUMORI.
SHOULD WE GO BACK TO SCHOOL?
UM...
SURE.
HUH? WHERE'S SEN?
DID HE GO BACK TO CLASS ALREADY?
AT LEAST I COM-PLETED MY MISSION.
I MUST HURRY HOME AND REPORT EVERY-THING TO MY MASTER...
...INCLUD-ING...
...THAT HORRIFIC VISION OF THE KARA-SUMORI SITE!

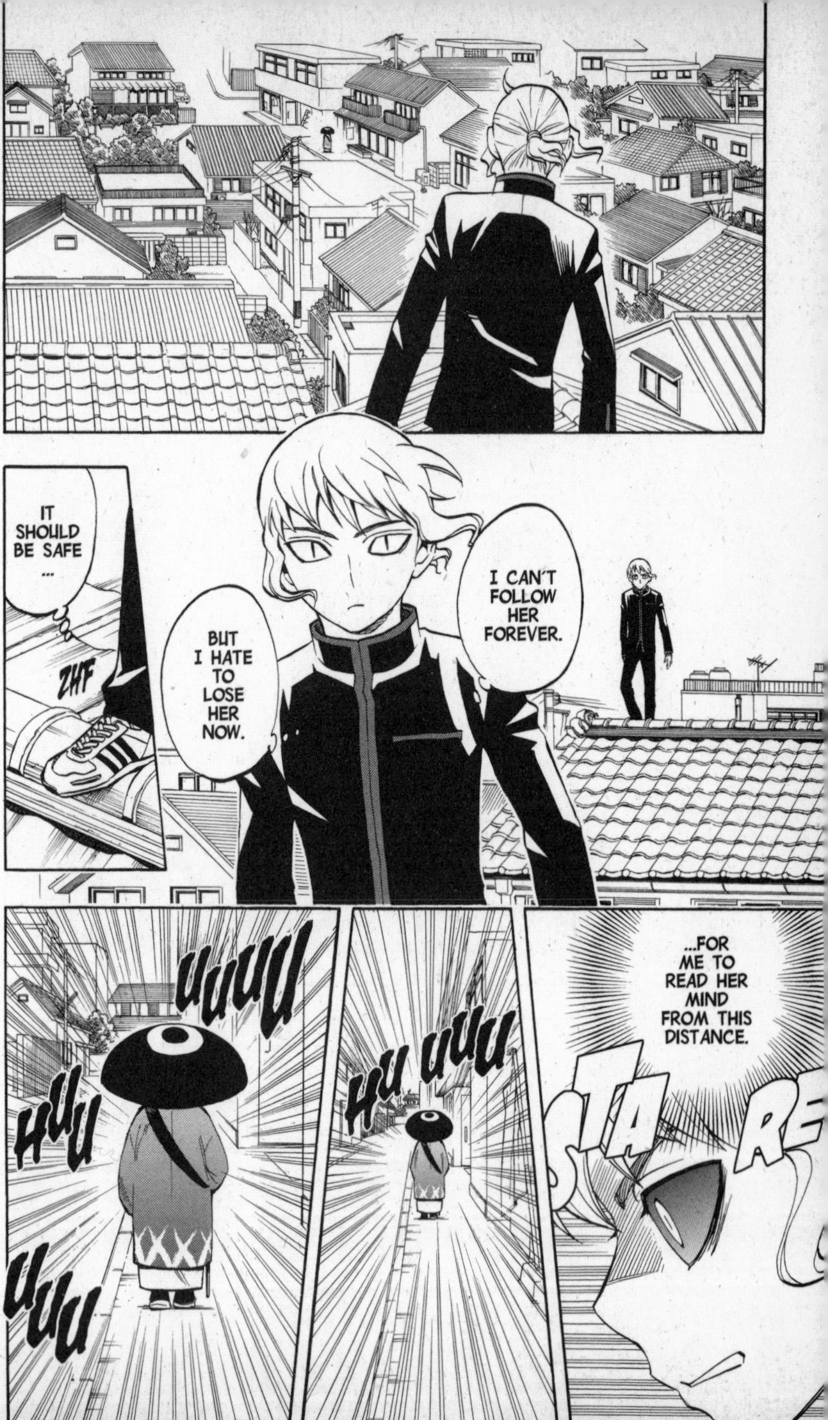
I CAN'T FOLLOW HER FOREVER.
BUT I HATE TO LOSE HER NOW.
IT SHOULD BE SAFE ...
ZHF
...FOR ME TO READ HER MIND FROM THIS DISTANCE.
TA
RE
HU UUU
UUUU
HUU
UUU

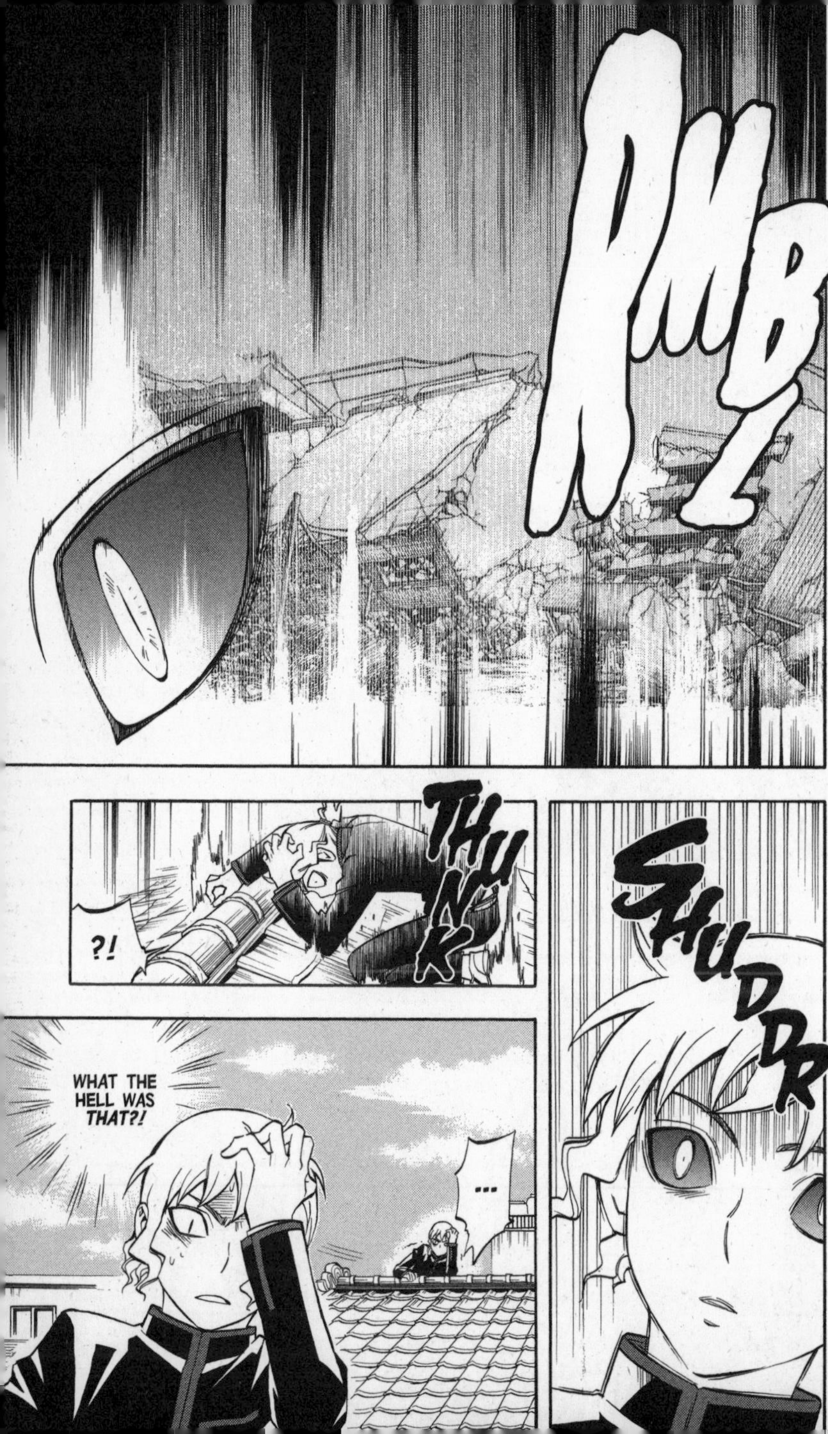

SHUDDR
THUNK
?!
WHAT THE HELL WAS *THAT*?!
...

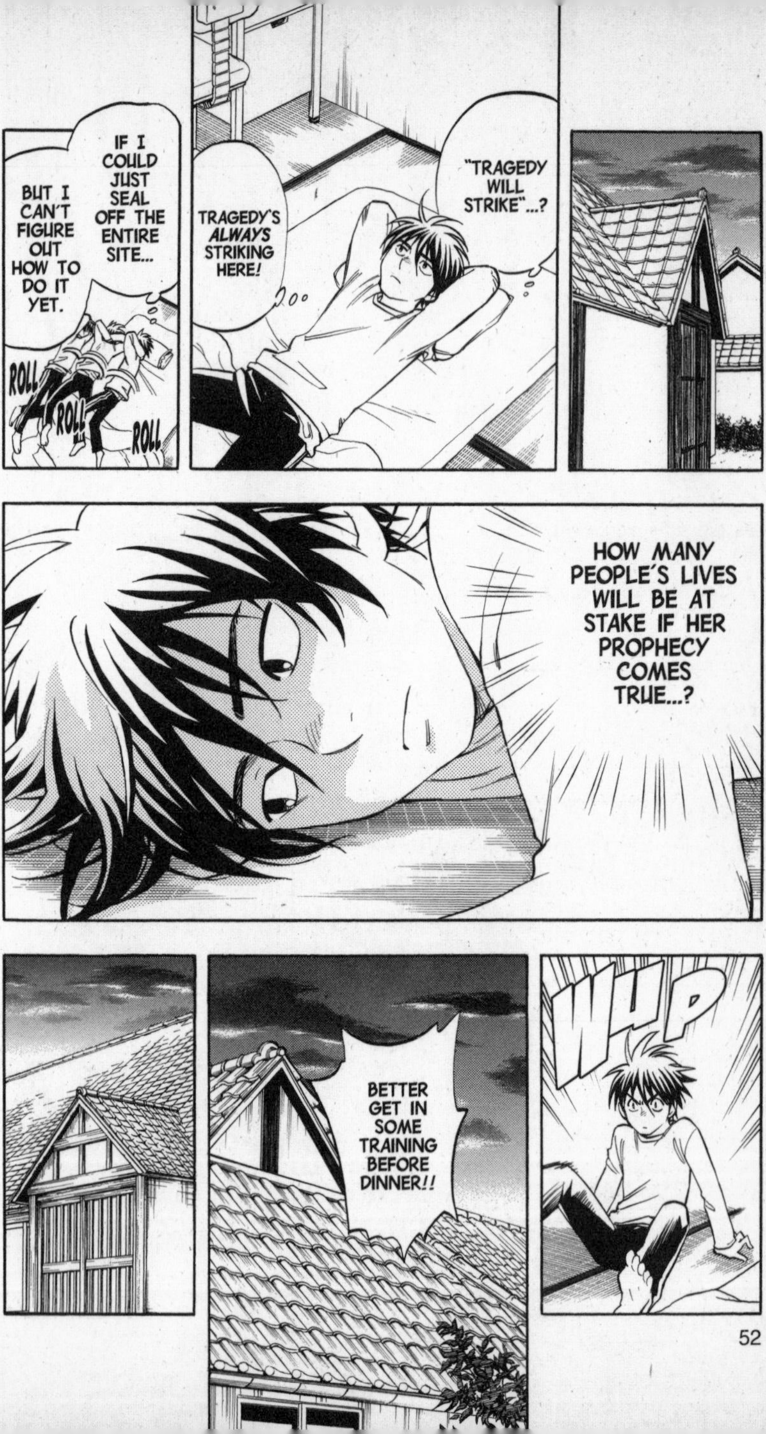
"TRAGEDY WILL STRIKE"...?
TRAGEDY'S *ALWAYS* STRIKING HERE!
IF I COULD JUST SEAL OFF THE ENTIRE SITE...
BUT I CAN'T FIGURE OUT HOW TO DO IT YET.
ROLL
ROLL
ROLL
HOW MANY PEOPLE'S LIVES WILL BE AT STAKE IF HER PROPHECY COMES TRUE...?
WHUP
BETTER GET IN SOME TRAINING BEFORE DINNER!!

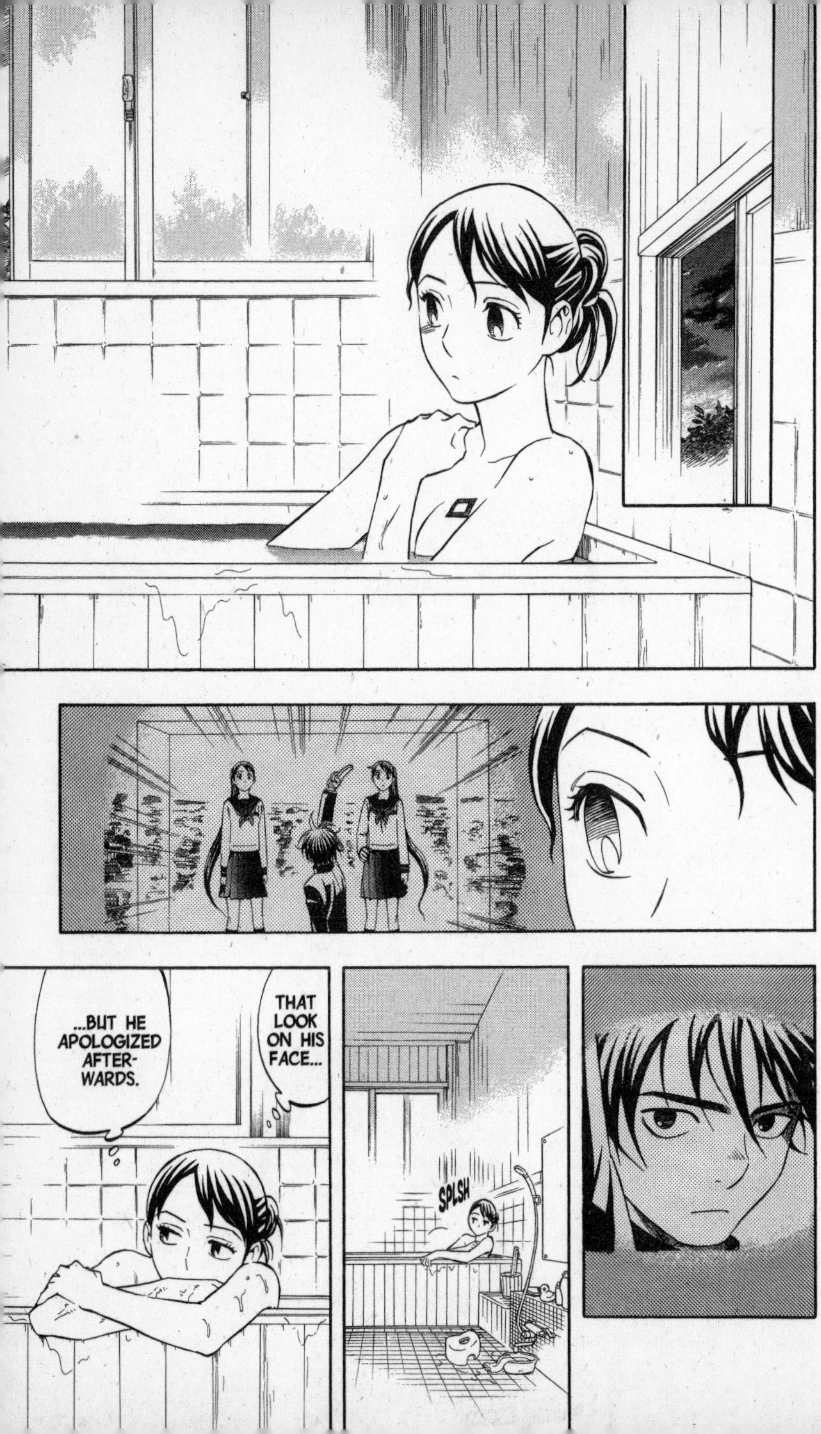
SPLSH
THAT LOOK ON HIS FACE...
...BUT HE APOLOGIZED AFTER-WARDS.

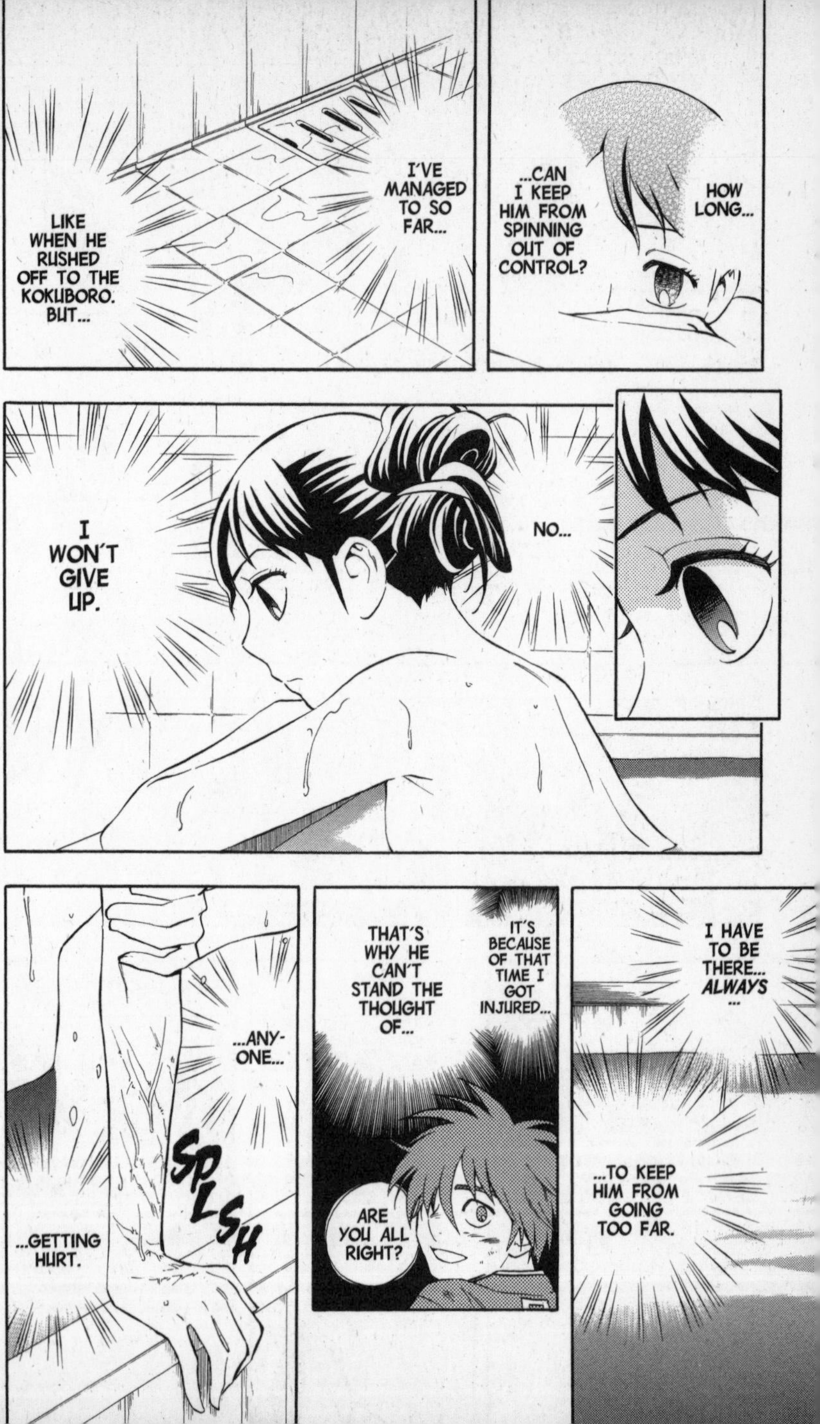
HOW LONG...
...CAN I KEEP HIM FROM SPINNING OUT OF CONTROL?
I'VE MANAGED TO SO FAR...
LIKE WHEN HE RUSHED OFF TO THE KOKUBORO. BUT...
NO...
I WON'T GIVE UP.
I HAVE TO BE THERE... *ALWAYS* ...
...TO KEEP HIM FROM GOING TOO FAR.
IT'S BECAUSE OF THAT TIME I GOT INJURED...
THAT'S WHY HE CAN'T STAND THE THOUGHT OF...
ARE YOU ALL RIGHT?
...ANY-ONE...
SPLSH
...GETTING HURT.

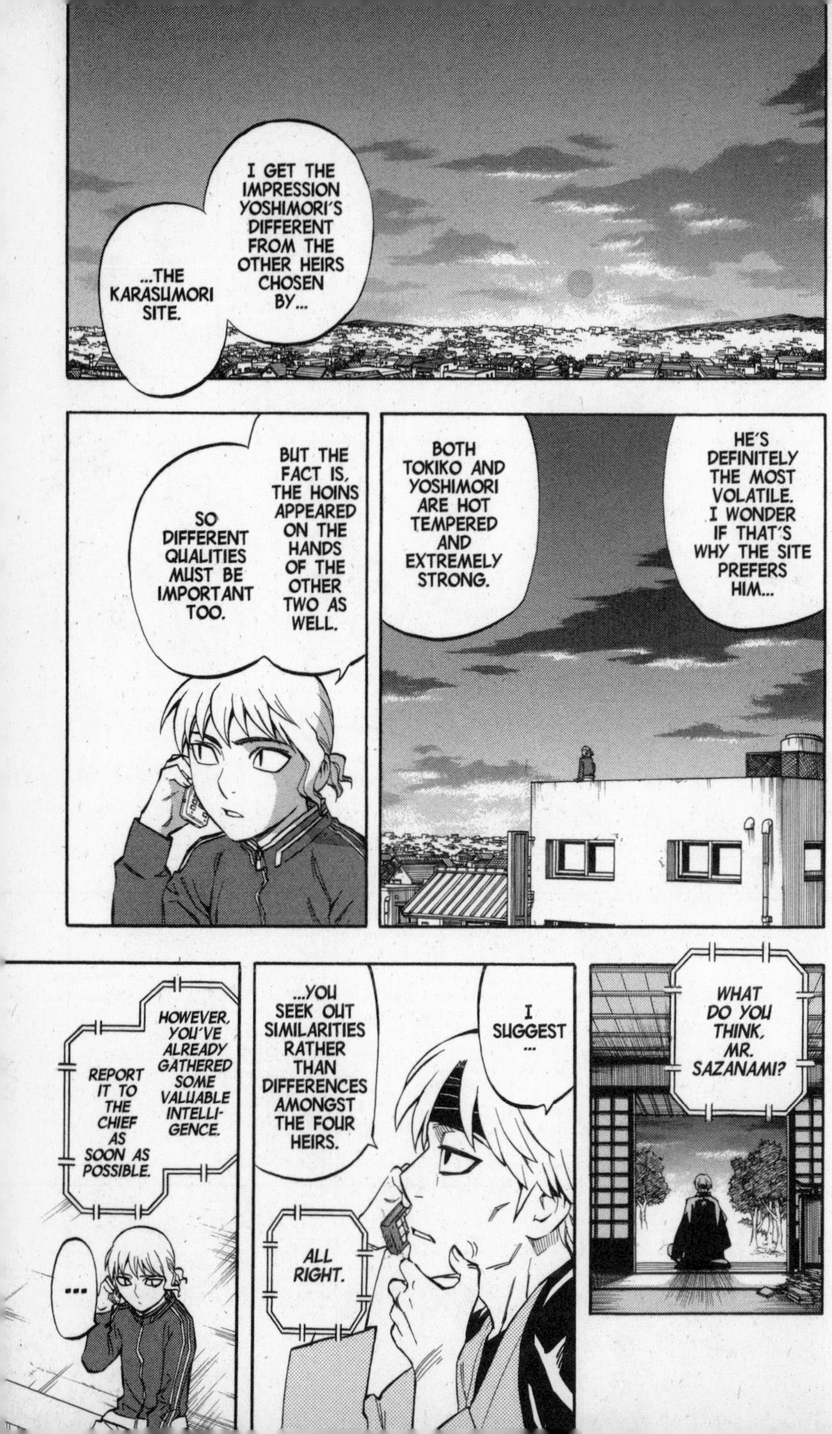
I GET THE IMPRESSION YOSHIMORI'S DIFFERENT FROM THE OTHER HEIRS CHOSEN BY...
...THE KARASUMORI SITE.
HE'S DEFINITELY THE MOST VOLATILE. I WONDER IF THAT'S WHY THE SITE PREFERS HIM...
BOTH TOKIKO AND YOSHIMORI ARE HOT TEMPERED AND EXTREMELY STRONG.
BUT THE FACT IS, THE HOINS APPEARED ON THE HANDS OF THE OTHER TWO AS WELL.
SO DIFFERENT QUALITIES MUST BE IMPORTANT TOO.
WHAT DO YOU THINK, MR. SAZANAMI?
I SUGGEST...
...YOU SEEK OUT SIMILARITIES RATHER THAN DIFFERENCES AMONGST THE FOUR HEIRS.
ALL RIGHT.
HOWEVER, YOU'VE ALREADY GATHERED SOME VALUABLE INTELLI-GENCE.
REPORT IT TO THE CHIEF AS SOON AS POSSIBLE.
...

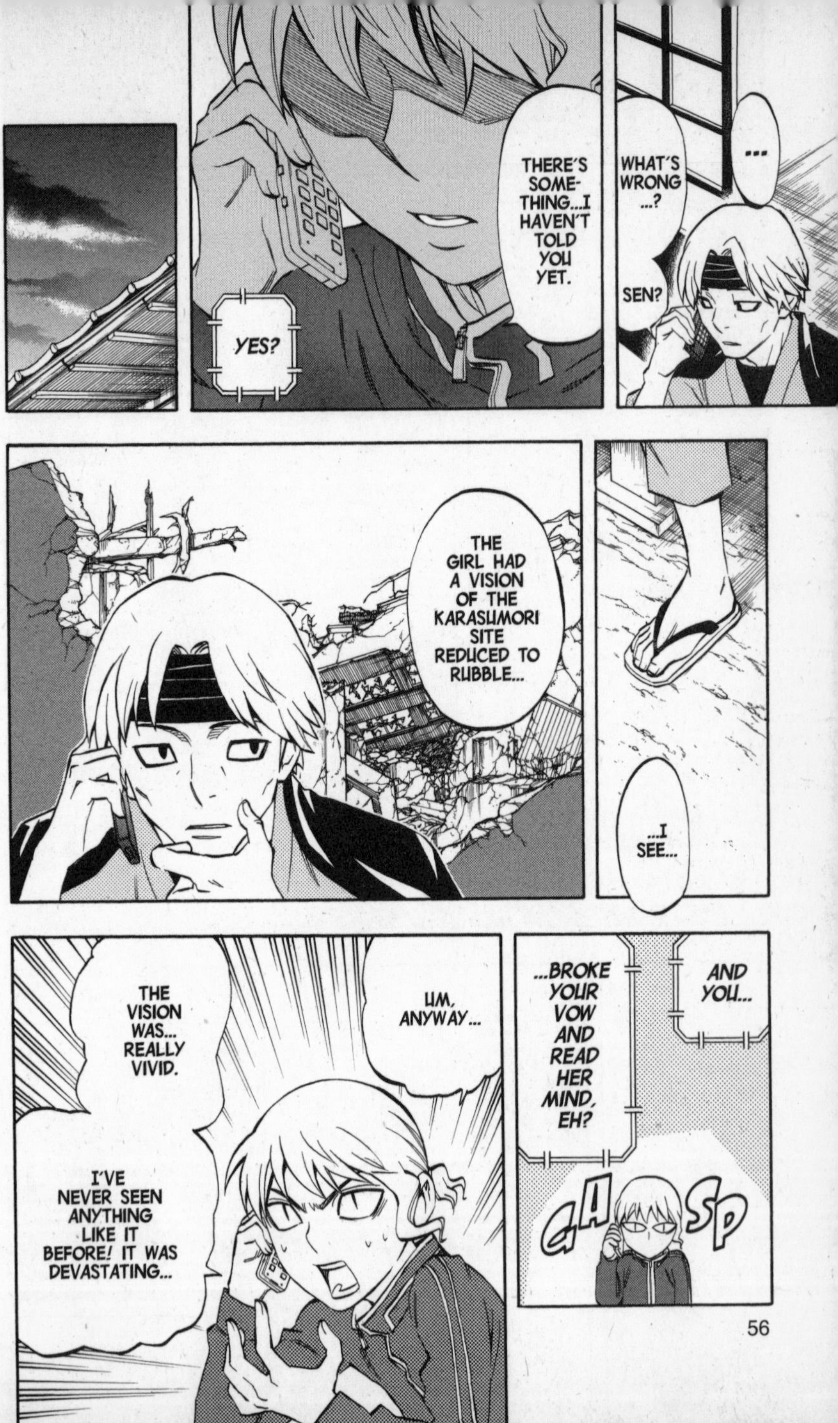
...
WHAT'S WRONG ...?
SEN?
THERE'S SOME-THING...I HAVEN'T TOLD YOU YET.
YES?
...I SEE...
THE GIRL HAD A VISION OF THE KARASUMORI SITE REDUCED TO RUBBLE...
AND YOU...
...BROKE YOUR VOW AND READ HER MIND, EH?
GASP
UM, ANYWAY...
THE VISION WAS... REALLY VIVID.
I'VE NEVER SEEN ANYTHING LIKE IT BEFORE! IT WAS DEVASTATING...

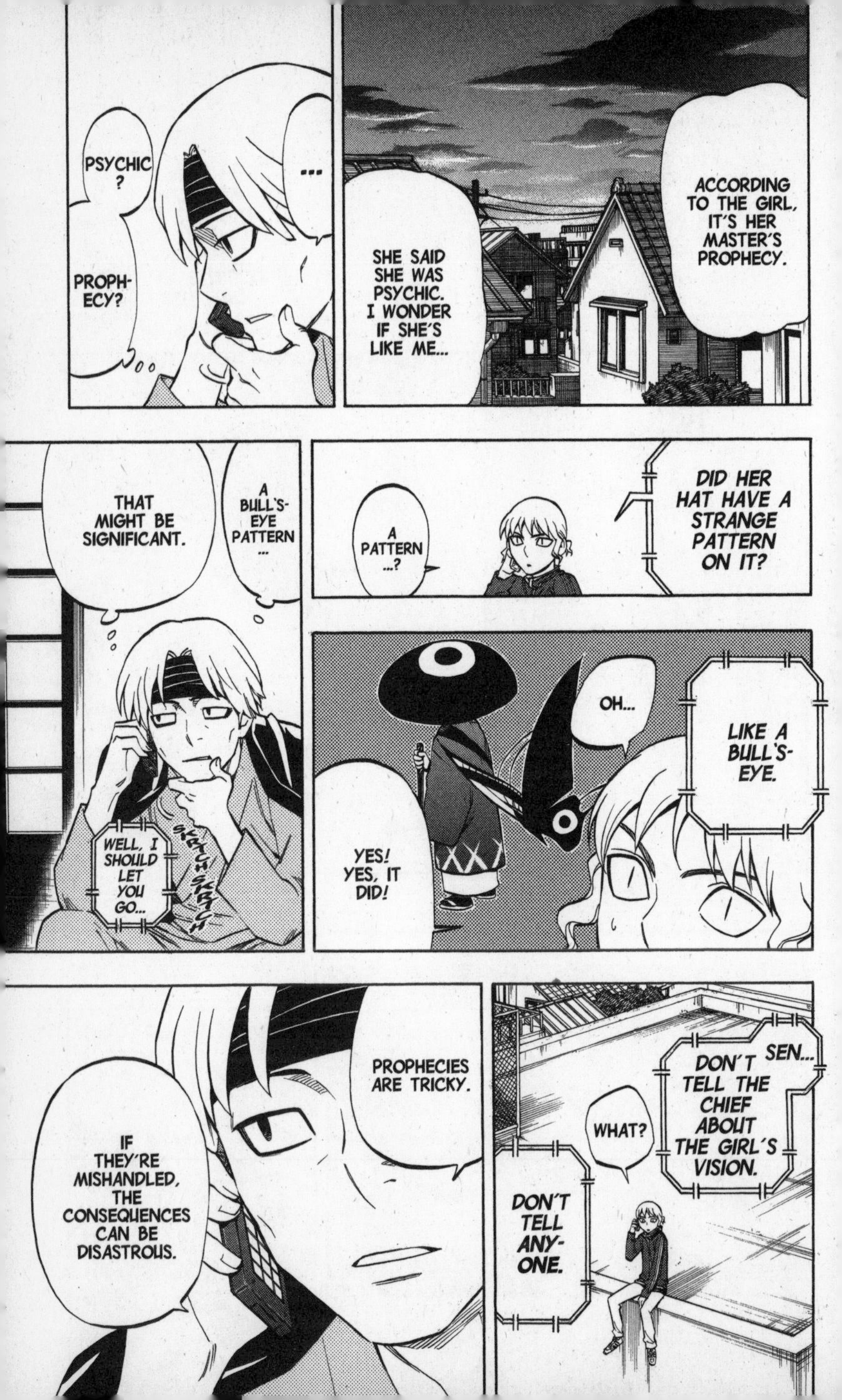

ACCORDING TO THE GIRL, IT'S HER MASTER'S PROPHECY.
SHE SAID SHE WAS PSYCHIC. I WONDER IF SHE'S LIKE ME...
...
PSYCHIC?
PROPHECY?
DID HER HAT HAVE A STRANGE PATTERN ON IT?
A PATTERN...?
LIKE A BULL'S-EYE.
OH...
YES! YES, IT DID!
A BULL'S-EYE PATTERN...
THAT MIGHT BE SIGNIFICANT.
WELL, I SHOULD LET YOU GO...
SKRTCH SKRTCH
SEN... DON'T TELL THE CHIEF ABOUT THE GIRL'S VISION.
WHAT?
DON'T TELL ANYONE.
PROPHECIES ARE TRICKY.
IF THEY'RE MISHANDLED, THE CONSEQUENCES CAN BE DISASTROUS.

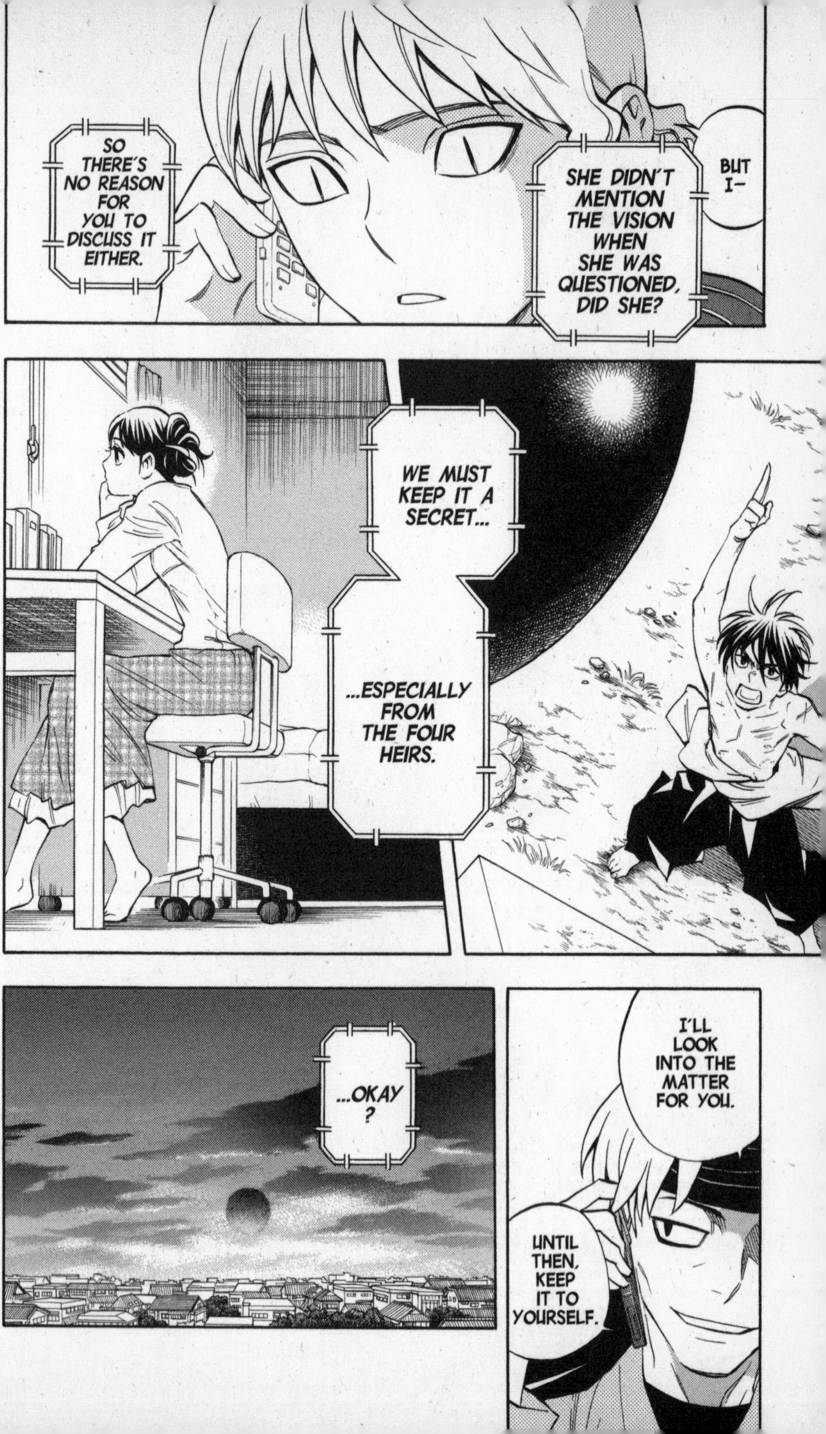
BUT I—
SHE DIDN'T MENTION THE VISION WHEN SHE WAS QUESTIONED, DID SHE?
SO THERE'S NO REASON FOR YOU TO DISCUSS IT EITHER.
WE MUST KEEP IT A SECRET...
...ESPECIALLY FROM THE FOUR HEIRS.
I'LL LOOK INTO THE MATTER FOR YOU.
UNTIL THEN, KEEP IT TO YOURSELF.
...OKAY?

Chapter 178: The Crows

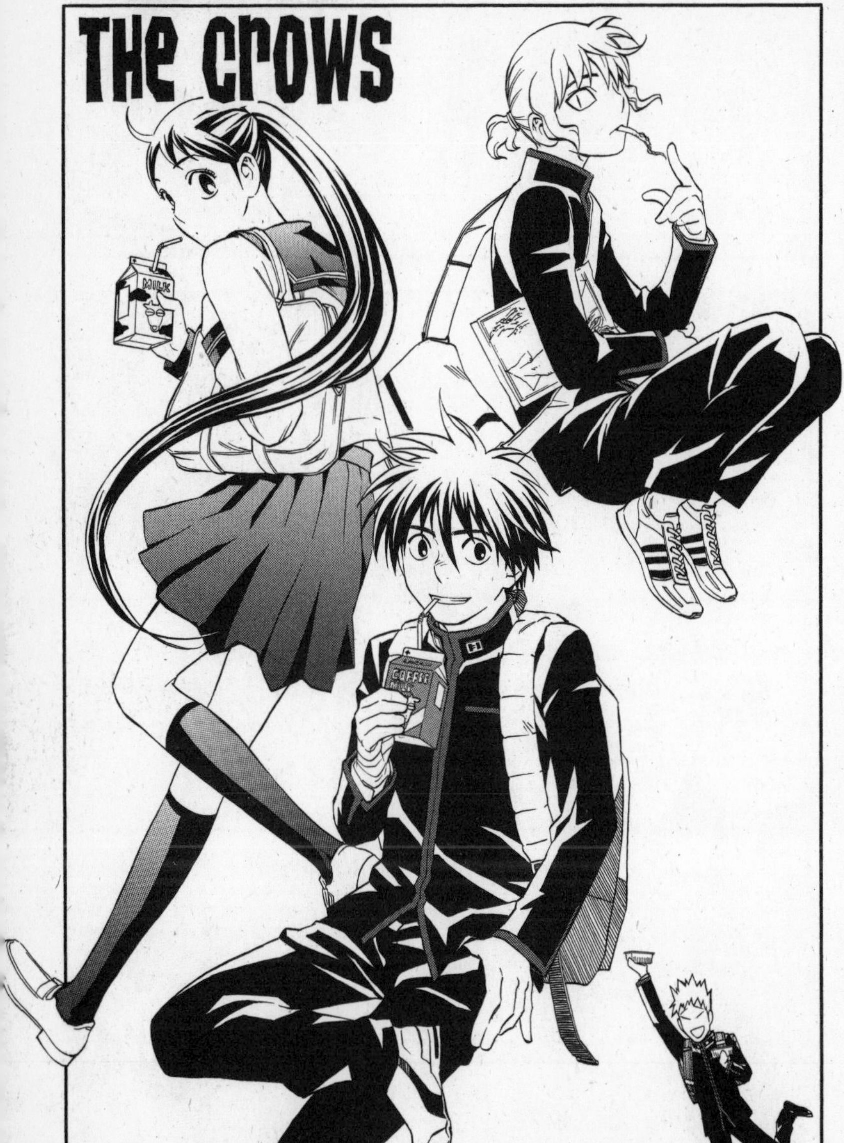
MILK
COFFEE MILK

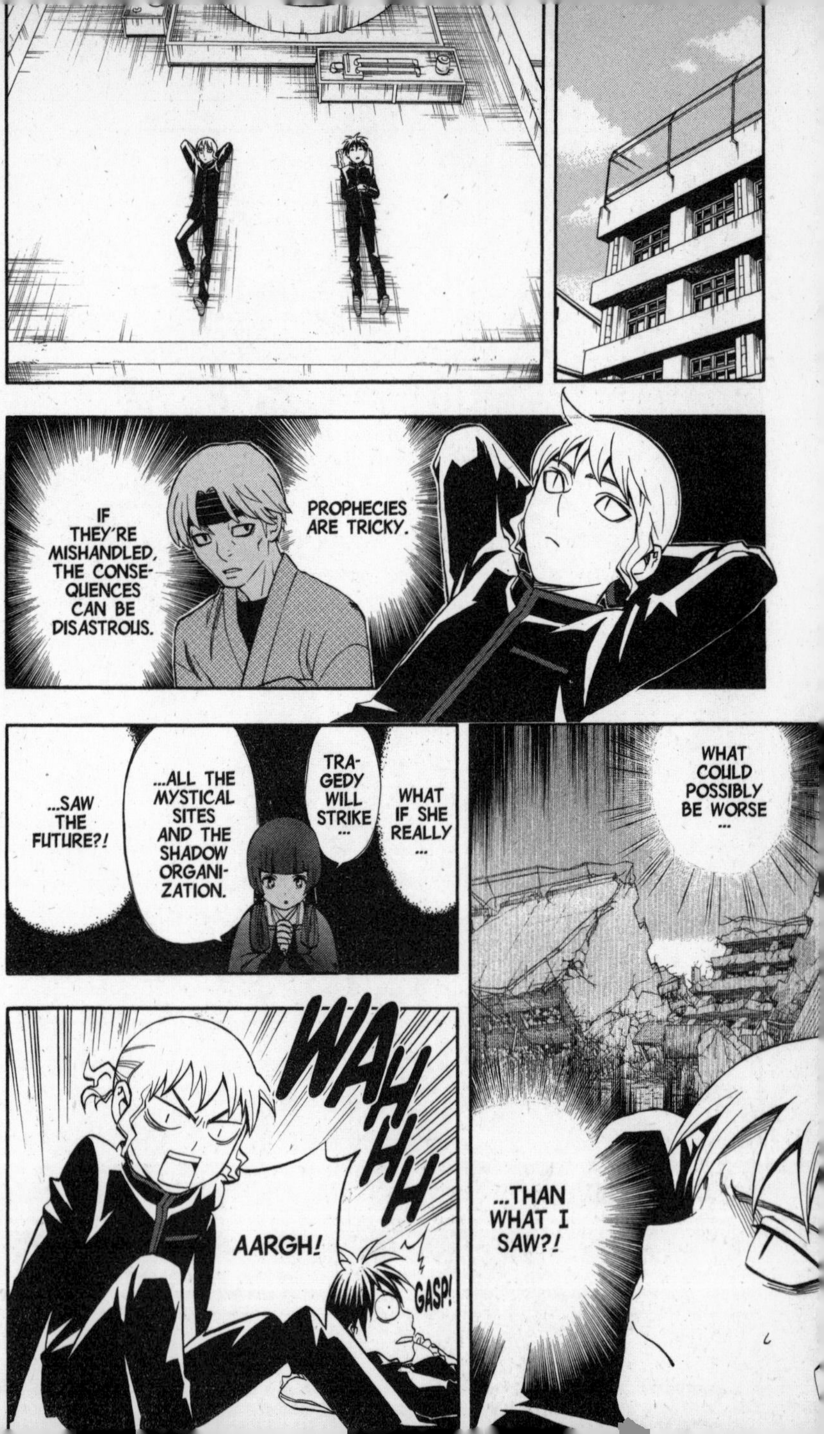
PROPHECIES ARE TRICKY.
IF THEY'RE MISHANDLED, THE CONSE-QUENCES CAN BE DISASTROUS.
WHAT COULD POSSIBLY BE WORSE ...
...THAN WHAT I SAW?!
WHAT IF SHE REALLY ...
TRA-GEDY WILL STRIKE ...
...ALL THE MYSTICAL SITES AND THE SHADOW ORGANI-ZATION.
...SAW THE FUTURE?!
WAHHH
AARGH!
GASP!

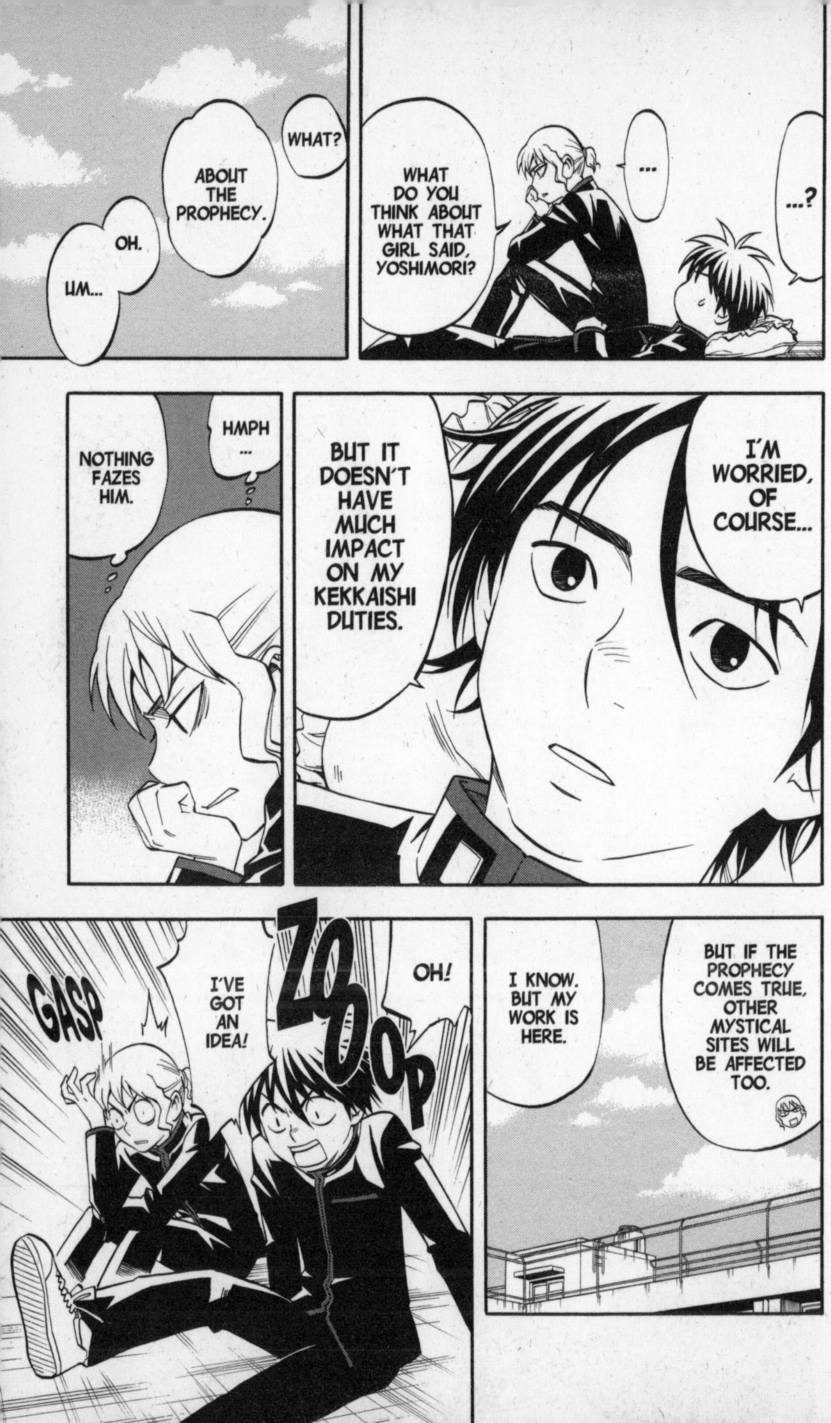
...?
...
WHAT DO YOU THINK ABOUT WHAT THAT GIRL SAID, YOSHIMORI?
WHAT?
ABOUT THE PROPHECY.
OH.
UM...
I'M WORRIED, OF COURSE...
BUT IT DOESN'T HAVE MUCH IMPACT ON MY KEKKAISHI DUTIES.
HMPH ...
NOTHING FAZES HIM.
BUT IF THE PROPHECY COMES TRUE, OTHER MYSTICAL SITES WILL BE AFFECTED TOO.
I KNOW. BUT MY WORK IS HERE.
OH!
ZOOOP
I'VE GOT AN IDEA!
GASP

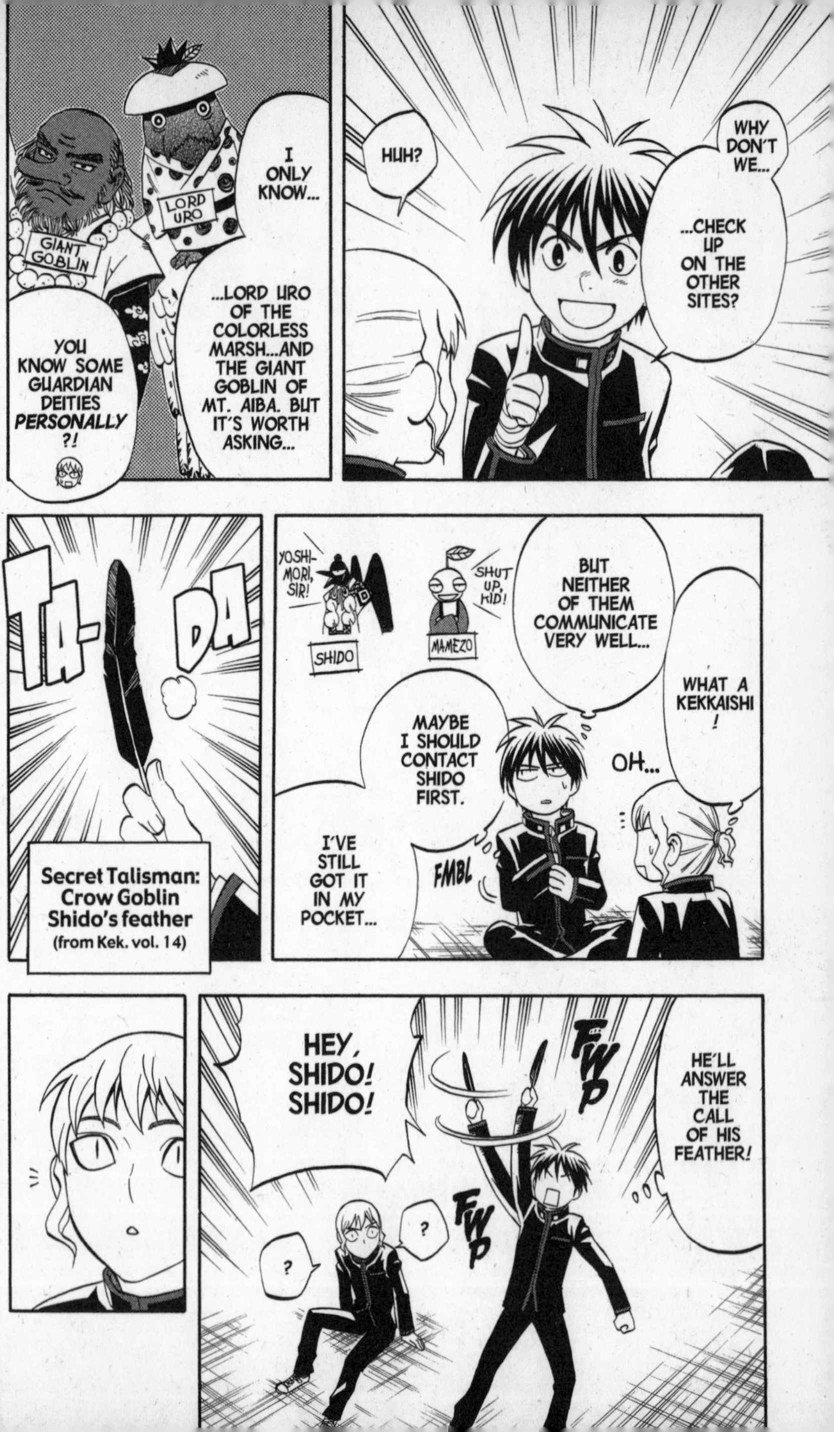
WHY DON'T WE...
...CHECK UP ON THE OTHER SITES?
HUH?
I ONLY KNOW...
...LORD URO OF THE COLORLESS MARSH...AND THE GIANT GOBLIN OF MT. AIBA. BUT IT'S WORTH ASKING...
LORD URO
GIANT GOBLIN
YOU KNOW SOME GUARDIAN DEITIES PERSONALLY ?!
WHAT A KEKKAISHI!
BUT NEITHER OF THEM COMMUNICATE VERY WELL...
SHUT UP, KID!
MAMEZO
YOSHI-MORI, SIR!
SHIDO
OH...
MAYBE I SHOULD CONTACT SHIDO FIRST.
I'VE STILL GOT IT IN MY POCKET...
FMBL
TA-DA
Secret Talisman: Crow Goblin Shido's feather
(from Kek. vol. 14)
HE'LL ANSWER THE CALL OF HIS FEATHER!
FWP
HEY, SHIDO! SHIDO!
FWP
?
?

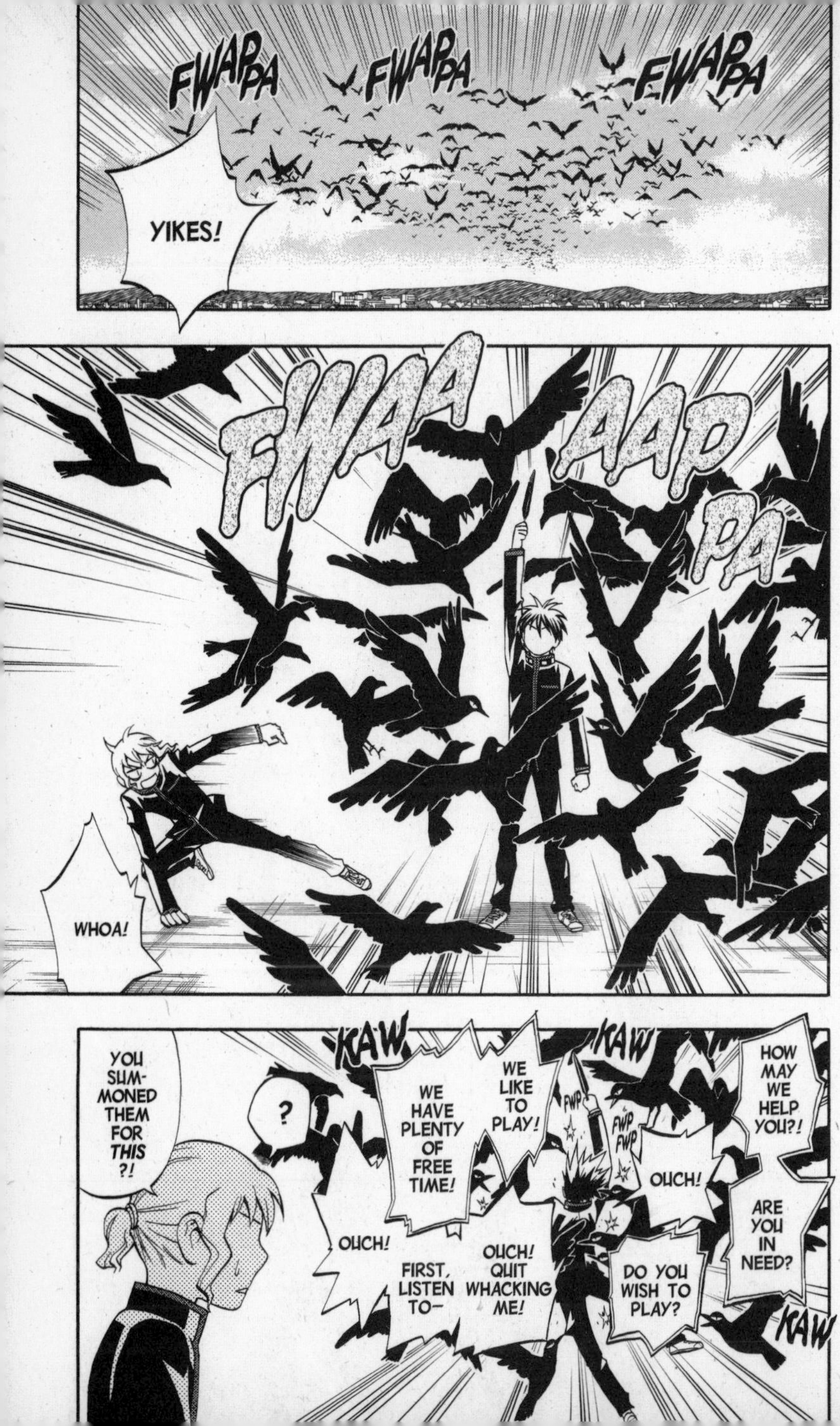
FWAPPA
FWAPPA
FWAPPA
YIKES!
FWAAAAPPA
WHOA!
KAW
HOW MAY WE HELP YOU?!
KAW
WE LIKE TO PLAY!
WE HAVE PLENTY OF FREE TIME!
KAW
?
YOU SUMMONED THEM FOR THIS?!
FWP
FWP FWP
OUCH!
ARE YOU IN NEED?
DO YOU WISH TO PLAY?
OUCH! QUIT WHACKING ME!
FIRST, LISTEN TO—
OUCH!
KAW

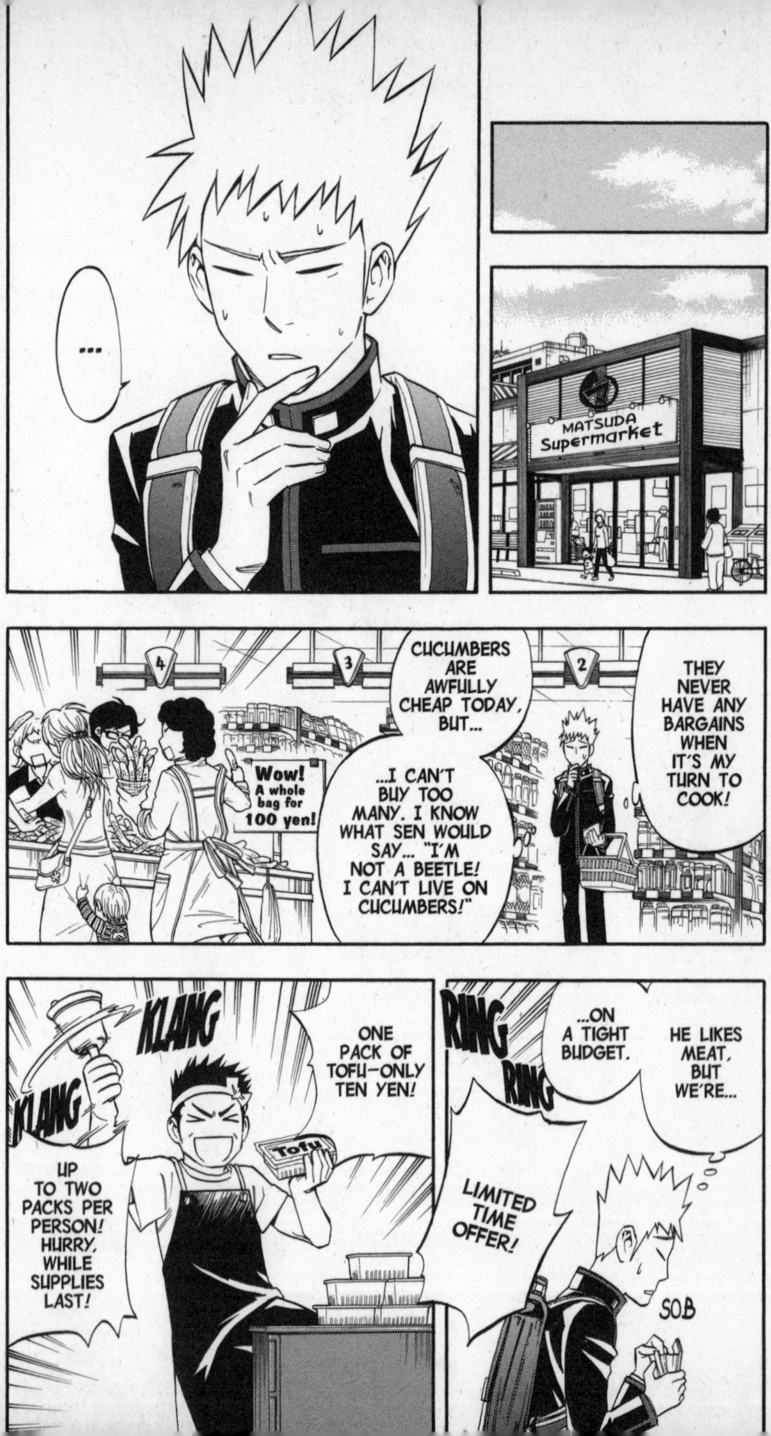
MATSUDA Supermarket
...
THEY NEVER HAVE ANY BARGAINS WHEN IT'S MY TURN TO COOK!
CUCUMBERS ARE AWFULLY CHEAP TODAY, BUT...
...I CAN'T BUY TOO MANY. I KNOW WHAT SEN WOULD SAY... "I'M NOT A BEETLE! I CAN'T LIVE ON CUCUMBERS!"
Wow! A whole bag for 100 yen!
HE LIKES MEAT, BUT WE'RE...
...ON A TIGHT BUDGET.
RING
RING
LIMITED TIME OFFER!
SOB
KLANG
ONE PACK OF TOFU—ONLY TEN YEN!
Tofu
KLANG
UP TO TWO PACKS PER PERSON! HURRY, WHILE SUPPLIES LAST!

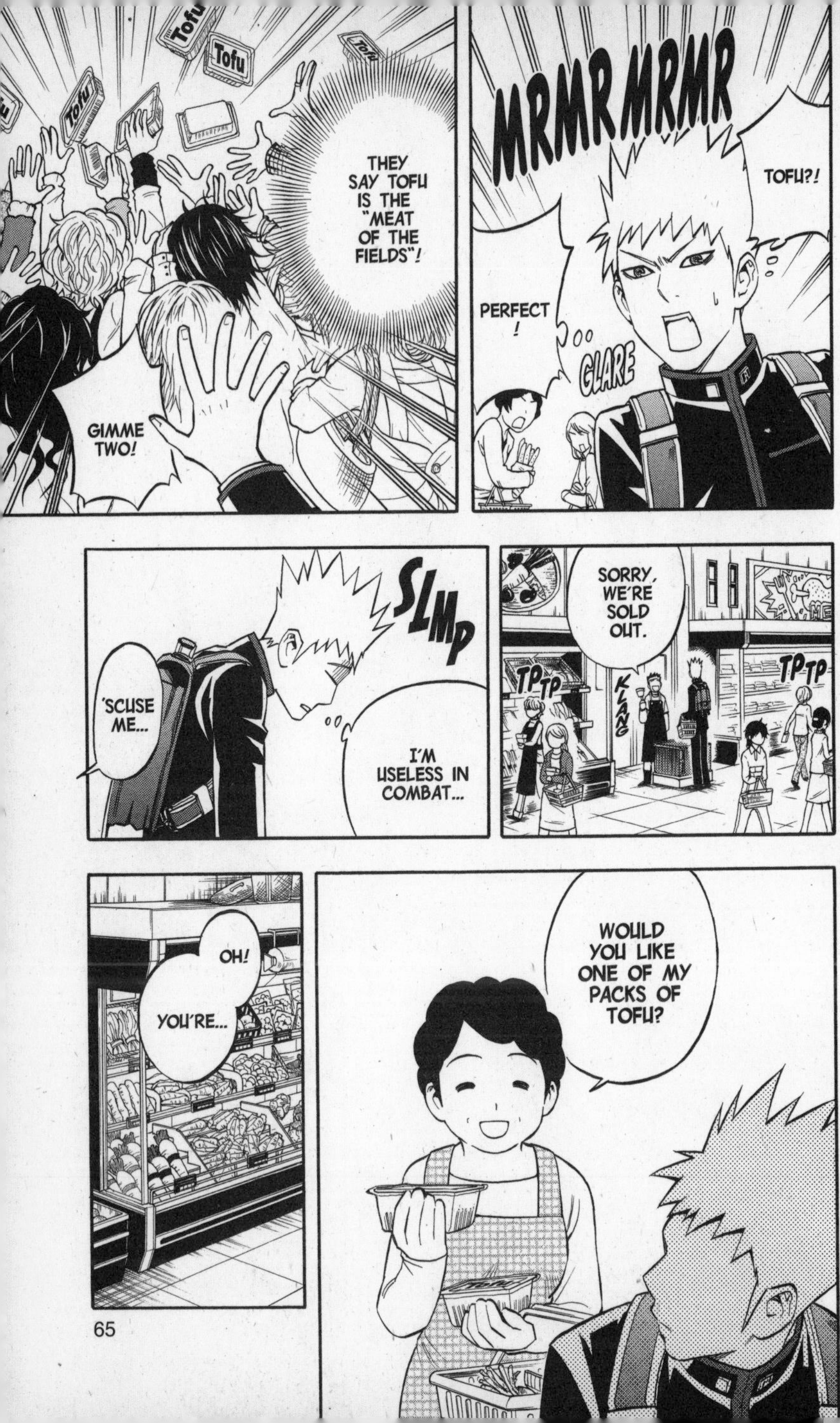
MRMR MRMR
TOFU?!
PERFECT!
GLARE
Tofu
THEY SAY TOFU IS THE "MEAT OF THE FIELDS"!
GIMME TWO!
SORRY, WE'RE SOLD OUT.
KLANG
TP TP
TP TP
SLMP
'SCUSE ME...
I'M USELESS IN COMBAT...
WOULD YOU LIKE ONE OF MY PACKS OF TOFU?
OH!
YOU'RE...

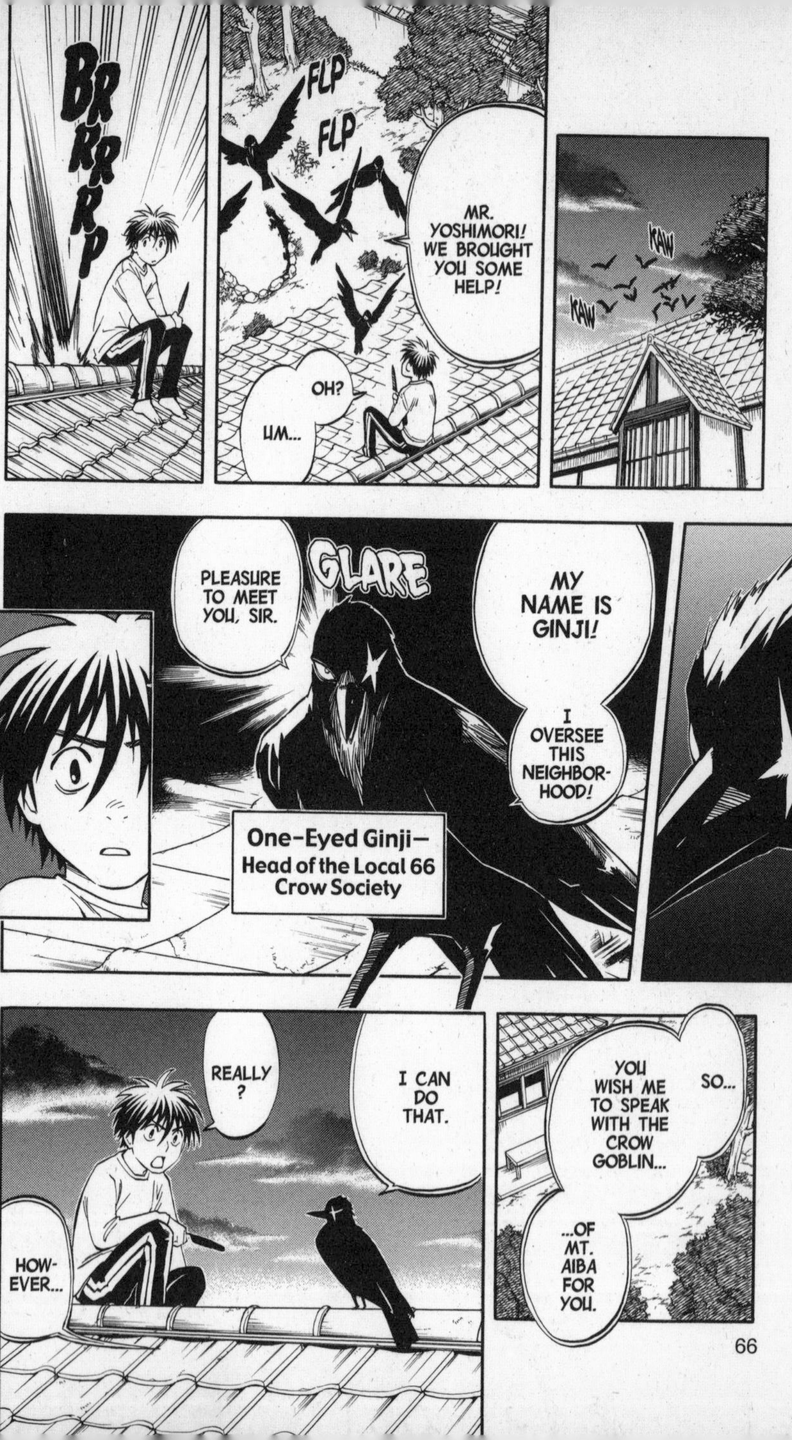
KAW
KAW
FLP
FLP
MR. YOSHIMORI! WE BROUGHT YOU SOME HELP!
OH?
UM...
BRRRRP
MY NAME IS GINJI!
I OVERSEE THIS NEIGHBOR-HOOD!
GLARE
PLEASURE TO MEET YOU, SIR.
One-Eyed Ginji—Head of the Local 66 Crow Society
SO...
YOU WISH ME TO SPEAK WITH THE CROW GOBLIN...
...OF MT. AIBA FOR YOU.
I CAN DO THAT.
REALLY?
HOW-EVER...

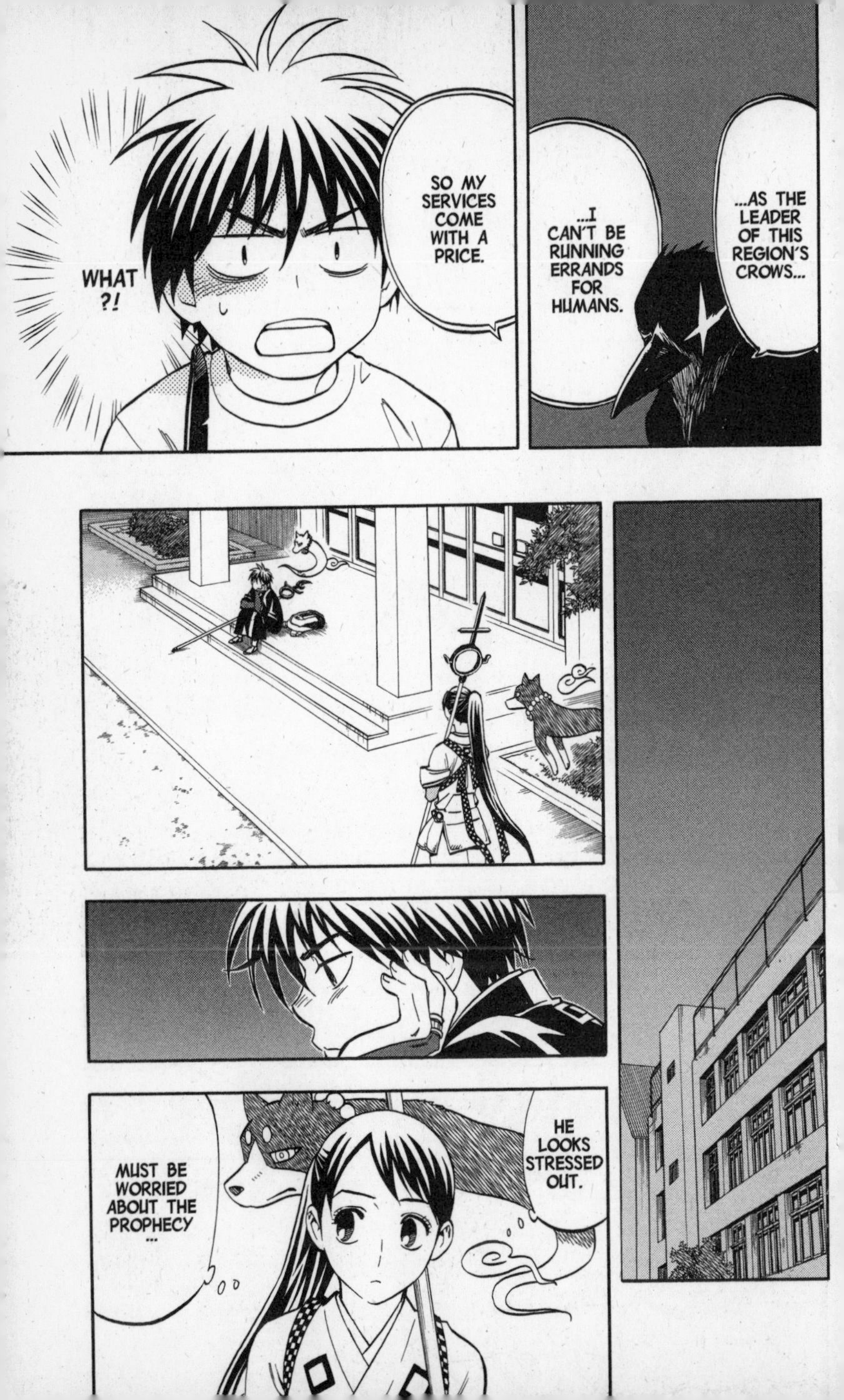
...AS THE LEADER OF THIS REGION'S CROWS...
...I CAN'T BE RUNNING ERRANDS FOR HUMANS.
SO MY SERVICES COME WITH A PRICE.
WHAT?!
HE LOOKS STRESSED OUT.
MUST BE WORRIED ABOUT THE PROPHECY...

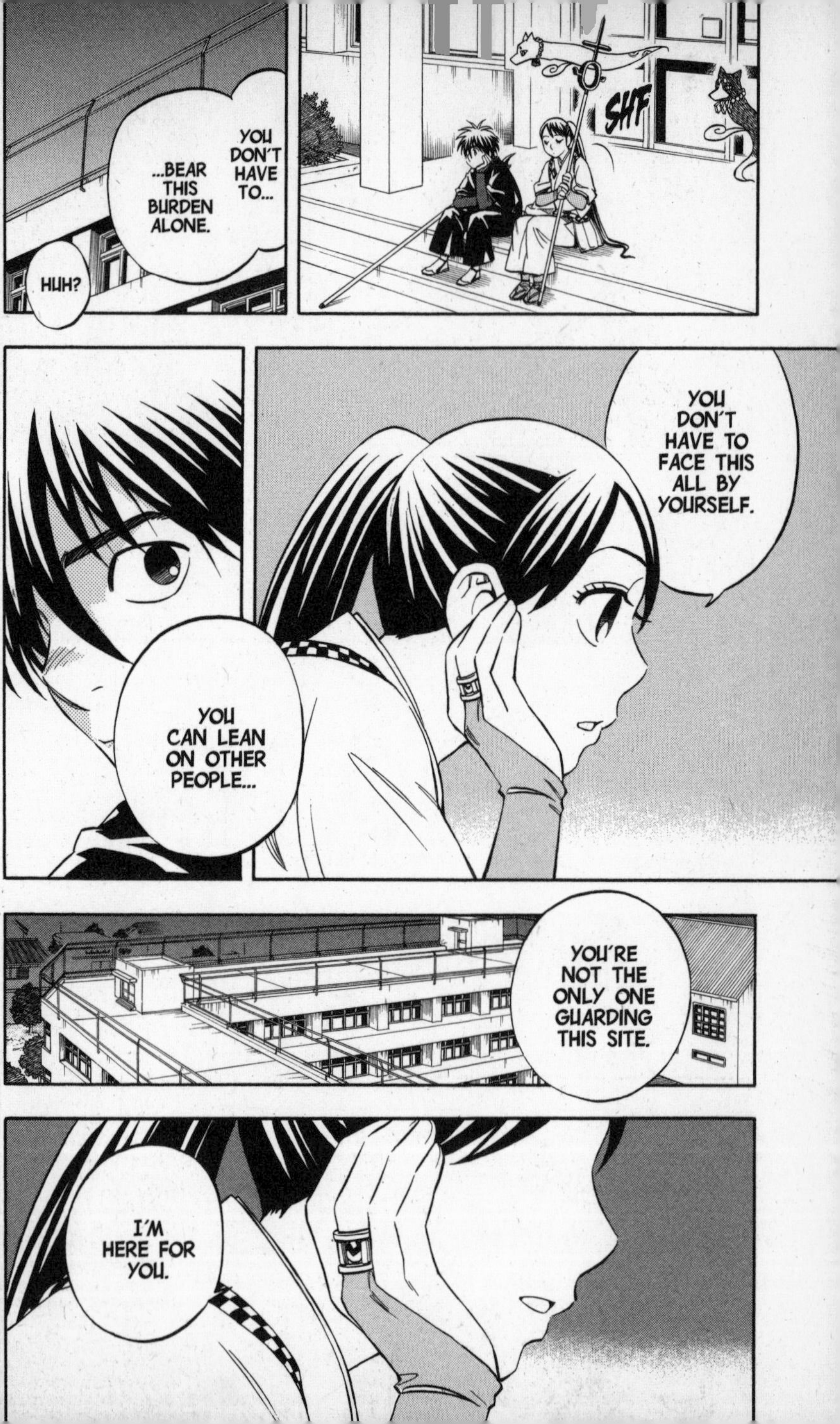
SHF
YOU DON'T HAVE TO...
...BEAR THIS BURDEN ALONE.
HUH?
YOU DON'T HAVE TO FACE THIS ALL BY YOURSELF.
YOU CAN LEAN ON OTHER PEOPLE...
YOU'RE NOT THE ONLY ONE GUARDING THIS SITE.
I'M HERE FOR YOU.

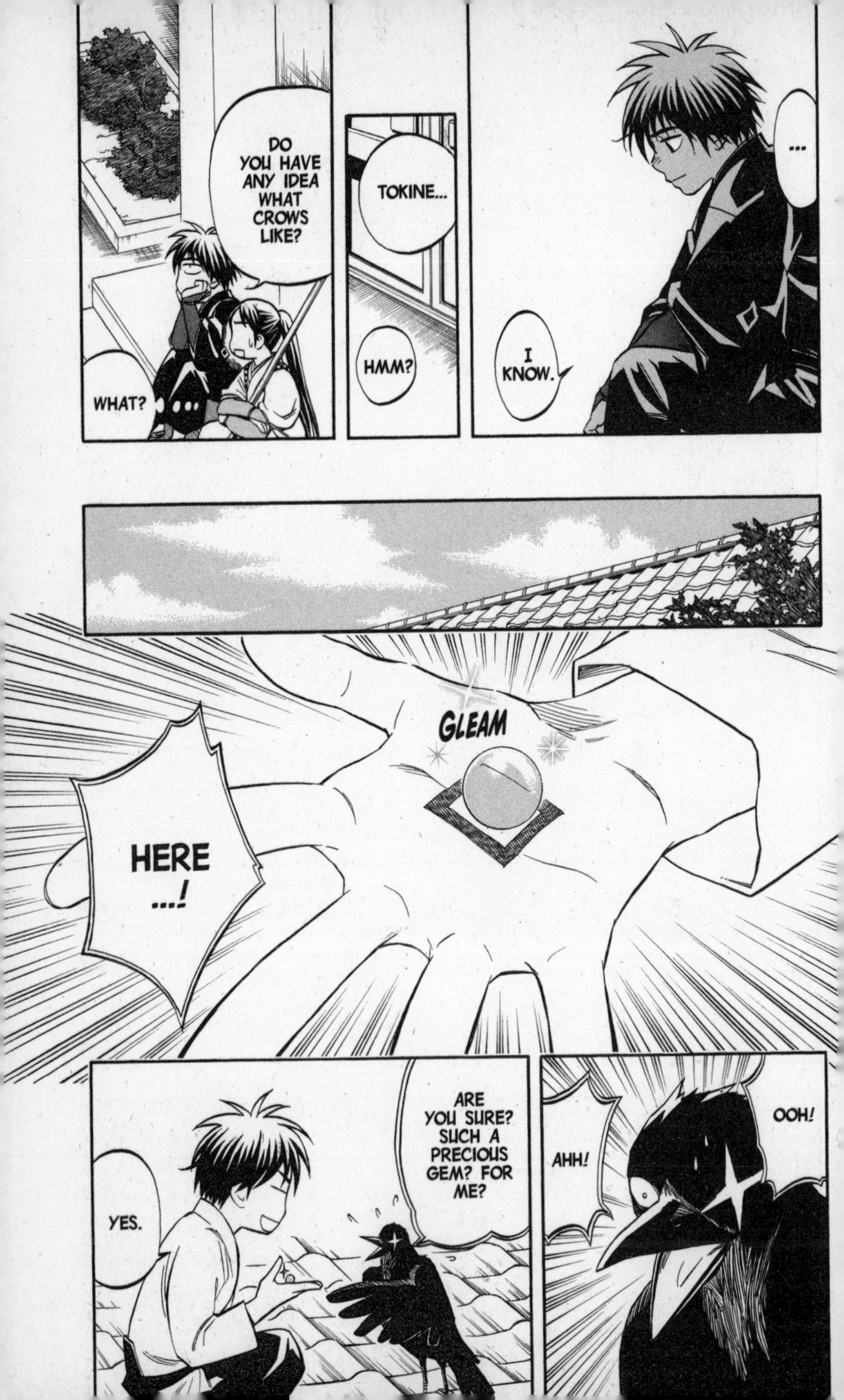
...
I KNOW.
TOKINE...
HMM?
DO YOU HAVE ANY IDEA WHAT CROWS LIKE?
WHAT?
GLEAM
HERE ...!
OOH!
AHH!
ARE YOU SURE? SUCH A PRECIOUS GEM? FOR ME?
YES.

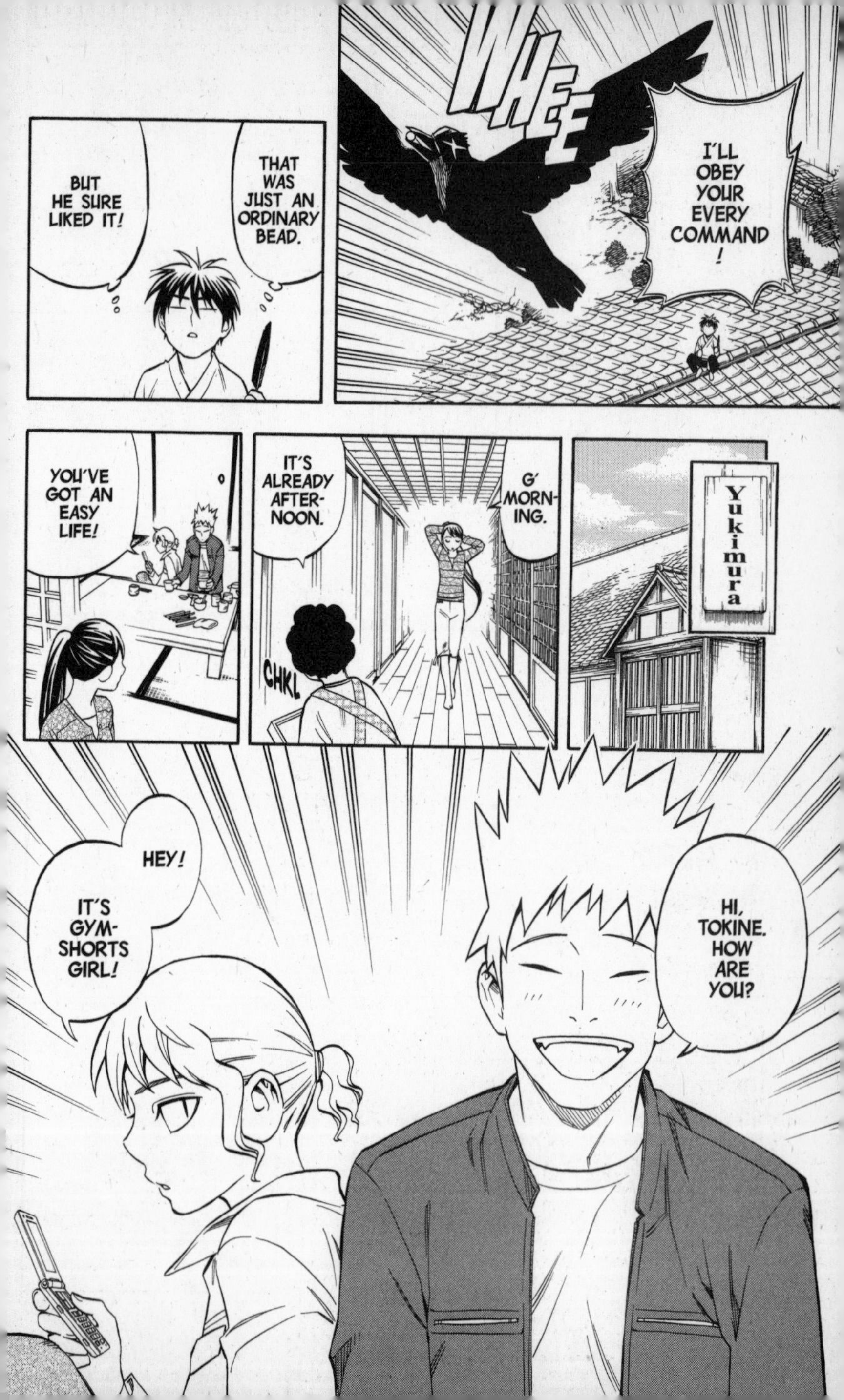
WHEE
I'LL OBEY YOUR EVERY COMMAND!
THAT WAS JUST AN ORDINARY BEAD.
BUT HE SURE LIKED IT!
Yukimura
G' MORNING.
IT'S ALREADY AFTERNOON.
CHKL
YOU'VE GOT AN EASY LIFE!
HI, TOKINE. HOW ARE YOU?
HEY!
IT'S GYM-SHORTS GIRL!

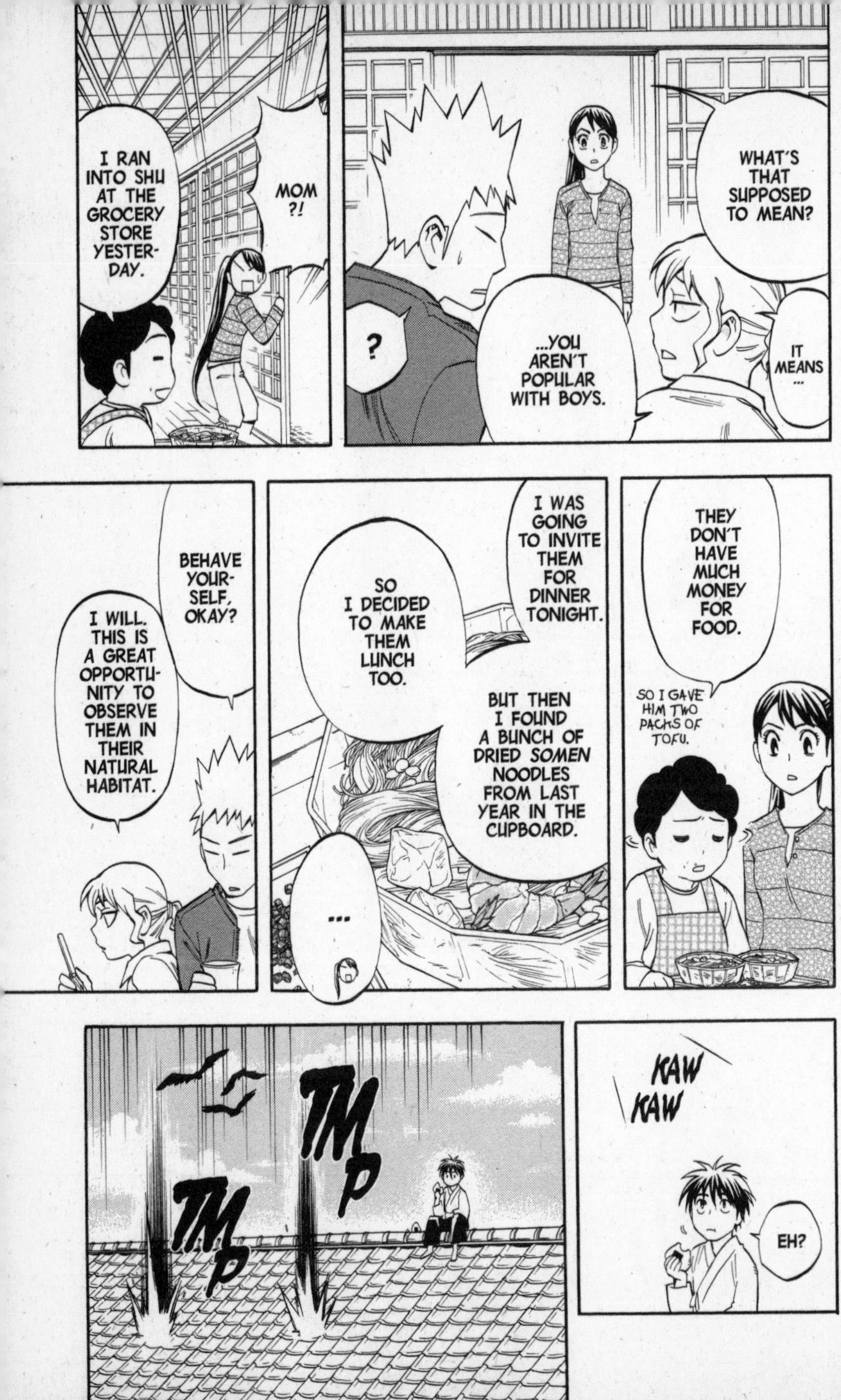
WHAT'S THAT SUPPOSED TO MEAN?
IT MEANS ...
...YOU AREN'T POPULAR WITH BOYS.
?
MOM ?!
I RAN INTO SHU AT THE GROCERY STORE YESTER-DAY.
THEY DON'T HAVE MUCH MONEY FOR FOOD.
SO I GAVE HIM TWO PACKS OF TOFU.
I WAS GOING TO INVITE THEM FOR DINNER TONIGHT.
BUT THEN I FOUND A BUNCH OF DRIED *SOMEN* NOODLES FROM LAST YEAR IN THE CUPBOARD.
SO I DECIDED TO MAKE THEM LUNCH TOO.
...
BEHAVE YOUR-SELF, OKAY?
I WILL. THIS IS A GREAT OPPORTU-NITY TO OBSERVE THEM IN THEIR NATURAL HABITAT.
KAW KAW
EH?
TMP
TMP

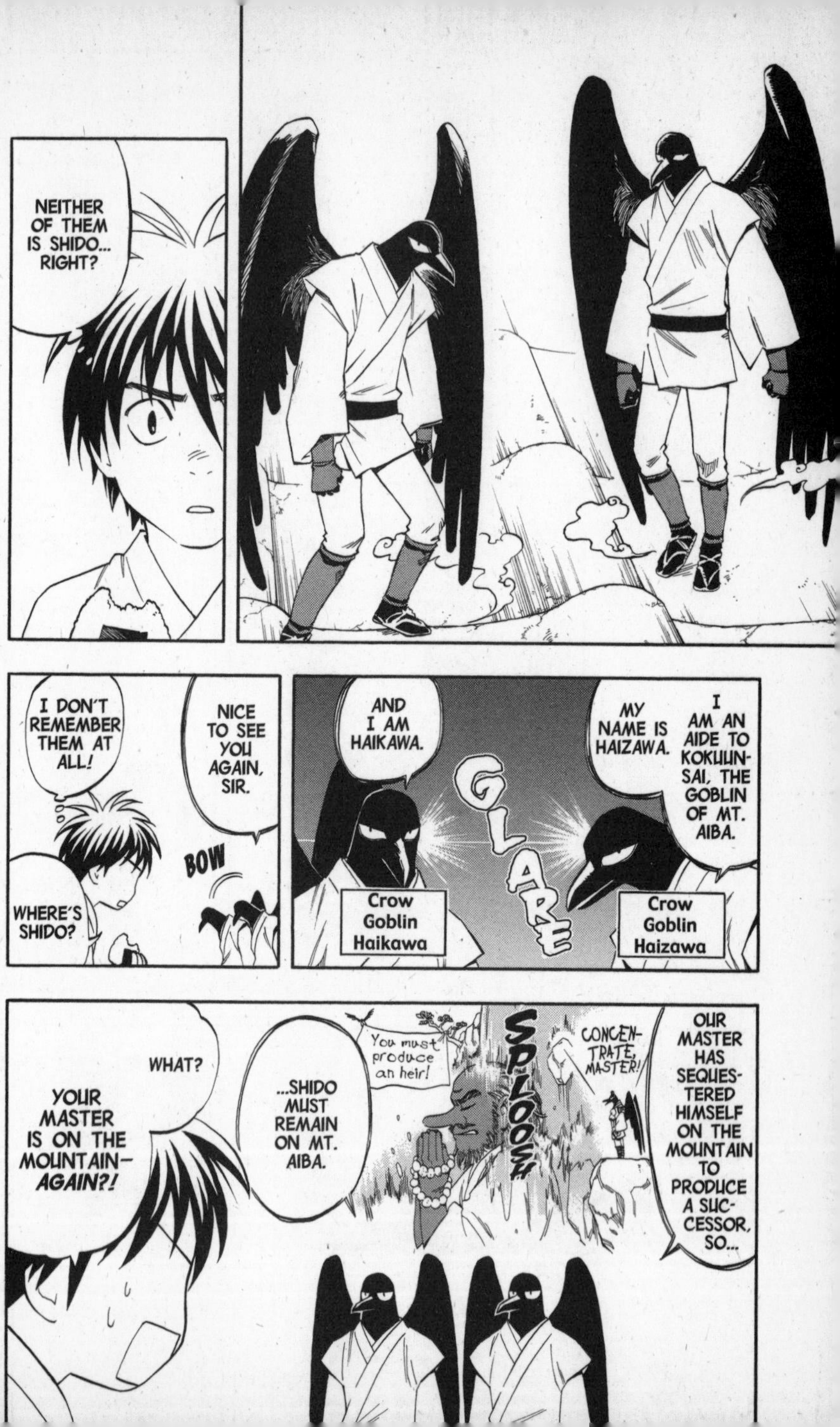
NEITHER OF THEM IS SHIDO... RIGHT?
MY NAME IS HAIZAWA.
I AM AN AIDE TO KOKUUNSAI, THE GOBLIN OF MT. AIBA.
GLARE
AND I AM HAIKAWA.
Crow Goblin Haizawa
Crow Goblin Haikawa
NICE TO SEE YOU AGAIN, SIR.
BOW
I DON'T REMEMBER THEM AT ALL!
WHERE'S SHIDO?
OUR MASTER HAS SEQUESTERED HIMSELF ON THE MOUNTAIN TO PRODUCE A SUCCESSOR, SO...
CONCENTRATE, MASTER!
SPLOOSH
You must produce an heir!
...SHIDO MUST REMAIN ON MT. AIBA.
WHAT?
YOUR MASTER IS ON THE MOUNTAIN—AGAIN?!

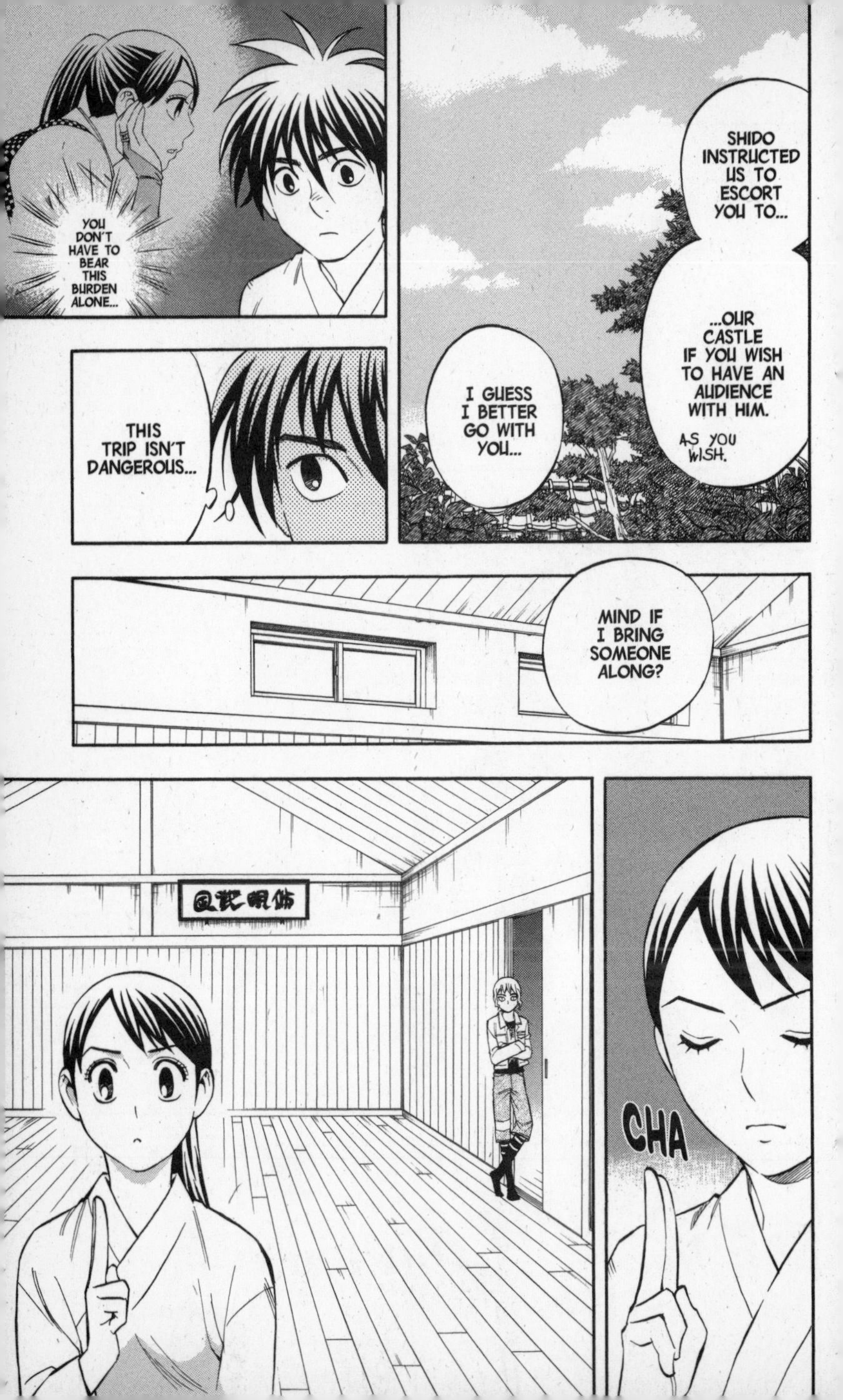
SHIDO INSTRUCTED US TO ESCORT YOU TO...
...OUR CASTLE IF YOU WISH TO HAVE AN AUDIENCE WITH HIM.
AS YOU WISH.
I GUESS I BETTER GO WITH YOU...
YOU DON'T HAVE TO BEAR THIS BURDEN ALONE...
THIS TRIP ISN'T DANGEROUS...
MIND IF I BRING SOMEONE ALONG?
CHA

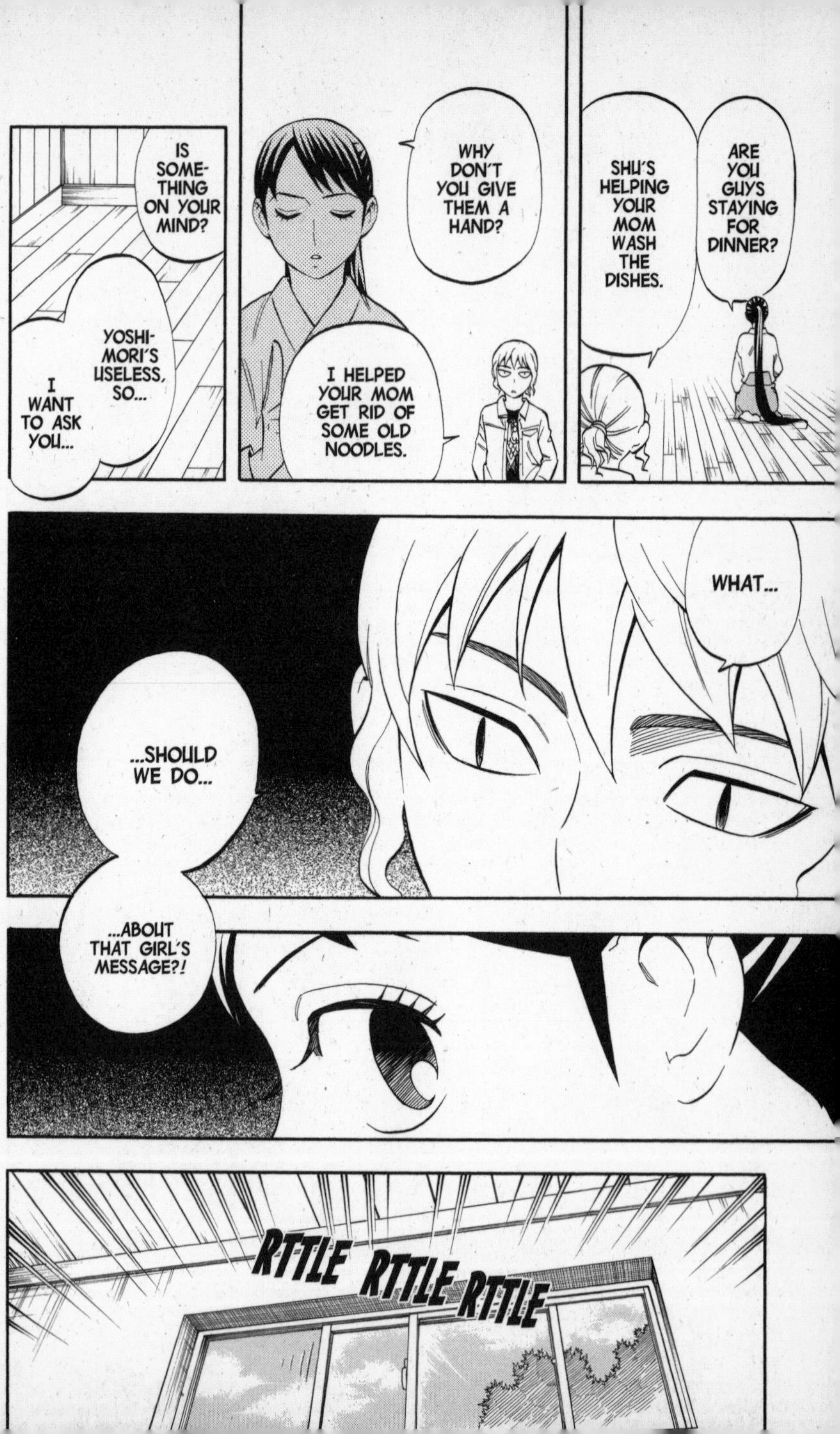
ARE YOU GUYS STAYING FOR DINNER?
SHU'S HELPING YOUR MOM WASH THE DISHES.
WHY DON'T YOU GIVE THEM A HAND?
I HELPED YOUR MOM GET RID OF SOME OLD NOODLES.
IS SOME-THING ON YOUR MIND?
YOSHI-MORI'S USELESS, SO...
I WANT TO ASK YOU...
WHAT...
...SHOULD WE DO...
...ABOUT THAT GIRL'S MESSAGE?!
RTTLE RTTLE RTTLE

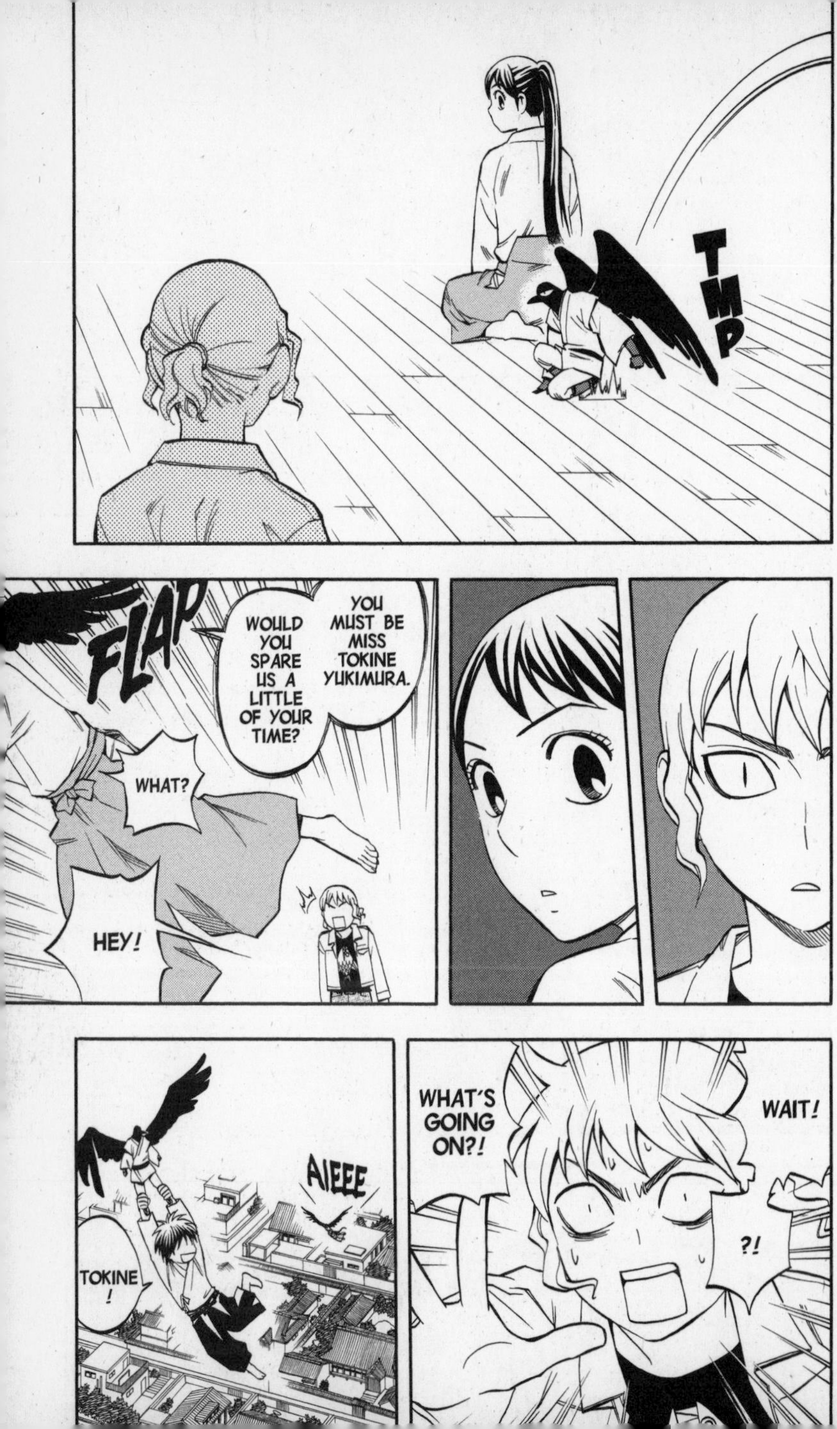
TMP
FLAP
YOU MUST BE MISS TOKINE YUKIMURA.
WOULD YOU SPARE US A LITTLE OF YOUR TIME?
WHAT?
HEY!
WAIT!
?!
WHAT'S GOING ON?!
AIEEE
TOKINE!

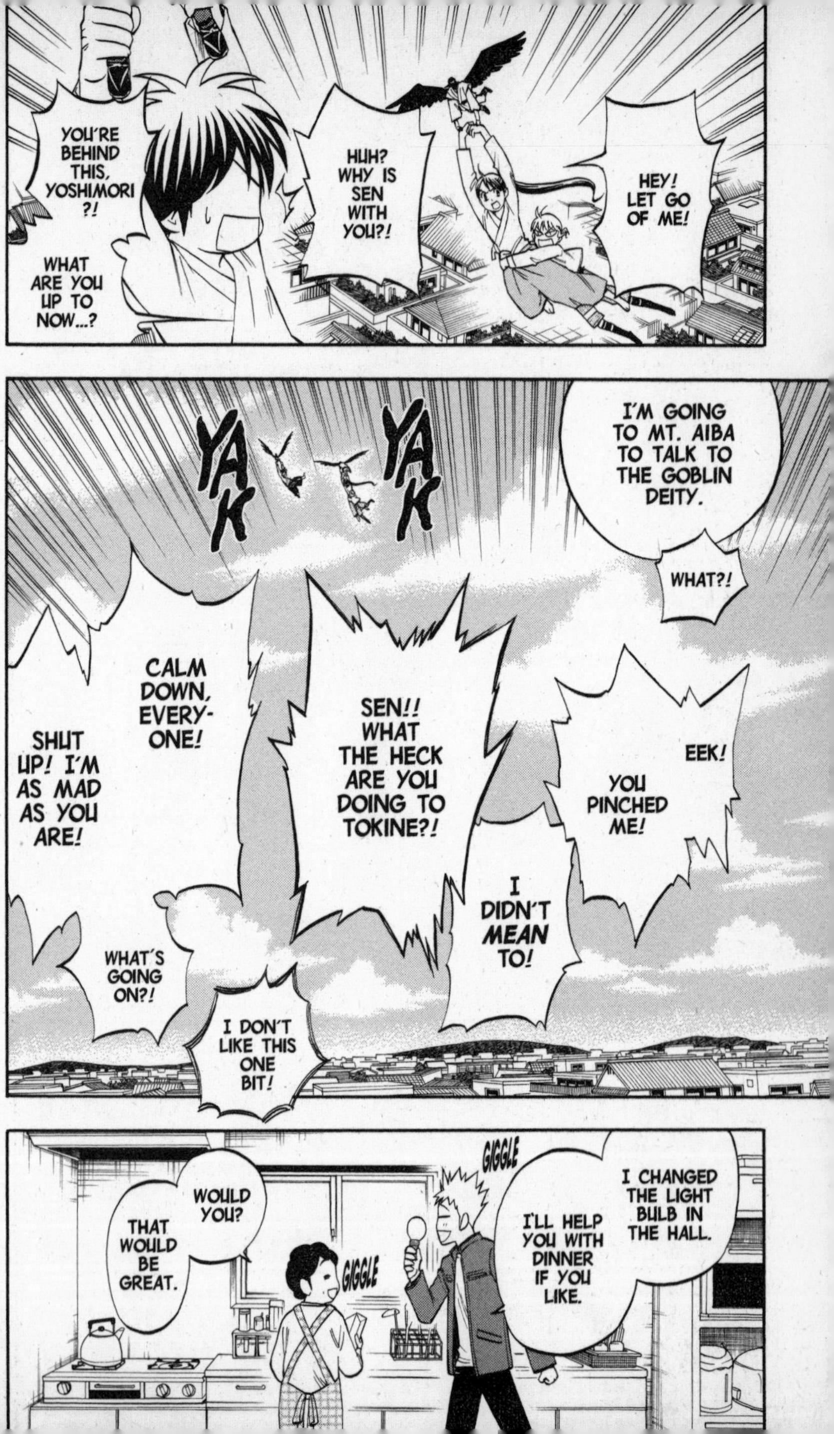
HEY! LET GO OF ME!
HUH? WHY IS SEN WITH YOU?!
YOU'RE BEHIND THIS, YOSHIMORI?!
WHAT ARE YOU UP TO NOW...?
I'M GOING TO MT. AIBA TO TALK TO THE GOBLIN DEITY.
YAK
YAK
WHAT?!
EEK!
YOU PINCHED ME!
SEN!! WHAT THE HECK ARE YOU DOING TO TOKINE?!
CALM DOWN, EVERY-ONE!
SHUT UP! I'M AS MAD AS YOU ARE!
I DIDN'T *MEAN* TO!
WHAT'S GOING ON?!
I DON'T LIKE THIS ONE BIT!
I CHANGED THE LIGHT BULB IN THE HALL.
I'LL HELP YOU WITH DINNER IF YOU LIKE.
GIGGLE
WOULD YOU?
THAT WOULD BE GREAT.
GIGGLE

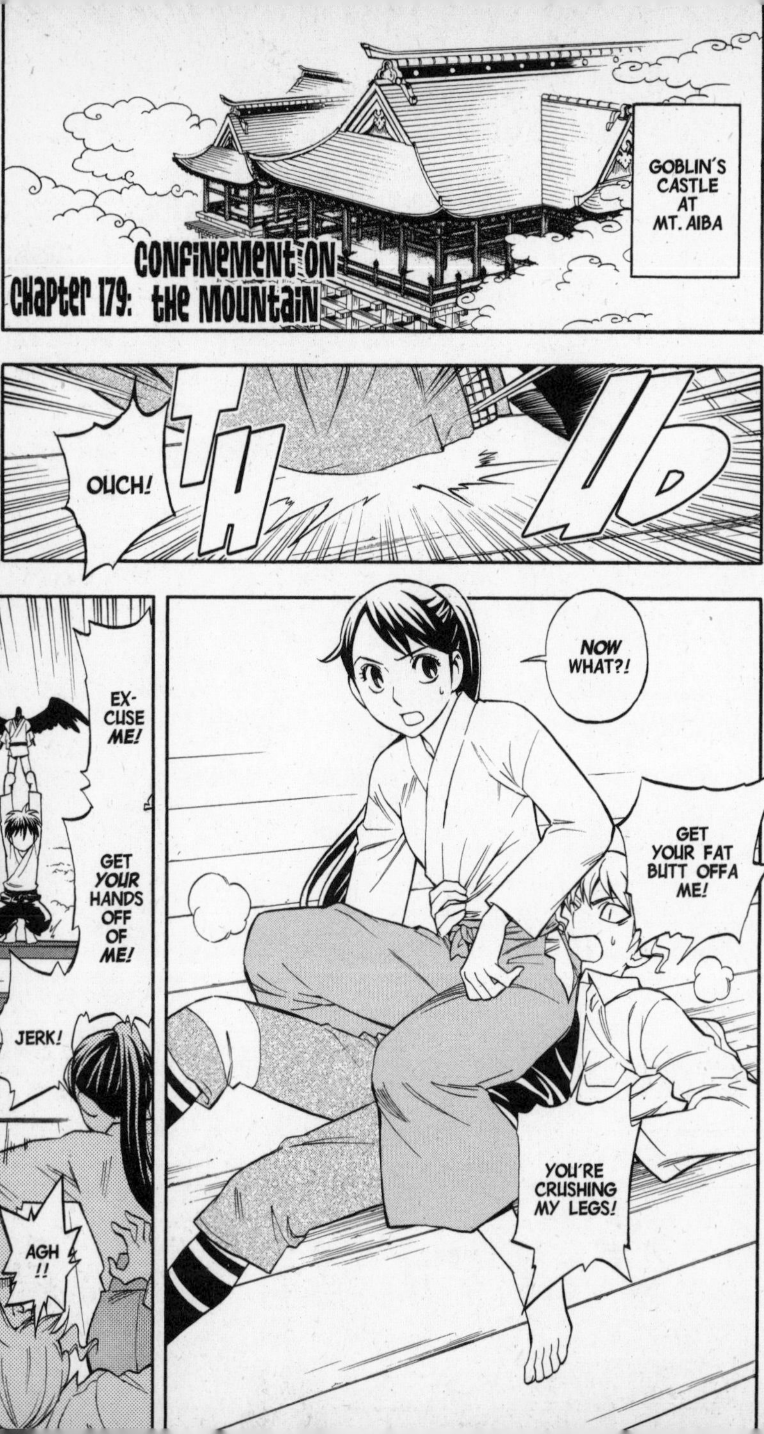
GOBLIN'S CASTLE AT MT. AIBA
CHAPTER 179: CONFINEMENT ON THE MOUNTAIN
THUD
OUCH!
NOW WHAT?!
GET YOUR FAT BUTT OFFA ME!
YOU'RE CRUSHING MY LEGS!
EX-CUSE ME!
TMP
GET YOUR HANDS OFF OF ME!
JERK!
AGH!!

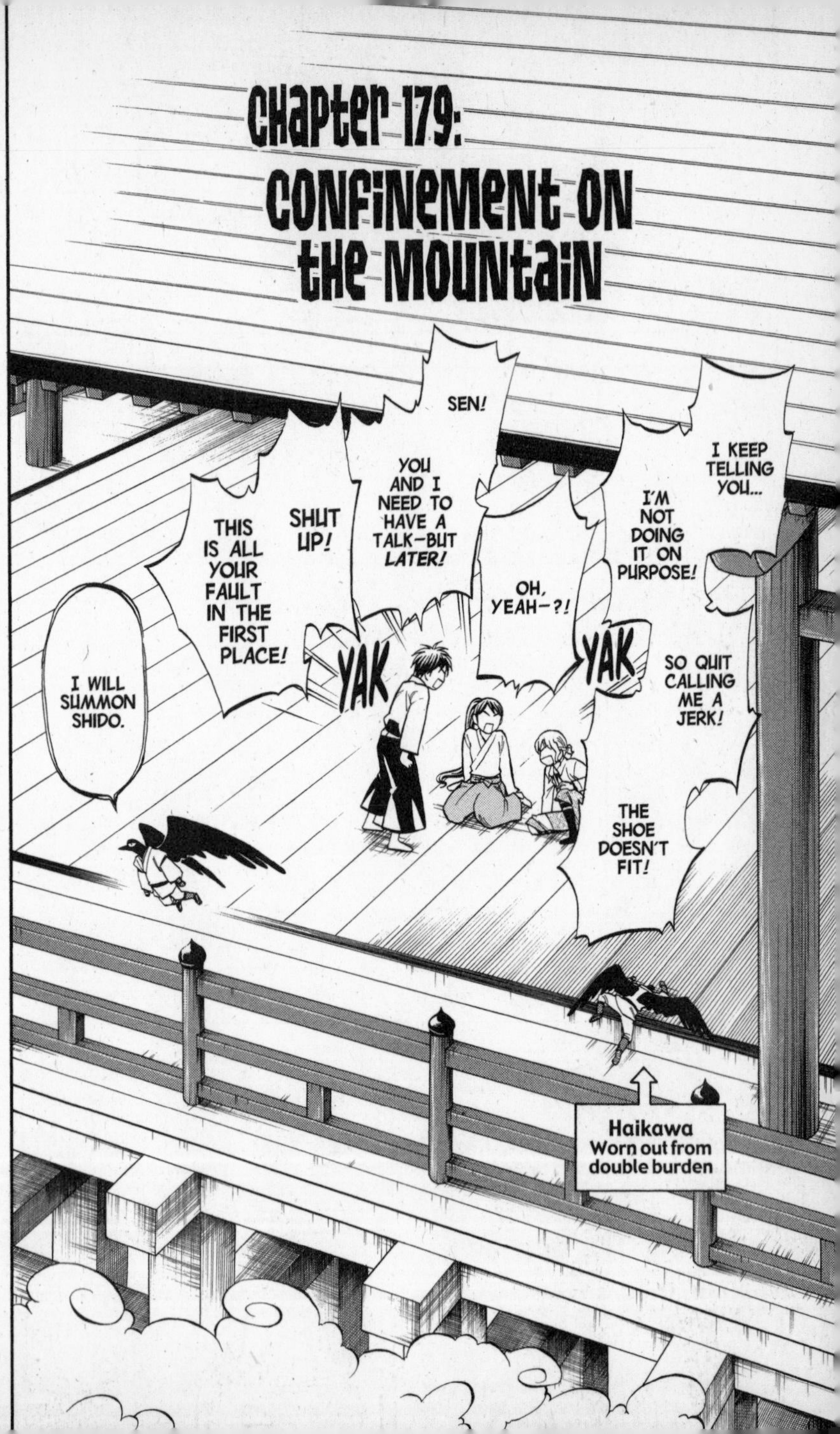
Chapter 179:
Confinement on the Mountain
I KEEP TELLING YOU...
I'M NOT DOING IT ON PURPOSE!
SO QUIT CALLING ME A JERK!
THE SHOE DOESN'T FIT!
YAK
OH, YEAH—?!
SEN!
YOU AND I NEED TO HAVE A TALK—BUT LATER!
YAK
SHUT UP!
THIS IS ALL YOUR FAULT IN THE FIRST PLACE!
I WILL SUMMON SHIDO.
Haikawa
Worn out from double burden

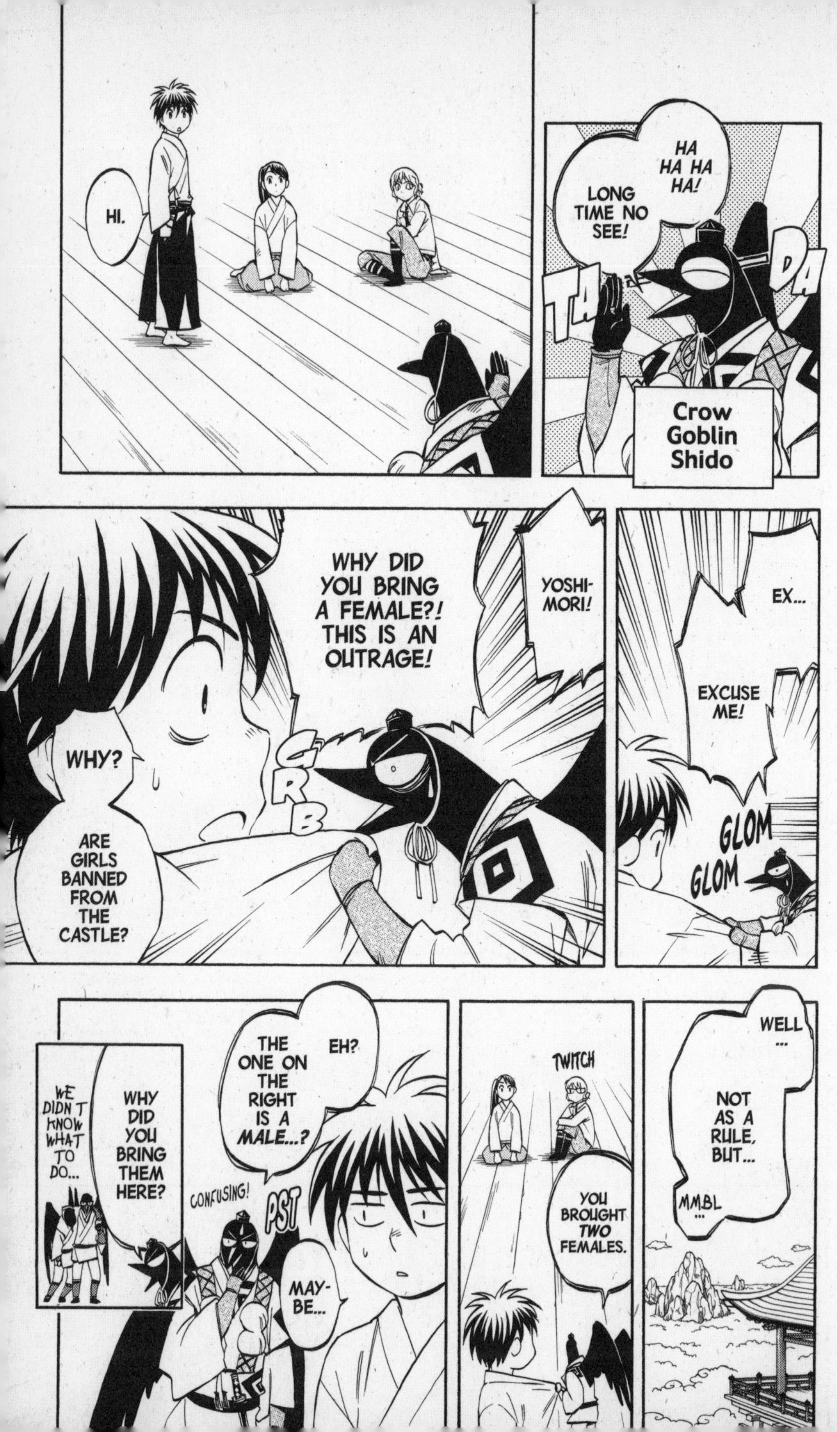
HA HA HA HA! LONG TIME NO SEE!
DA
TA
Crow Goblin Shido
HI.
EX...
EXCUSE ME!
GLOM GLOM
YOSHI-MORI!
WHY DID YOU BRING A FEMALE?! THIS IS AN OUTRAGE!
GRB
WHY?
ARE GIRLS BANNED FROM THE CASTLE?
WELL...
NOT AS A RULE, BUT...
MMBL...
TWITCH
YOU BROUGHT TWO FEMALES.
EH?
THE ONE ON THE RIGHT IS A MALE...?
CONFUSING!
PST
MAY-BE...
WHY DID YOU BRING THEM HERE?
WE DIDN'T KNOW WHAT TO DO...

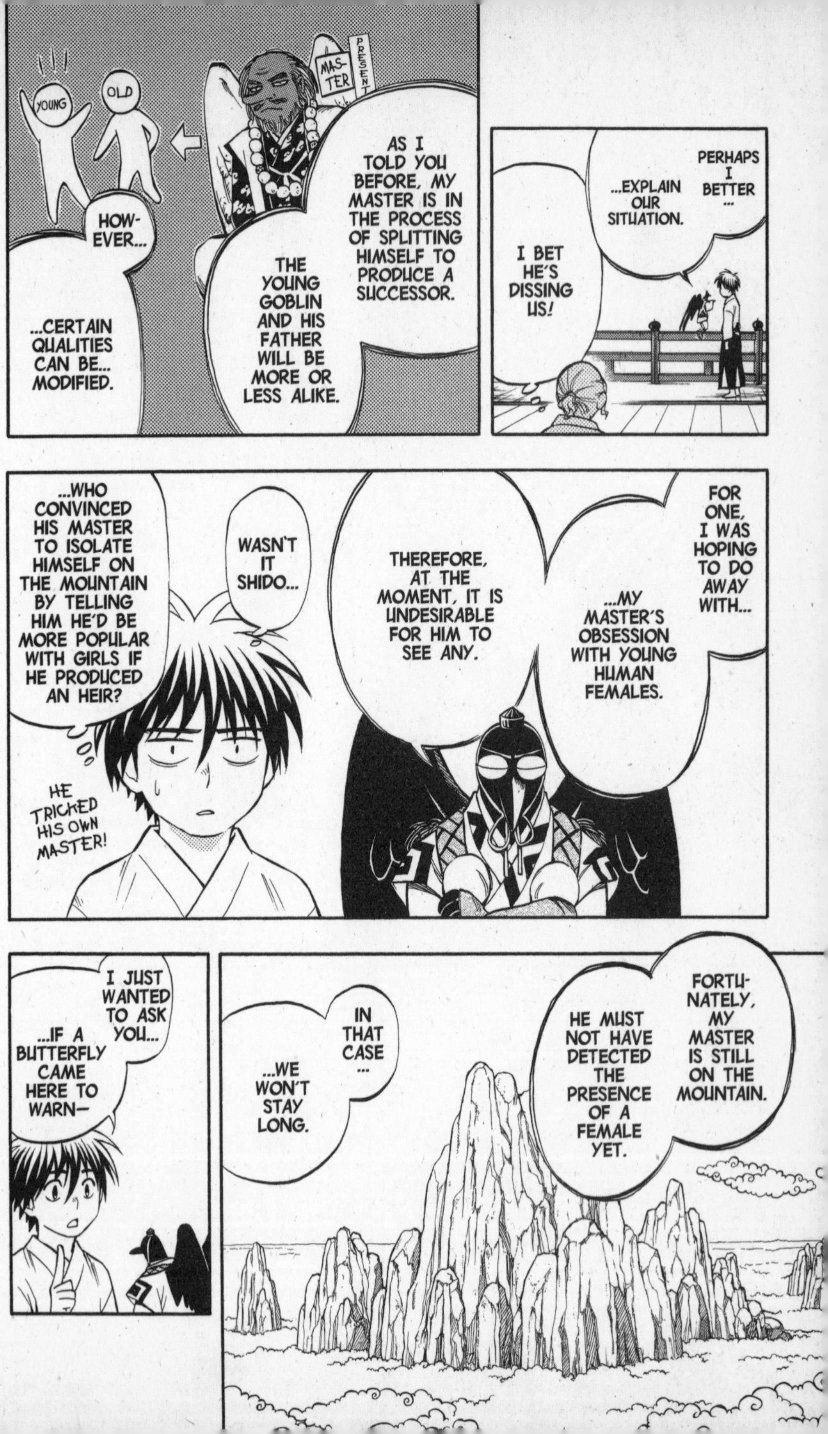
PERHAPS I BETTER...
...EXPLAIN OUR SITUATION.
I BET HE'S DISSING US!
PRESENT MASTER
AS I TOLD YOU BEFORE, MY MASTER IS IN THE PROCESS OF SPLITTING HIMSELF TO PRODUCE A SUCCESSOR.
THE YOUNG GOBLIN AND HIS FATHER WILL BE MORE OR LESS ALIKE.
OLD
YOUNG
HOW-EVER...
...CERTAIN QUALITIES CAN BE... MODIFIED.
FOR ONE, I WAS HOPING TO DO AWAY WITH...
...MY MASTER'S OBSESSION WITH YOUNG HUMAN FEMALES.
THEREFORE, AT THE MOMENT, IT IS UNDESIRABLE FOR HIM TO SEE ANY.
WASN'T IT SHIDO...
...WHO CONVINCED HIS MASTER TO ISOLATE HIMSELF ON THE MOUNTAIN BY TELLING HIM HE'D BE MORE POPULAR WITH GIRLS IF HE PRODUCED AN HEIR?
HE TRICKED HIS OWN MASTER!
FORTU-NATELY, MY MASTER IS STILL ON THE MOUNTAIN.
HE MUST NOT HAVE DETECTED THE PRESENCE OF A FEMALE YET.
IN THAT CASE...
...WE WON'T STAY LONG.
I JUST WANTED TO ASK YOU...
...IF A BUTTERFLY CAME HERE TO WARN—

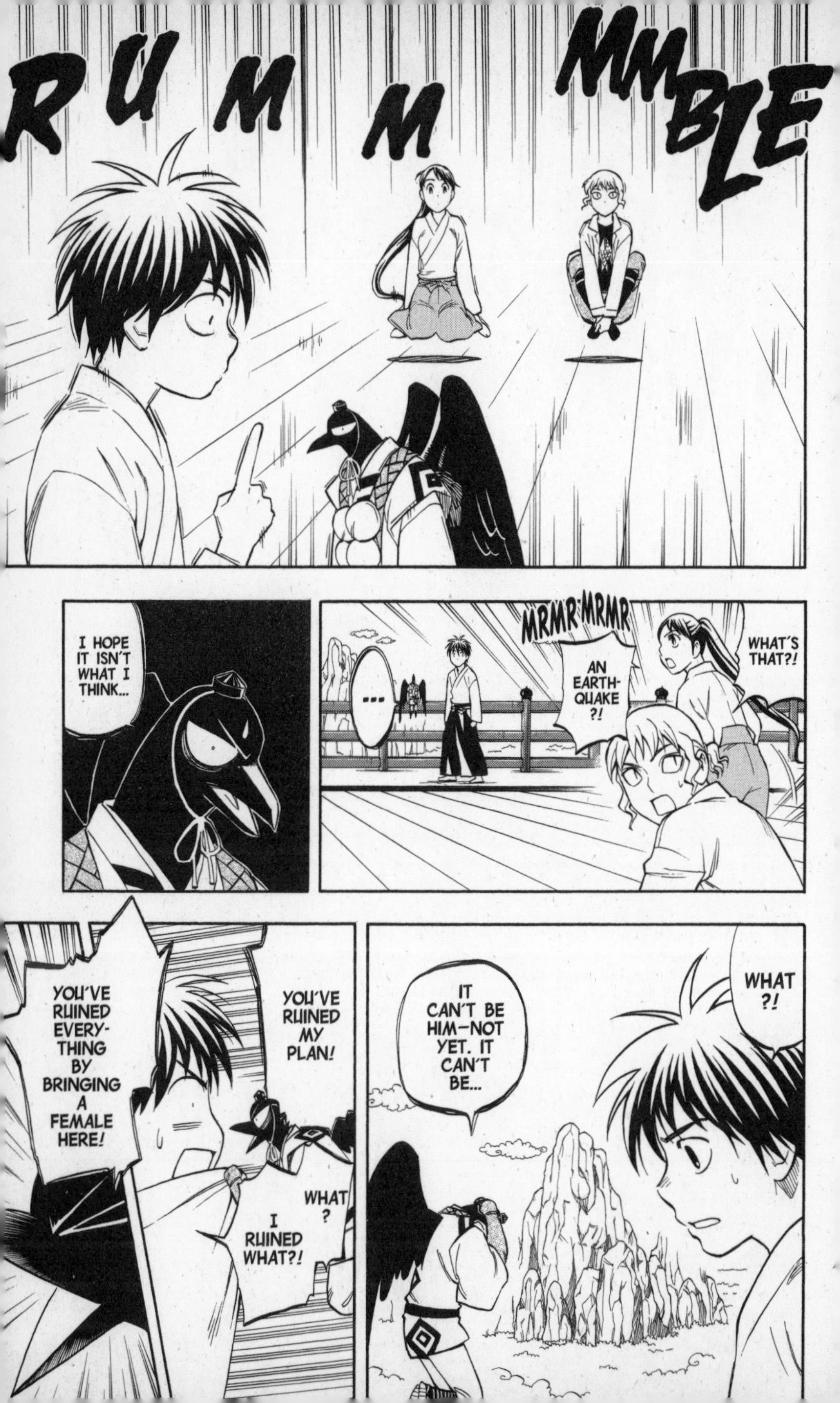
RUMMMMBLE
MRMR MRMR
WHAT'S THAT?!
AN EARTHQUAKE?!
...
I HOPE IT ISN'T WHAT I THINK...
WHAT?!
IT CAN'T BE HIM—NOT YET. IT CAN'T BE...
YOU'VE RUINED MY PLAN!
YOU'VE RUINED EVERYTHING BY BRINGING A FEMALE HERE!
WHAT?
I RUINED WHAT?!

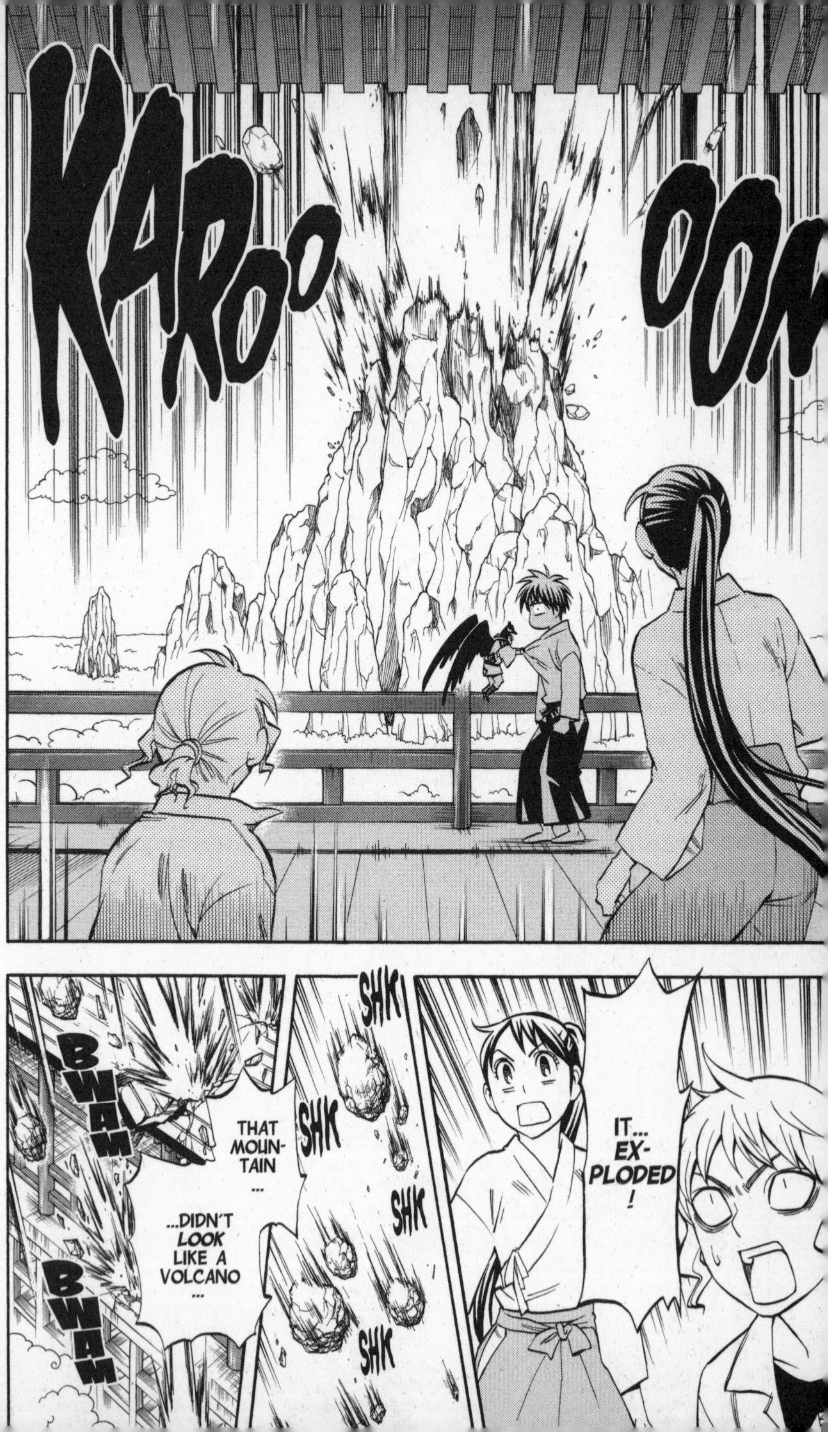
KAROOOOOM
IT... EX-PLODED!
SHK
SHK
SHK
SHK
THAT MOUN-TAIN ...
...DIDN'T LOOK LIKE A VOLCANO ...
BWAM
BWAM

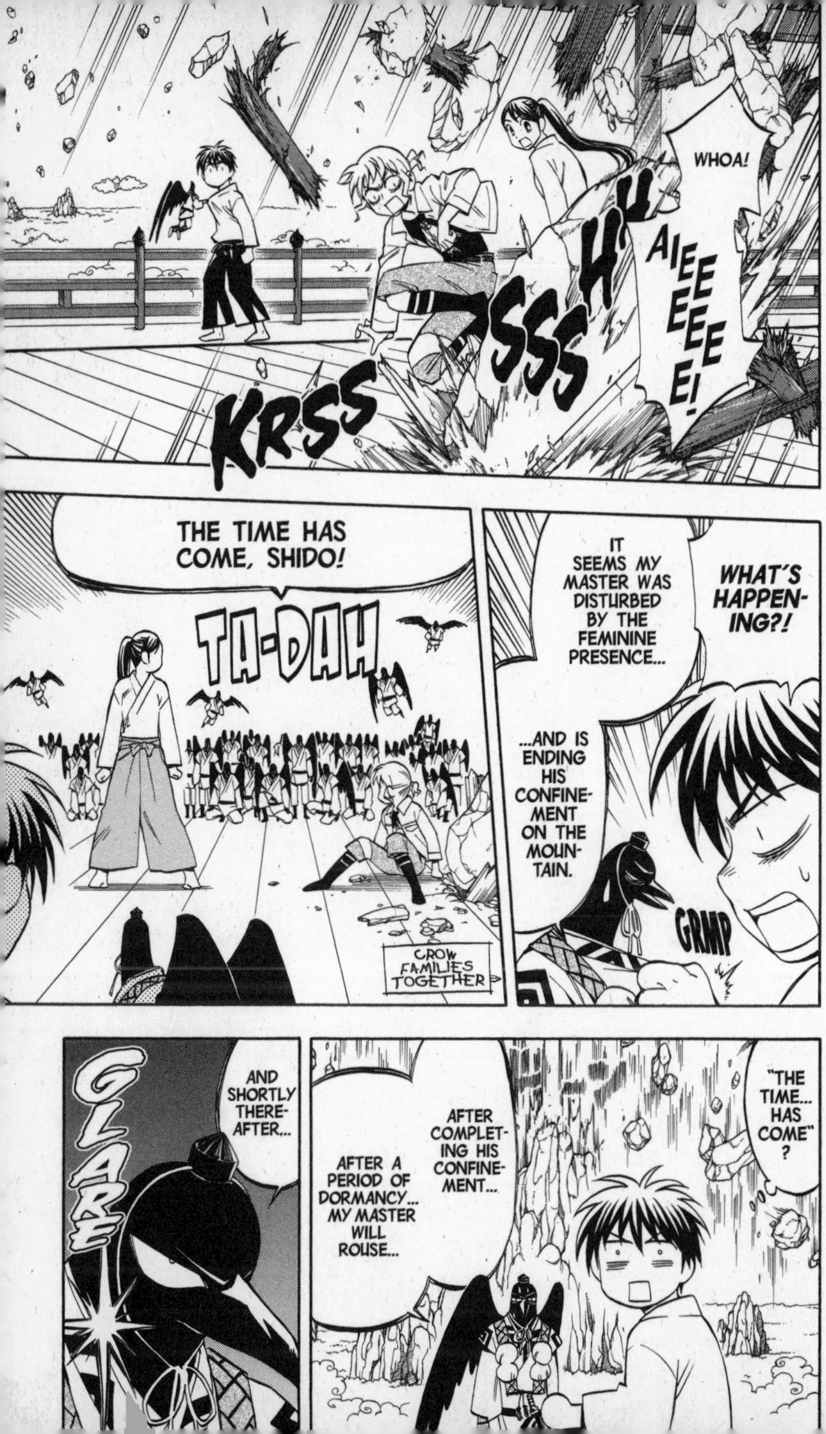
WHOA!
AIEEEEEE!
SSSHH
KRSS
WHAT'S HAPPEN-ING?!
IT SEEMS MY MASTER WAS DISTURBED BY THE FEMININE PRESENCE...
...AND IS ENDING HIS CONFINE-MENT ON THE MOUN-TAIN.
GRMP
THE TIME HAS COME, SHIDO!
TA-DAH
CROW FAMILIES TOGETHER
"THE TIME... HAS COME"?
AFTER COMPLET-ING HIS CONFINE-MENT...
AFTER A PERIOD OF DORMANCY... MY MASTER WILL ROUSE...
AND SHORTLY THERE-AFTER...
GLARE

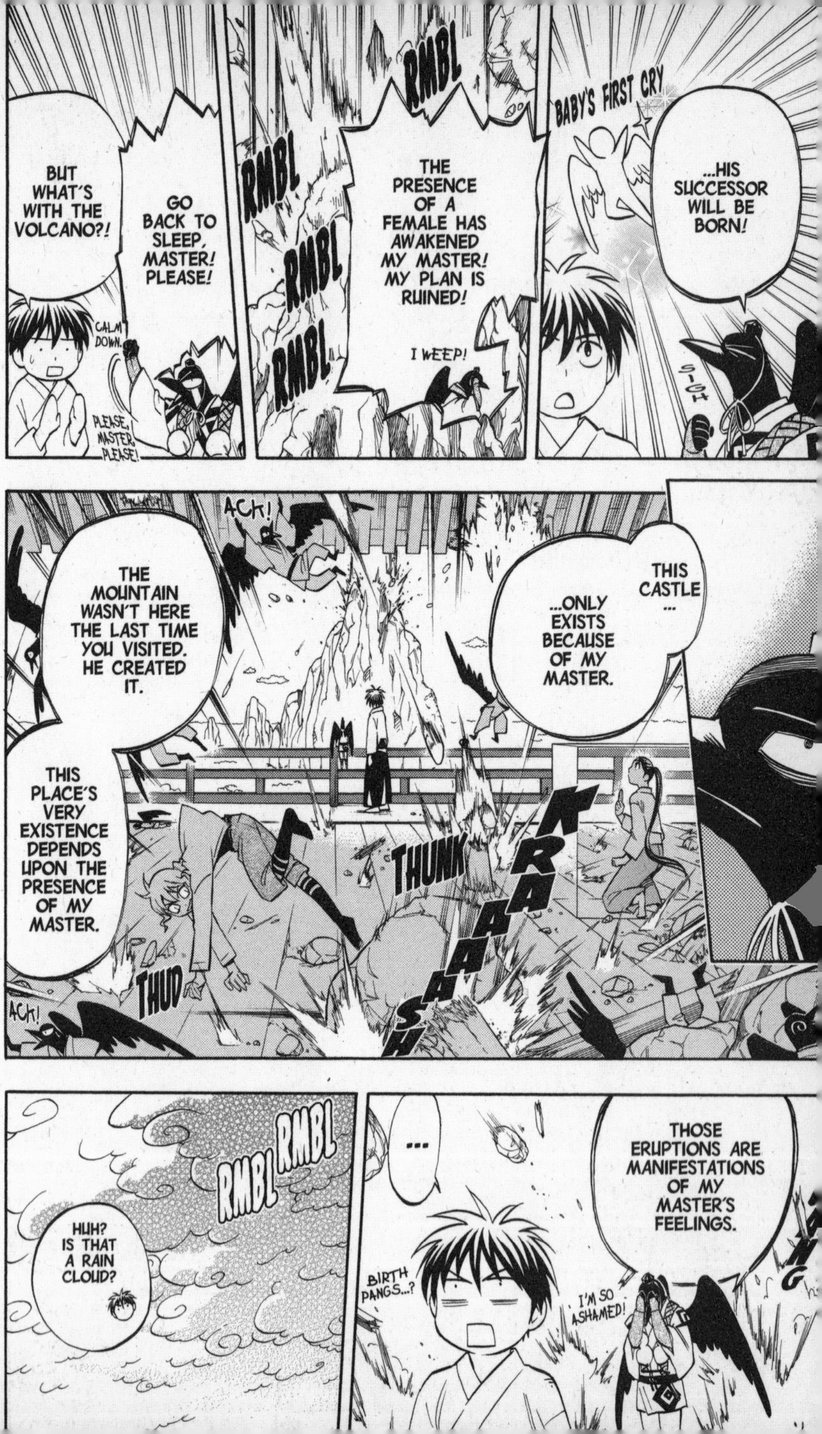
BABY'S FIRST CRY
...HIS SUCCESSOR WILL BE BORN!
SIGH
RMBL
THE PRESENCE OF A FEMALE HAS AWAKENED MY MASTER! MY PLAN IS RUINED!
RMBL
RMBL
RMBL
I WEEP!
GO BACK TO SLEEP, MASTER! PLEASE!
BUT WHAT'S WITH THE VOLCANO?!
CALM DOWN.
PLEASE, MASTER, PLEASE!
THIS CASTLE...
...ONLY EXISTS BECAUSE OF MY MASTER.
ACK!
THE MOUNTAIN WASN'T HERE THE LAST TIME YOU VISITED. HE CREATED IT.
THIS PLACE'S VERY EXISTENCE DEPENDS UPON THE PRESENCE OF MY MASTER.
KRAAAASH
THUNK
THUD
ACK!
THOSE ERUPTIONS ARE MANIFESTATIONS OF MY MASTER'S FEELINGS.
...
BIRTH PANGS...?
I'M SO ASHAMED!
RMBL
RMBL
HUH? IS THAT A RAIN CLOUD?

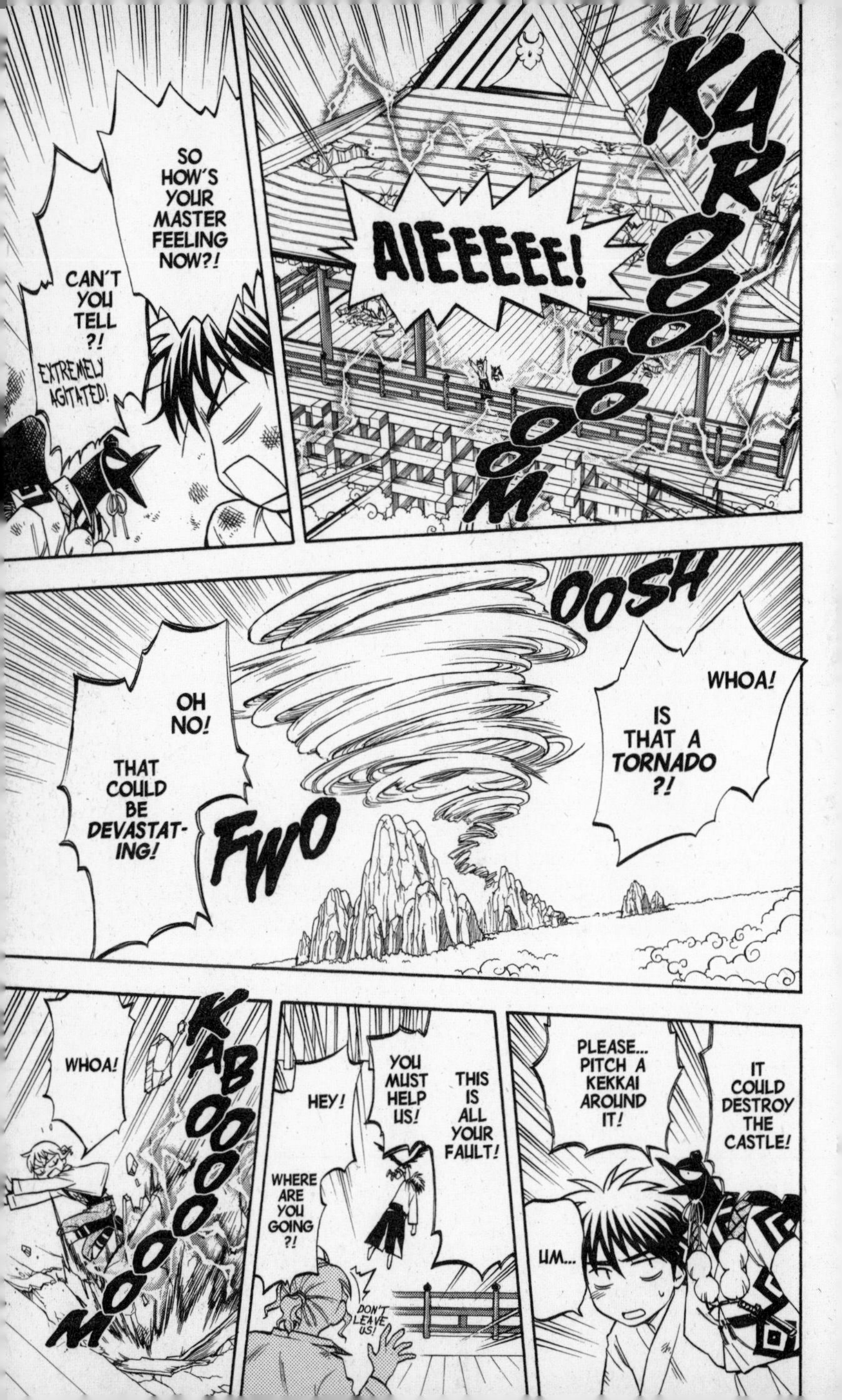
KAROOOOOOOM
AIEEEEEE!
SO HOW'S YOUR MASTER FEELING NOW?!
CAN'T YOU TELL?!
EXTREMELY AGITATED!
OOSH
WHOA!
IS THAT A TORNADO?!
FWO
OH NO!
THAT COULD BE DEVASTATING!
IT COULD DESTROY THE CASTLE!
PLEASE... PITCH A KEKKAI AROUND IT!
UM...
THIS IS ALL YOUR FAULT!
YOU MUST HELP US!
HEY!
WHERE ARE YOU GOING?!
DON'T LEAVE US!
KABOOOOOOOM
WHOA!

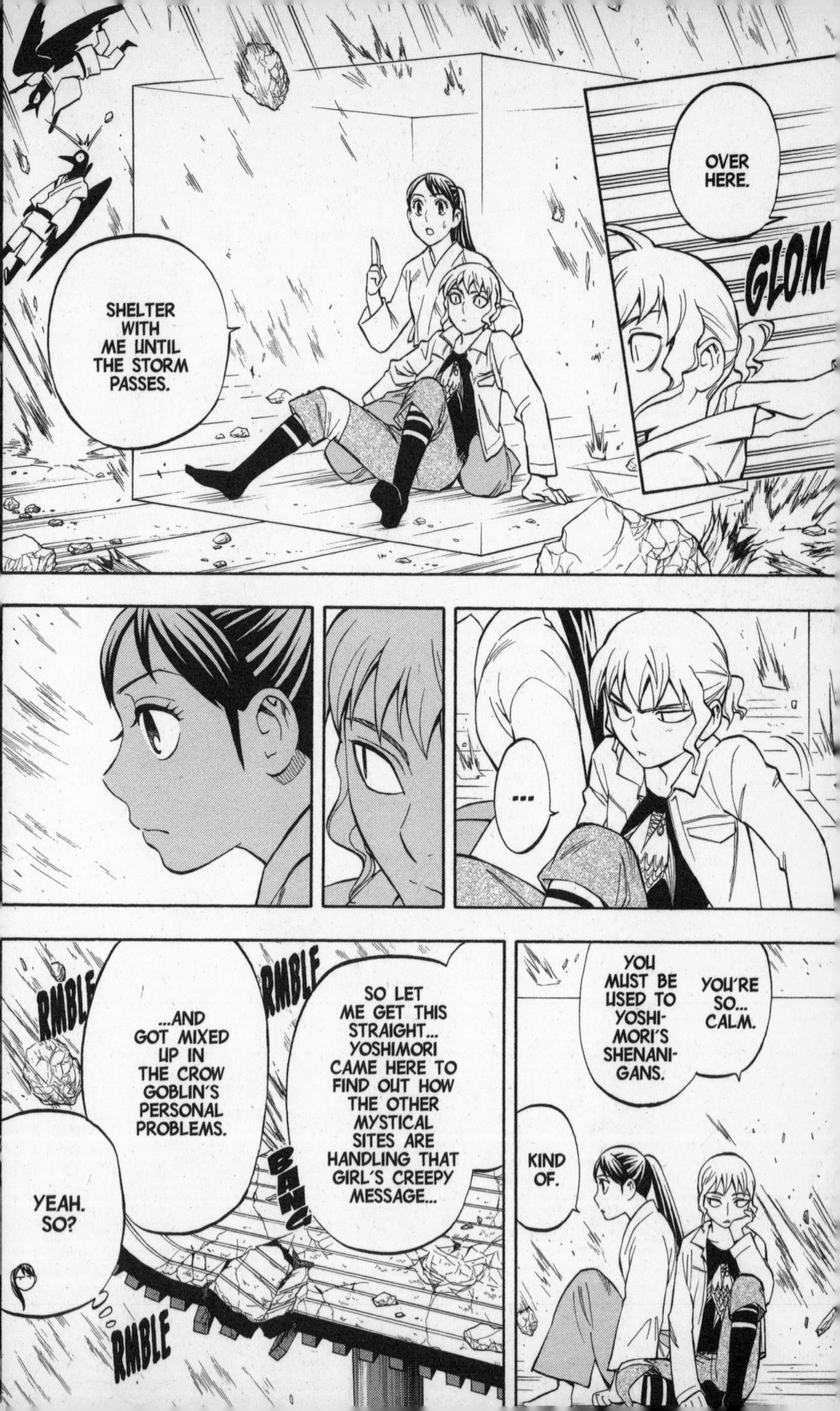
OVER HERE.
GLOM
SHELTER WITH ME UNTIL THE STORM PASSES.
...
YOU'RE SO... CALM.
YOU MUST BE USED TO YOSHIMORI'S SHENANIGANS.
KIND OF.
RMBLE
RMBLE
SO LET ME GET THIS STRAIGHT... YOSHIMORI CAME HERE TO FIND OUT HOW THE OTHER MYSTICAL SITES ARE HANDLING THAT GIRL'S CREEPY MESSAGE...
...AND GOT MIXED UP IN THE CROW GOBLIN'S PERSONAL PROBLEMS.
BANG
YEAH. SO?
RMBLE

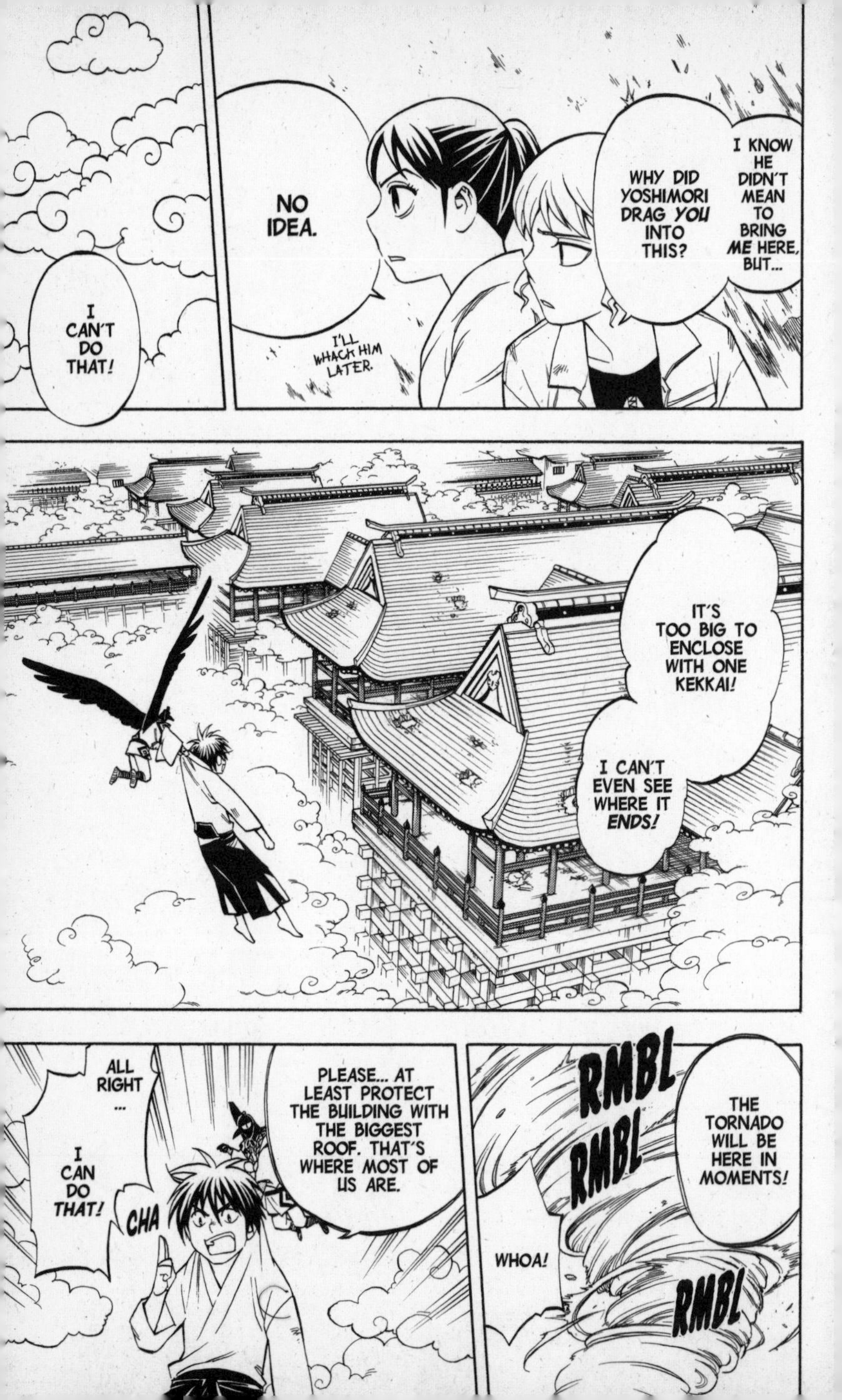
I KNOW HE DIDN'T MEAN TO BRING *ME* HERE, BUT...
WHY DID YOSHIMORI DRAG *YOU* INTO THIS?
NO IDEA.
I'LL WHACK HIM LATER.
I CAN'T DO THAT!
IT'S TOO BIG TO ENCLOSE WITH ONE KEKKAI!
I CAN'T EVEN SEE WHERE IT *ENDS!*
RMBL
RMBL
THE TORNADO WILL BE HERE IN MOMENTS!
WHOA!
RMBL
PLEASE... AT LEAST PROTECT THE BUILDING WITH THE BIGGEST ROOF. THAT'S WHERE MOST OF US ARE.
ALL RIGHT...
I CAN DO *THAT!*
CHA

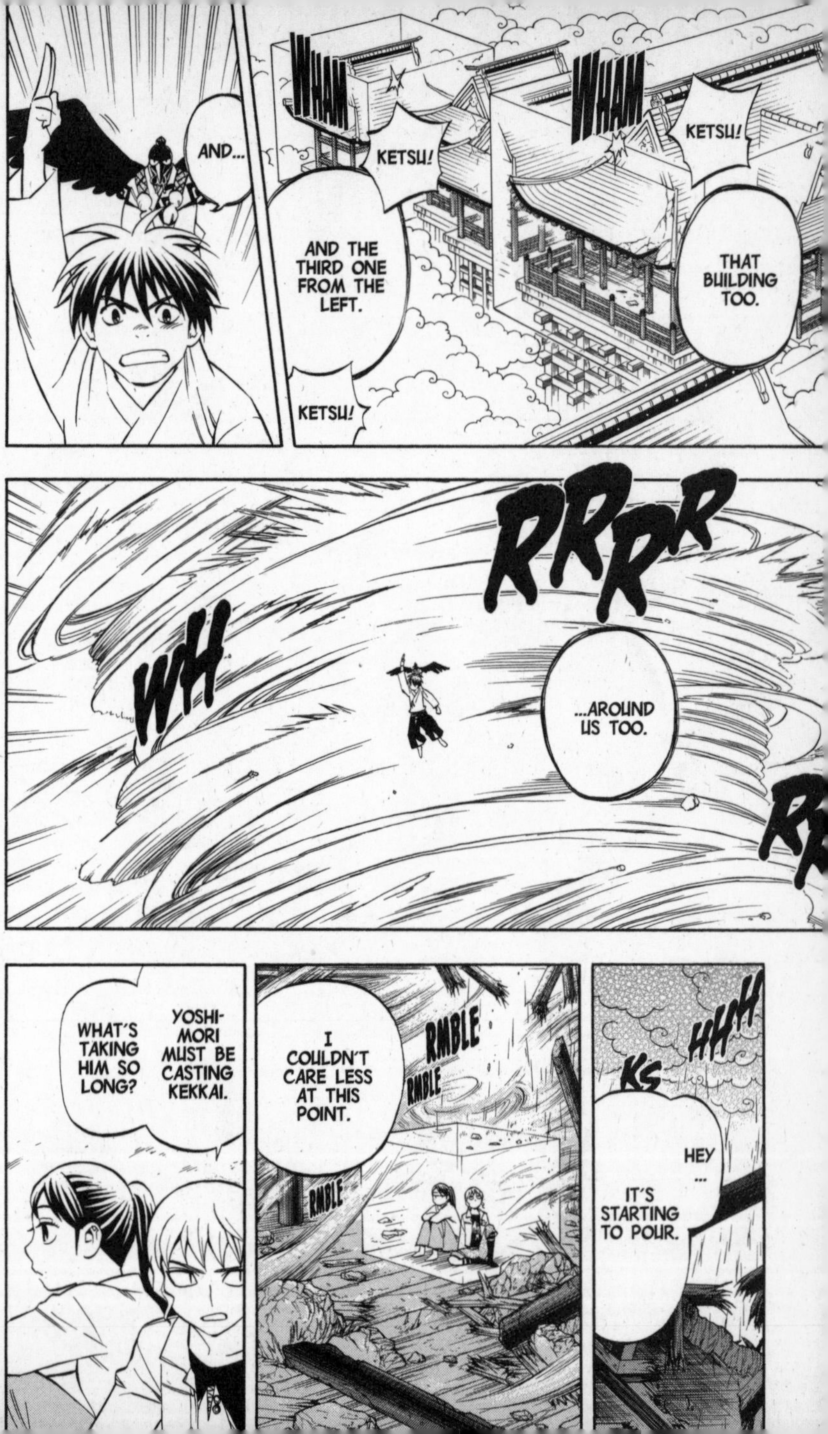
WHAM
KETSU!
THAT BUILDING TOO.
WHAM
KETSU!
AND THE THIRD ONE FROM THE LEFT.
KETSU!
AND...
RRRR
...AROUND US TOO.
RR
WH
HHH
KS
HEY ...
IT'S STARTING TO POUR.
RMBLE
RMBLE
I COULDN'T CARE LESS AT THIS POINT.
RMBLE
YOSHIMORI MUST BE CASTING KEKKAI.
WHAT'S TAKING HIM SO LONG?

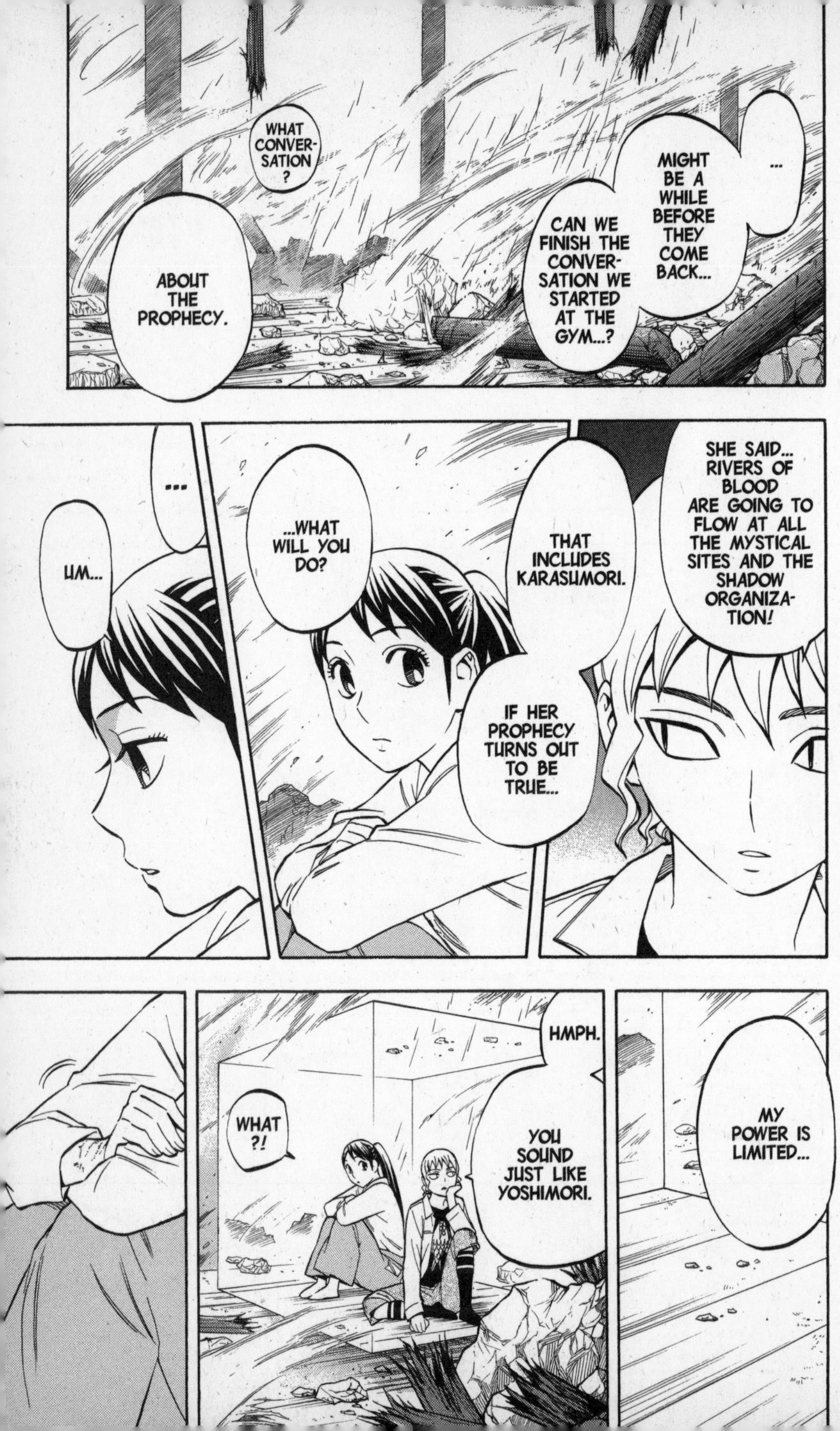
...
MIGHT BE A WHILE BEFORE THEY COME BACK...
CAN WE FINISH THE CONVER-SATION WE STARTED AT THE GYM...?
WHAT CONVER-SATION?
ABOUT THE PROPHECY.
SHE SAID... RIVERS OF BLOOD ARE GOING TO FLOW AT ALL THE MYSTICAL SITES AND THE SHADOW ORGANIZA-TION!
THAT INCLUDES KARASUMORI.
IF HER PROPHECY TURNS OUT TO BE TRUE...
...WHAT WILL YOU DO?
...
UM...
MY POWER IS LIMITED...
HMPH.
YOU SOUND JUST LIKE YOSHIMORI.
WHAT?!

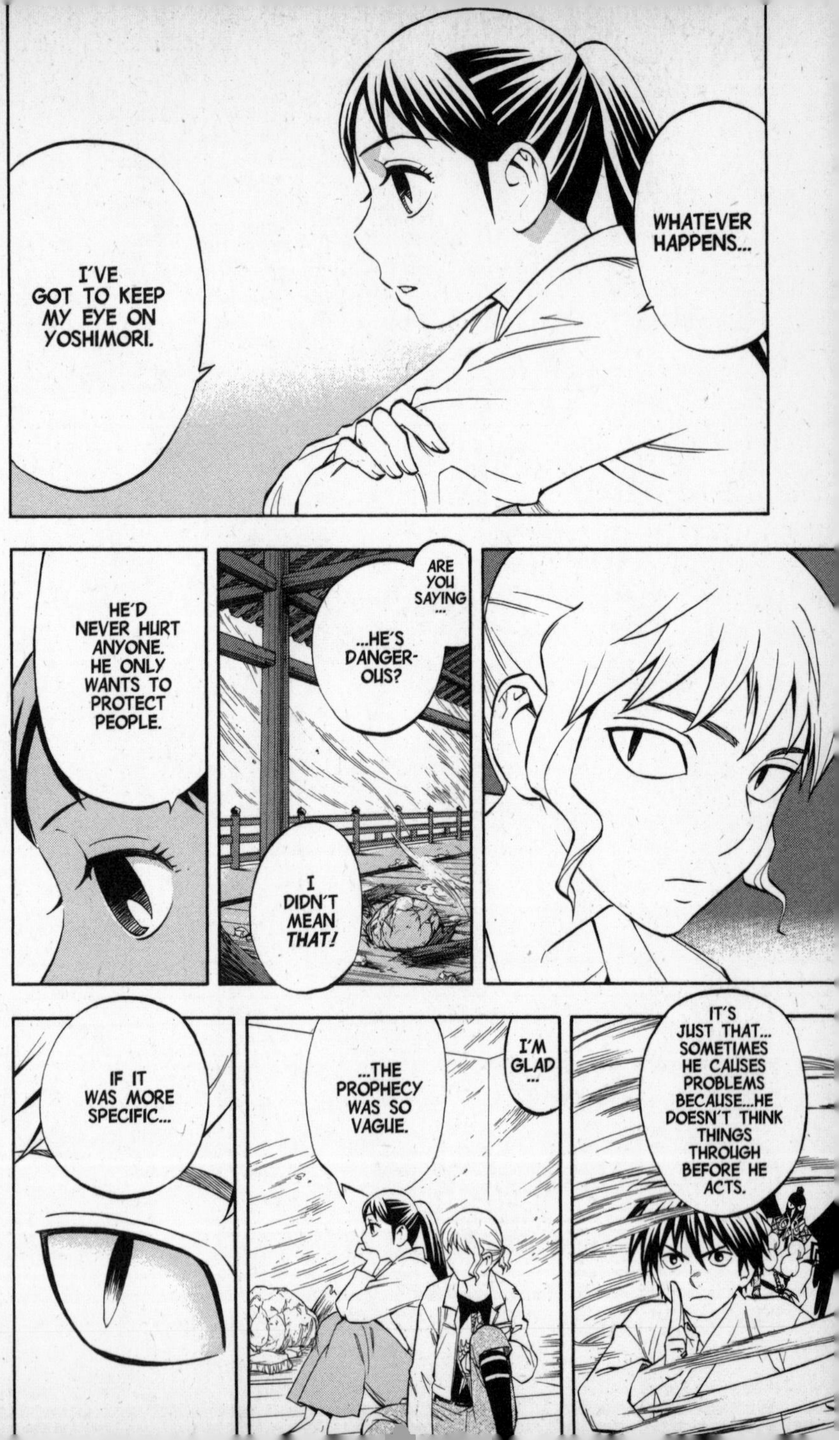
WHATEVER HAPPENS...
I'VE GOT TO KEEP MY EYE ON YOSHIMORI.
ARE YOU SAYING ...
...HE'S DANGER-OUS?
I DIDN'T MEAN *THAT!*
HE'D NEVER HURT ANYONE. HE ONLY WANTS TO PROTECT PEOPLE.
IT'S JUST THAT... SOMETIMES HE CAUSES PROBLEMS BECAUSE...HE DOESN'T THINK THINGS THROUGH BEFORE HE ACTS.
I'M GLAD ...
...THE PROPHECY WAS SO VAGUE.
IF IT WAS MORE SPECIFIC...

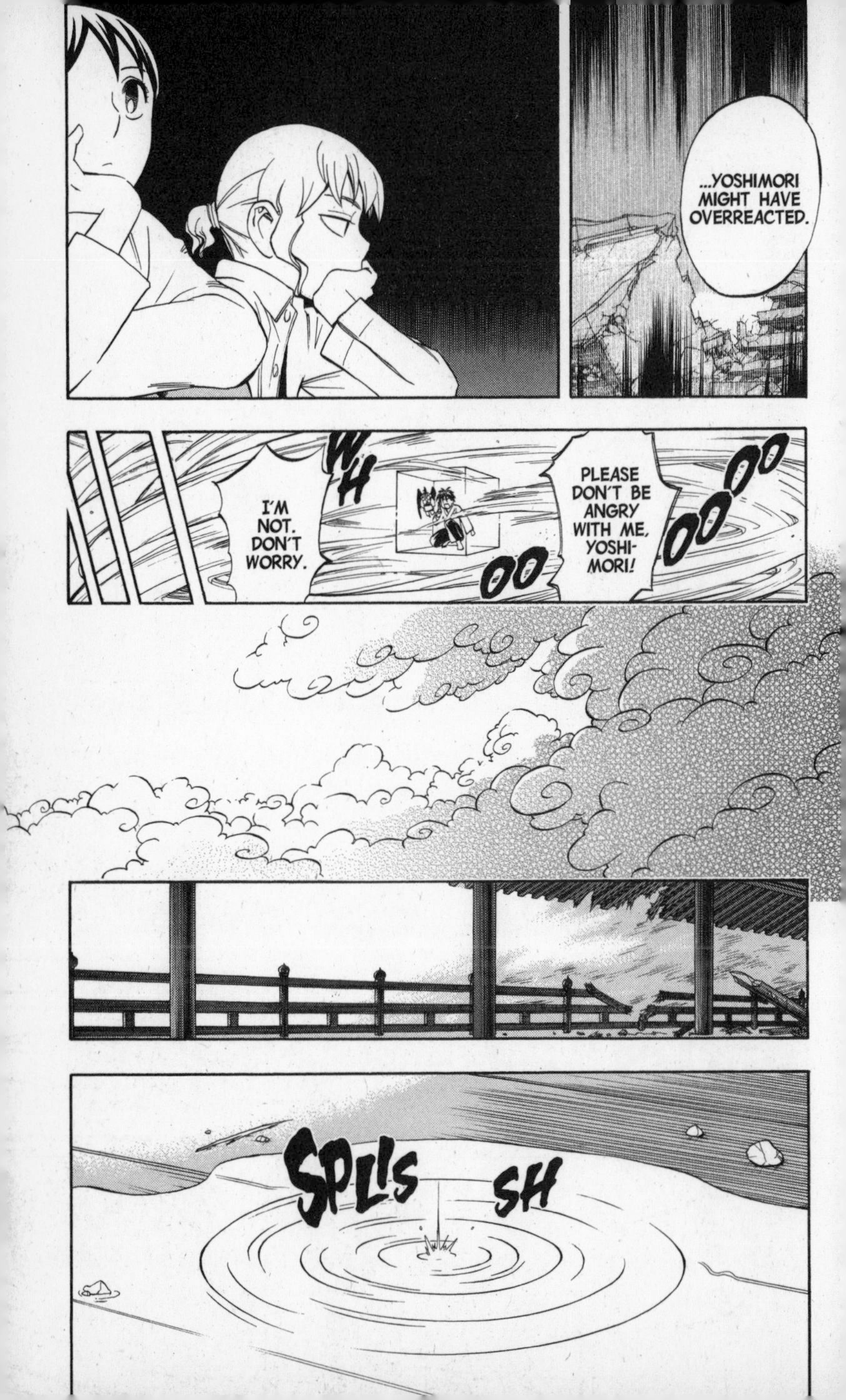
...YOSHIMORI MIGHT HAVE OVERREACTED.
PLEASE DON'T BE ANGRY WITH ME, YOSHIMORI!
OOOOO
WH
OO
I'M NOT. DON'T WORRY.
SPLIS
SH

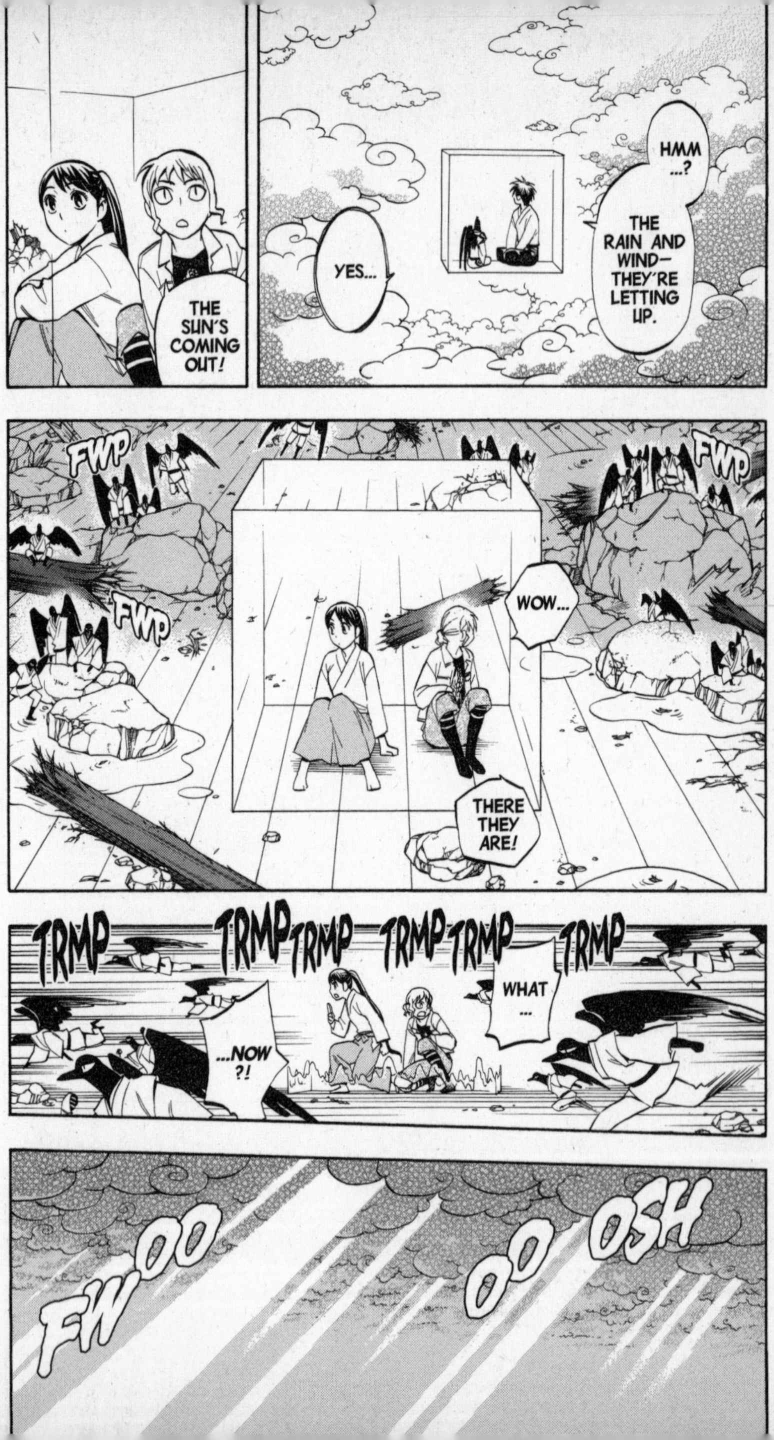
HMM ...?
THE RAIN AND WIND—THEY'RE LETTING UP.
YES...
THE SUN'S COMING OUT!
FWP
WOW...
FWP
FWP
THERE THEY ARE!
TRMP
TRMP
TRMP
TRMP
TRMP
TRMP
WHAT ...
...NOW ?!
FWOOOOOSH

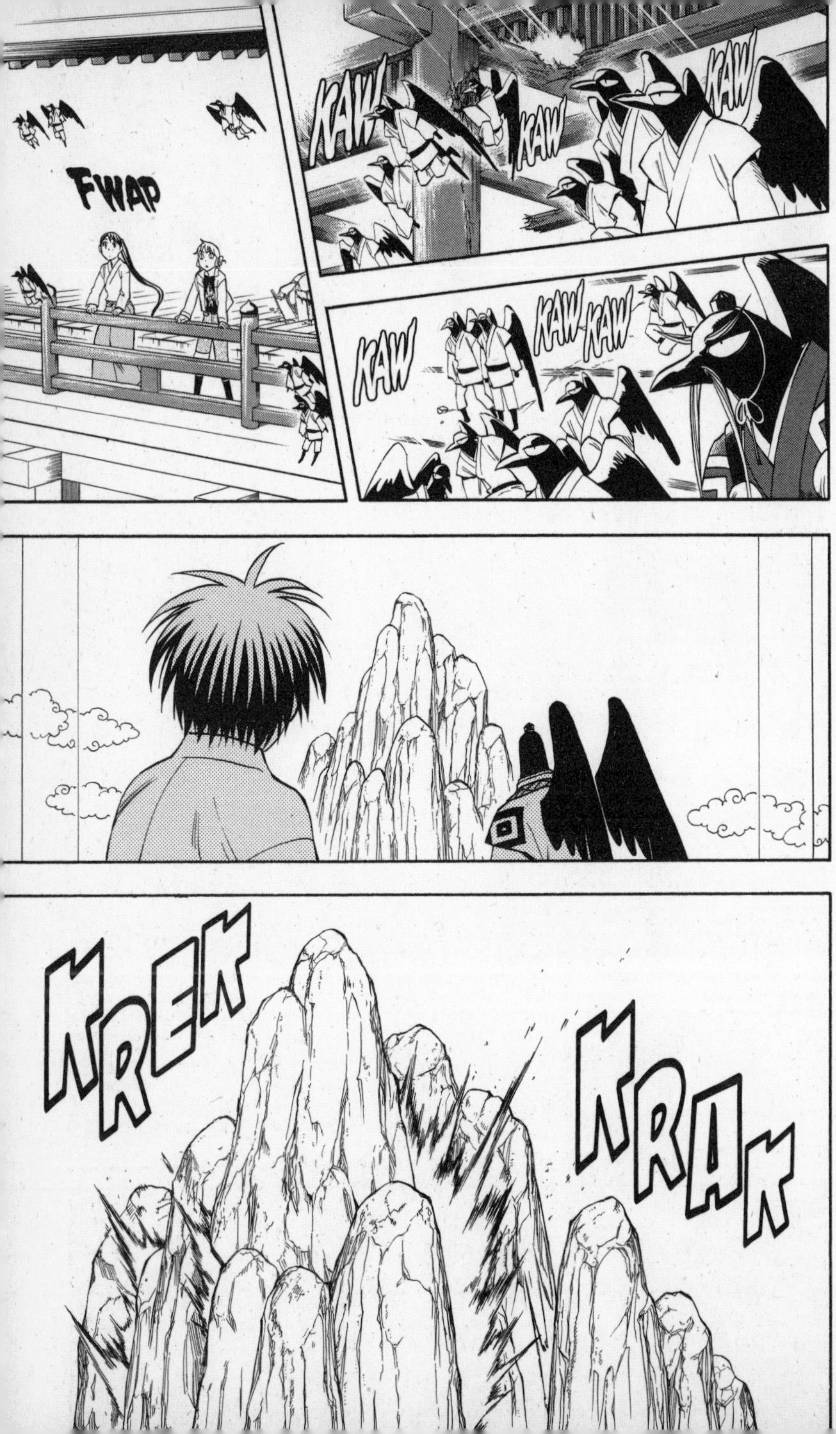
KAW
KAW
KAW
KAW
KAW
KAW
FWAP
KRAK
KREK

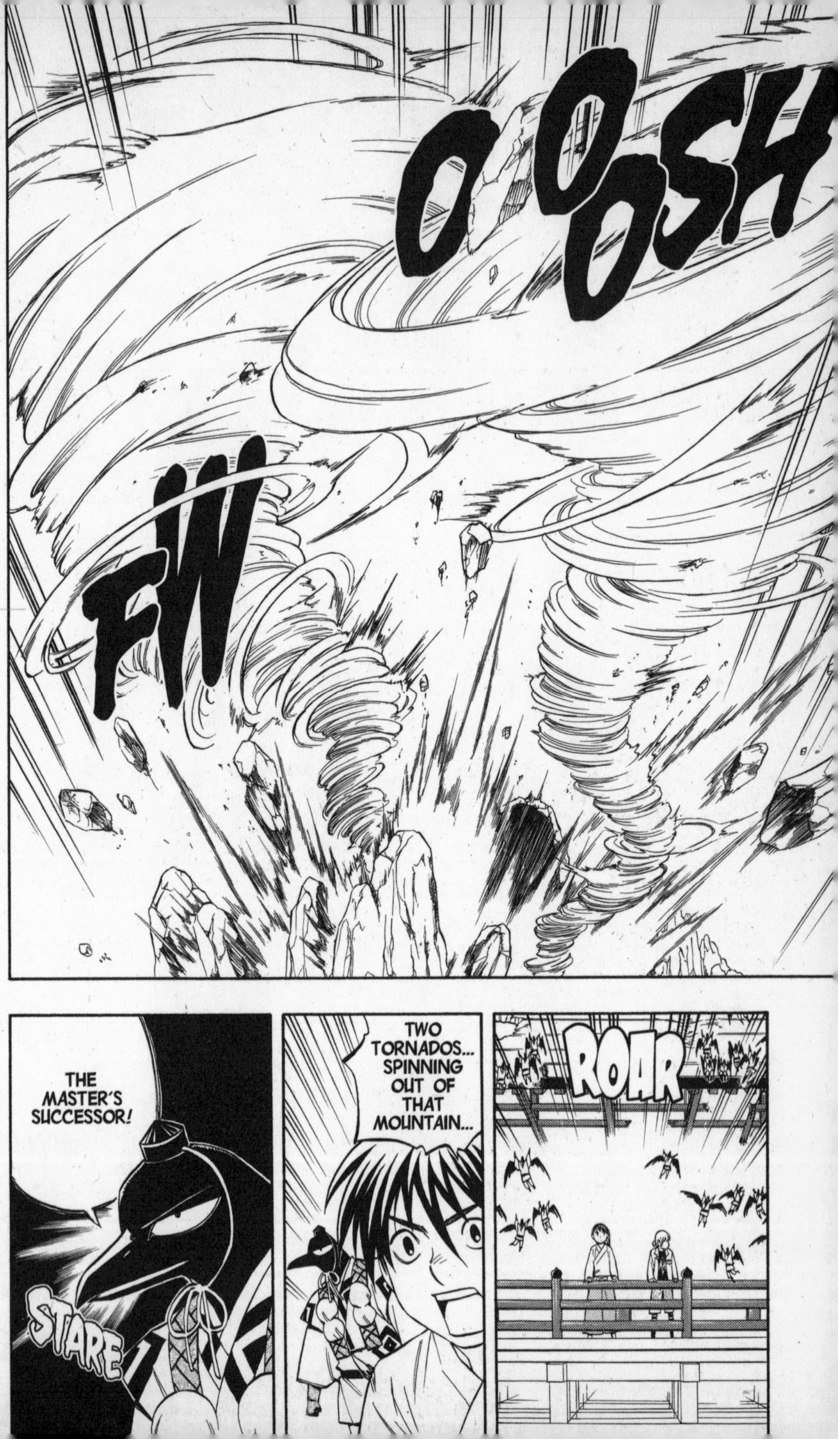
OOOSH
FW
ROAR
TWO TORNADOS... SPINNING OUT OF THAT MOUNTAIN...
THE MASTER'S SUCCESSOR!
STARE

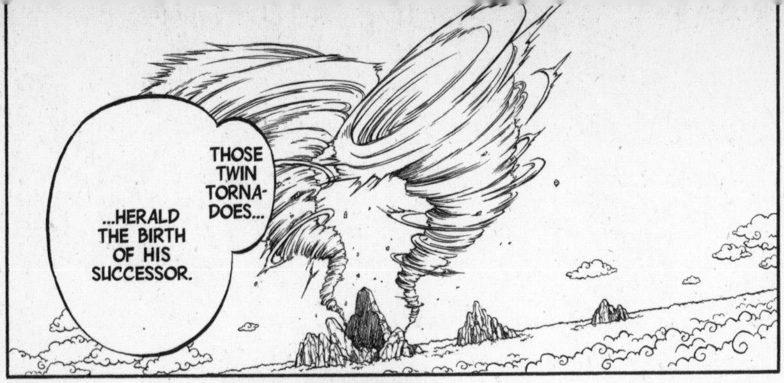
THOSE TWIN TORNADOES...
...HERALD THE BIRTH OF HIS SUCCESSOR.

Chapter 180: TOBIMARU

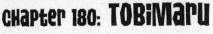

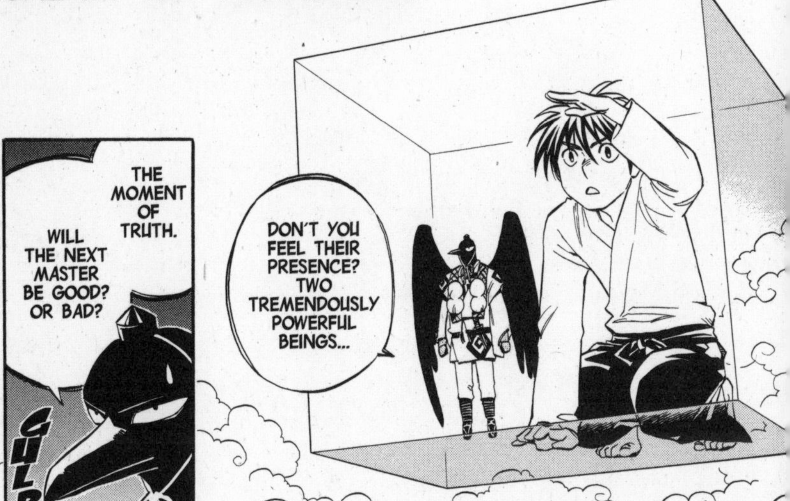
DON'T YOU FEEL THEIR PRESENCE? TWO TREMENDOUSLY POWERFUL BEINGS...
THE MOMENT OF TRUTH.
WILL THE NEXT MASTER BE GOOD? OR BAD?
GULP

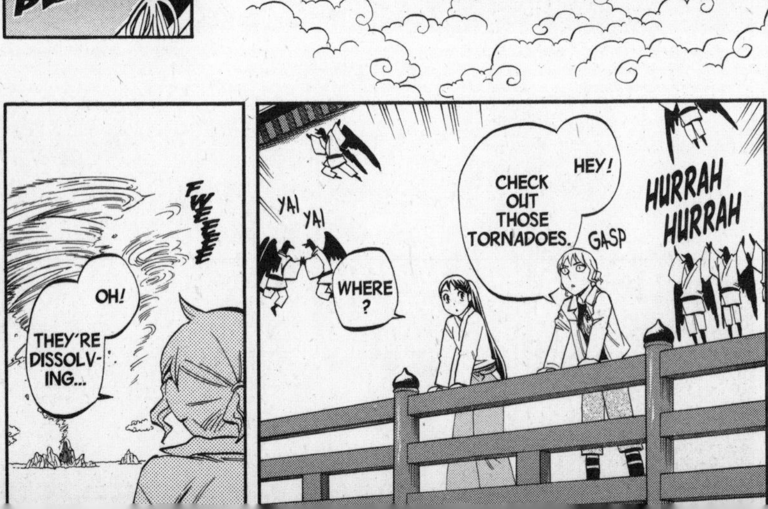
HURRAH HURRAH
HEY!
CHECK OUT THOSE TORNADOES.
GASP
YAI YAI
WHERE?
OH!
THEY'RE DISSOLVING...

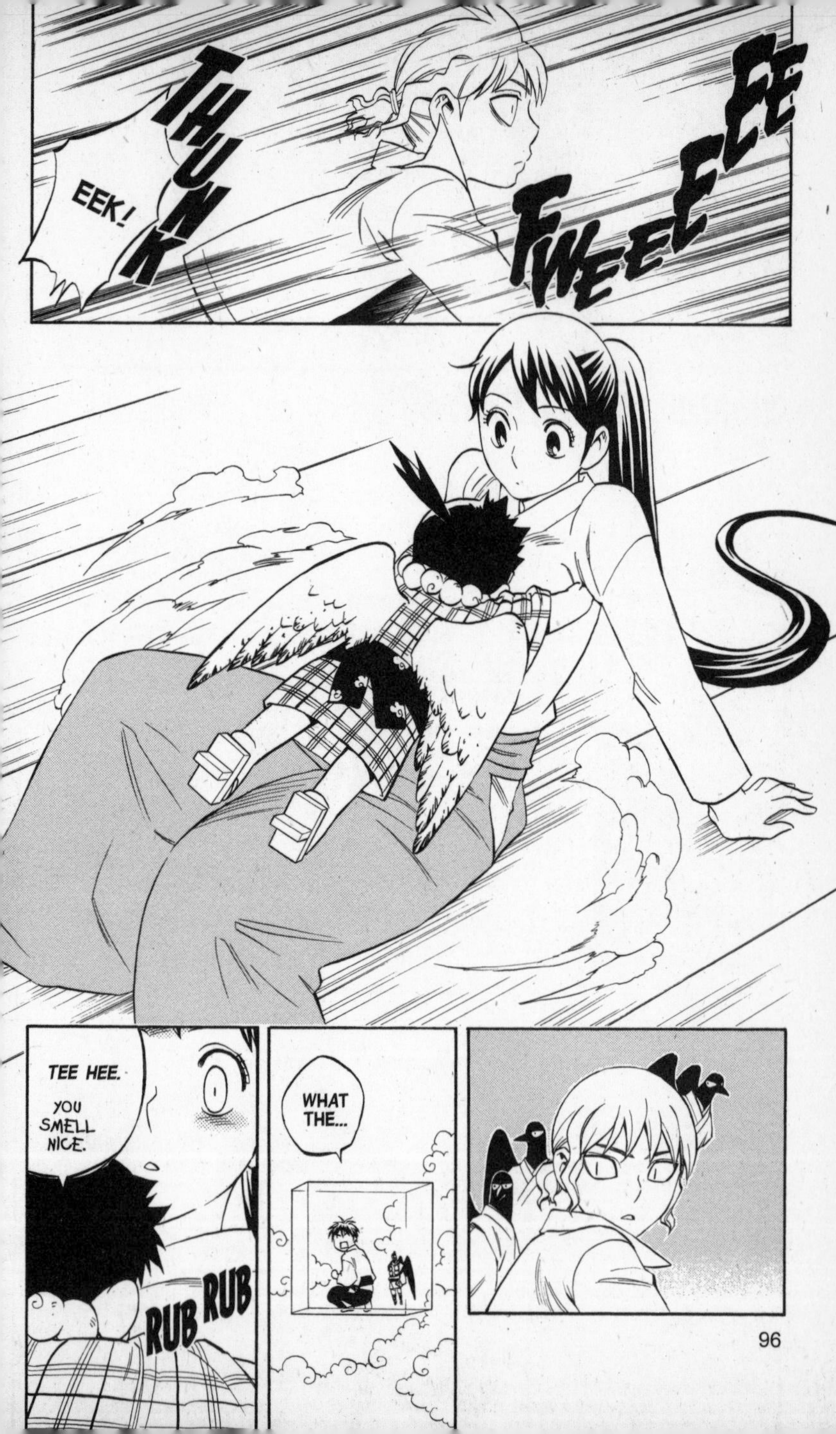
FWEEEEEE
THUNK
EEK!
WHAT THE...
TEE HEE.
YOU SMELL NICE.
RUB RUB

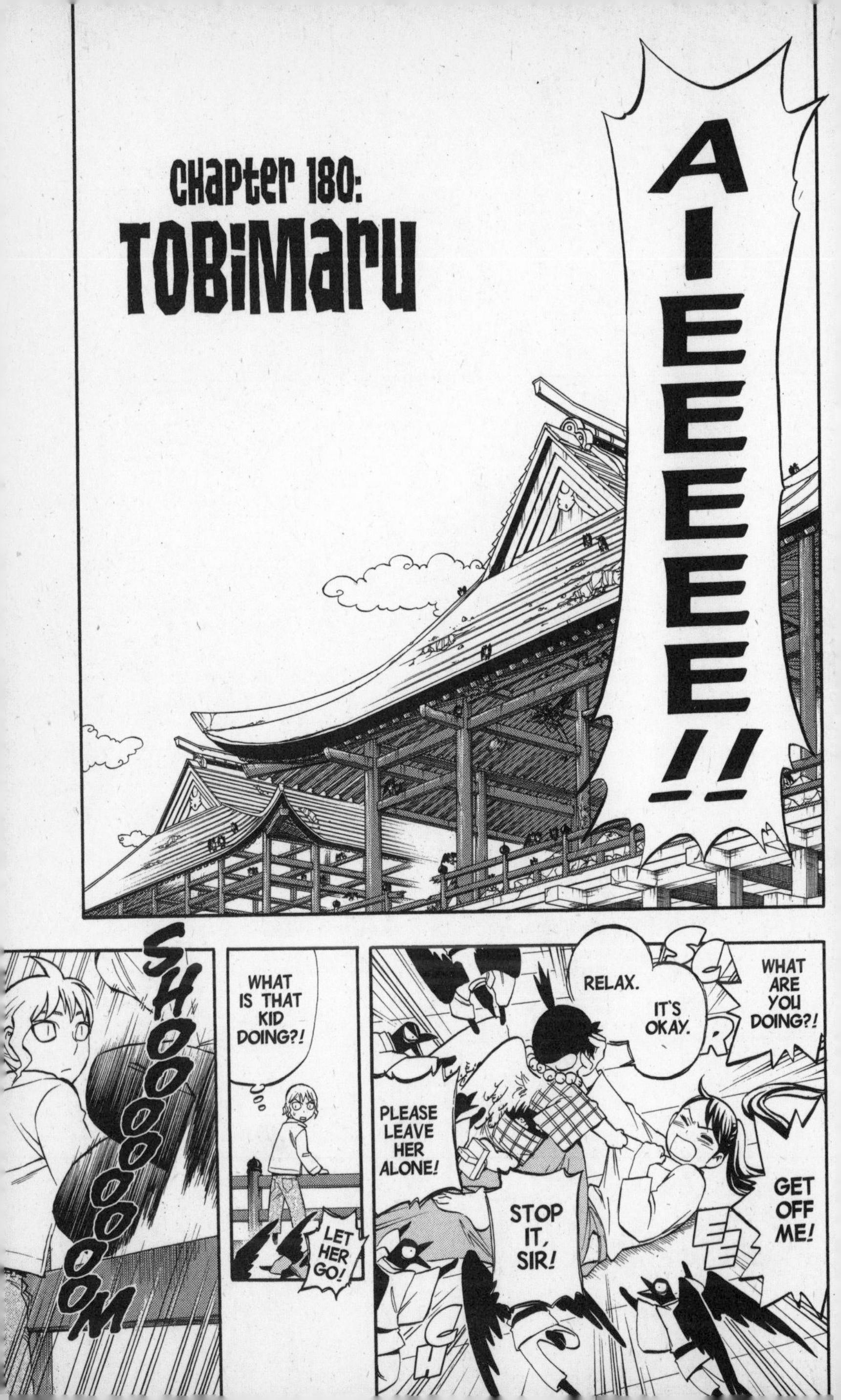
AIEEEEE!!
Chapter 180:
TOBIMARU
WHAT ARE YOU DOING?!
RELAX.
IT'S OKAY.
PLEASE LEAVE HER ALONE!
GET OFF ME!
STOP IT, SIR!
WHAT IS THAT KID DOING?!
LET HER GO!
SHOOOOOOOOOOM

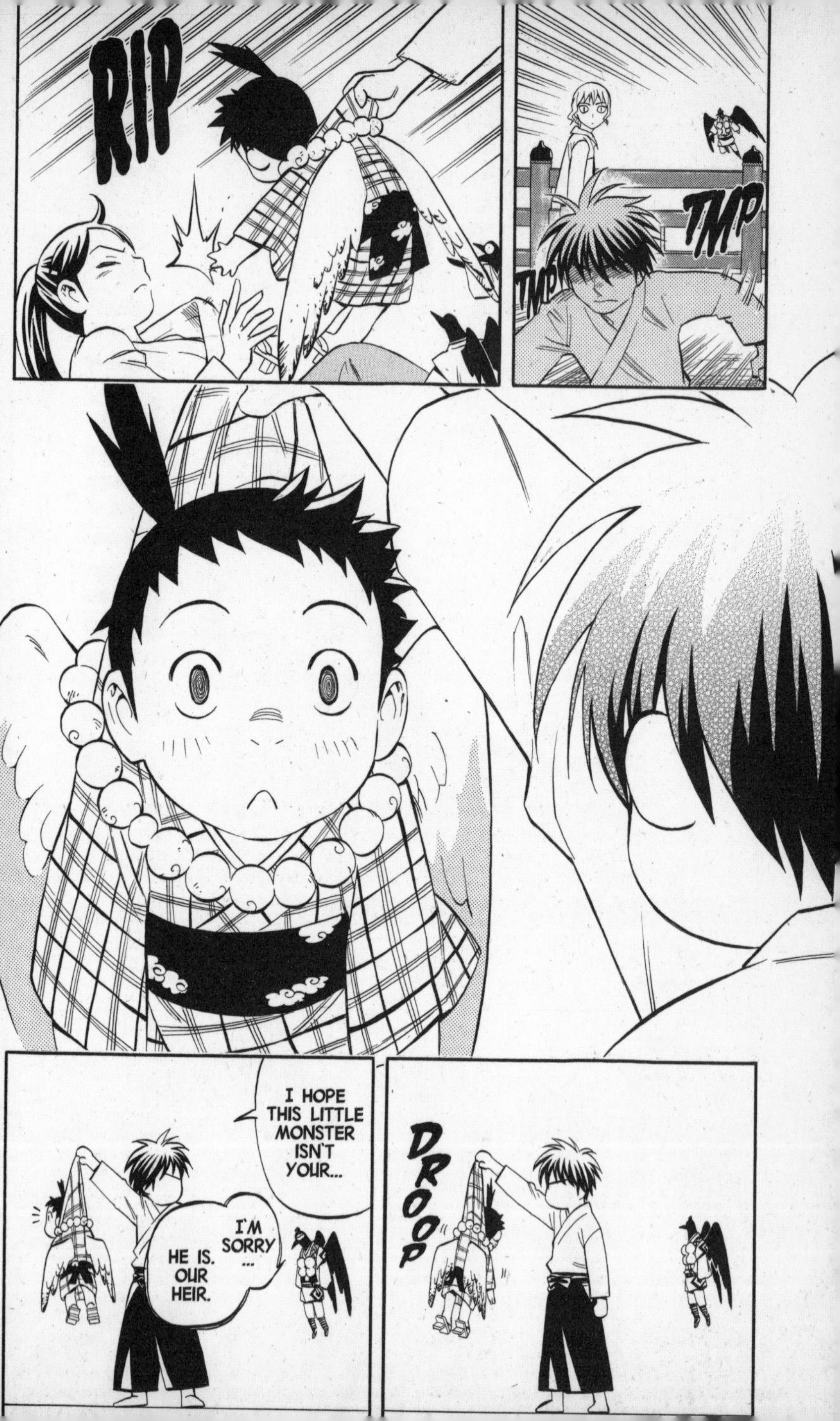
TMP
TMP
RIP
DROOOP
I HOPE THIS LITTLE MONSTER ISN'T YOUR...
I'M SORRY ...
HE IS. OUR HEIR.

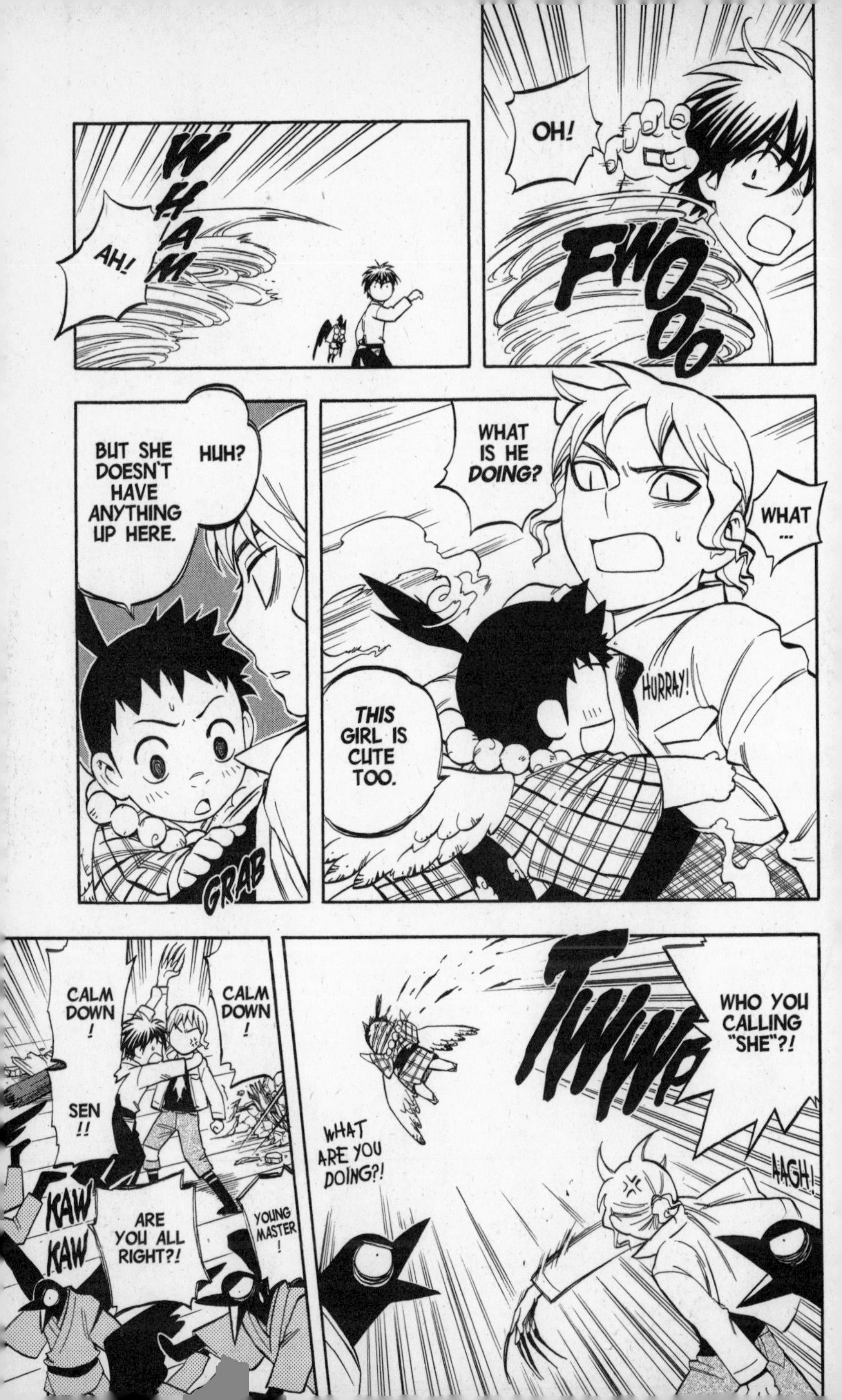
OH!
FWOOOO
WHAM
AH!
WHAT IS HE DOING?
WHAT ---
THIS GIRL IS CUTE TOO.
HURRAY!
HUH?
BUT SHE DOESN'T HAVE ANYTHING UP HERE.
GRAB
WHO YOU CALLING "SHE"?!
AAGH!
WHAT ARE YOU DOING?!
CALM DOWN!
CALM DOWN!
SEN!!
YOUNG MASTER!
ARE YOU ALL RIGHT?!
KAW KAW

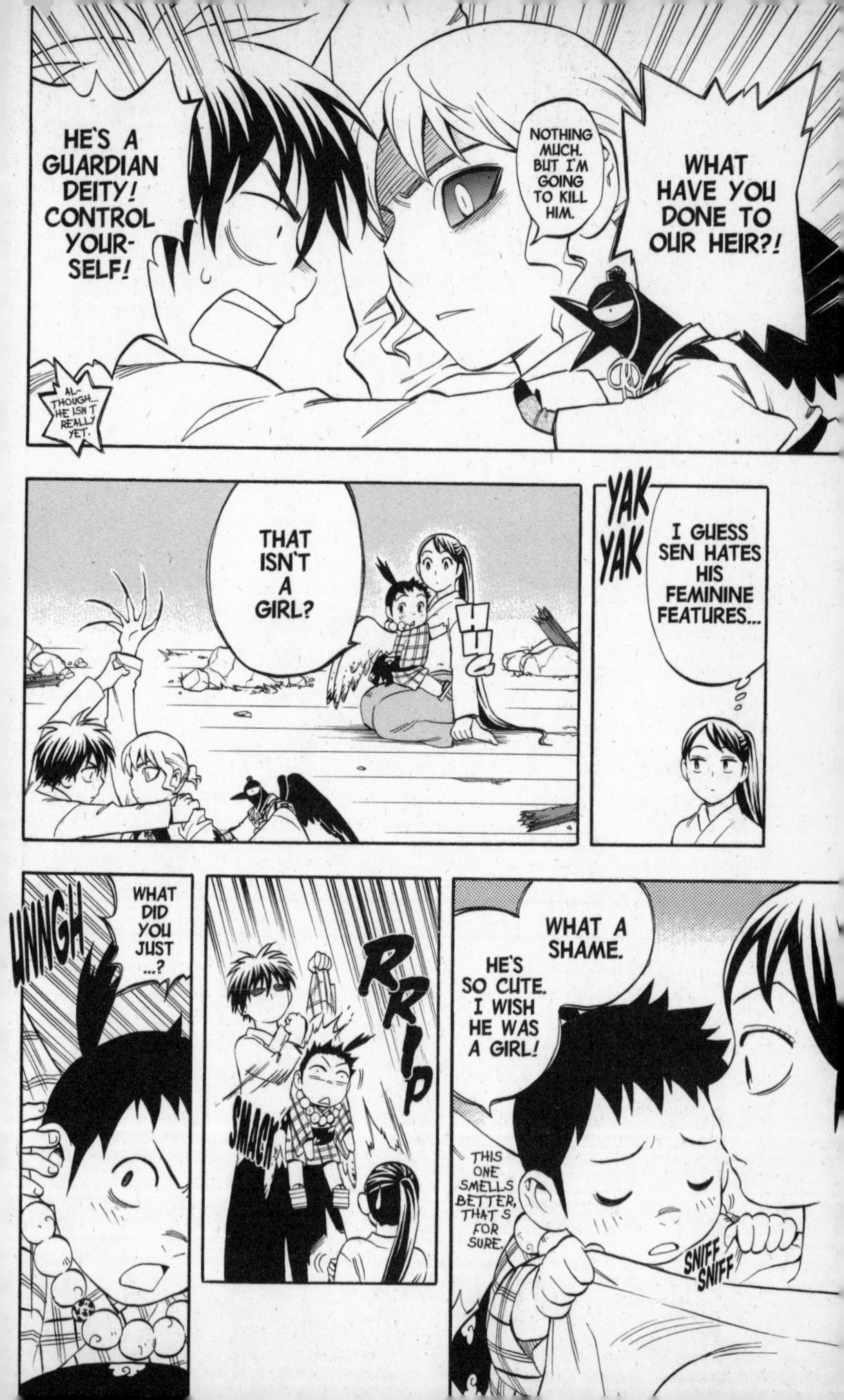
WHAT HAVE YOU DONE TO OUR HEIR?!
NOTHING MUCH. BUT I'M GOING TO KILL HIM.
HE'S A GUARDIAN DEITY! CONTROL YOUR-SELF!
AL-THOUGH... HE ISN'T REALLY YET.
YAK YAK
I GUESS SEN HATES HIS FEMININE FEATURES...
THAT ISN'T A GIRL?
HUH
WHAT A SHAME.
HE'S SO CUTE. I WISH HE WAS A GIRL!
THIS ONE SMELLS BETTER, THAT'S FOR SURE.
SNIFF SNIFF
RRIP
SMACK
UNNGH
WHAT DID YOU JUST ...?

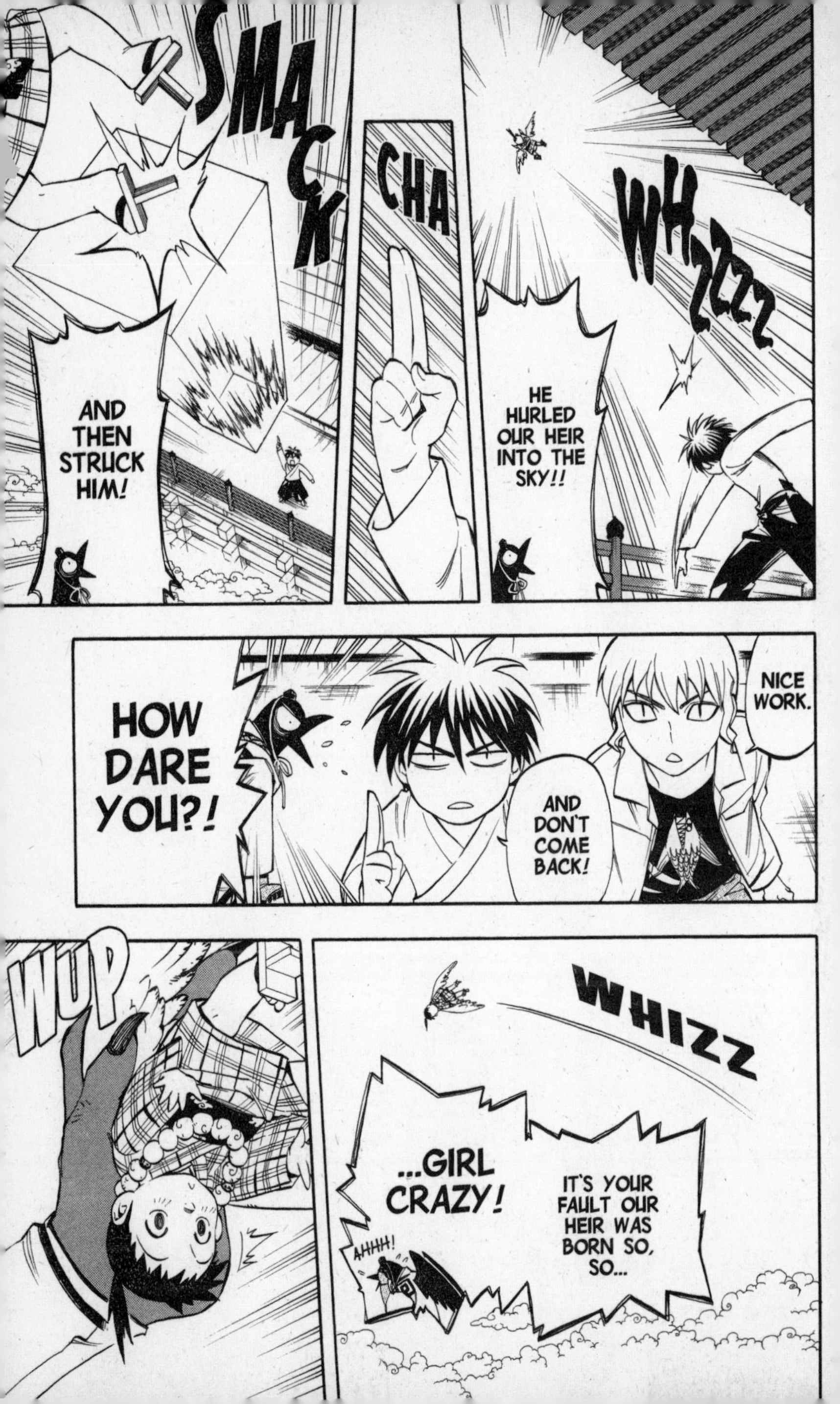
WHZZZZ
HE HURLED OUR HEIR INTO THE SKY!!
CHA
SMACK
AND THEN STRUCK HIM!
NICE WORK.
AND DON'T COME BACK!
HOW DARE YOU?!
WHIZZ
IT'S YOUR FAULT OUR HEIR WAS BORN SO, SO...
...GIRL CRAZY!
AHHH!
WUP

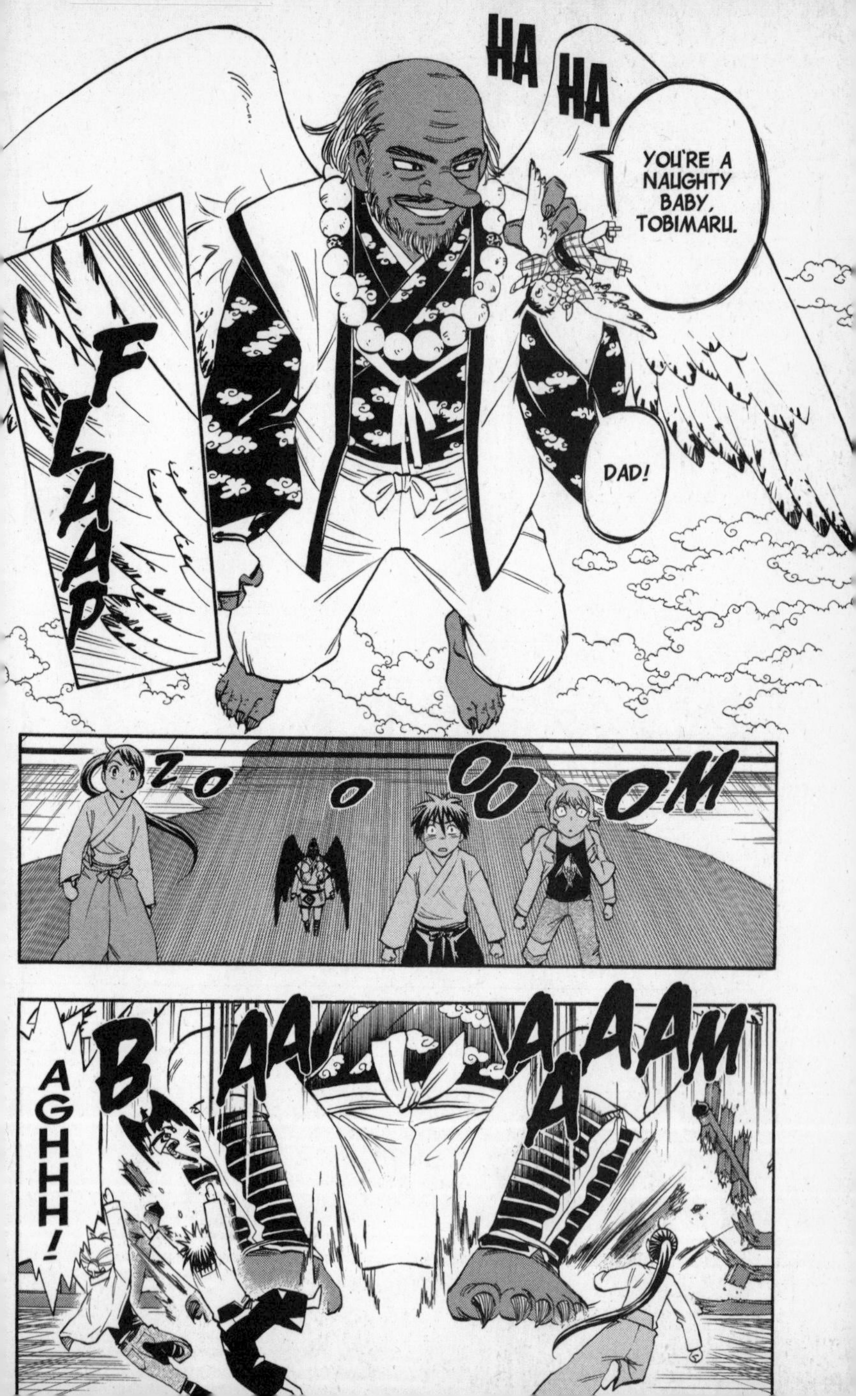
HA HA
YOU'RE A NAUGHTY BABY, TOBIMARU.
DAD!
FLAP
ZOOOOOM
BAAAAAAM
AGHHH!

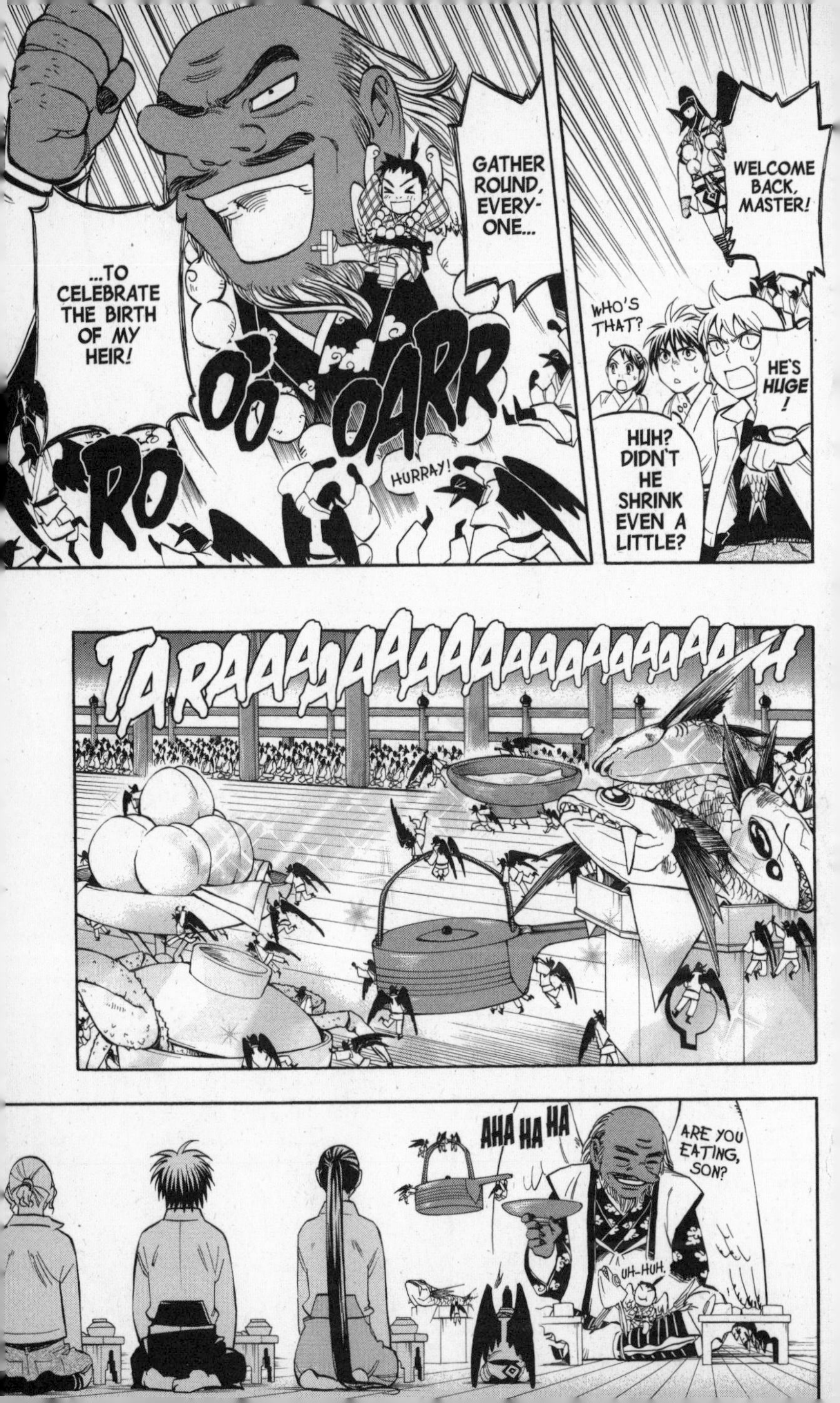
WELCOME BACK, MASTER!
WHO'S THAT?
HE'S HUGE!
HUH? DIDN'T HE SHRINK EVEN A LITTLE?
GATHER ROUND, EVERY-ONE...
...TO CELEBRATE THE BIRTH OF MY HEIR!
ROOOOARR
HURRAY!
TARAAAAAAAAAAAAAAAAAAH
ARE YOU EATING, SON?
AHAHAHA
UH-HUH.

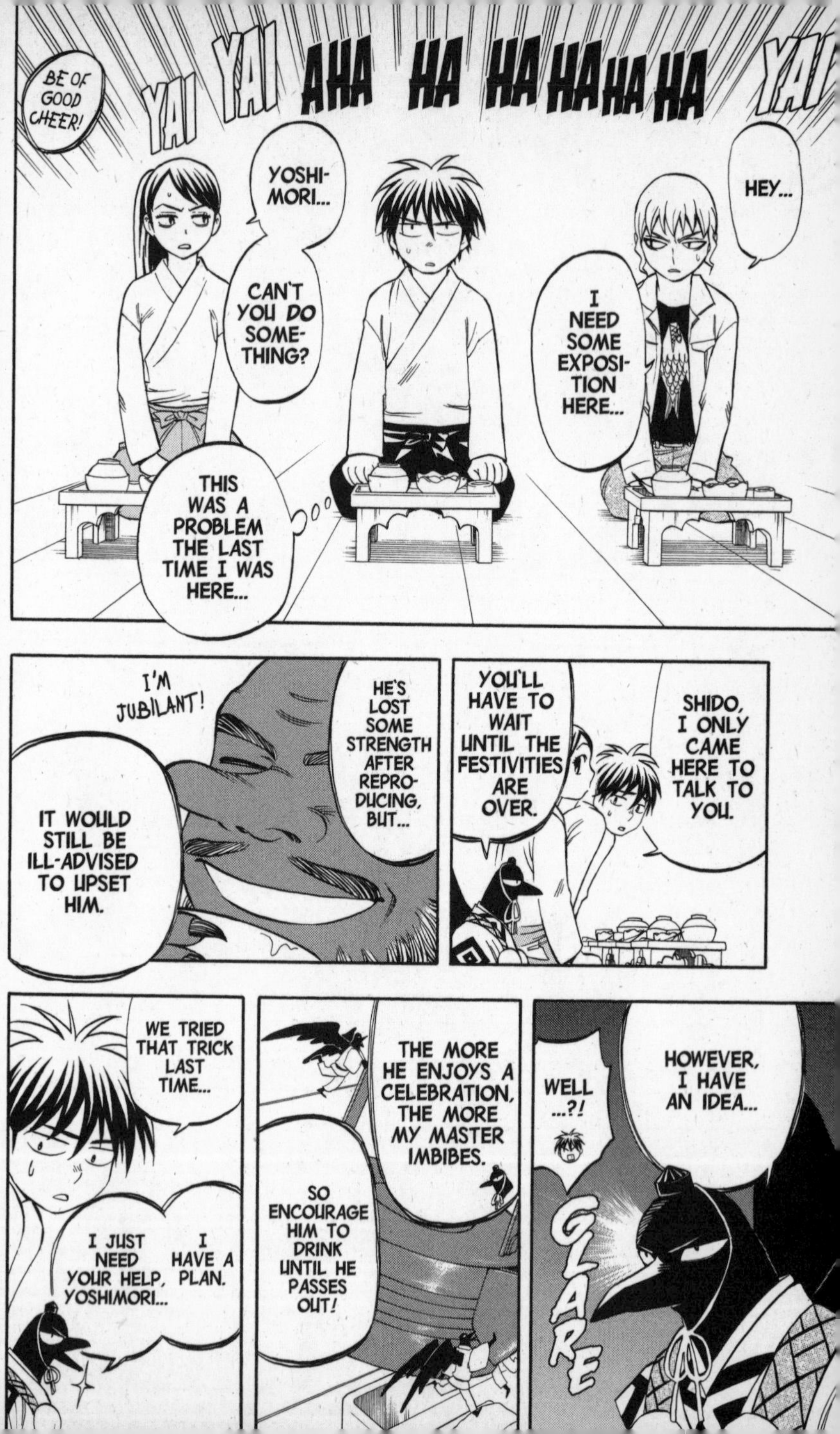
YAI YAI AHA HA HA HAHAHA HA YAI
HEY...
I NEED SOME EXPOSITION HERE...
YOSHIMORI...
CAN'T YOU DO SOMETHING?
BE OF GOOD CHEER!
THIS WAS A PROBLEM THE LAST TIME I WAS HERE...
SHIDO, I ONLY CAME HERE TO TALK TO YOU.
YOU'LL HAVE TO WAIT UNTIL THE FESTIVITIES ARE OVER.
HE'S LOST SOME STRENGTH AFTER REPRODUCING, BUT...
I'M JUBILANT!
IT WOULD STILL BE ILL-ADVISED TO UPSET HIM.
HOWEVER, I HAVE AN IDEA...
WELL ...?!
GLARE
THE MORE HE ENJOYS A CELEBRATION, THE MORE MY MASTER IMBIBES.
SO ENCOURAGE HIM TO DRINK UNTIL HE PASSES OUT!
WE TRIED THAT TRICK LAST TIME...
I HAVE A PLAN.
I JUST NEED YOUR HELP, YOSHIMORI...

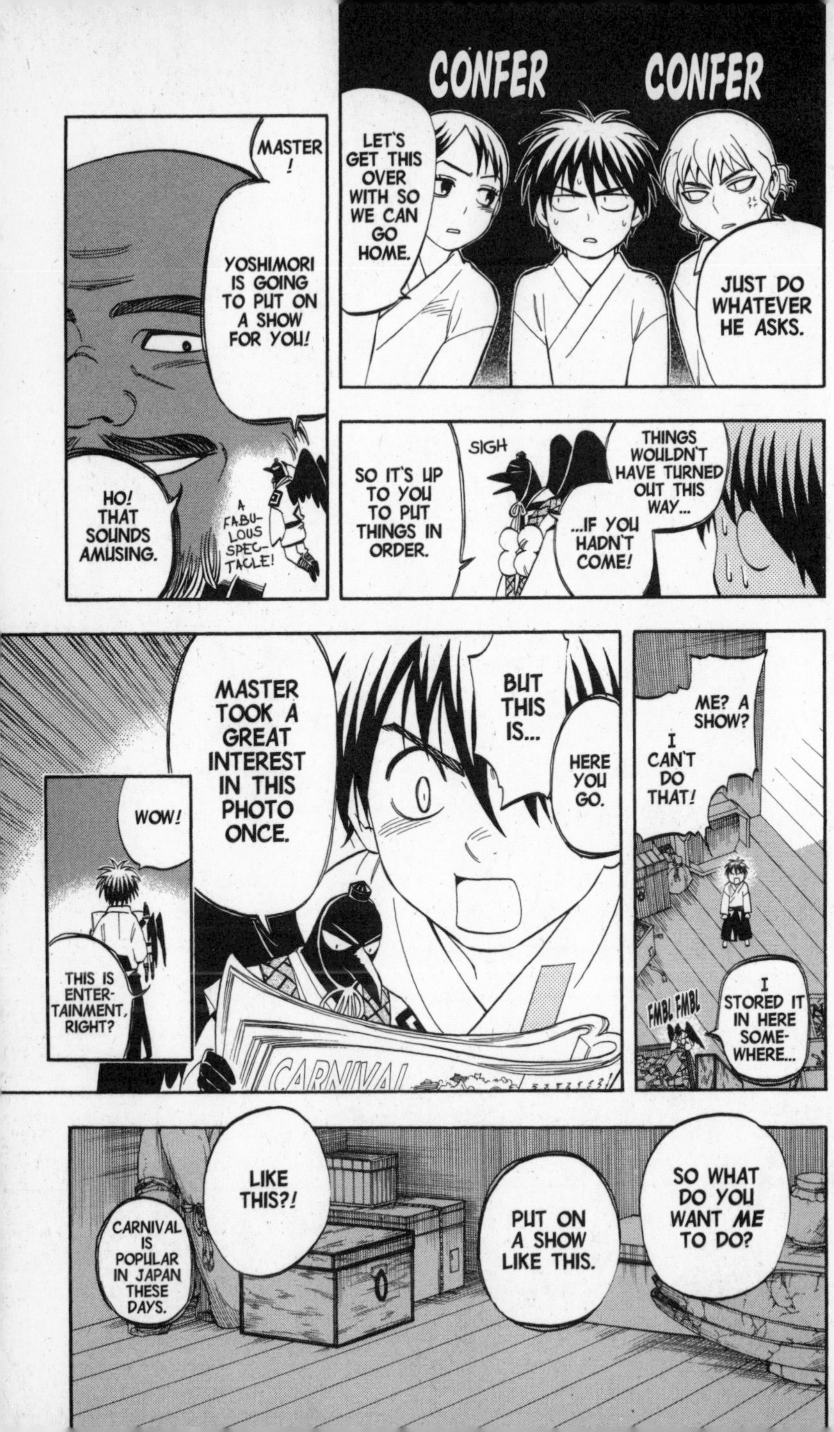
CONFER CONFER
JUST DO WHATEVER HE ASKS.
LET'S GET THIS OVER WITH SO WE CAN GO HOME.
THINGS WOULDN'T HAVE TURNED OUT THIS WAY...
...IF YOU HADN'T COME!
SIGH
SO IT'S UP TO YOU TO PUT THINGS IN ORDER.
MASTER!
YOSHIMORI IS GOING TO PUT ON A SHOW FOR YOU!
A FABULOUS SPECTACLE!
HO! THAT SOUNDS AMUSING.
ME? A SHOW?
I CAN'T DO THAT!
I STORED IT IN HERE SOMEWHERE...
FMBL FMBL
BUT THIS IS...
HERE YOU GO.
MASTER TOOK A GREAT INTEREST IN THIS PHOTO ONCE.
CARNIVAL
WOW!
THIS IS ENTERTAINMENT, RIGHT?
SO WHAT DO YOU WANT ME TO DO?
PUT ON A SHOW LIKE THIS.
LIKE THIS?!
CARNIVAL IS POPULAR IN JAPAN THESE DAYS.

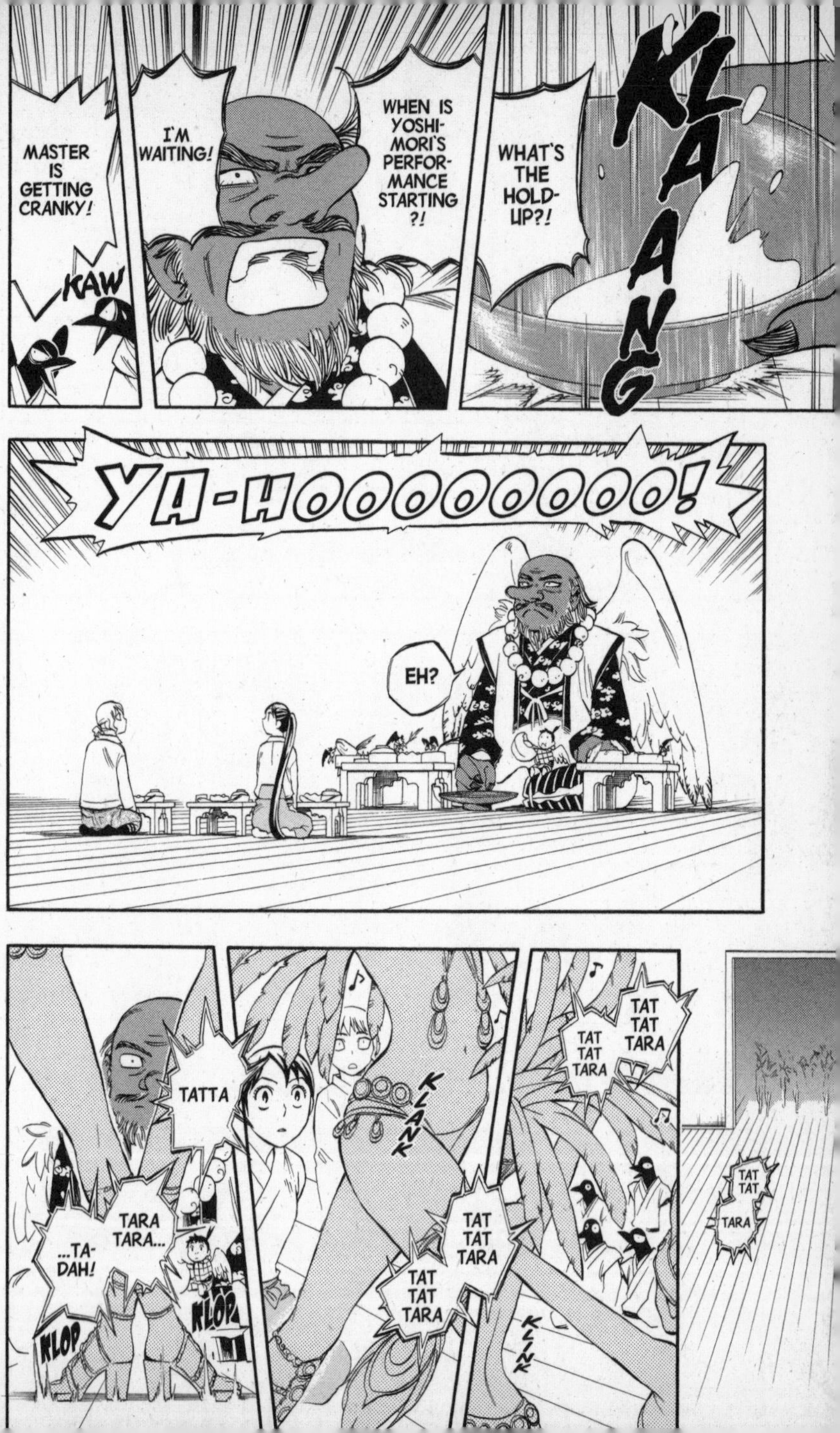
KLAANG
WHAT'S THE HOLD-UP?!
WHEN IS YOSHIMORI'S PERFORMANCE STARTING?!
I'M WAITING!
MASTER IS GETTING CRANKY!
KAW
YA-HOOOOOOOO!
EH?
TAT TAT TARA
TAT TAT TARA
TAT TAT TARA
KLANK
TAT TAT TARA
TAT TAT TARA
KLINK
TATTA
TARA TARA...
...TA-DAH!
KLOP
KLOP

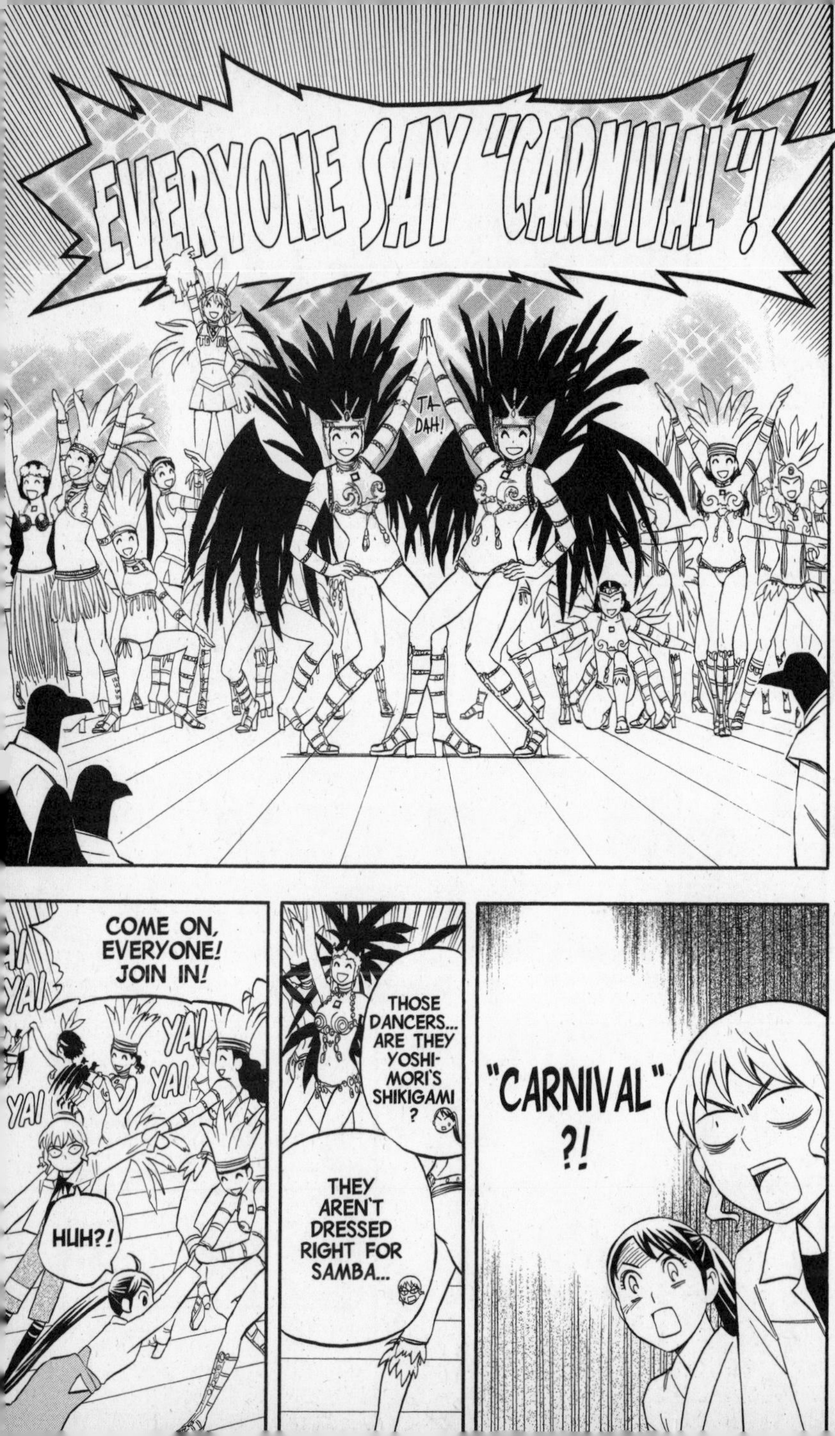
EVERYONE SAY "CARNIVAL"!
TA-DAH!
"CARNIVAL" ?!
THOSE DANCERS... ARE THEY YOSHIMORI'S SHIKIGAMI?
THEY AREN'T DRESSED RIGHT FOR SAMBA...
COME ON, EVERYONE! JOIN IN!
YAI
YAI
YAI
YAI
YAI
HUH?!

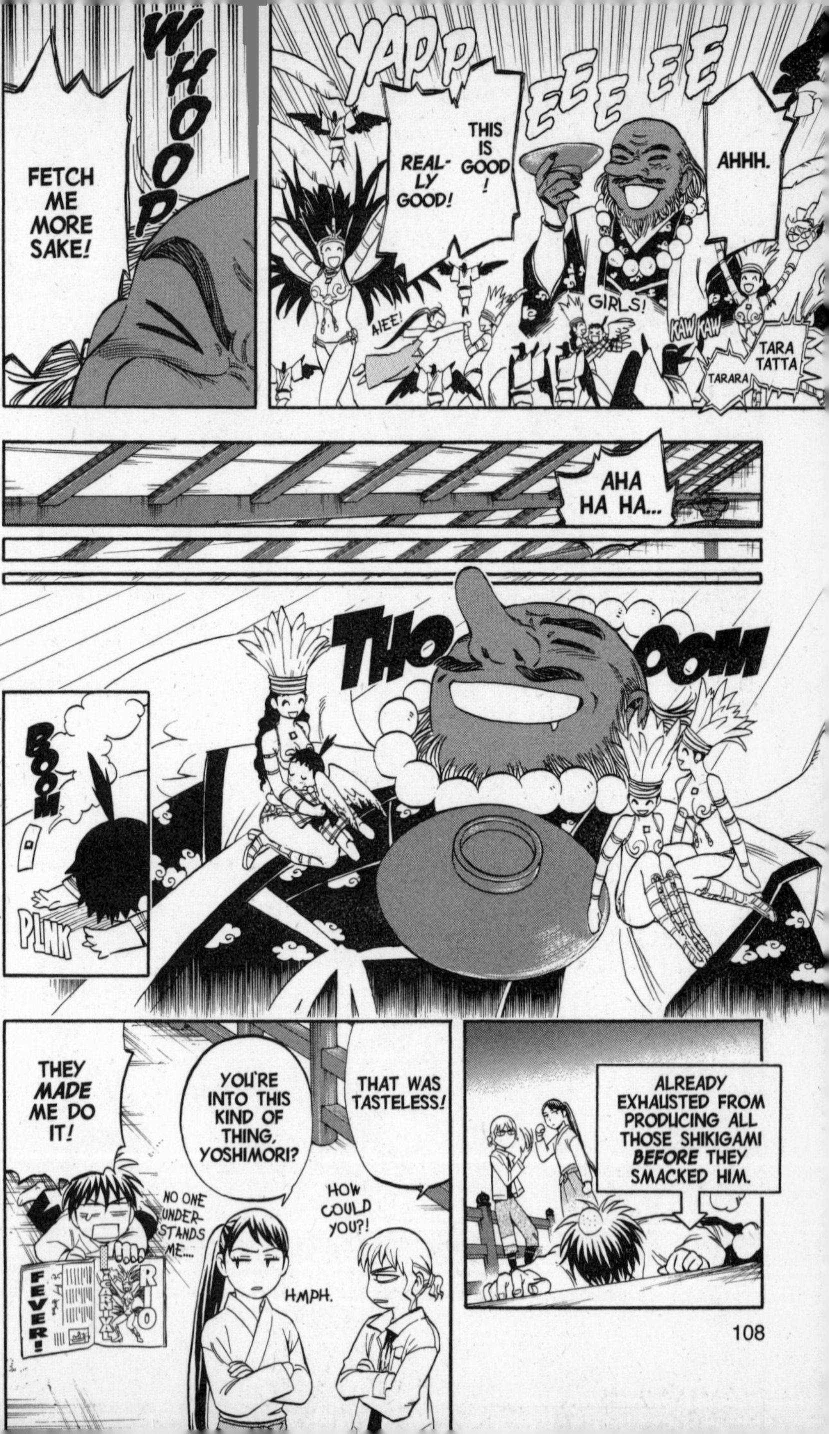
AHHH.
THIS IS GOOD!
REALLY GOOD!
YAPPEEEEE
GIRLS!
TARA TATTA
TARARA
KAW KAW
AIEE!
WHOOOP
FETCH ME MORE SAKE!
AHA HA HA...
THOOOM
BOOM
PLINK
ALREADY EXHAUSTED FROM PRODUCING ALL THOSE SHIKIGAMI *BEFORE* THEY SMACKED HIM.
THAT WAS TASTELESS!
YOU'RE INTO THIS KIND OF THING, YOSHIMORI?
HOW COULD YOU?!
THEY *MADE* ME DO IT!
NO ONE UNDERSTANDS ME...
HMPH.
FEVER!
RIO

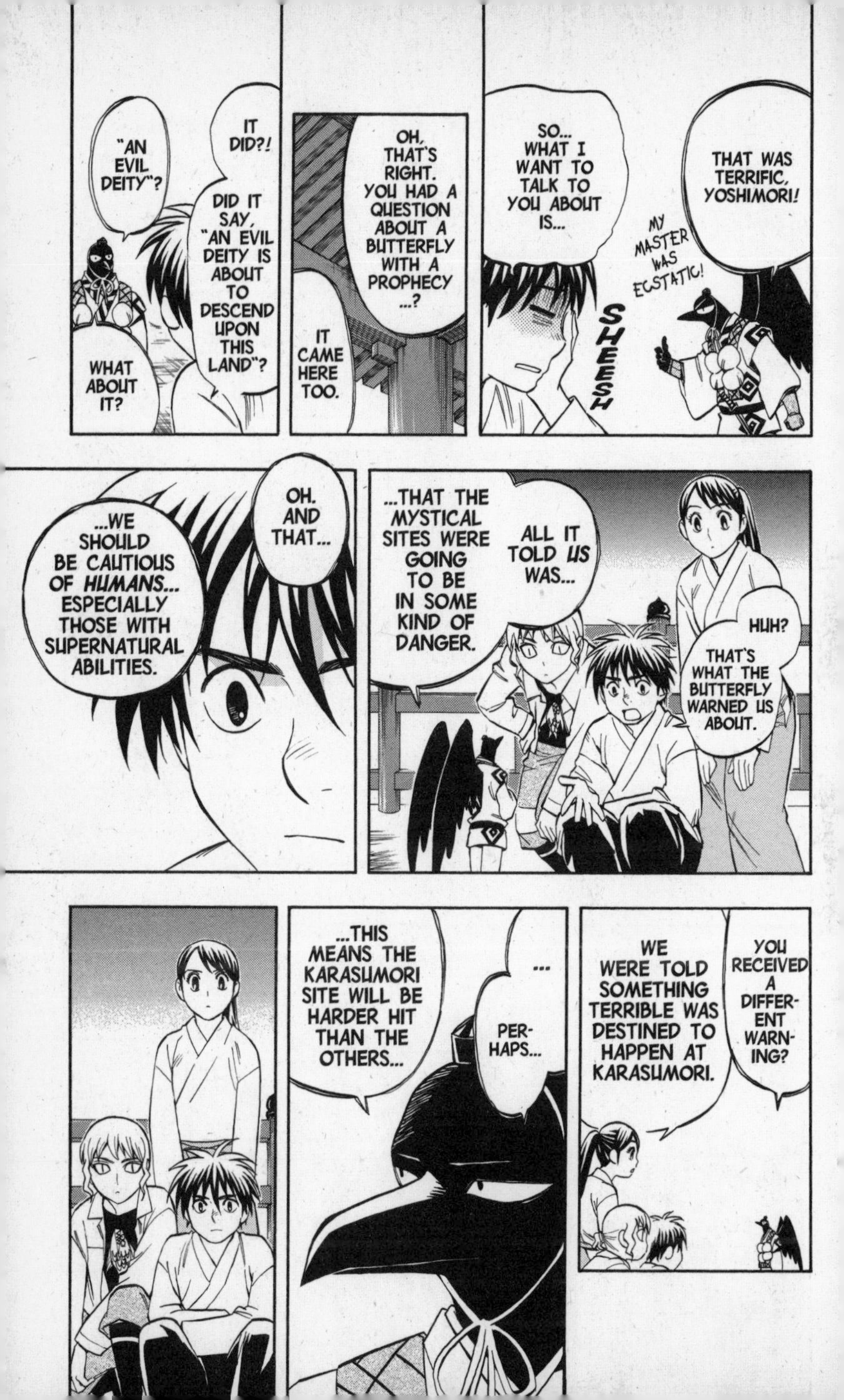

THAT WAS TERRIFIC, YOSHIMORI!
MY MASTER WAS ECSTATIC!
SO... WHAT I WANT TO TALK TO YOU ABOUT IS...
SHEESH
OH, THAT'S RIGHT. YOU HAD A QUESTION ABOUT A BUTTERFLY WITH A PROPHECY ...?
IT CAME HERE TOO.
IT DID?!
DID IT SAY, "AN EVIL DEITY IS ABOUT TO DESCEND UPON THIS LAND"?
"AN EVIL DEITY"?
WHAT ABOUT IT?
HUH?
THAT'S WHAT THE BUTTERFLY WARNED US ABOUT.
ALL IT TOLD *US* WAS...
...THAT THE MYSTICAL SITES WERE GOING TO BE IN SOME KIND OF DANGER.
OH. AND THAT...
...WE SHOULD BE CAUTIOUS OF *HUMANS*... ESPECIALLY THOSE WITH SUPERNATURAL ABILITIES.
YOU RECEIVED A DIFFERENT WARNING?
WE WERE TOLD SOMETHING TERRIBLE WAS DESTINED TO HAPPEN AT KARASUMORI.
...
PERHAPS...
...THIS MEANS THE KARASUMORI SITE WILL BE HARDER HIT THAN THE OTHERS...

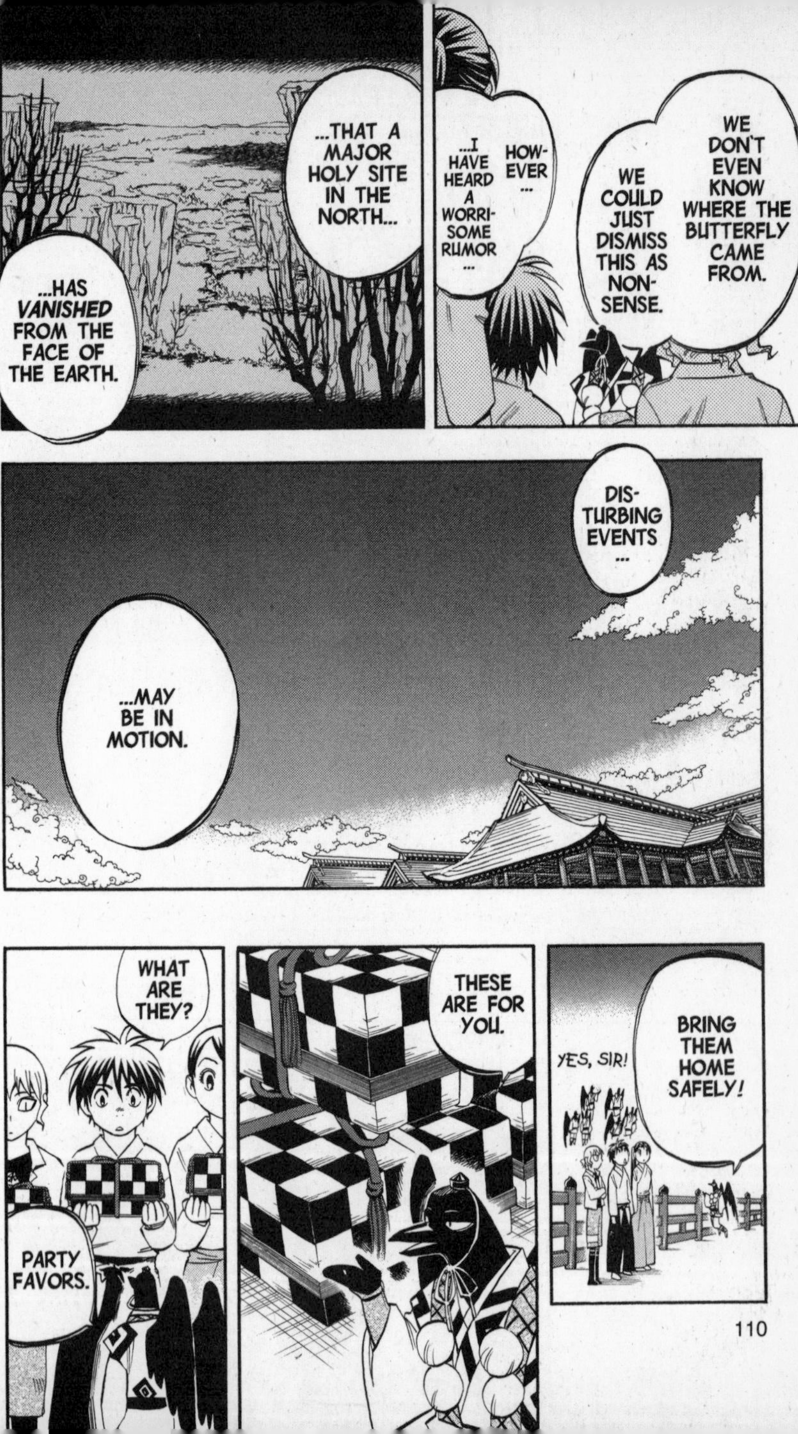
WE DON'T EVEN KNOW WHERE THE BUTTERFLY CAME FROM.
WE COULD JUST DISMISS THIS AS NONSENSE.
HOWEVER...
...I HAVE HEARD A WORRISOME RUMOR...
...THAT A MAJOR HOLY SITE IN THE NORTH...
...HAS *VANISHED* FROM THE FACE OF THE EARTH.
DISTURBING EVENTS...
...MAY BE IN MOTION.
BRING THEM HOME SAFELY!
YES, SIR!
THESE ARE FOR YOU.
WHAT ARE THEY?
PARTY FAVORS.

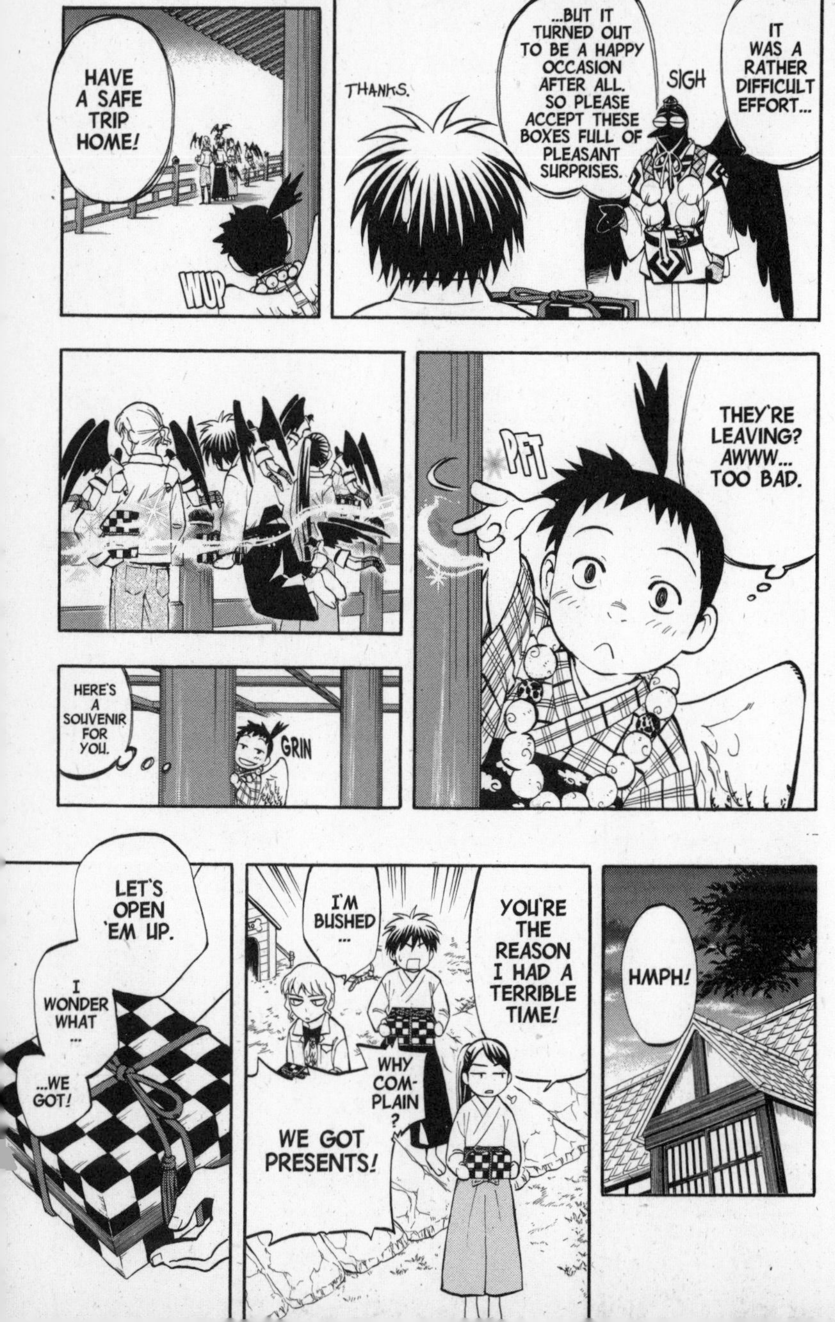
IT WAS A RATHER DIFFICULT EFFORT...
SIGH
...BUT IT TURNED OUT TO BE A HAPPY OCCASION AFTER ALL. SO PLEASE ACCEPT THESE BOXES FULL OF PLEASANT SURPRISES.
THANKS.
HAVE A SAFE TRIP HOME!
WUP
THEY'RE LEAVING? AWWW... TOO BAD.
PFT
HERE'S A SOUVENIR FOR YOU.
GRIN
HMPH!
YOU'RE THE REASON I HAD A TERRIBLE TIME!
I'M BUSHED...
WHY COM-PLAIN?
WE GOT PRESENTS!
LET'S OPEN 'EM UP.
I WONDER WHAT...
...WE GOT!

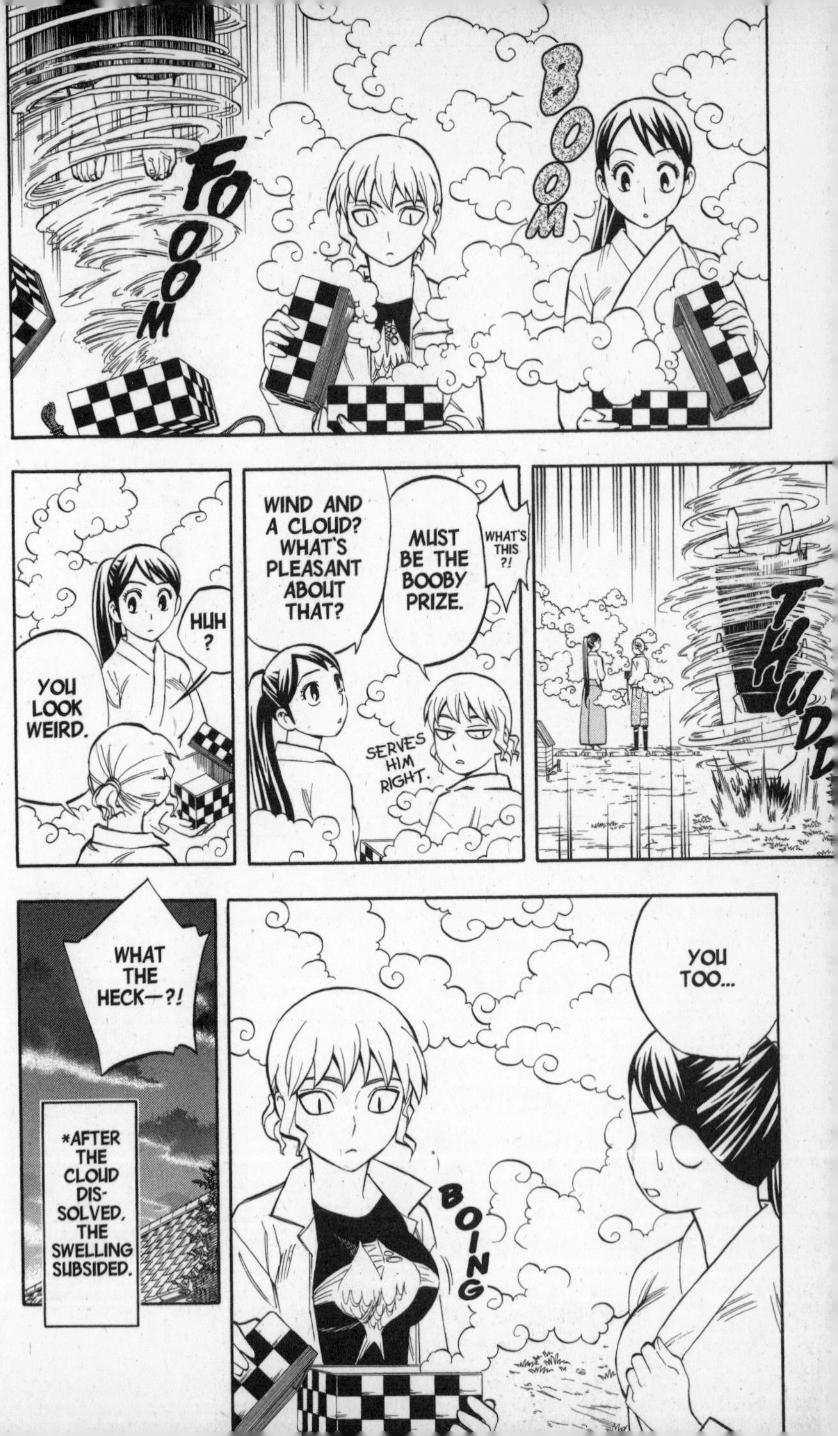
BOOOM
FOOOM
WHAT'S THIS?!
THUD
MUST BE THE BOOBY PRIZE.
WIND AND A CLOUD? WHAT'S PLEASANT ABOUT THAT?
SERVES HIM RIGHT.
HUH?
YOU LOOK WEIRD.
YOU TOO...
BOING
WHAT THE HECK—?!
*AFTER THE CLOUD DIS-SOLVED, THE SWELLING SUBSIDED.

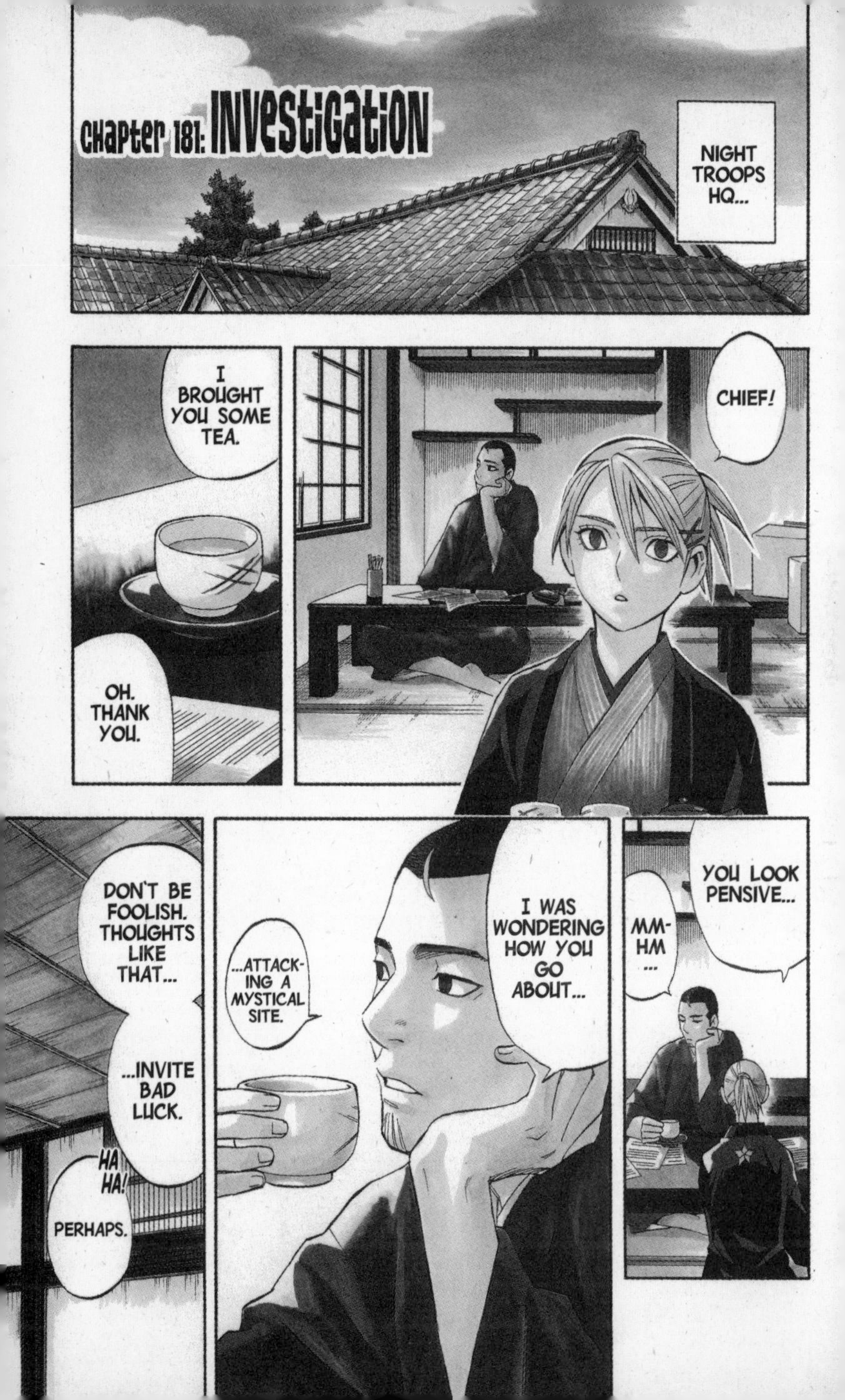
Chapter 181: Investigation
NIGHT TROOPS HQ...
CHIEF!
I BROUGHT YOU SOME TEA.
OH. THANK YOU.
YOU LOOK PENSIVE...
MM-HM...
I WAS WONDERING HOW YOU GO ABOUT...
...ATTACKING A MYSTICAL SITE.
DON'T BE FOOLISH. THOUGHTS LIKE THAT...
...INVITE BAD LUCK.
HA HA!
PERHAPS.

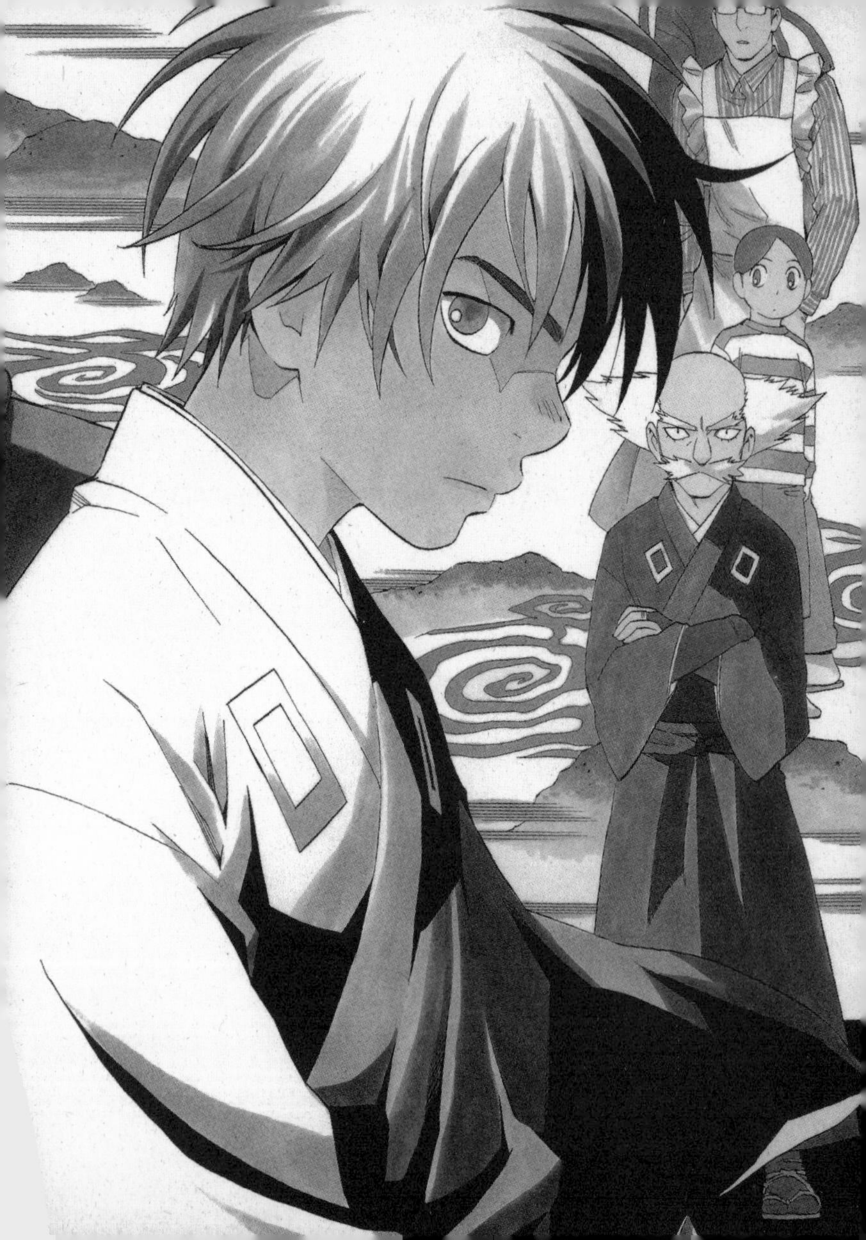

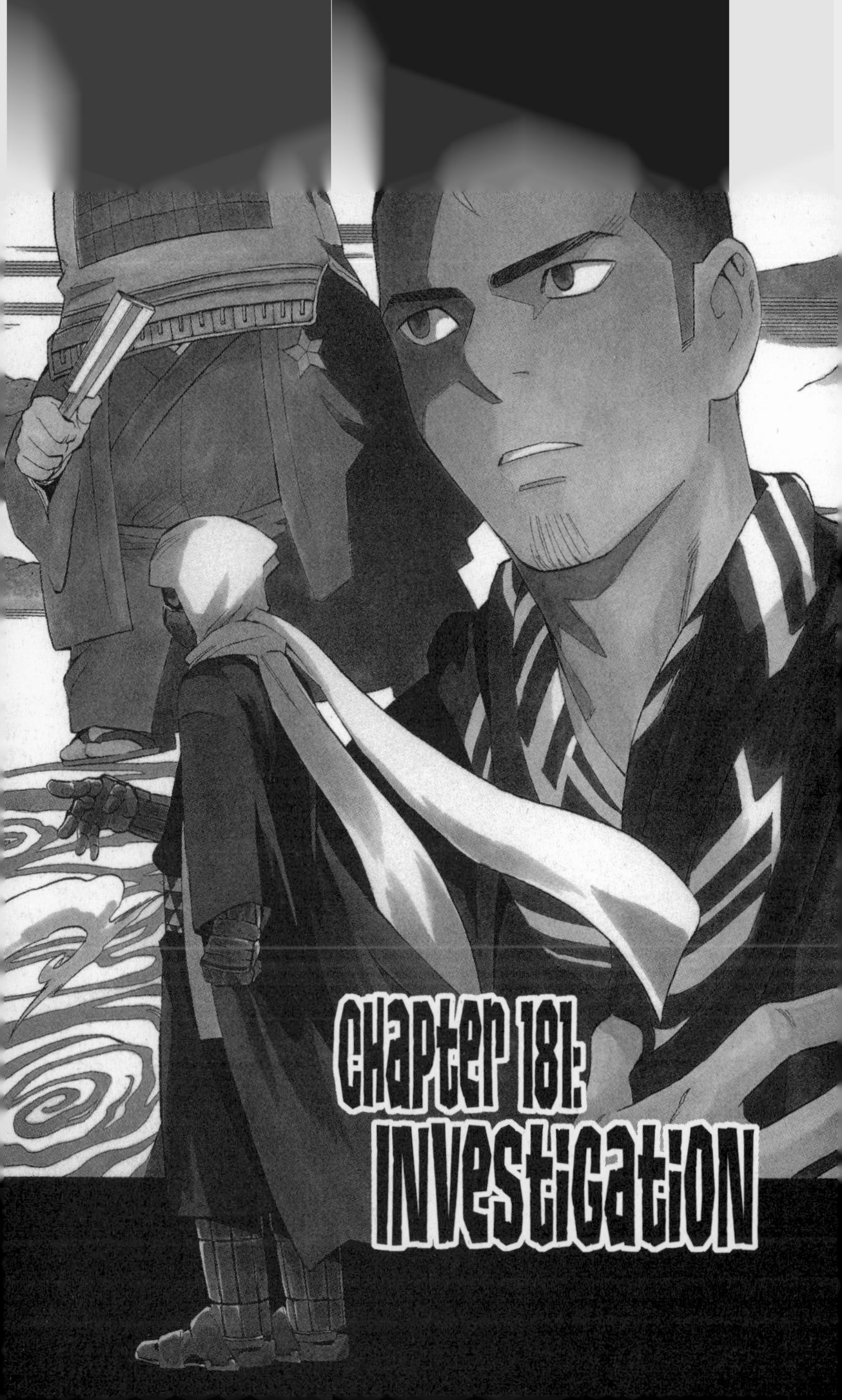
CHAPTER 181:
INVESTIGATION

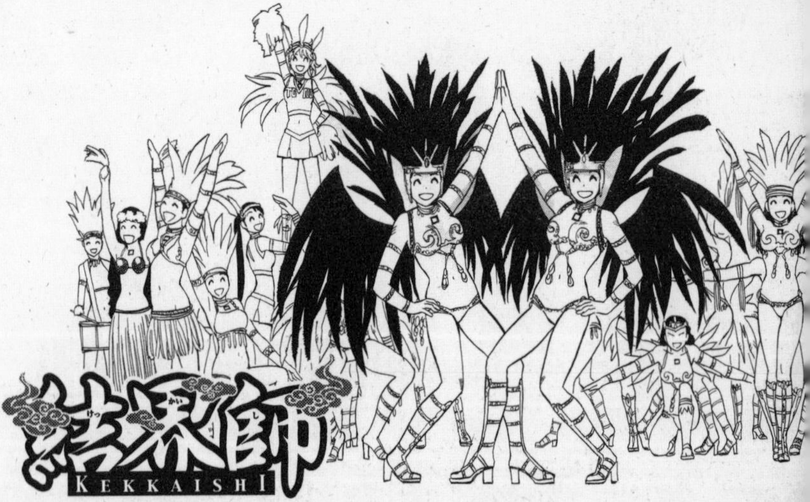
結界師
KEKKAISHI

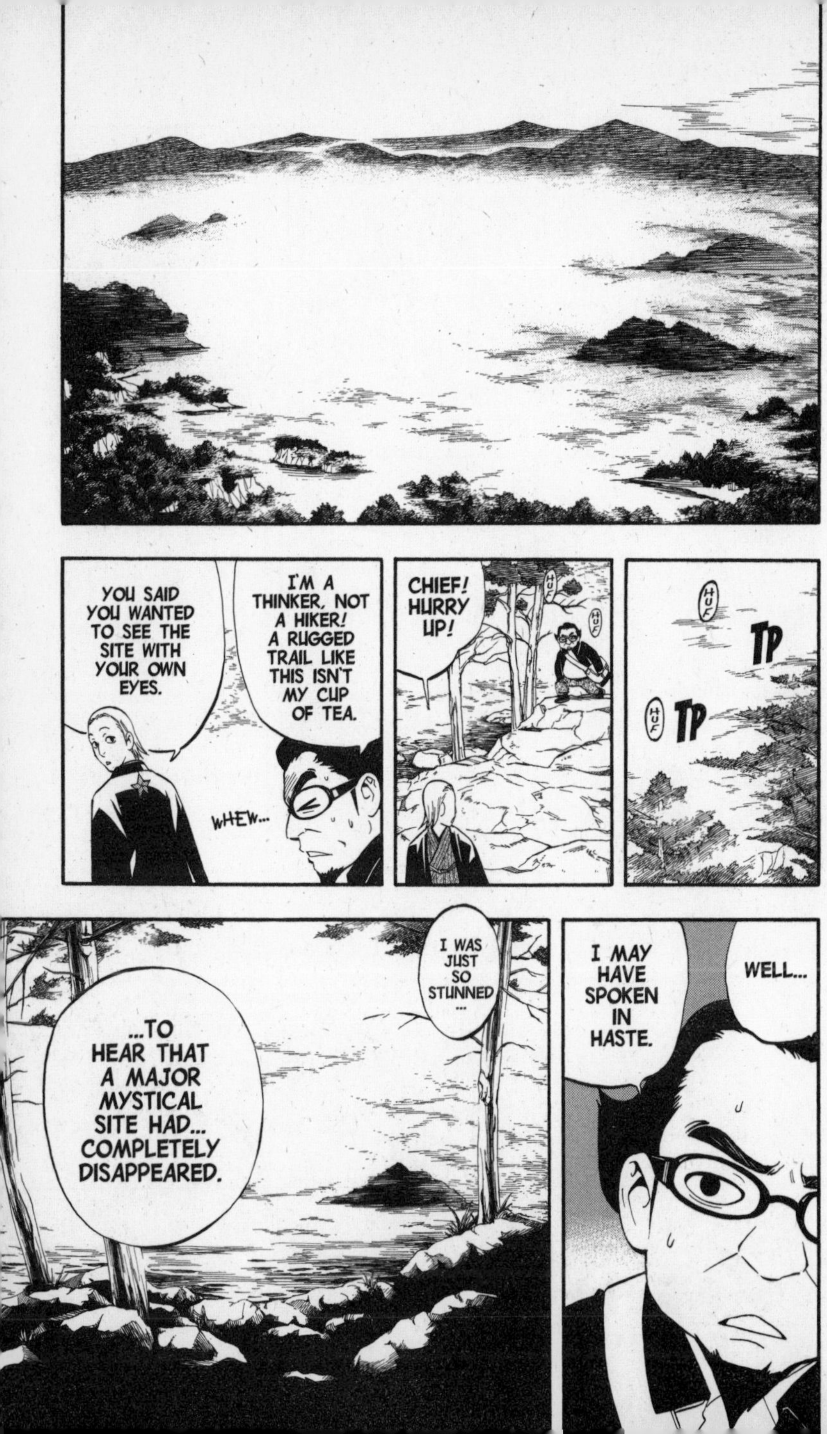
HUF
TP
HUF
TP
CHIEF! HURRY UP!
HUF
HUF
I'M A THINKER, NOT A HIKER! A RUGGED TRAIL LIKE THIS ISN'T MY CUP OF TEA.
YOU SAID YOU WANTED TO SEE THE SITE WITH YOUR OWN EYES.
WHEW...
WELL...
I MAY HAVE SPOKEN IN HASTE.
I WAS JUST SO STUNNED...
...TO HEAR THAT A MAJOR MYSTICAL SITE HAD... COMPLETELY DISAPPEARED.

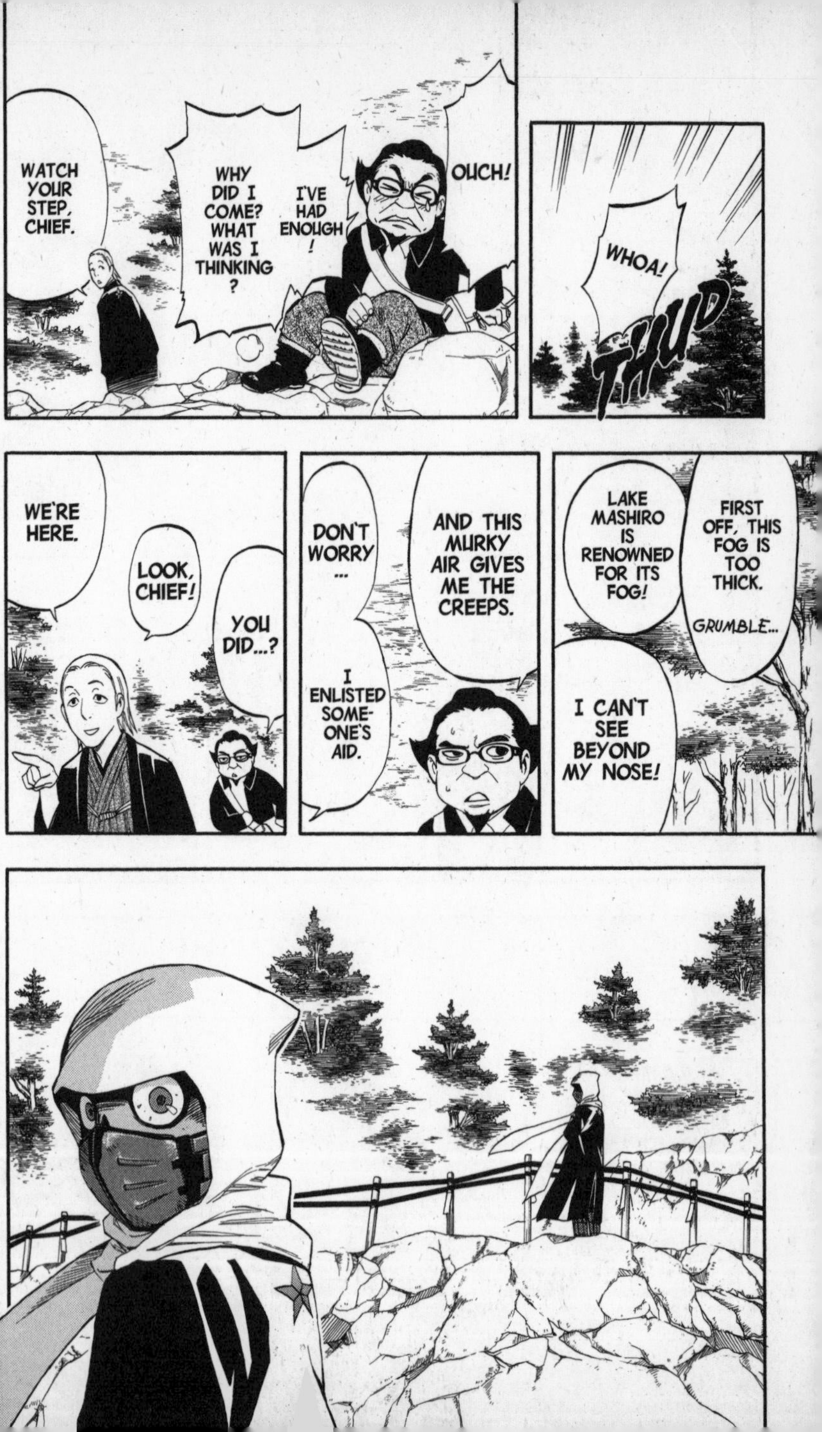
WHOA!
THUD
OUCH!
I'VE HAD ENOUGH!
WHY DID I COME? WHAT WAS I THINKING?
WATCH YOUR STEP, CHIEF.
FIRST OFF, THIS FOG IS TOO THICK.
GRUMBLE...
LAKE MASHIRO IS RENOWNED FOR ITS FOG!
I CAN'T SEE BEYOND MY NOSE!
AND THIS MURKY AIR GIVES ME THE CREEPS.
DON'T WORRY...
I ENLISTED SOMEONE'S AID.
YOU DID...?
LOOK, CHIEF!
WE'RE HERE.

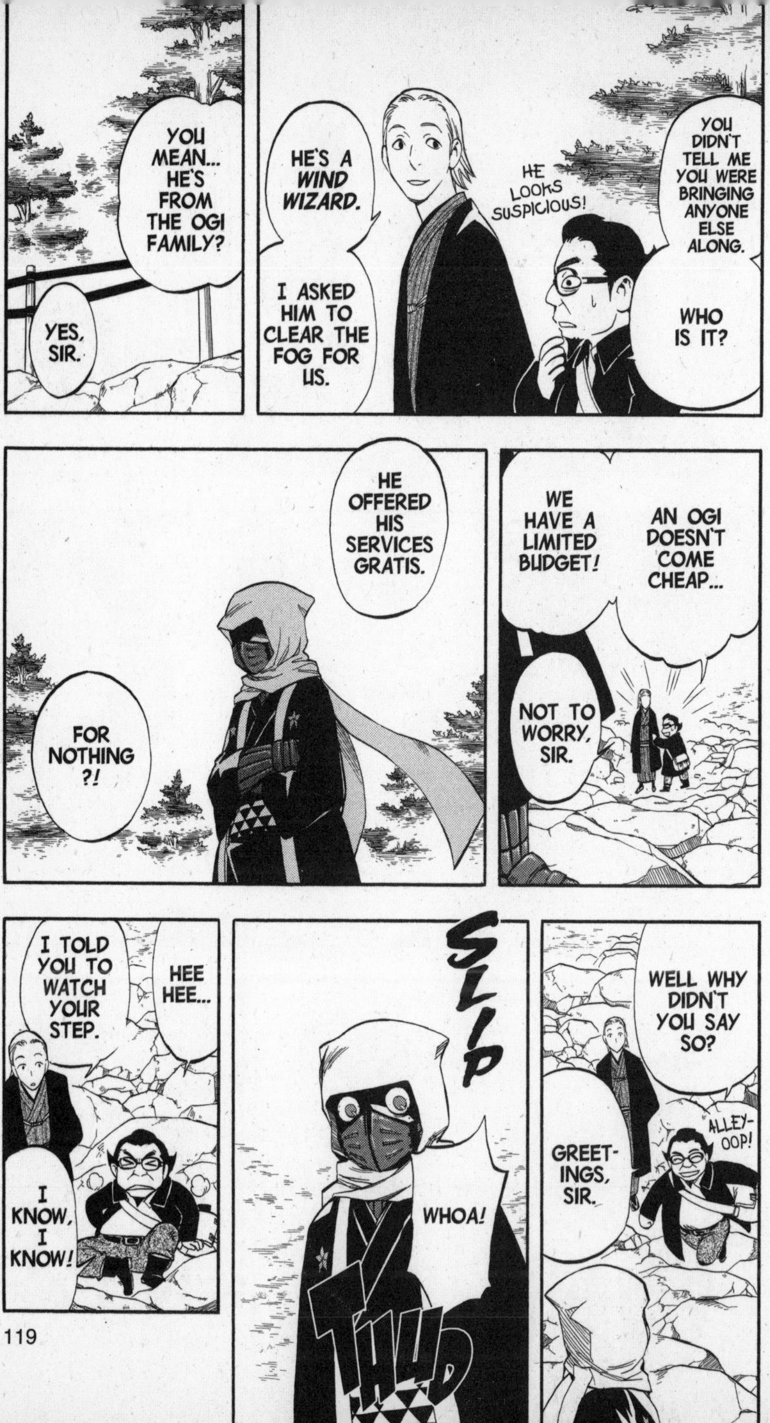
YOU DIDN'T TELL ME YOU WERE BRINGING ANYONE ELSE ALONG.
HE LOOKS SUSPICIOUS!
WHO IS IT?
HE'S A WIND WIZARD.
I ASKED HIM TO CLEAR THE FOG FOR US.
YOU MEAN... HE'S FROM THE OGI FAMILY?
YES, SIR.
AN OGI DOESN'T COME CHEAP...
WE HAVE A LIMITED BUDGET!
NOT TO WORRY, SIR.
HE OFFERED HIS SERVICES GRATIS.
FOR NOTHING?!
WELL WHY DIDN'T YOU SAY SO?
ALLEY-OOP!
GREET-INGS, SIR.
SLIP
WHOA!
THUD
HEE HEE...
I TOLD YOU TO WATCH YOUR STEP.
I KNOW, I KNOW!

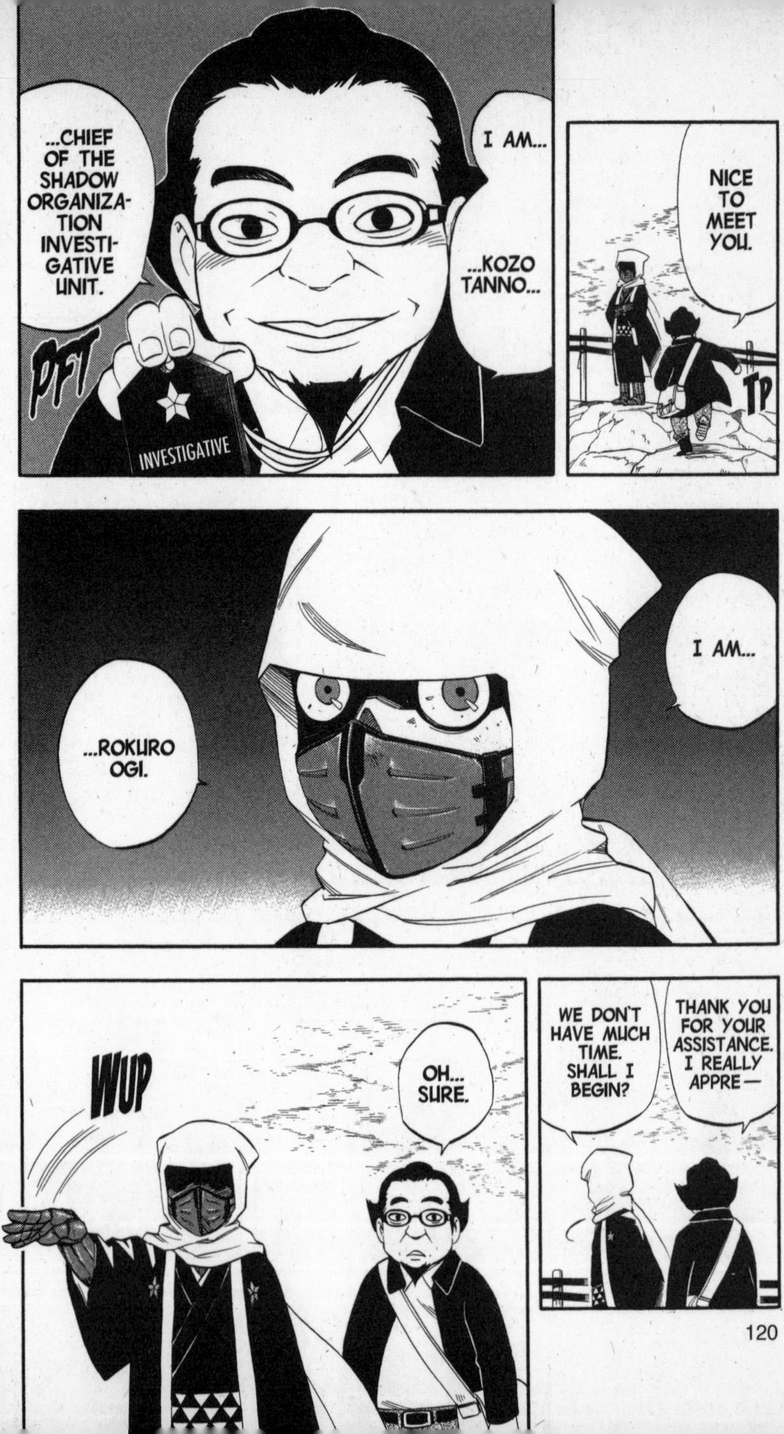
NICE TO MEET YOU.
TP
I AM...
...KOZO TANNO...
...CHIEF OF THE SHADOW ORGANIZATION INVESTIGATIVE UNIT.
PFT
INVESTIGATIVE
I AM...
...ROKURO OGI.
THANK YOU FOR YOUR ASSISTANCE. I REALLY APPRE—
WE DON'T HAVE MUCH TIME. SHALL I BEGIN?
OH... SURE.
WUP

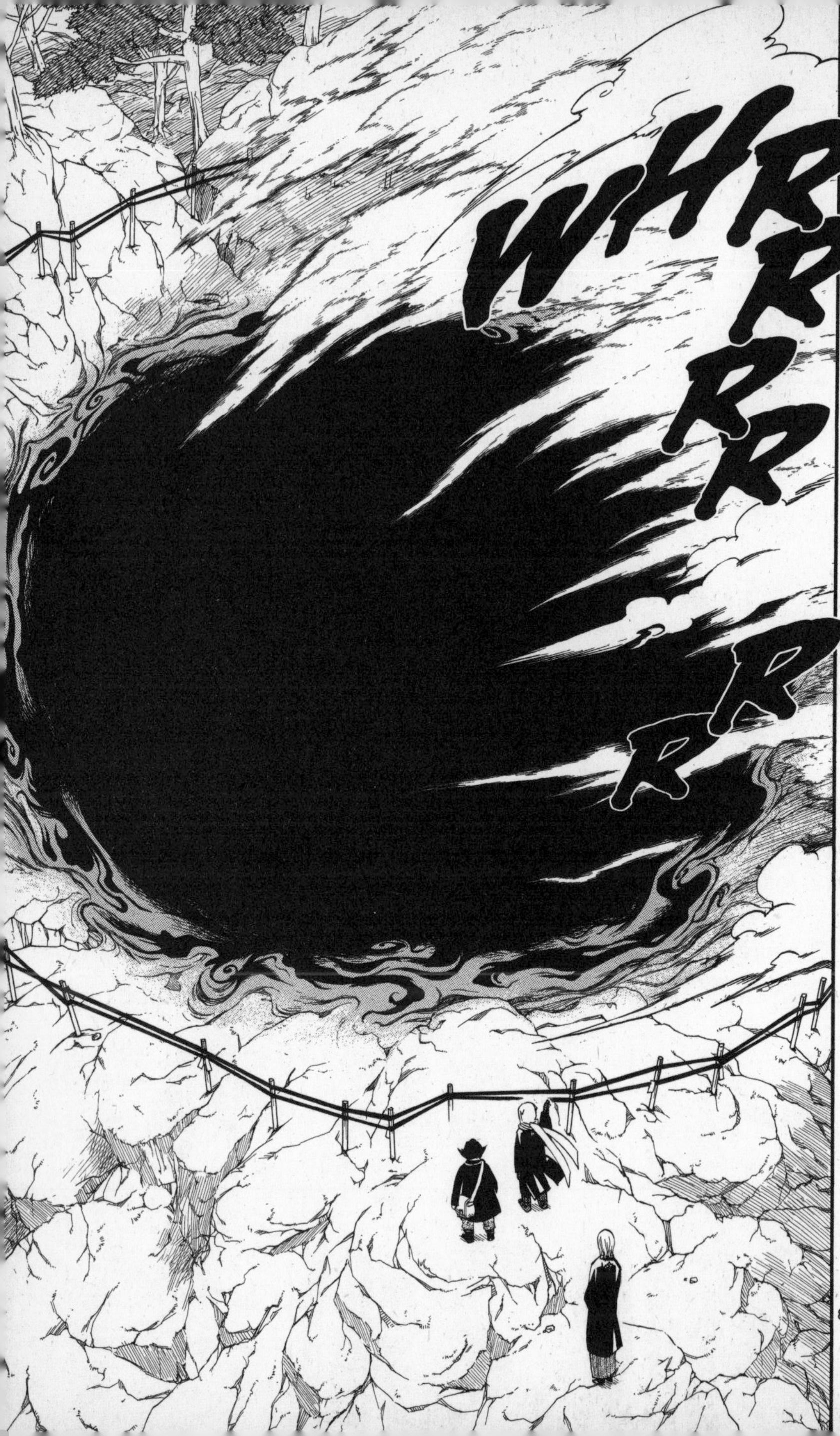
WHRRRRRR

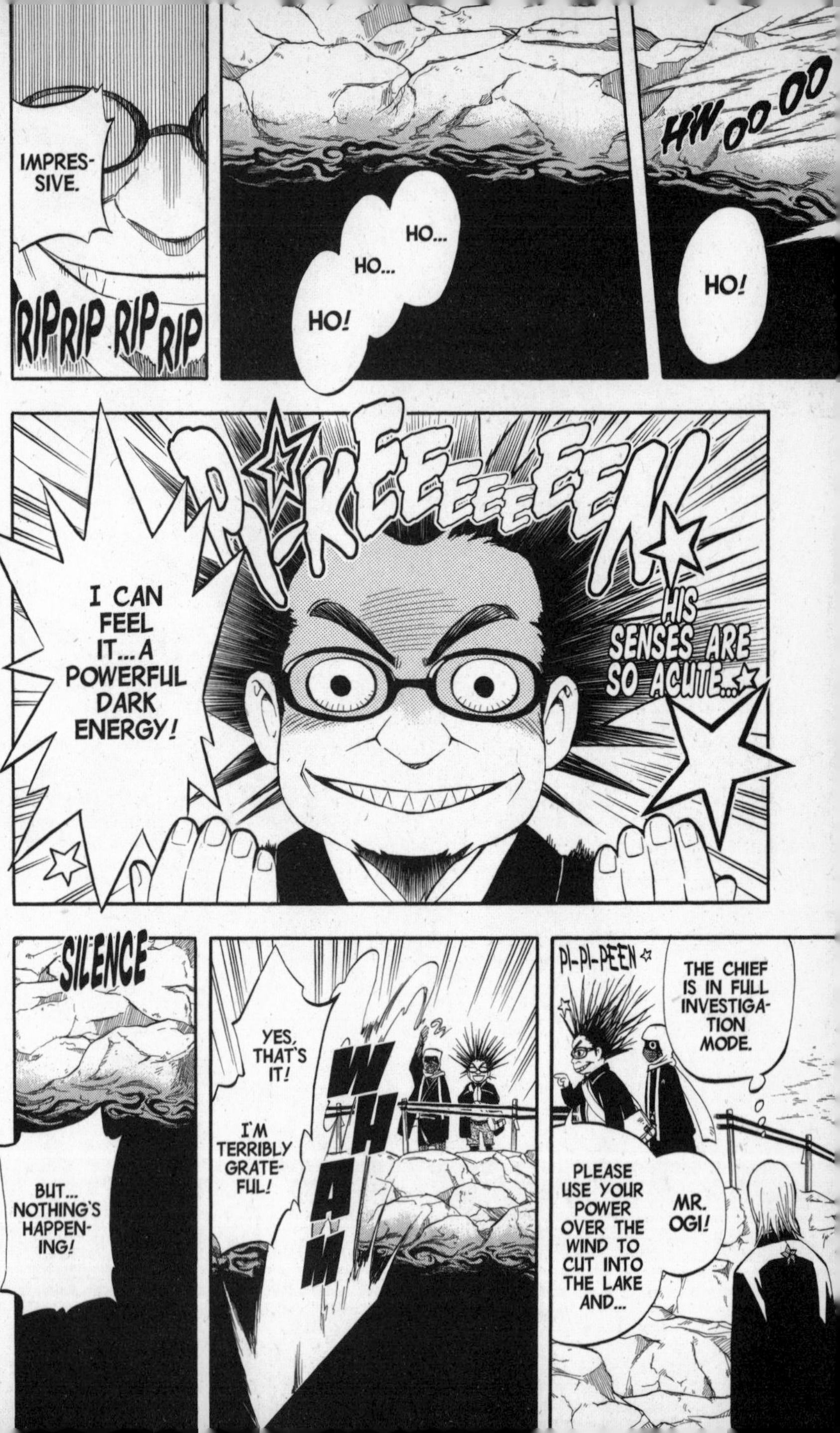
HWOO-OO
HO!
HO...
HO...
HO!
IMPRESSIVE.
RIP RIP RIP RIP
KEEEEEEN
HIS SENSES ARE SO ACUTE...☆
I CAN FEEL IT... A POWERFUL DARK ENERGY!
PI-PI-PEEN☆
THE CHIEF IS IN FULL INVESTIGATION MODE.
MR. OGI!
PLEASE USE YOUR POWER OVER THE WIND TO CUT INTO THE LAKE AND...
YES, THAT'S IT!
I'M TERRIBLY GRATEFUL!
WHAM
SILENCE
BUT... NOTHING'S HAPPENING!

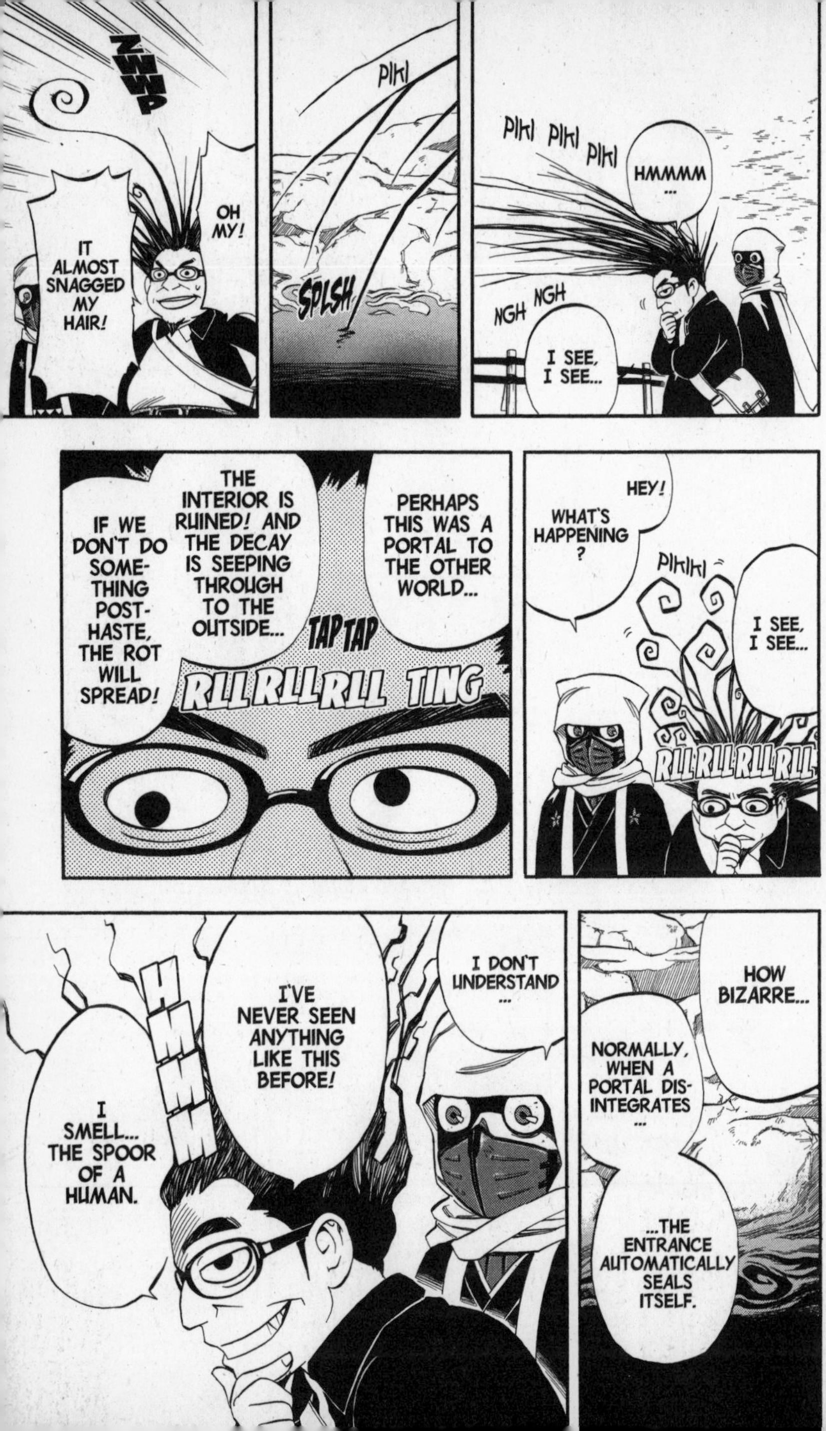
PIKI PIKI PIKI
HMMMM ...
NGH NGH
I SEE, I SEE...
PIKI
SPLSH
ZWWP
OH MY!
IT ALMOST SNAGGED MY HAIR!
HEY!
WHAT'S HAPPENING ?
PIKIKI
I SEE, I SEE...
RLLRLLRLLRLL
PERHAPS THIS WAS A PORTAL TO THE OTHER WORLD...
THE INTERIOR IS RUINED! AND THE DECAY IS SEEPING THROUGH TO THE OUTSIDE...
IF WE DON'T DO SOME-THING POST-HASTE, THE ROT WILL SPREAD!
TAP TAP
RLLRLLRLL TING
HOW BIZARRE...
NORMALLY, WHEN A PORTAL DIS-INTEGRATES ...
...THE ENTRANCE AUTOMATICALLY SEALS ITSELF.
I DON'T UNDERSTAND ...
I'VE NEVER SEEN ANYTHING LIKE THIS BEFORE!
HMMMM
I SMELL... THE SPOOR OF A HUMAN.

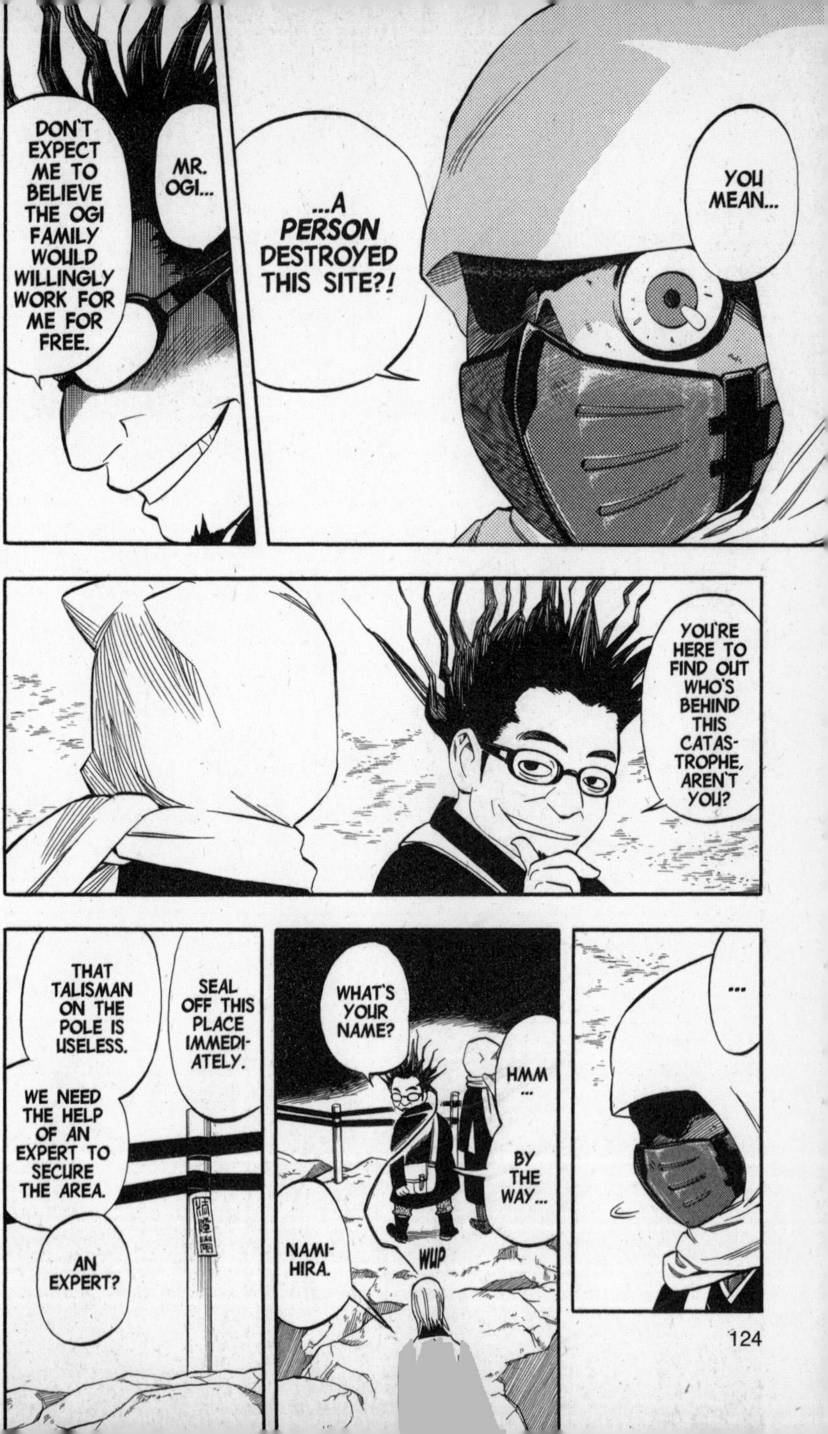
YOU MEAN...
...A PERSON DESTROYED THIS SITE?!
MR. OGI...
DON'T EXPECT ME TO BELIEVE THE OGI FAMILY WOULD WILLINGLY WORK FOR ME FOR FREE.
YOU'RE HERE TO FIND OUT WHO'S BEHIND THIS CATAS-TROPHE, AREN'T YOU?
...
HMM...
BY THE WAY...
WHAT'S YOUR NAME?
WUP
NAMI-HIRA.
SEAL OFF THIS PLACE IMMEDI-ATELY.
THAT TALISMAN ON THE POLE IS USELESS.
WE NEED THE HELP OF AN EXPERT TO SECURE THE AREA.
AN EXPERT?

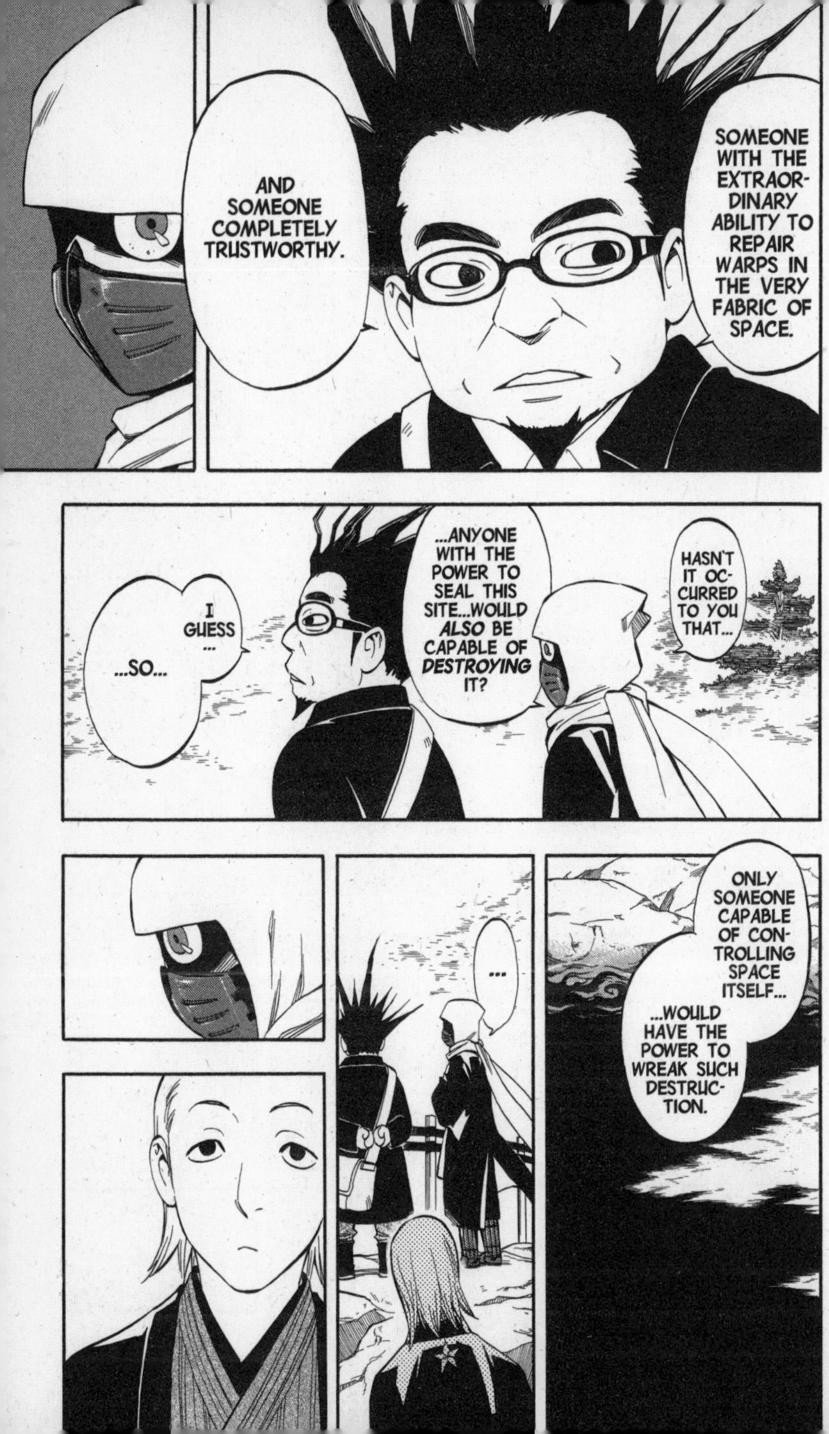
SOMEONE WITH THE EXTRAORDINARY ABILITY TO REPAIR WARPS IN THE VERY FABRIC OF SPACE.
AND SOMEONE COMPLETELY TRUSTWORTHY.
HASN'T IT OCCURRED TO YOU THAT...
...ANYONE WITH THE POWER TO SEAL THIS SITE...WOULD *ALSO* BE CAPABLE OF *DESTROYING* IT?
I GUESS ...
...SO...
ONLY SOMEONE CAPABLE OF CONTROLLING SPACE ITSELF...
...WOULD HAVE THE POWER TO WREAK SUCH DESTRUCTION.
...

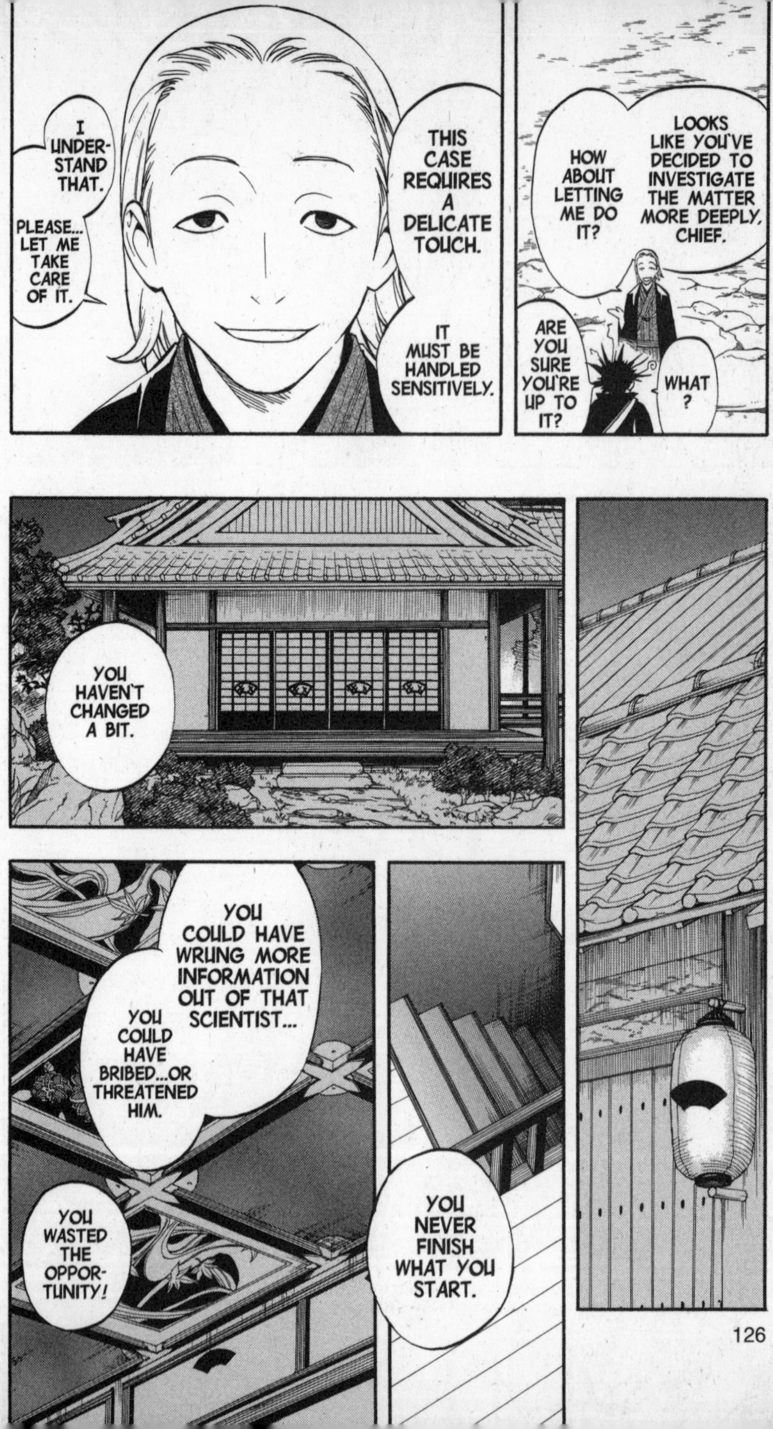
LOOKS LIKE YOU'VE DECIDED TO INVESTIGATE THE MATTER MORE DEEPLY, CHIEF.
HOW ABOUT LETTING ME DO IT?
WHAT?
ARE YOU SURE YOU'RE UP TO IT?
THIS CASE REQUIRES A DELICATE TOUCH.
IT MUST BE HANDLED SENSITIVELY.
I UNDER-STAND THAT.
PLEASE... LET ME TAKE CARE OF IT.
YOU HAVEN'T CHANGED A BIT.
YOU NEVER FINISH WHAT YOU START.
YOU COULD HAVE WRUNG MORE INFORMATION OUT OF THAT SCIENTIST...
YOU COULD HAVE BRIBED...OR THREATENED HIM.
YOU WASTED THE OPPOR-TUNITY!

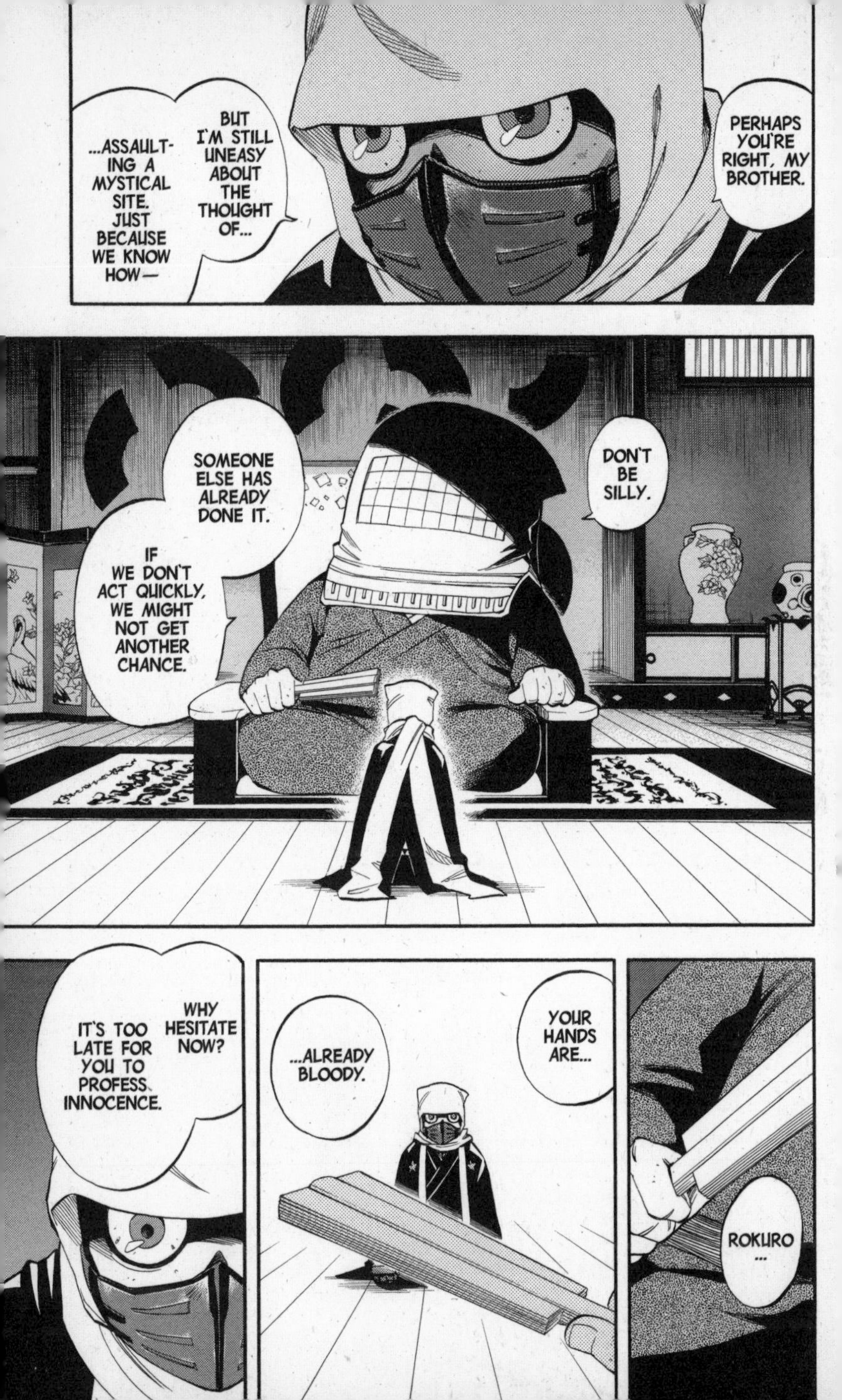
PERHAPS YOU'RE RIGHT, MY BROTHER.
BUT I'M STILL UNEASY ABOUT THE THOUGHT OF...
...ASSAULTING A MYSTICAL SITE. JUST BECAUSE WE KNOW HOW—
DON'T BE SILLY.
SOMEONE ELSE HAS ALREADY DONE IT.
IF WE DON'T ACT QUICKLY, WE MIGHT NOT GET ANOTHER CHANCE.
ROKURO...
YOUR HANDS ARE...
...ALREADY BLOODY.
WHY HESITATE NOW?
IT'S TOO LATE FOR YOU TO PROFESS INNOCENCE.

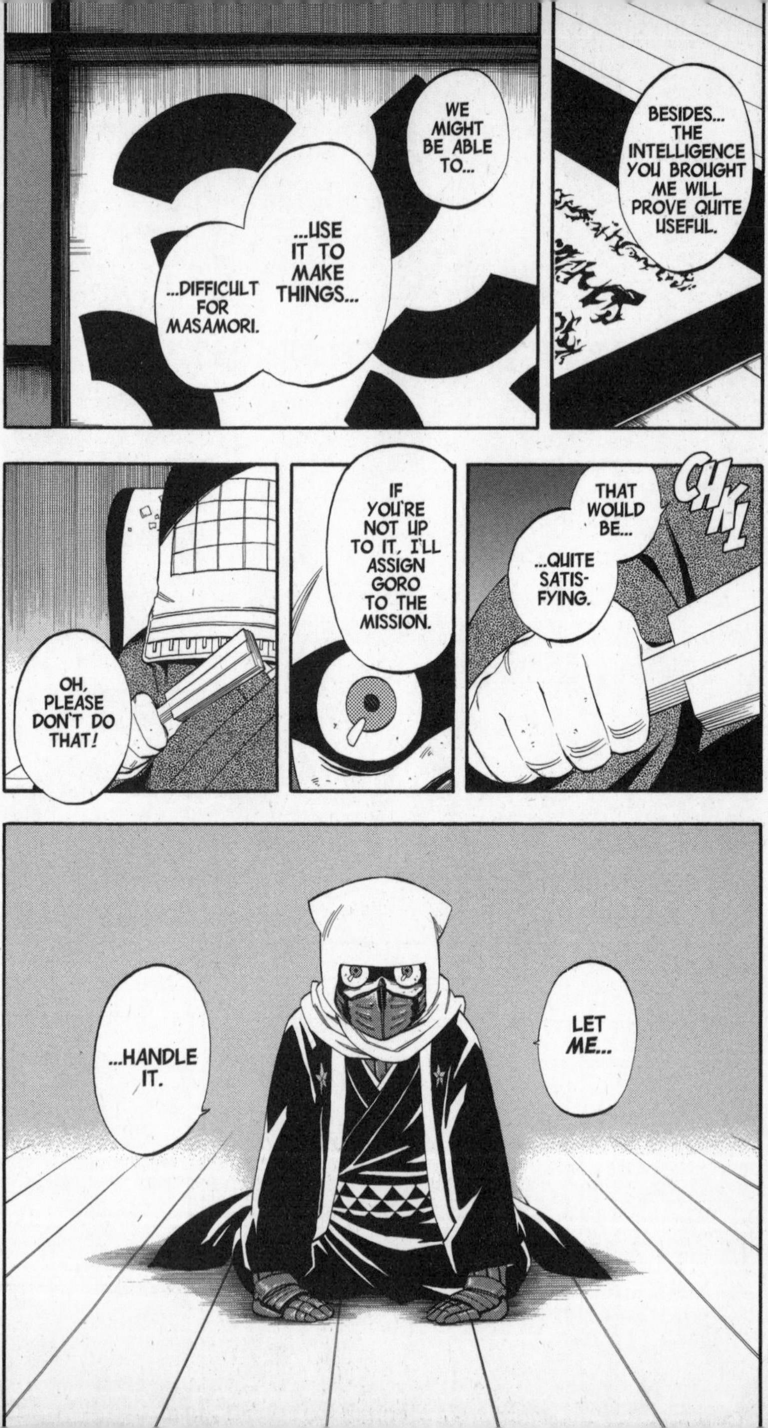
BESIDES... THE INTELLIGENCE YOU BROUGHT ME WILL PROVE QUITE USEFUL.
WE MIGHT BE ABLE TO...
...USE IT TO MAKE THINGS...
...DIFFICULT FOR MASAMORI.
THAT WOULD BE...
...QUITE SATIS-FYING.
CHK!
IF YOU'RE NOT UP TO IT, I'LL ASSIGN GORO TO THE MISSION.
OH, PLEASE DON'T DO THAT!
LET ME...
...HANDLE IT.

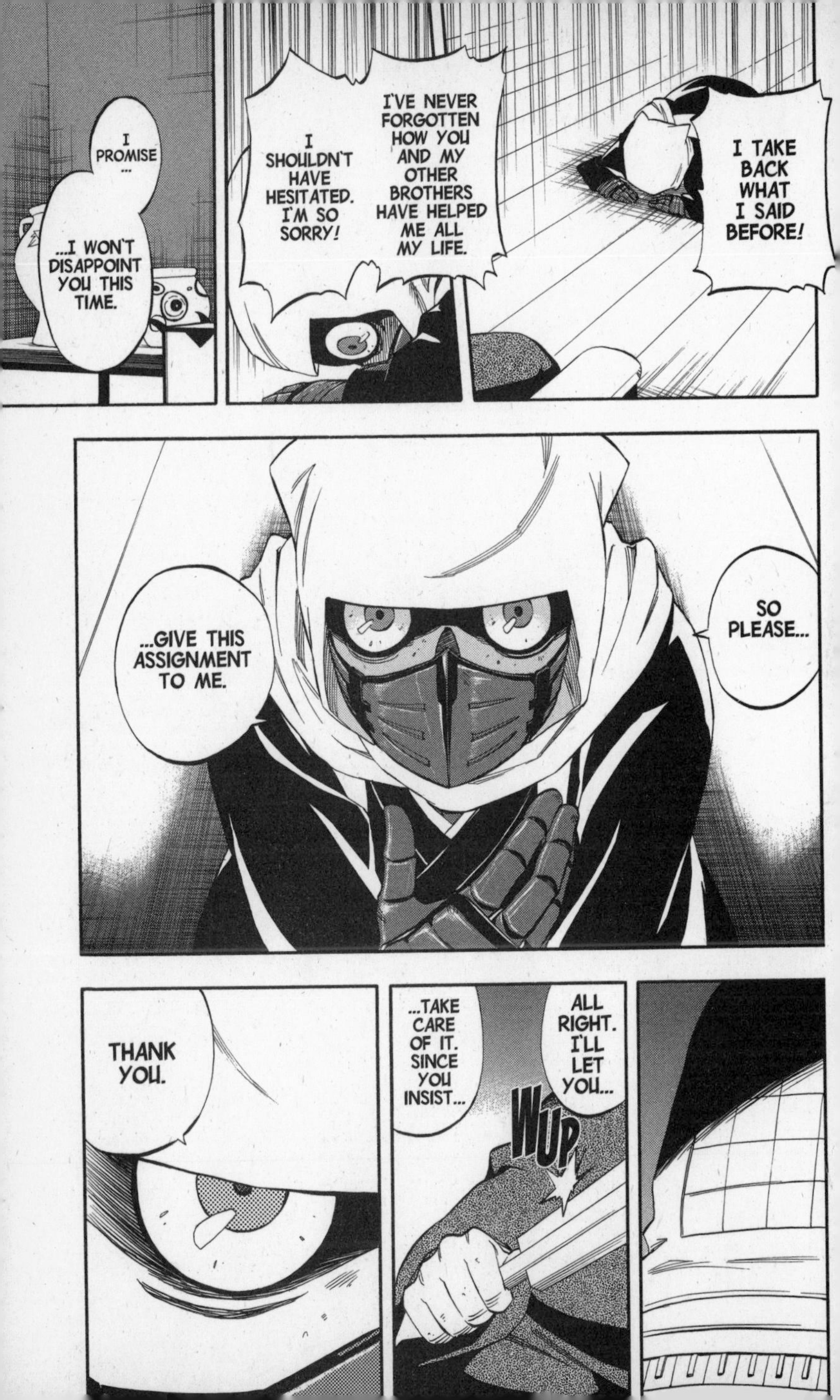
I TAKE BACK WHAT I SAID BEFORE!
I'VE NEVER FORGOTTEN HOW YOU AND MY OTHER BROTHERS HAVE HELPED ME ALL MY LIFE.
I SHOULDN'T HAVE HESITATED. I'M SO SORRY!
I PROMISE...
...I WON'T DISAPPOINT YOU THIS TIME.
SO PLEASE...
...GIVE THIS ASSIGNMENT TO ME.
ALL RIGHT. I'LL LET YOU...
...TAKE CARE OF IT. SINCE YOU INSIST...
WUP
THANK YOU.

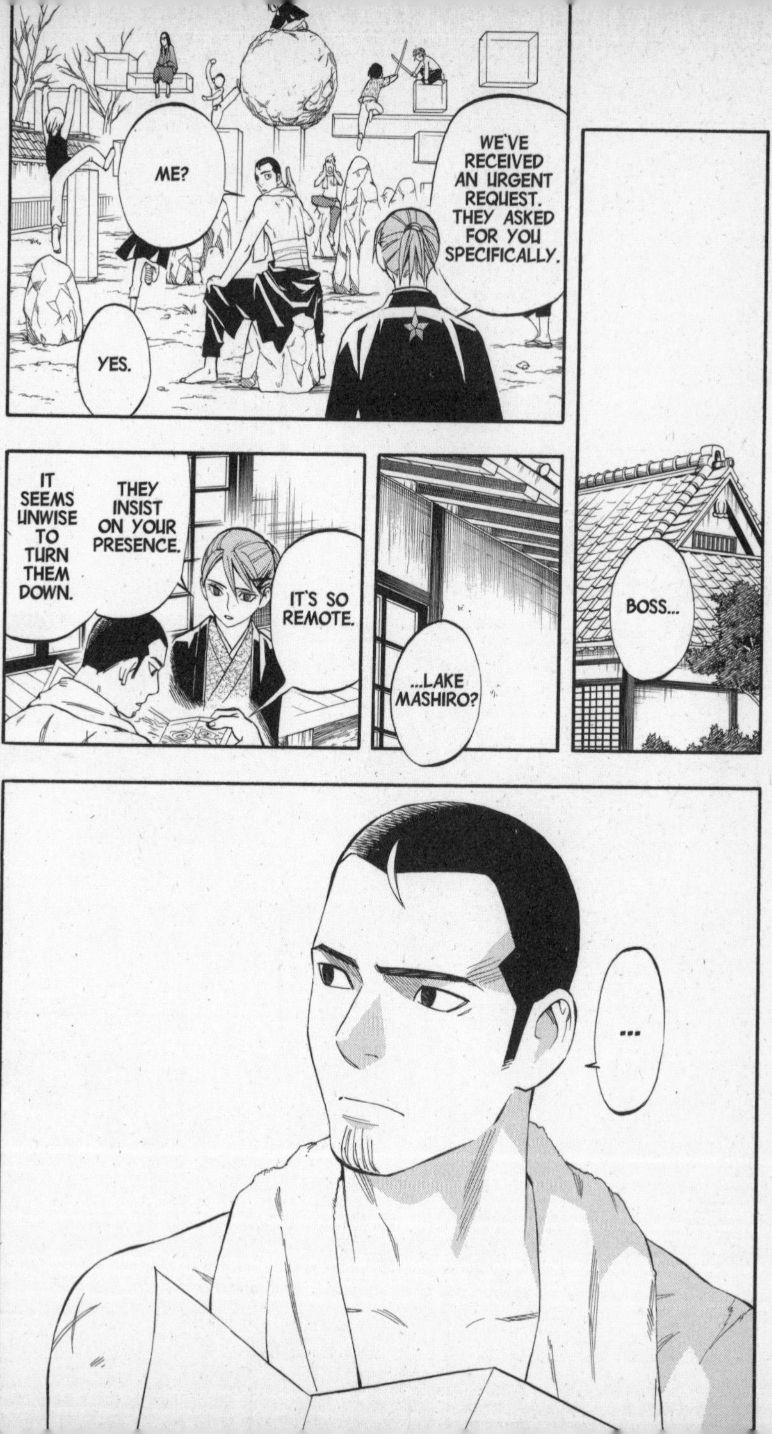
BOSS...
WE'VE RECEIVED AN URGENT REQUEST. THEY ASKED FOR YOU SPECIFICALLY.
ME?
YES.
...LAKE MASHIRO?
IT'S SO REMOTE.
THEY INSIST ON YOUR PRESENCE.
IT SEEMS UNWISE TO TURN THEM DOWN.
...

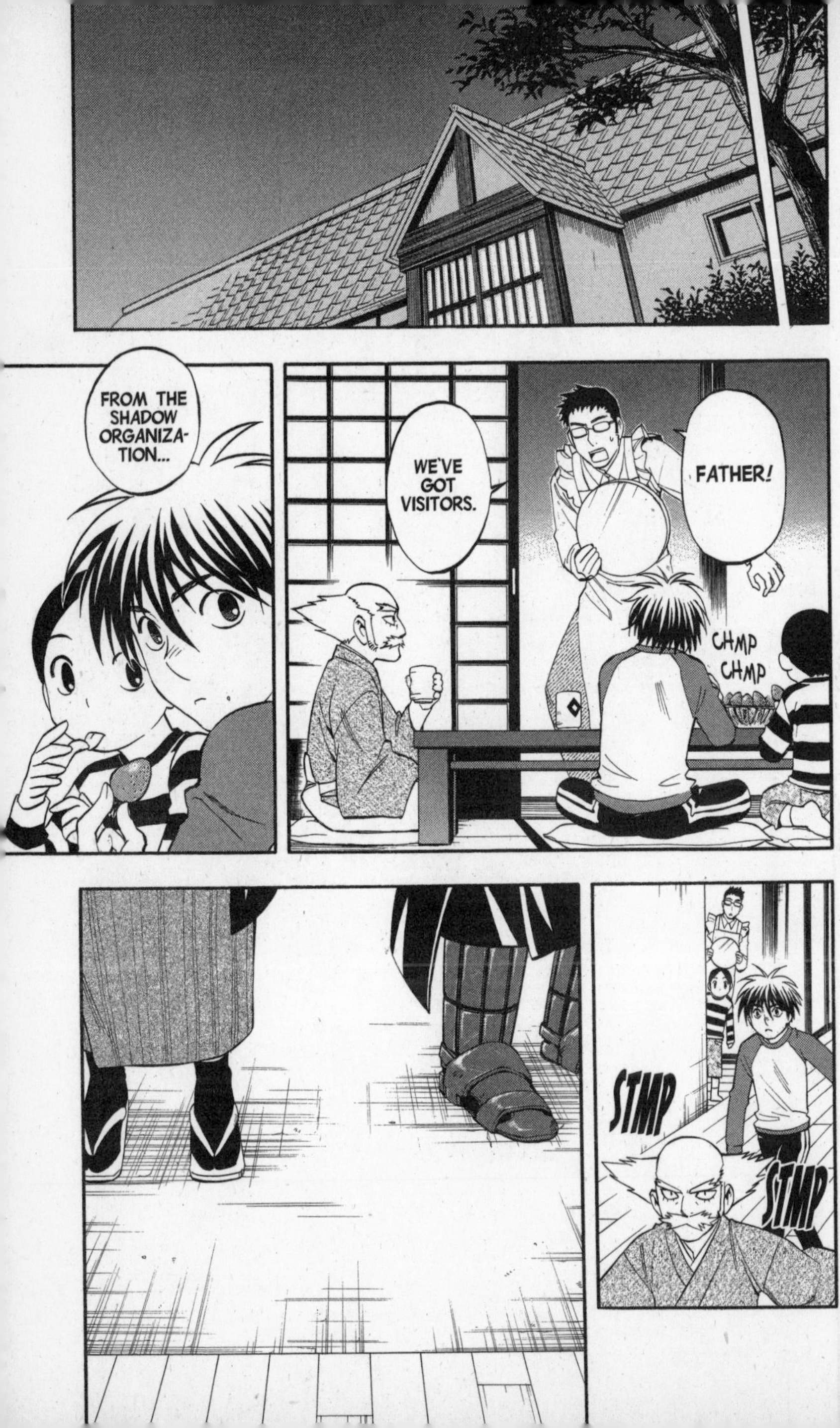
FATHER!
WE'VE GOT VISITORS.
CHMP CHMP
FROM THE SHADOW ORGANIZATION...
STMP
STMP

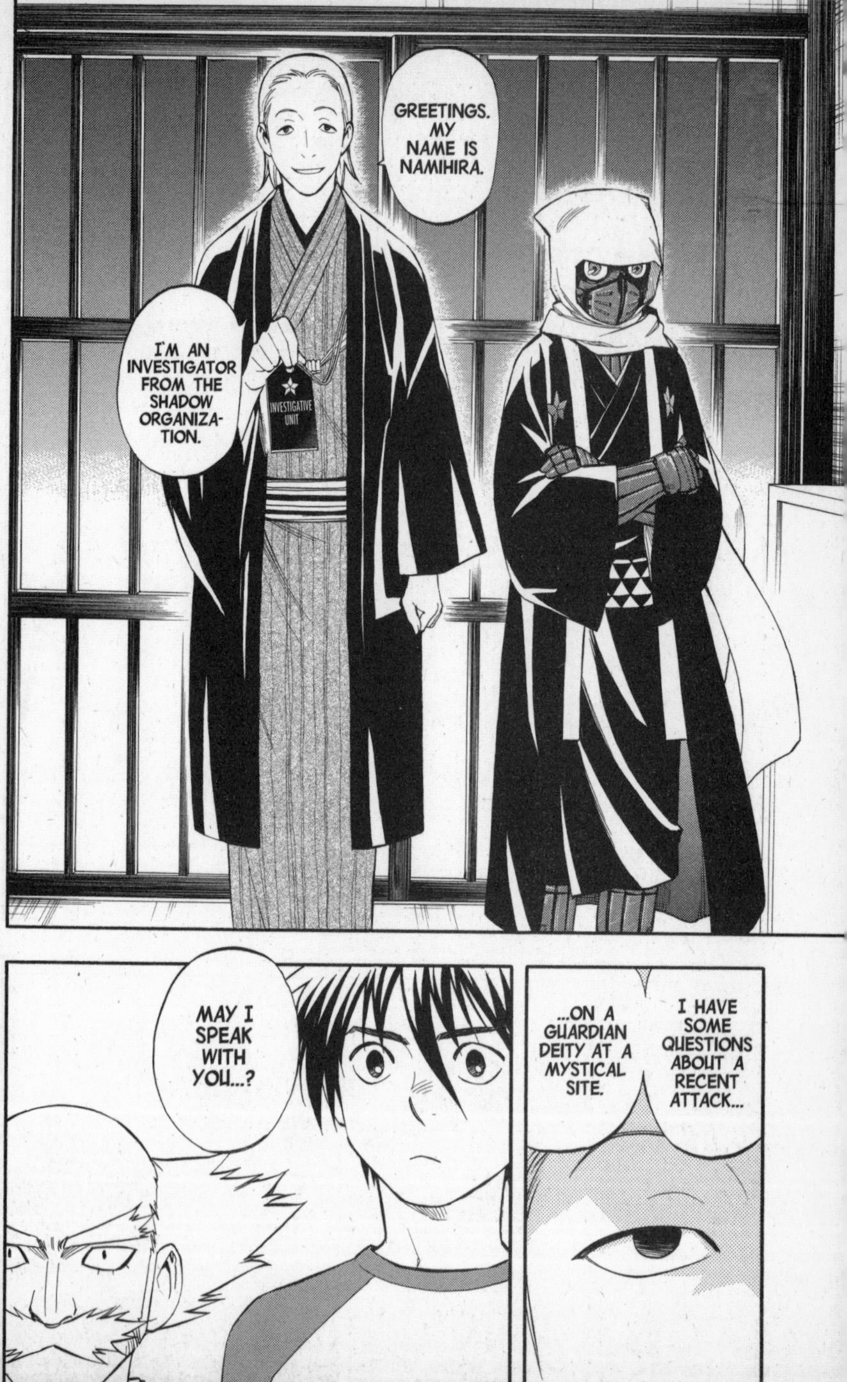
GREETINGS. MY NAME IS NAMIHIRA.
INVESTIGATIVE UNIT
I'M AN INVESTIGATOR FROM THE SHADOW ORGANIZA- TION.
I HAVE SOME QUESTIONS ABOUT A RECENT ATTACK...
...ON A GUARDIAN DEITY AT A MYSTICAL SITE.
MAY I SPEAK WITH YOU...?

Chapter 182: The Visit

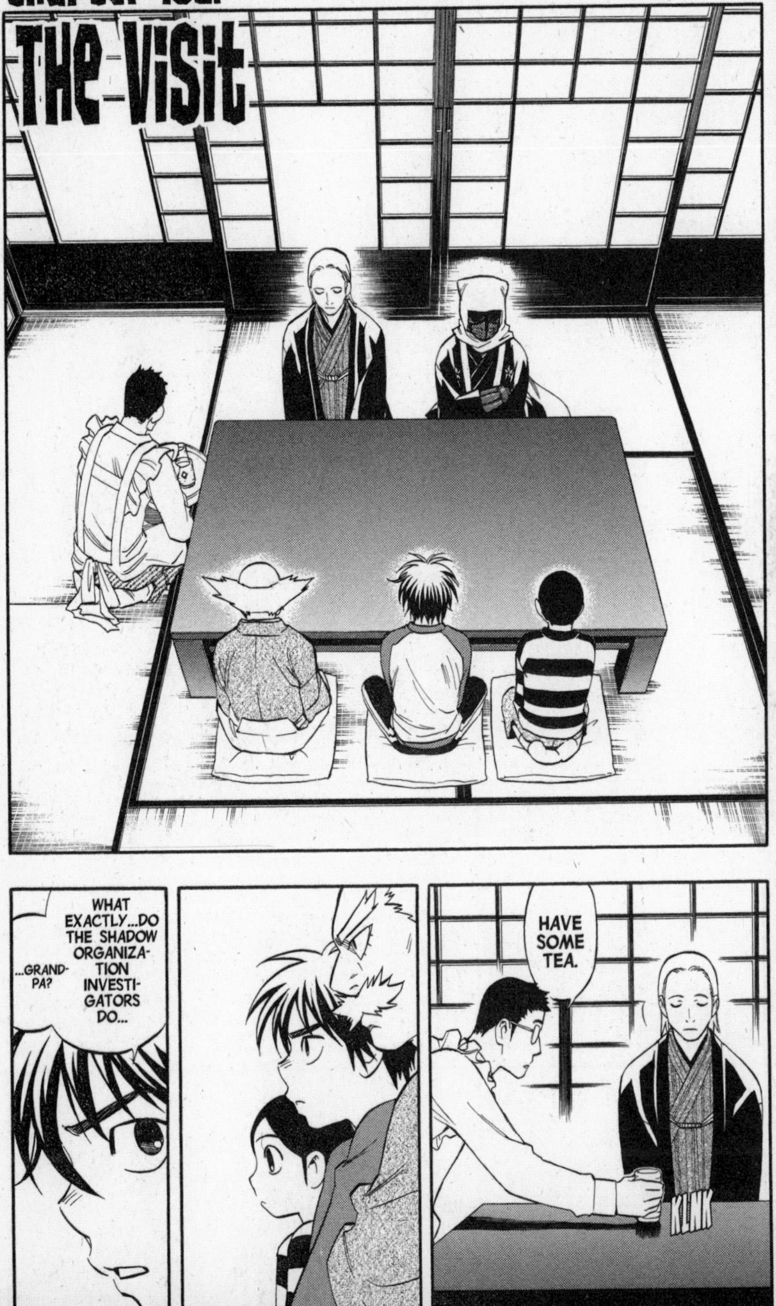
HAVE SOME TEA.
KLNK
WHAT EXACTLY...DO THE SHADOW ORGANIZATION INVESTIGATORS DO...
...GRANDPA?

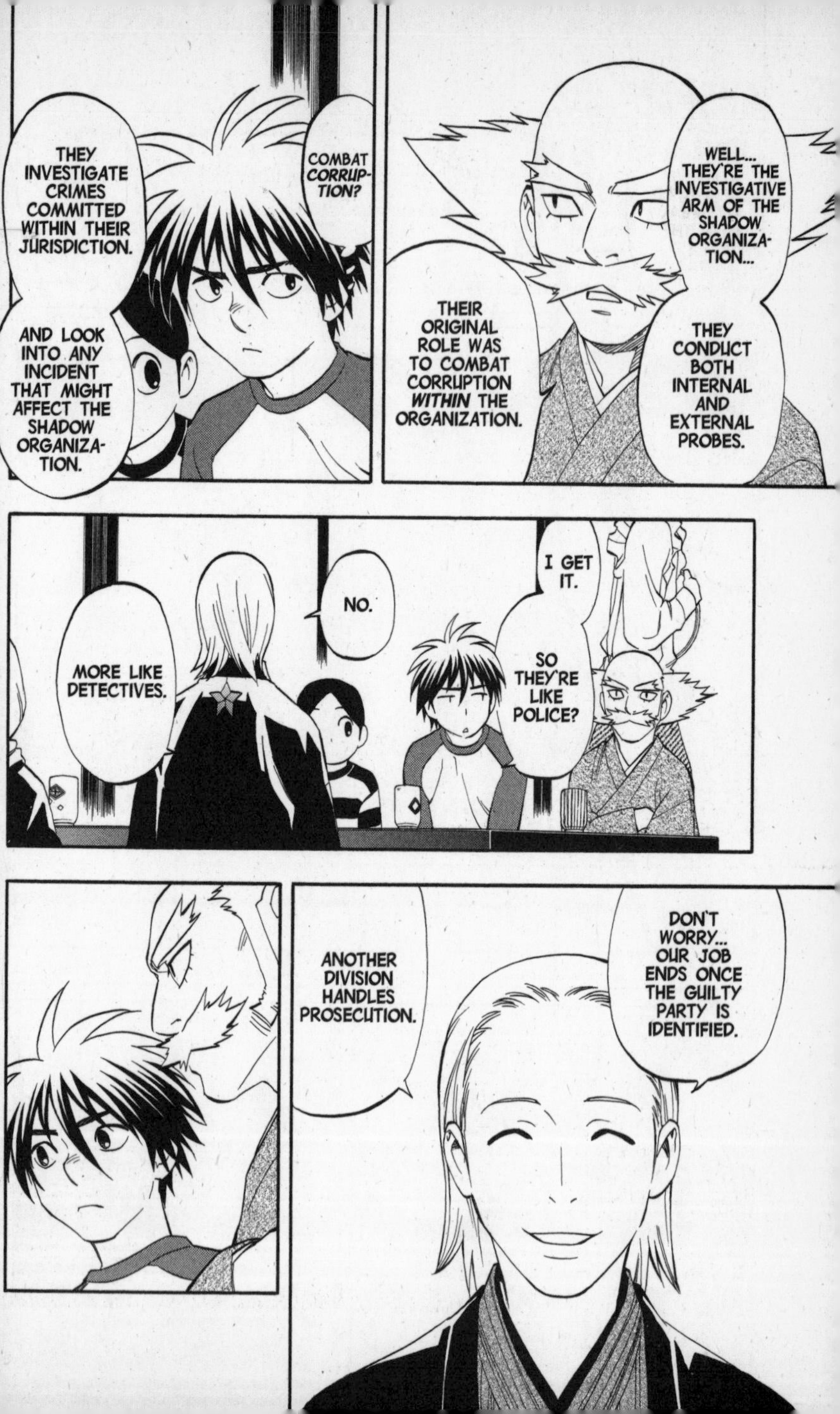
WELL... THEY'RE THE INVESTIGATIVE ARM OF THE SHADOW ORGANIZATION...
THEY CONDUCT BOTH INTERNAL AND EXTERNAL PROBES.
THEIR ORIGINAL ROLE WAS TO COMBAT CORRUPTION *WITHIN* THE ORGANIZATION.
COMBAT CORRUPTION?
THEY INVESTIGATE CRIMES COMMITTED WITHIN THEIR JURISDICTION.
AND LOOK INTO ANY INCIDENT THAT MIGHT AFFECT THE SHADOW ORGANIZATION.
I GET IT.
SO THEY'RE LIKE POLICE?
NO.
MORE LIKE DETECTIVES.
DON'T WORRY... OUR JOB ENDS ONCE THE GUILTY PARTY IS IDENTIFIED.
ANOTHER DIVISION HANDLES PROSECUTION.

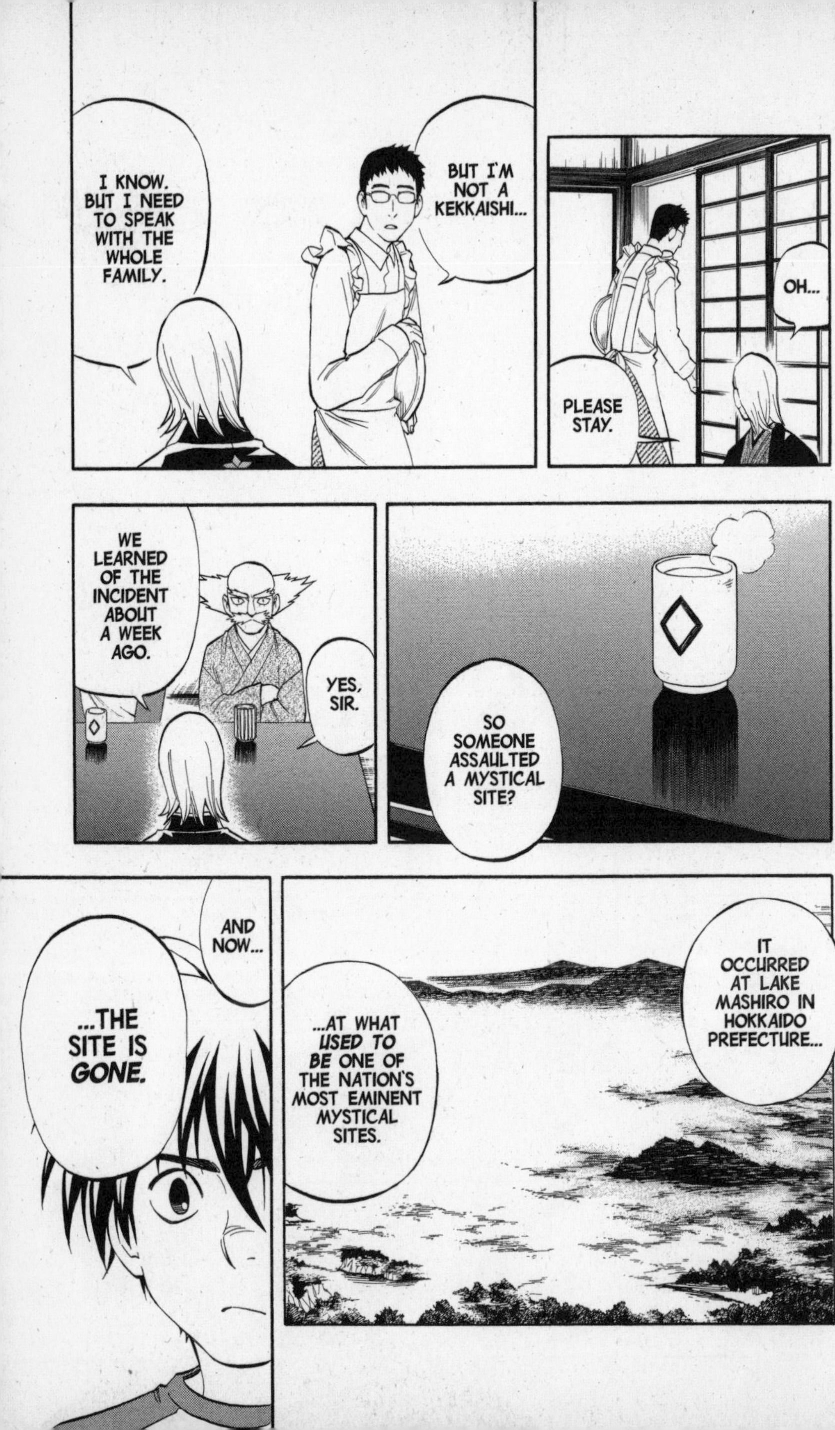
OH...
PLEASE STAY.
BUT I'M NOT A KEKKAISHI...
I KNOW. BUT I NEED TO SPEAK WITH THE WHOLE FAMILY.
SO SOMEONE ASSAULTED A MYSTICAL SITE?
WE LEARNED OF THE INCIDENT ABOUT A WEEK AGO.
YES, SIR.
IT OCCURRED AT LAKE MASHIRO IN HOKKAIDO PREFECTURE...
...AT WHAT *USED TO BE* ONE OF THE NATION'S MOST EMINENT MYSTICAL SITES.
AND NOW...
...THE SITE IS *GONE.*

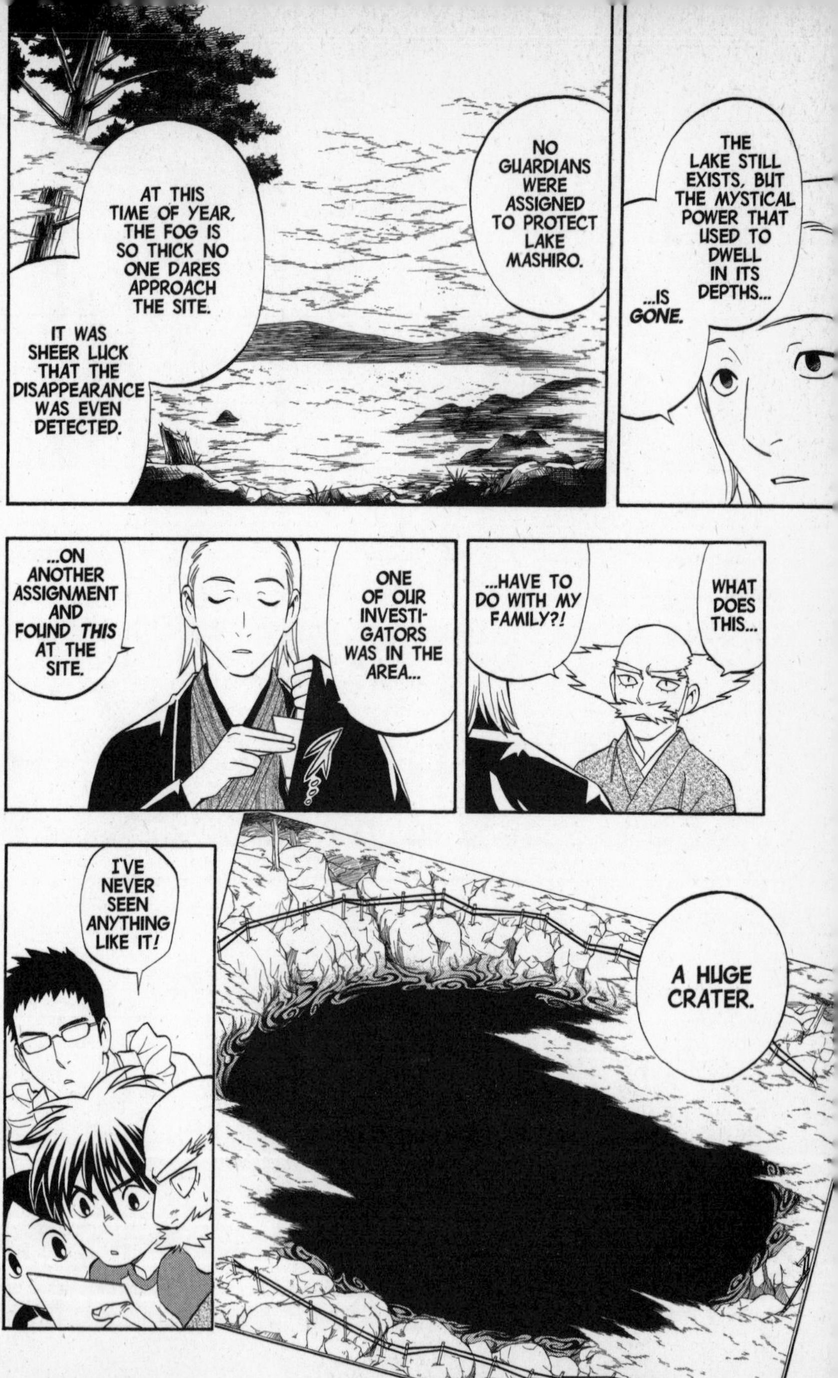
THE LAKE STILL EXISTS, BUT THE MYSTICAL POWER THAT USED TO DWELL IN ITS DEPTHS...
...IS *GONE.*
NO GUARDIANS WERE ASSIGNED TO PROTECT LAKE MASHIRO.
AT THIS TIME OF YEAR, THE FOG IS SO THICK NO ONE DARES APPROACH THE SITE.
IT WAS SHEER LUCK THAT THE DISAPPEARANCE WAS EVEN DETECTED.
WHAT DOES THIS...
...HAVE TO DO WITH MY FAMILY?!
ONE OF OUR INVESTI-GATORS WAS IN THE AREA...
...ON ANOTHER ASSIGNMENT AND FOUND *THIS* AT THE SITE.
A HUGE CRATER.
I'VE NEVER SEEN ANYTHING LIKE IT!

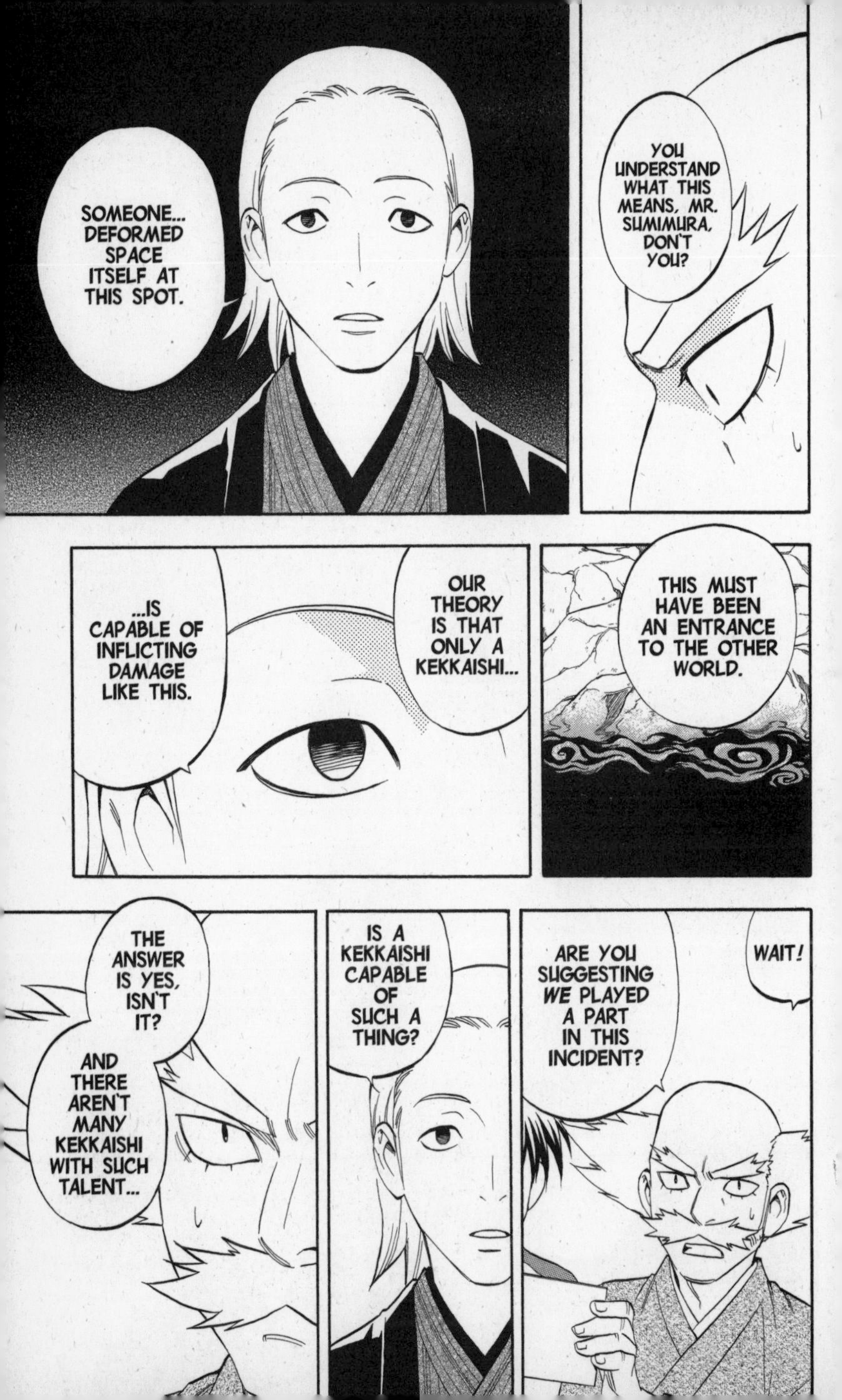
YOU UNDERSTAND WHAT THIS MEANS, MR. SUMIMURA, DON'T YOU?
SOMEONE... DEFORMED SPACE ITSELF AT THIS SPOT.
THIS MUST HAVE BEEN AN ENTRANCE TO THE OTHER WORLD.
OUR THEORY IS THAT ONLY A KEKKAISHI...
...IS CAPABLE OF INFLICTING DAMAGE LIKE THIS.
WAIT!
ARE YOU SUGGESTING *WE* PLAYED A PART IN THIS INCIDENT?
IS A KEKKAISHI CAPABLE OF SUCH A THING?
THE ANSWER IS *YES*, ISN'T IT?
AND THERE AREN'T *MANY* KEKKAISHI WITH SUCH TALENT...

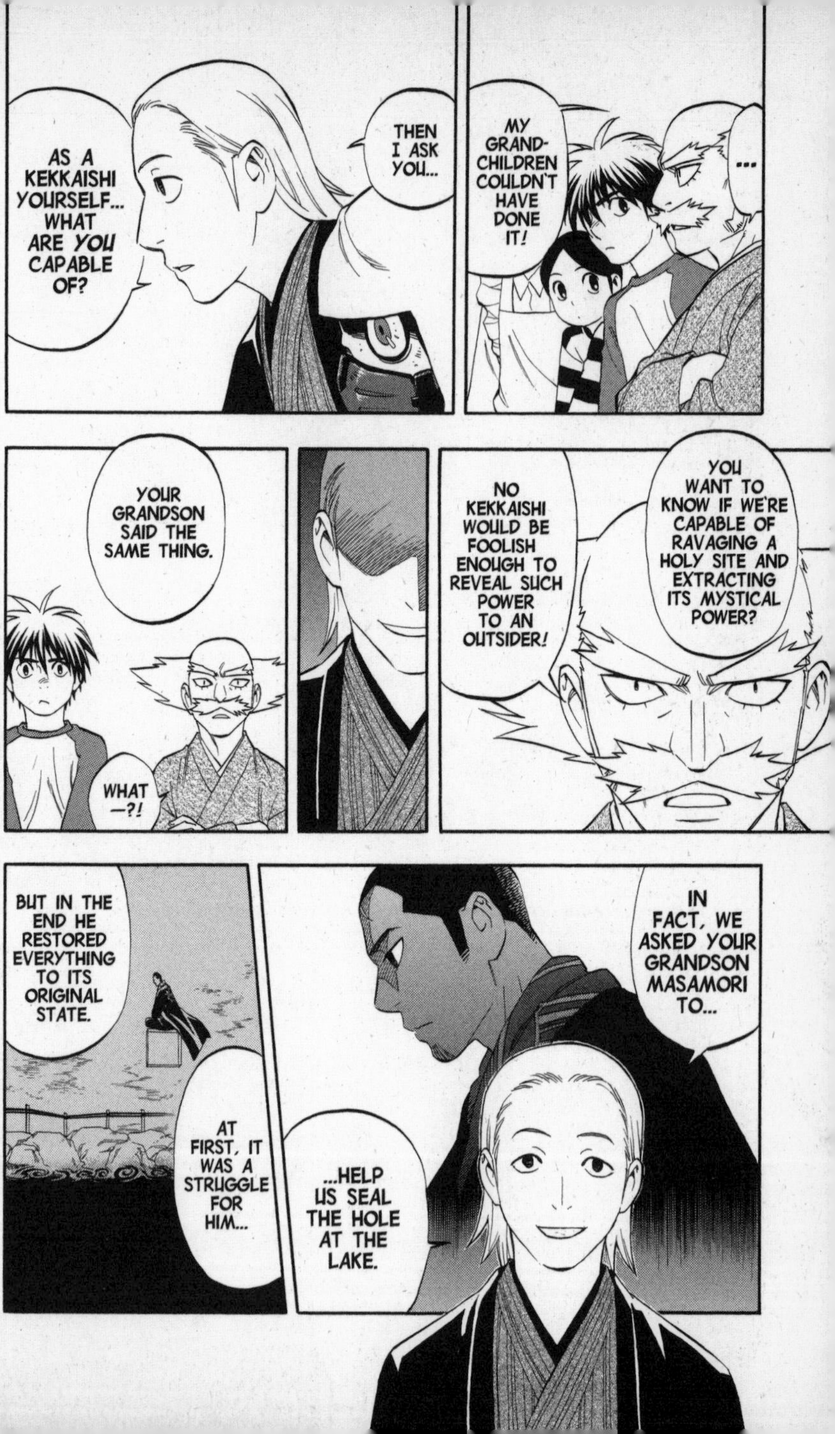
...
MY GRANDCHILDREN COULDN'T HAVE DONE IT!
THEN I ASK YOU...
AS A KEKKAISHI YOURSELF... WHAT ARE YOU CAPABLE OF?
YOU WANT TO KNOW IF WE'RE CAPABLE OF RAVAGING A HOLY SITE AND EXTRACTING ITS MYSTICAL POWER?
NO KEKKAISHI WOULD BE FOOLISH ENOUGH TO REVEAL SUCH POWER TO AN OUTSIDER!
YOUR GRANDSON SAID THE SAME THING.
WHAT—?!
IN FACT, WE ASKED YOUR GRANDSON MASAMORI TO...
...HELP US SEAL THE HOLE AT THE LAKE.
AT FIRST, IT WAS A STRUGGLE FOR HIM...
BUT IN THE END HE RESTORED EVERYTHING TO ITS ORIGINAL STATE.

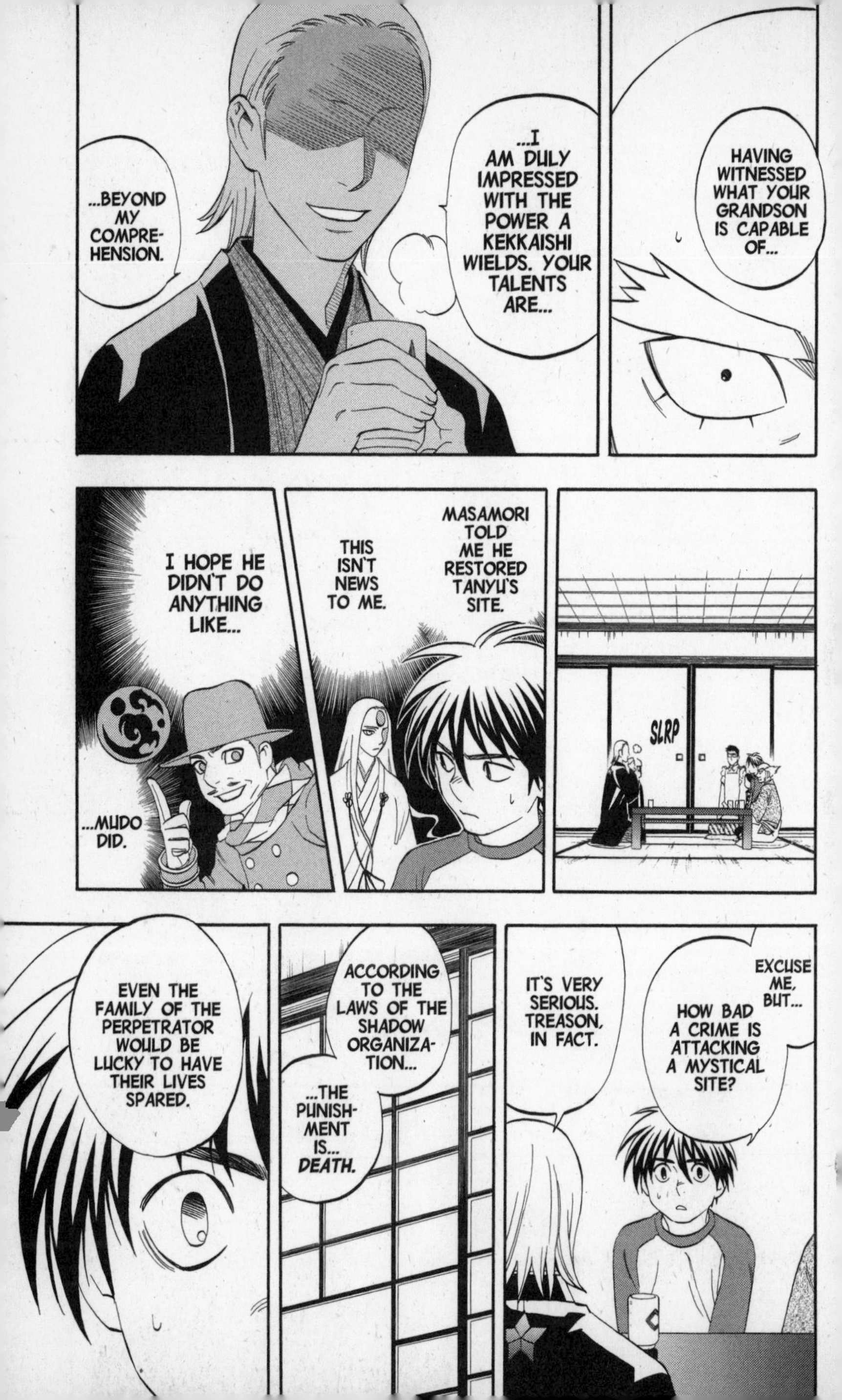
HAVING WITNESSED WHAT YOUR GRANDSON IS CAPABLE OF...
...I AM DULY IMPRESSED WITH THE POWER A KEKKAISHI WIELDS. YOUR TALENTS ARE...
...BEYOND MY COMPREHENSION.
SLRP
MASAMORI TOLD ME HE RESTORED TANYU'S SITE.
THIS ISN'T NEWS TO ME.
I HOPE HE DIDN'T DO ANYTHING LIKE...
...MUDO DID.
EXCUSE ME, BUT...
HOW BAD A CRIME IS ATTACKING A MYSTICAL SITE?
IT'S VERY SERIOUS. TREASON, IN FACT.
ACCORDING TO THE LAWS OF THE SHADOW ORGANIZATION...
...THE PUNISHMENT IS... *DEATH.*
EVEN THE FAMILY OF THE PERPETRATOR WOULD BE LUCKY TO HAVE THEIR LIVES SPARED.

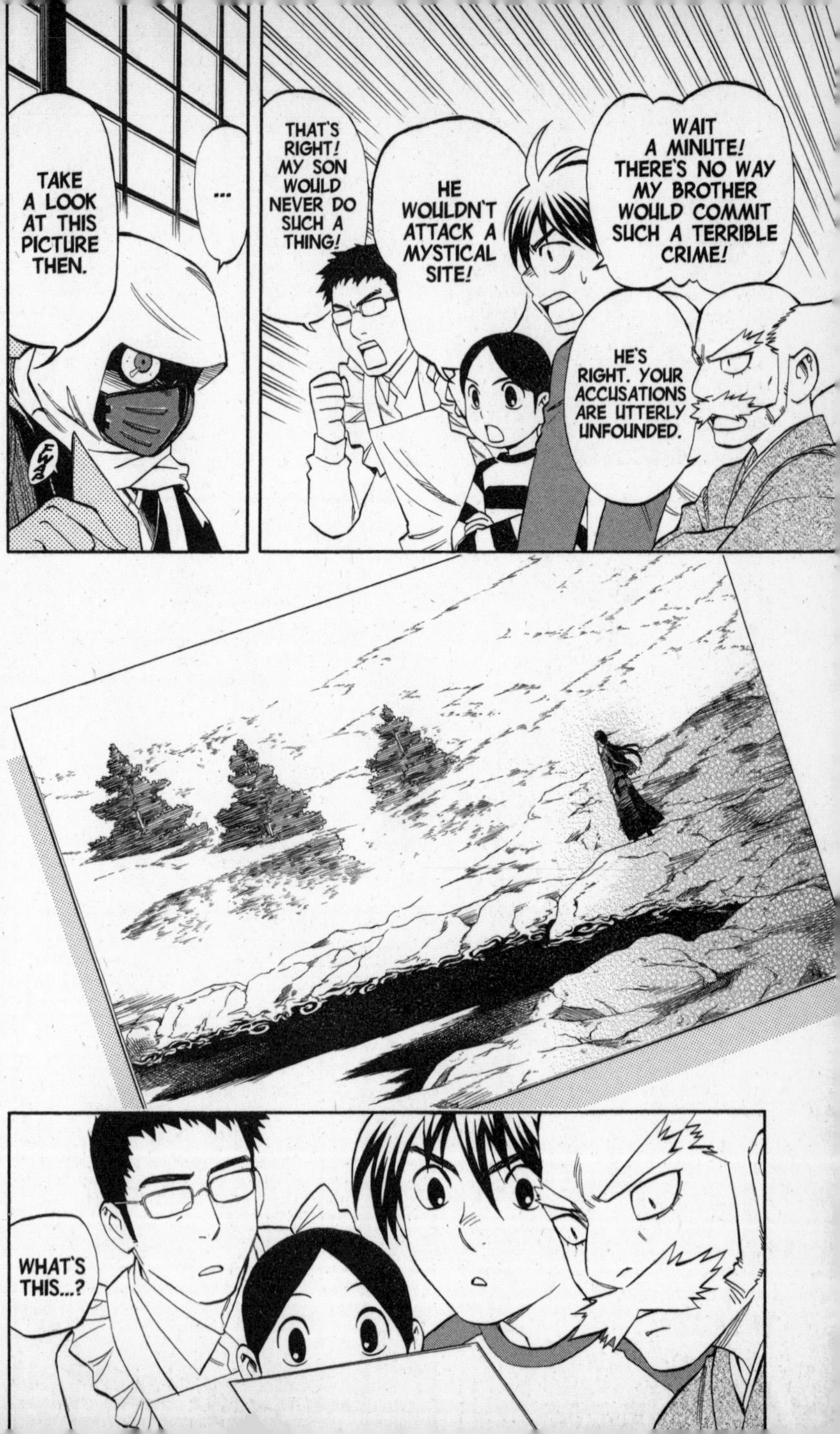
WAIT A MINUTE! THERE'S NO WAY MY BROTHER WOULD COMMIT SUCH A TERRIBLE CRIME!
HE WOULDN'T ATTACK A MYSTICAL SITE!
THAT'S RIGHT! MY SON WOULD NEVER DO SUCH A THING!
HE'S RIGHT. YOUR ACCUSATIONS ARE UTTERLY UNFOUNDED.
...
TAKE A LOOK AT THIS PICTURE THEN.
FWAP
WHAT'S THIS...?

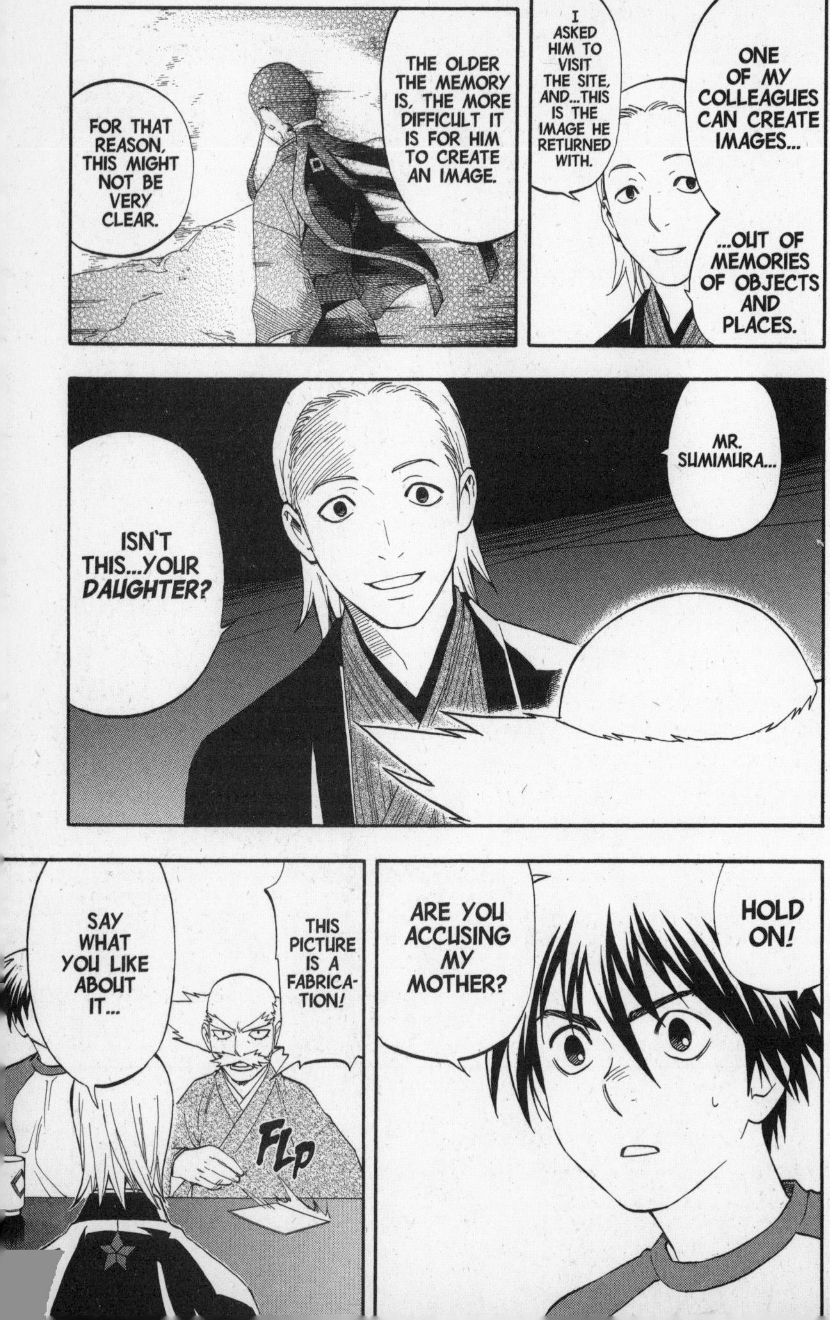
ONE OF MY COLLEAGUES CAN CREATE IMAGES...
...OUT OF MEMORIES OF OBJECTS AND PLACES.
I ASKED HIM TO VISIT THE SITE, AND...THIS IS THE IMAGE HE RETURNED WITH.
THE OLDER THE MEMORY IS, THE MORE DIFFICULT IT IS FOR HIM TO CREATE AN IMAGE.
FOR THAT REASON, THIS MIGHT NOT BE VERY CLEAR.
MR. SUMIMURA...
ISN'T THIS...YOUR *DAUGHTER?*
HOLD ON!
ARE YOU ACCUSING MY MOTHER?
THIS PICTURE IS A FABRICA-TION!
FLP
SAY WHAT YOU LIKE ABOUT IT...

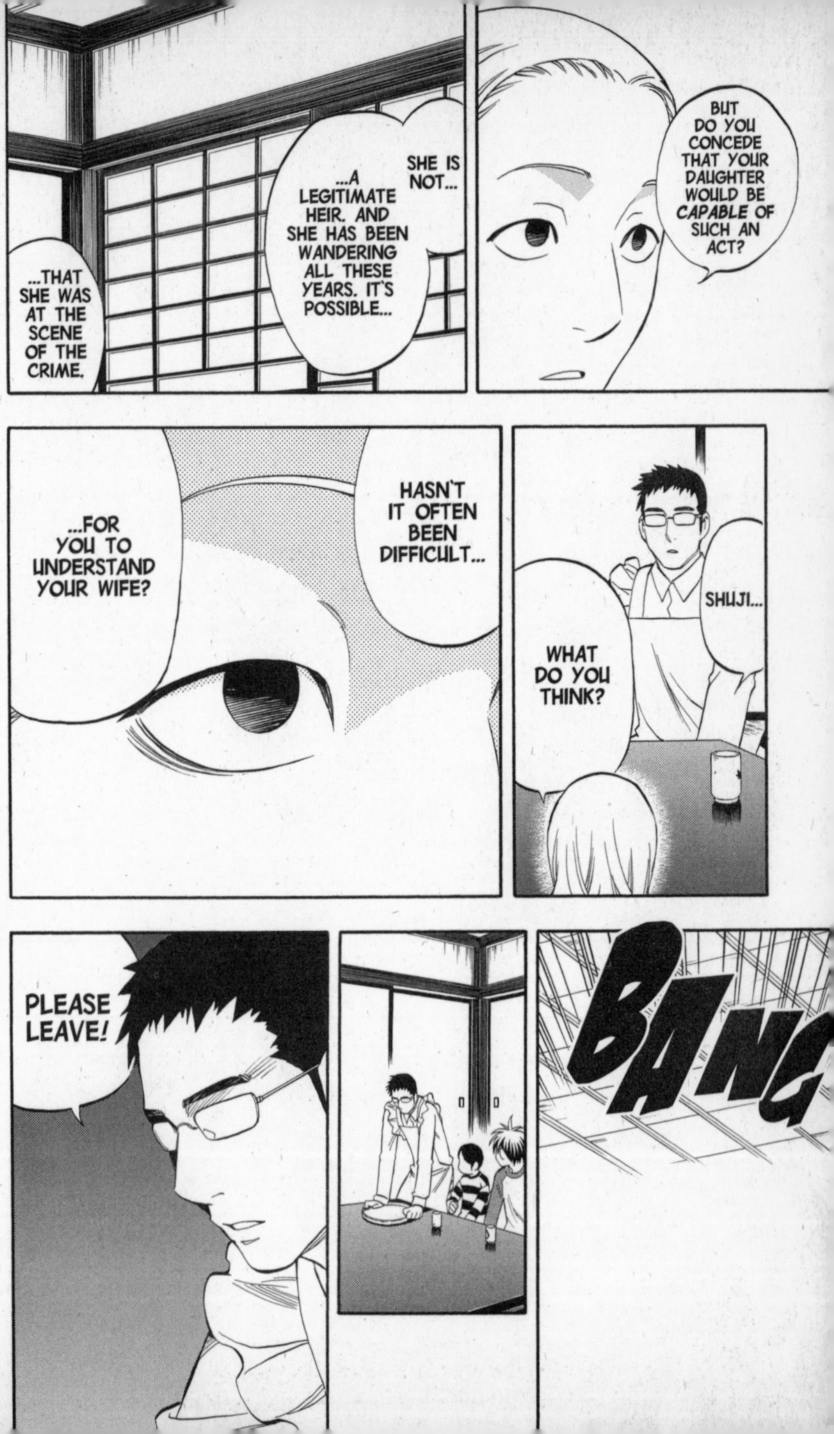
BUT DO YOU CONCEDE THAT YOUR DAUGHTER WOULD BE *CAPABLE* OF SUCH AN ACT?
SHE IS NOT...
...A LEGITIMATE HEIR. AND SHE HAS BEEN WANDERING ALL THESE YEARS. IT'S POSSIBLE...
...THAT SHE WAS AT THE SCENE OF THE CRIME.
SHUJI...
WHAT DO YOU THINK?
HASN'T IT OFTEN BEEN DIFFICULT...
...FOR YOU TO UNDERSTAND YOUR WIFE?
BANG
PLEASE LEAVE!

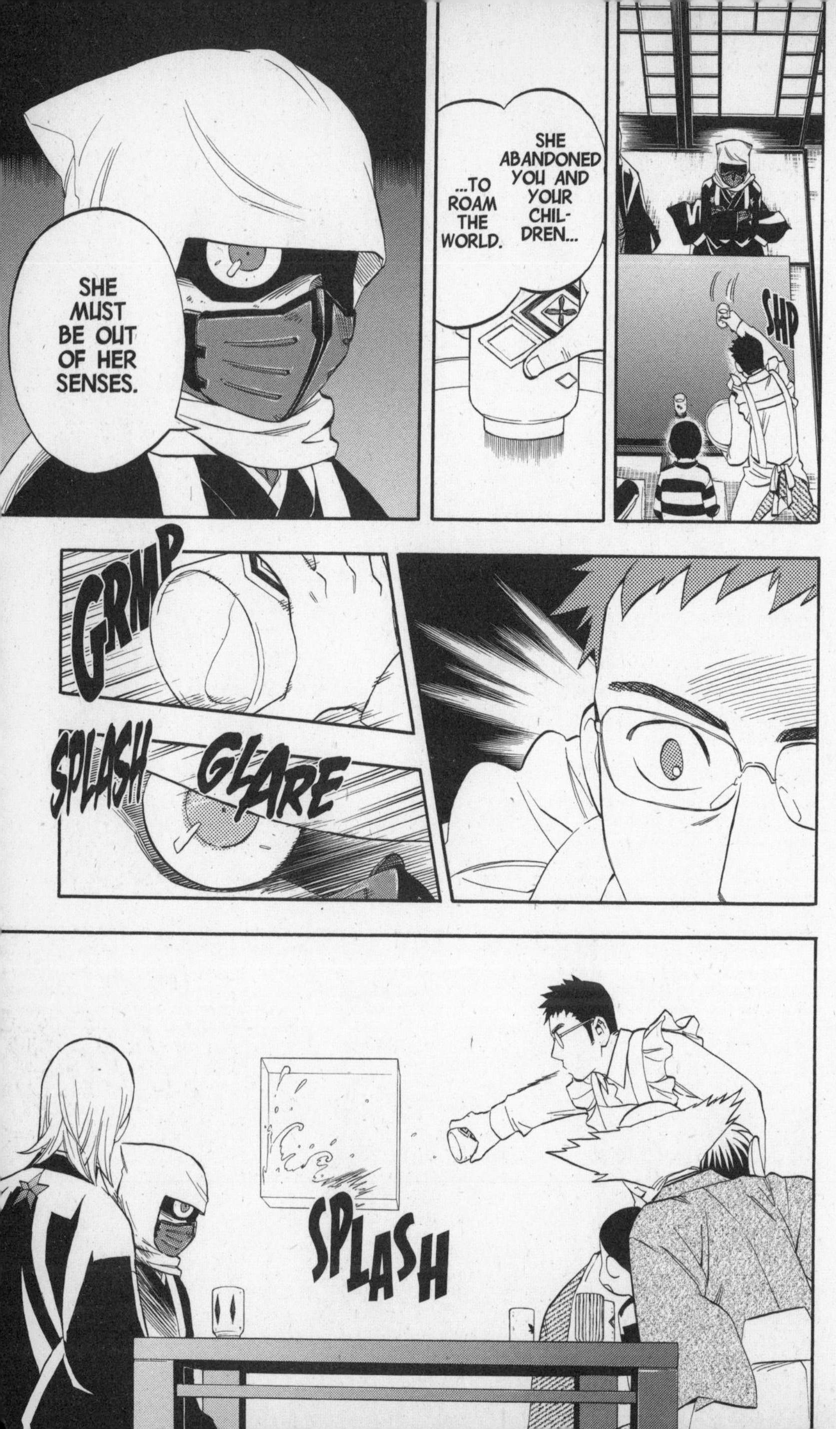
SHP
SHE ABANDONED YOU AND YOUR CHIL-DREN...
...TO ROAM THE WORLD.
SHE MUST BE OUT OF HER SENSES.
GRMP
SPLASH
GLARE
SPLASH

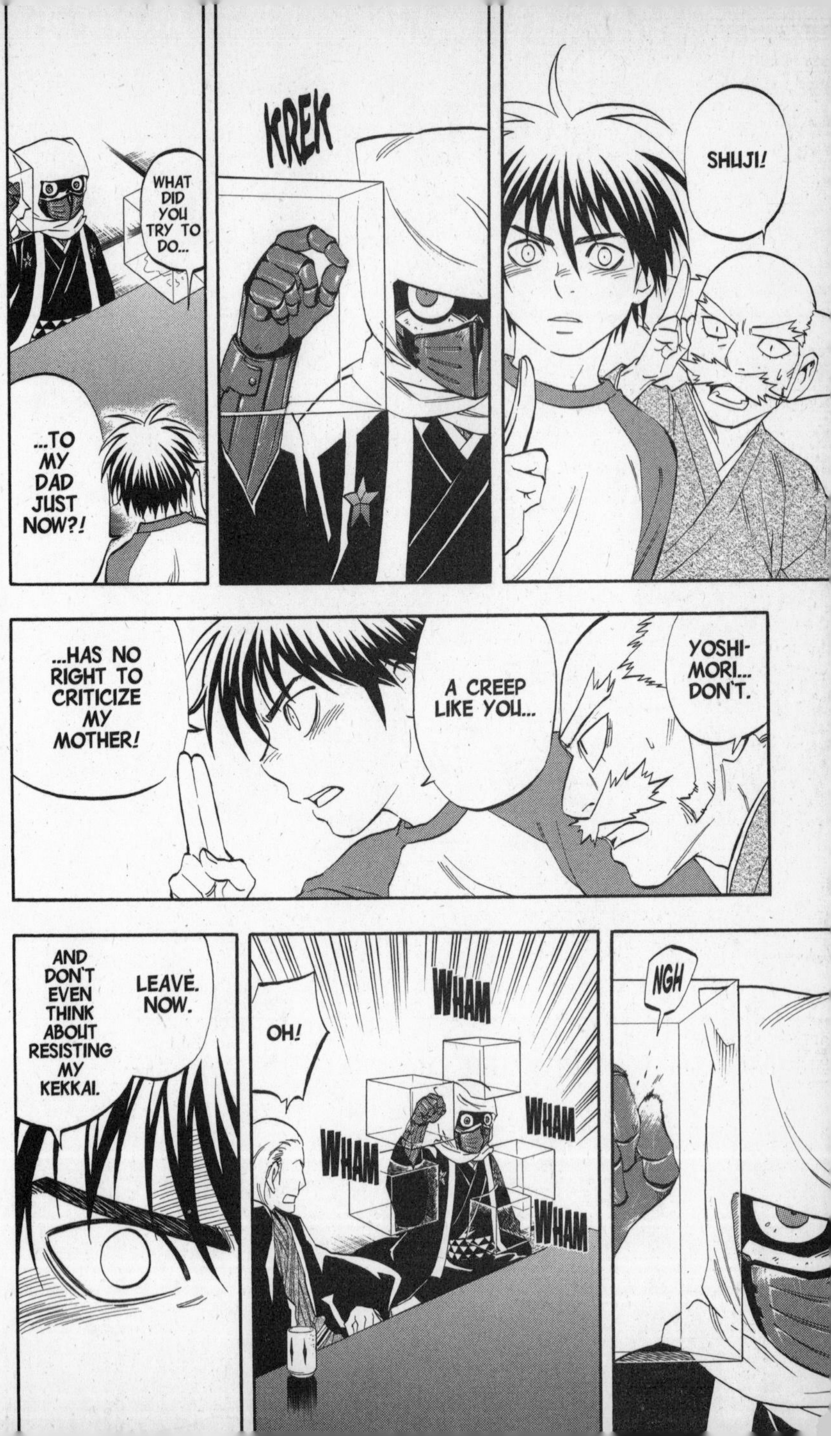
SHUJI!
KREK
WHAT DID YOU TRY TO DO...
...TO MY DAD JUST NOW?!
YOSHI-MORI... DON'T.
A CREEP LIKE YOU...
...HAS NO RIGHT TO CRITICIZE MY MOTHER!
NGH
WHAM
WHAM
OH!
WHAM
WHAM
LEAVE. NOW.
AND DON'T EVEN THINK ABOUT RESISTING MY KEKKAI.

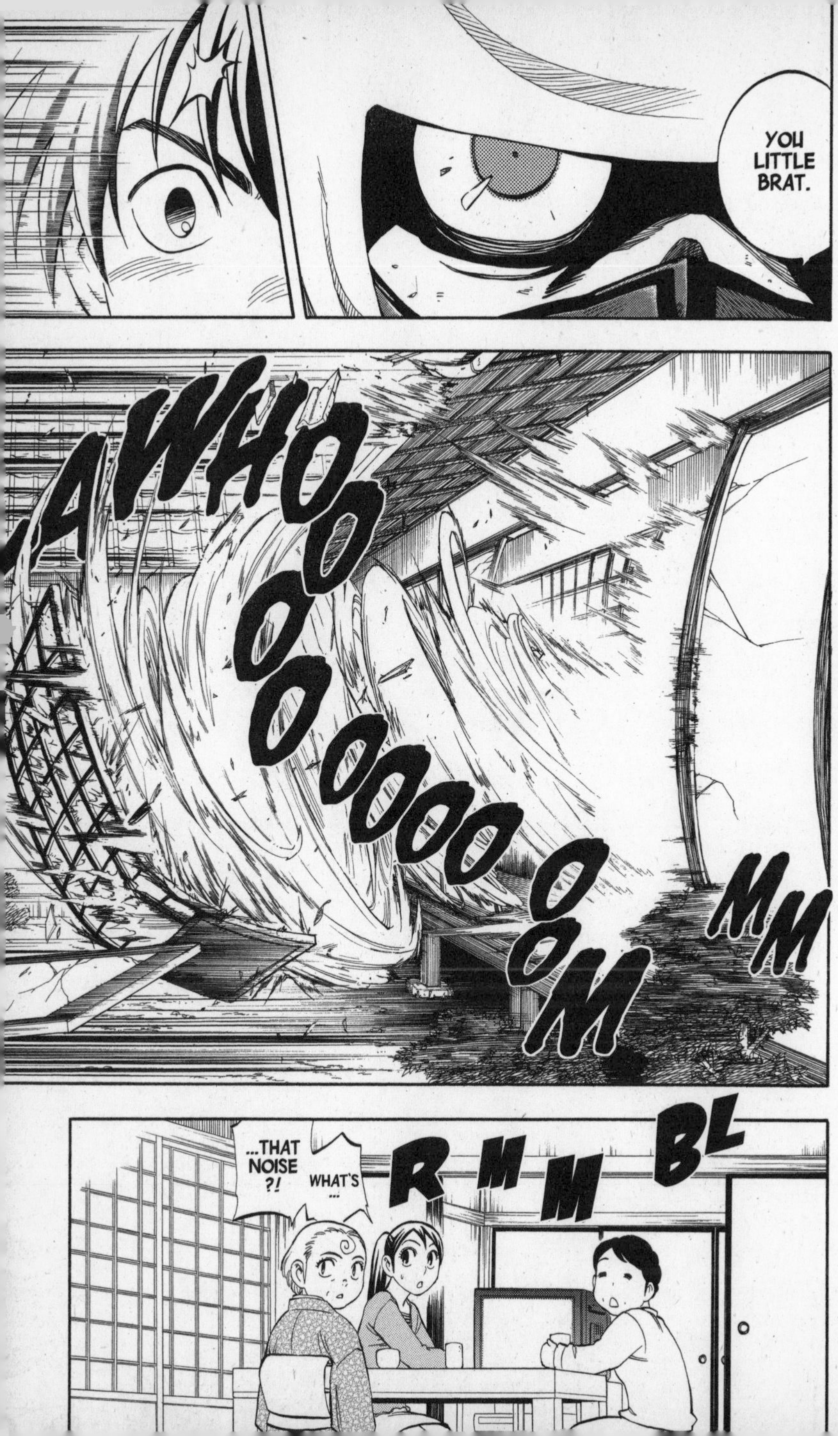
YOU LITTLE BRAT.
WHOOOOOOOOOOOOM
MM
WHAT'S ...
...THAT NOISE ?!
RMMMBL

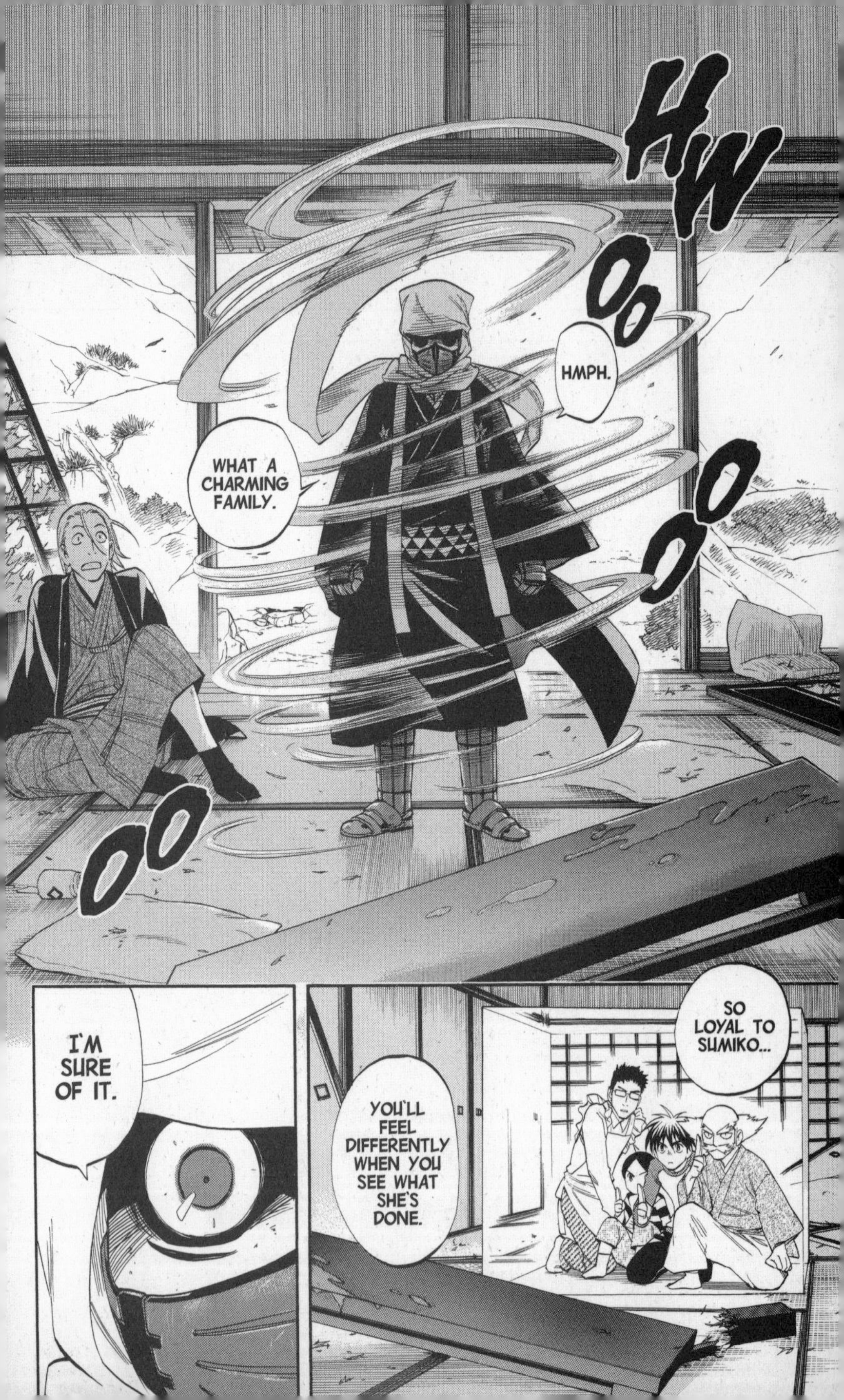
HWOOOOOOO
HMPH.
WHAT A CHARMING FAMILY.
SO LOYAL TO SUMIKO...
YOU'LL FEEL DIFFERENTLY WHEN YOU SEE WHAT SHE'S DONE.
I'M SURE OF IT.

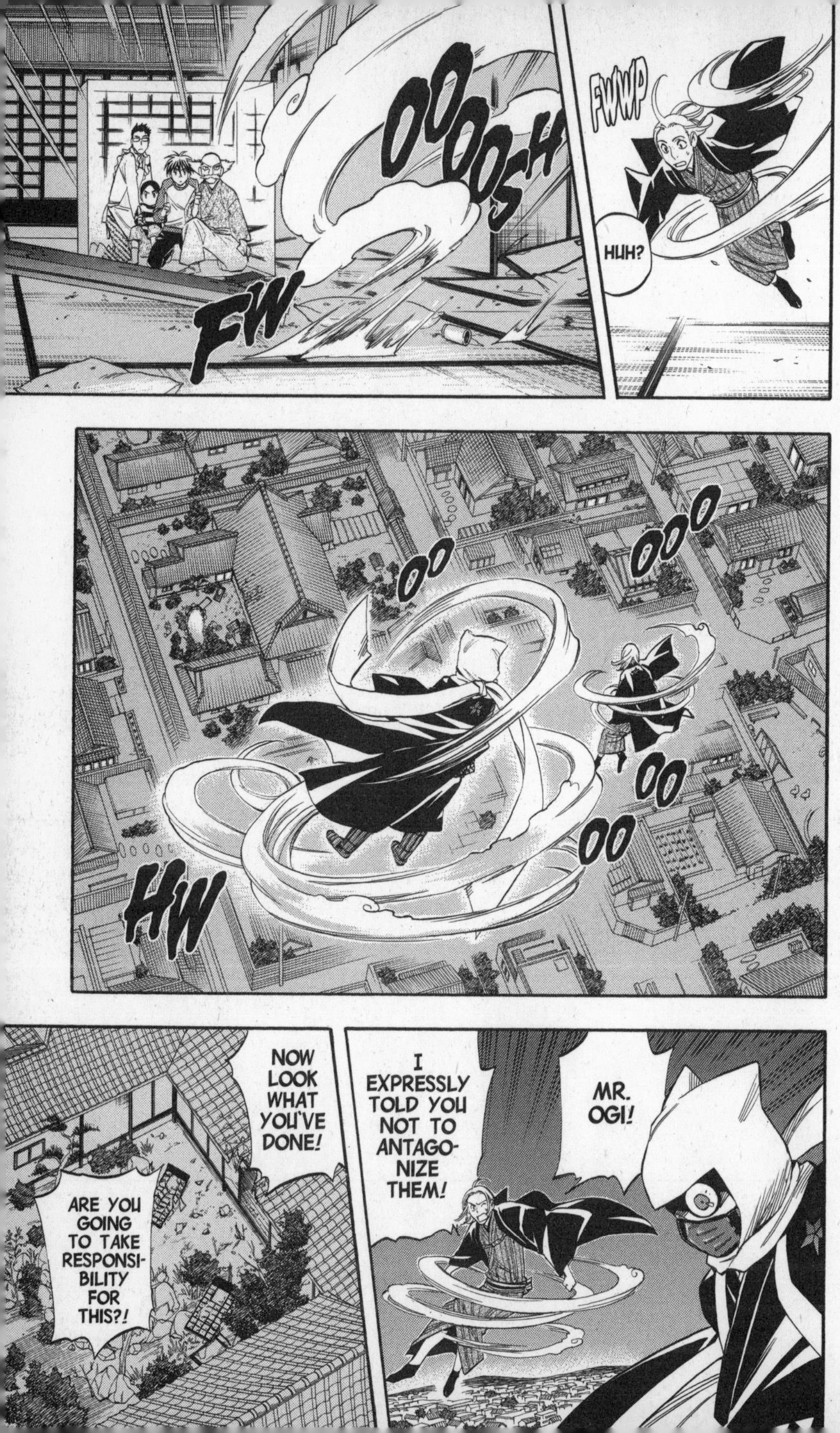

FWWP
HUH?
OOOOOSH
FW
OOO
OO
OO
OO
HW
MR. OGI!
I EXPRESSLY TOLD YOU NOT TO ANTAGONIZE THEM!
NOW LOOK WHAT YOU'VE DONE!
ARE YOU GOING TO TAKE RESPONSIBILITY FOR THIS?!

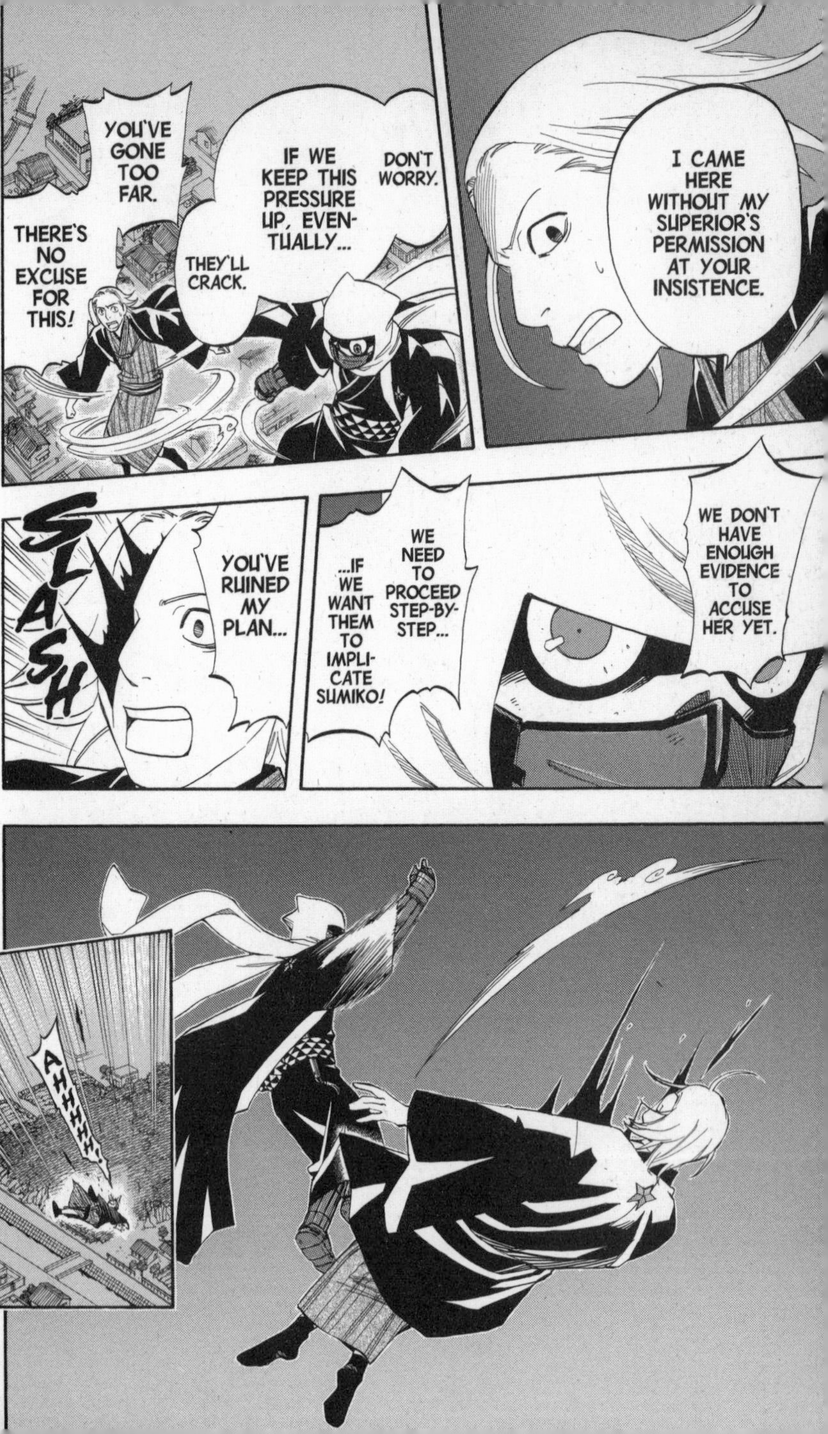
I CAME HERE WITHOUT MY SUPERIOR'S PERMISSION AT YOUR INSISTENCE.
DON'T WORRY.
IF WE KEEP THIS PRESSURE UP, EVENTUALLY...
THEY'LL CRACK.
YOU'VE GONE TOO FAR.
THERE'S NO EXCUSE FOR THIS!
WE DON'T HAVE ENOUGH EVIDENCE TO ACCUSE HER YET.
WE NEED TO PROCEED STEP-BY-STEP...
...IF WE WANT THEM TO IMPLICATE SUMIKO!
YOU'VE RUINED MY PLAN...
SLASH
AHHHHH!

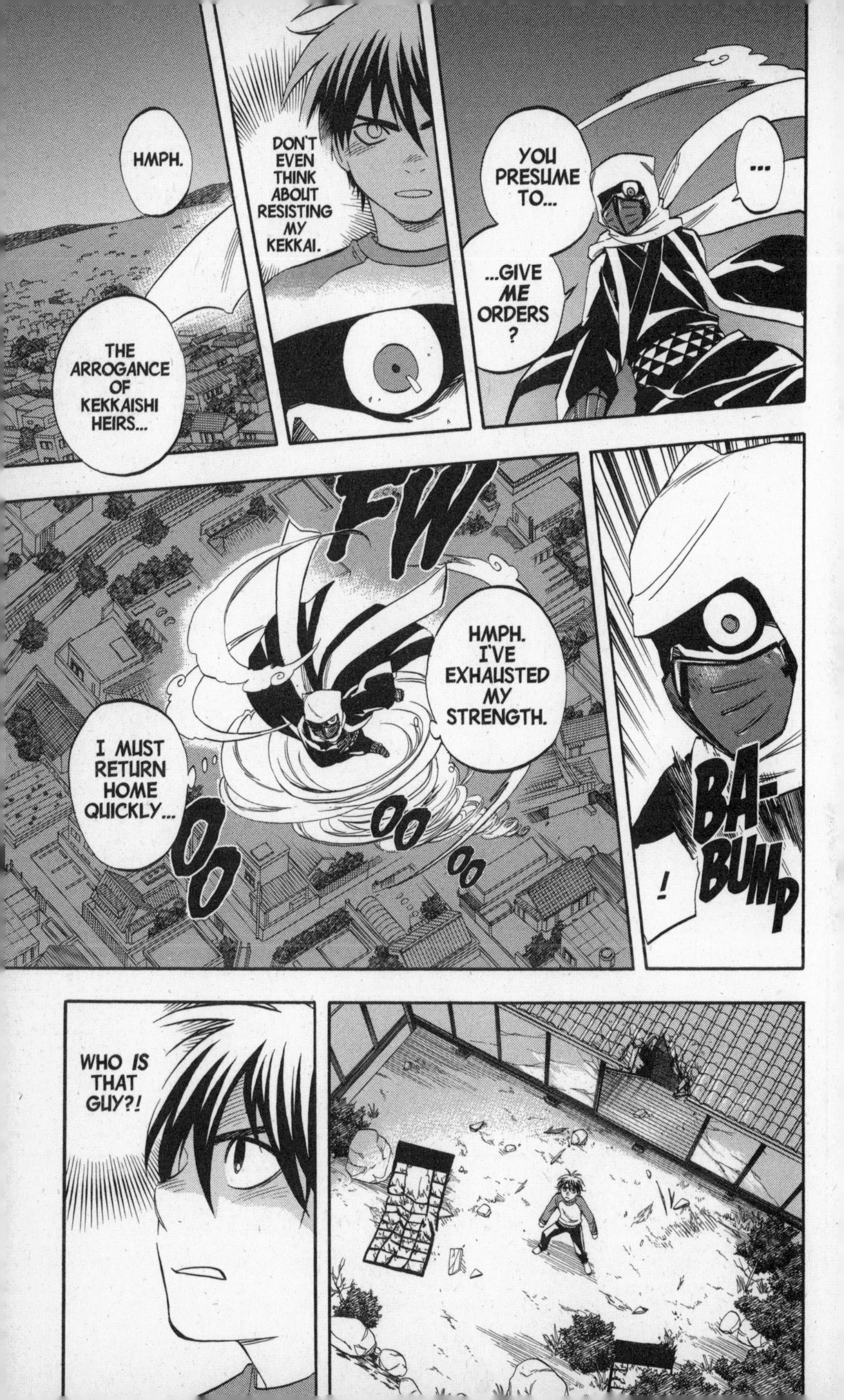
...
YOU PRESUME TO...
...GIVE *ME* ORDERS?
DON'T EVEN THINK ABOUT RESISTING MY KEKKAI.
HMPH.
THE ARROGANCE OF KEKKAISHI HEIRS...
BA-BUMP
!
FW
HMPH. I'VE EXHAUSTED MY STRENGTH.
OO OO
I MUST RETURN HOME QUICKLY...
OO
WHO *IS* THAT GUY?!

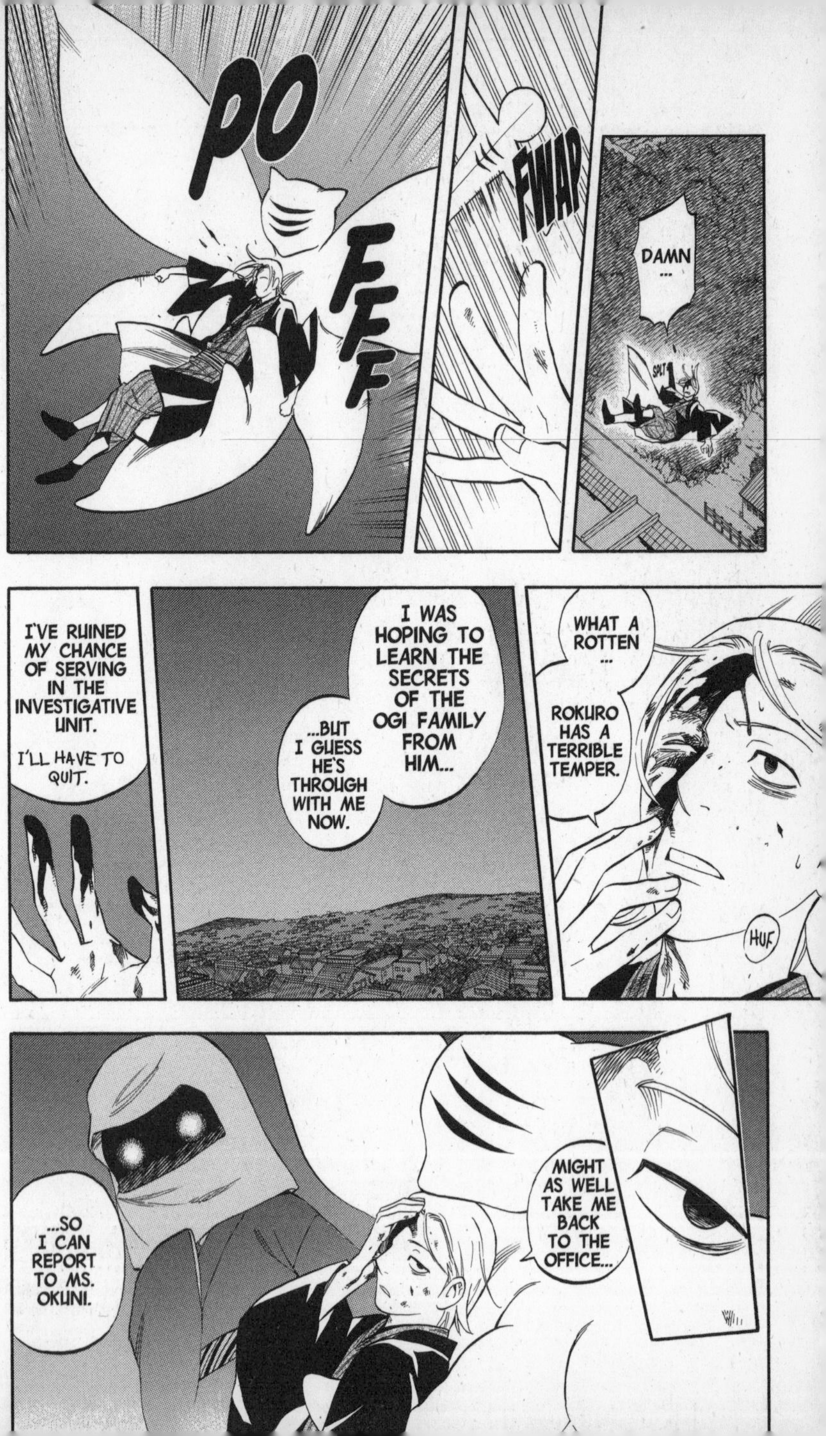
DAMN ...
SPLT
FWAP
PO
FFF
WHAT A ROTTEN ...
ROKURO HAS A TERRIBLE TEMPER.
HUF
I WAS HOPING TO LEARN THE SECRETS OF THE OGI FAMILY FROM HIM...
...BUT I GUESS HE'S THROUGH WITH ME NOW.
I'VE RUINED MY CHANCE OF SERVING IN THE INVESTIGATIVE UNIT.
I'LL HAVE TO QUIT.
MIGHT AS WELL TAKE ME BACK TO THE OFFICE...
...SO I CAN REPORT TO MS. OKUNI.

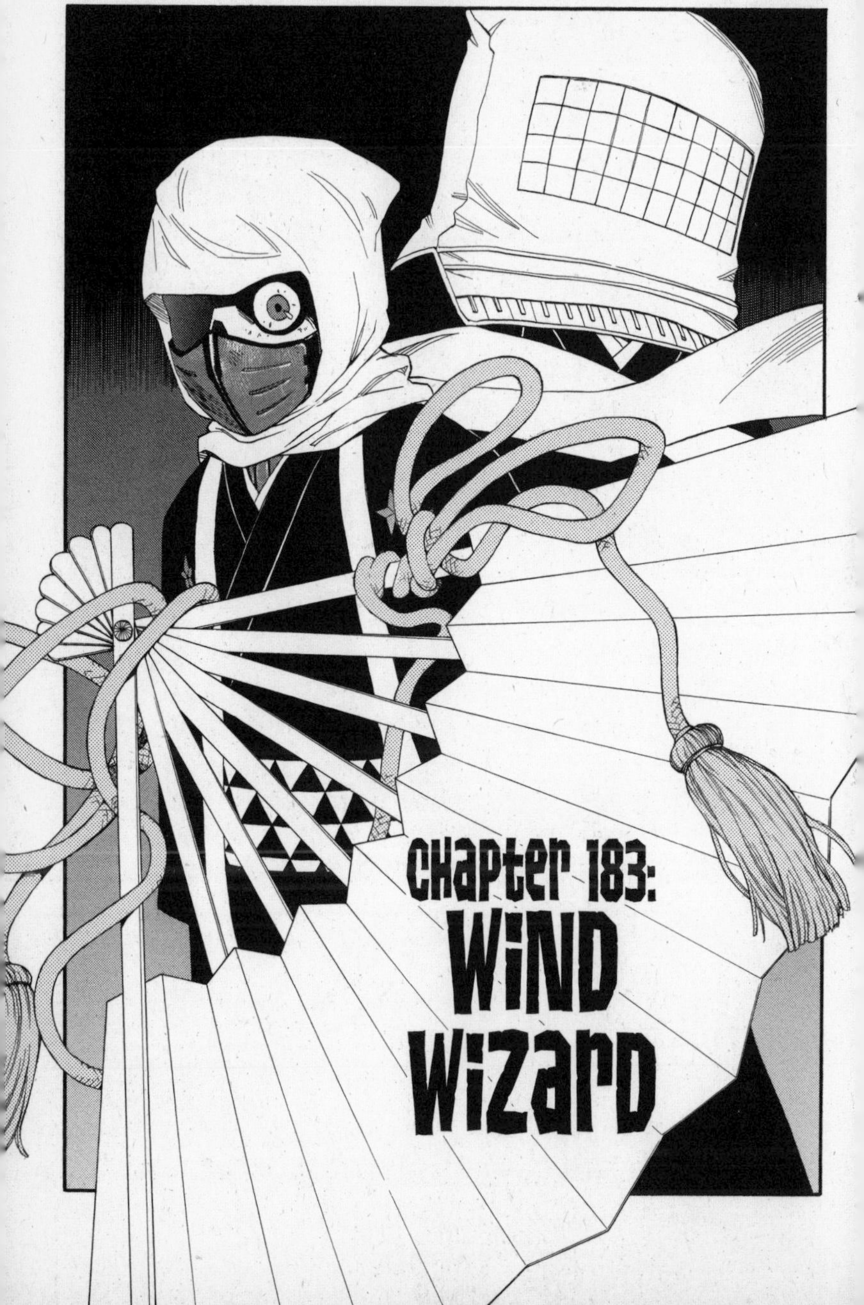
CHAPTER 183:
WIND
WIZARD

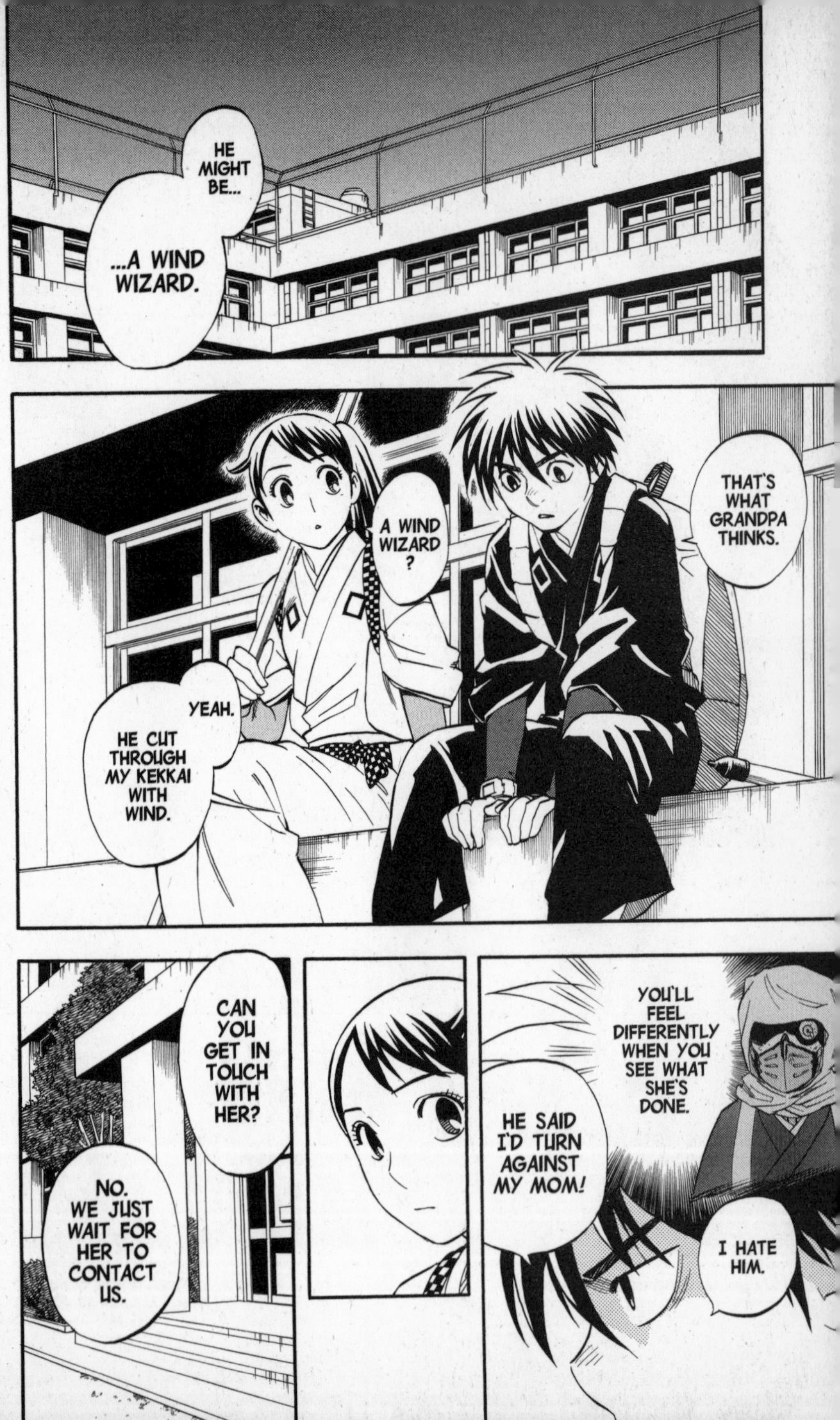
HE MIGHT BE...
...A WIND WIZARD.
THAT'S WHAT GRANDPA THINKS.
A WIND WIZARD?
YEAH.
HE CUT THROUGH MY KEKKAI WITH WIND.
YOU'LL FEEL DIFFERENTLY WHEN YOU SEE WHAT SHE'S DONE.
HE SAID I'D TURN AGAINST MY MOM!
I HATE HIM.
CAN YOU GET IN TOUCH WITH HER?
NO. WE JUST WAIT FOR HER TO CONTACT US.

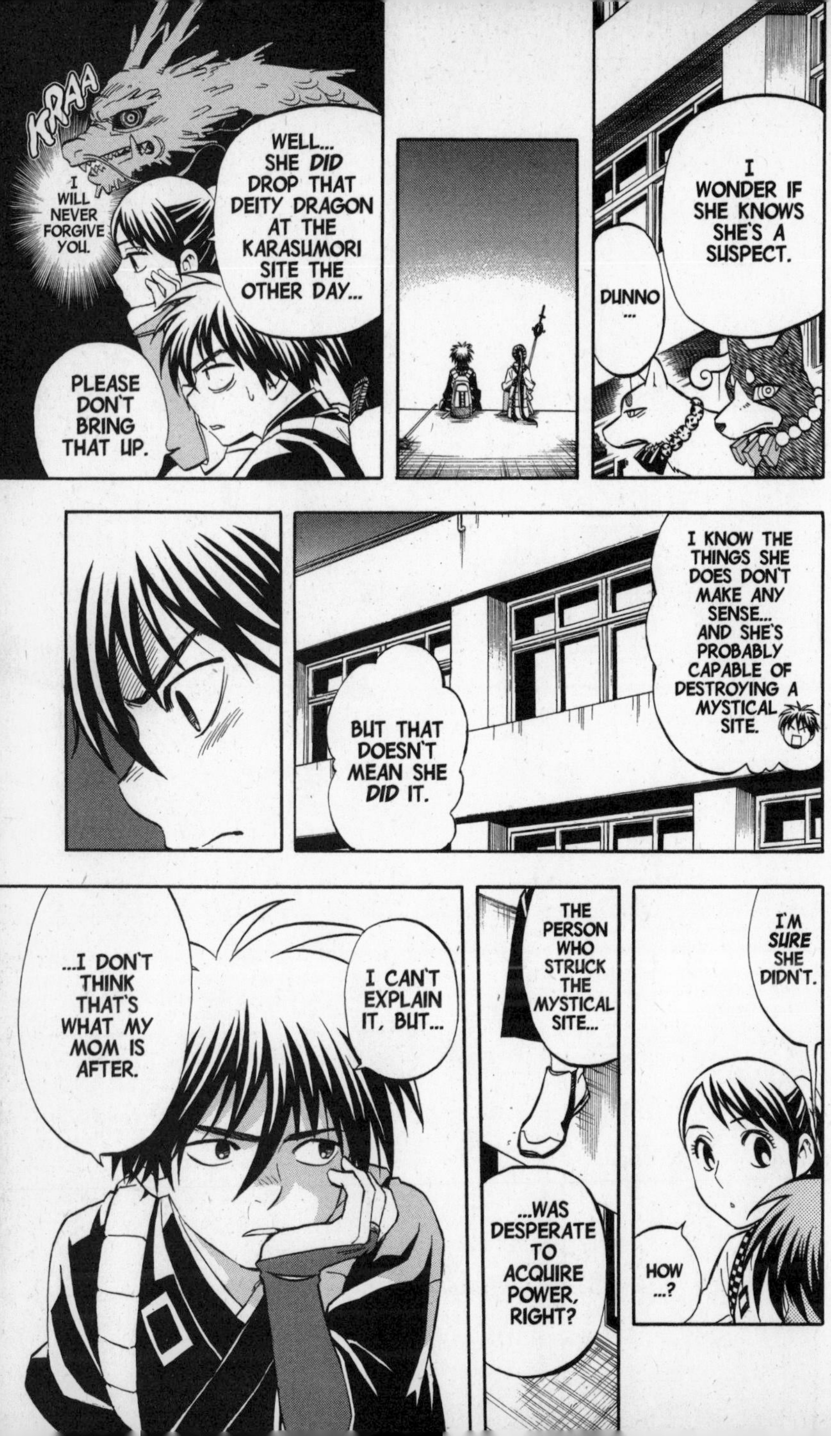
I WONDER IF SHE KNOWS SHE'S A SUSPECT.
DUNNO...
WELL... SHE *DID* DROP THAT DEITY DRAGON AT THE KARASUMORI SITE THE OTHER DAY...
KRAA
I WILL NEVER FORGIVE YOU.
PLEASE DON'T BRING THAT UP.
I KNOW THE THINGS SHE DOES DON'T MAKE ANY SENSE... AND SHE'S PROBABLY CAPABLE OF DESTROYING A MYSTICAL SITE.
BUT THAT DOESN'T MEAN SHE *DID* IT.
I'M *SURE* SHE DIDN'T.
HOW...?
THE PERSON WHO STRUCK THE MYSTICAL SITE...
...WAS DESPERATE TO ACQUIRE POWER, RIGHT?
I CAN'T EXPLAIN IT, BUT...
...I DON'T THINK THAT'S WHAT MY MOM IS AFTER.

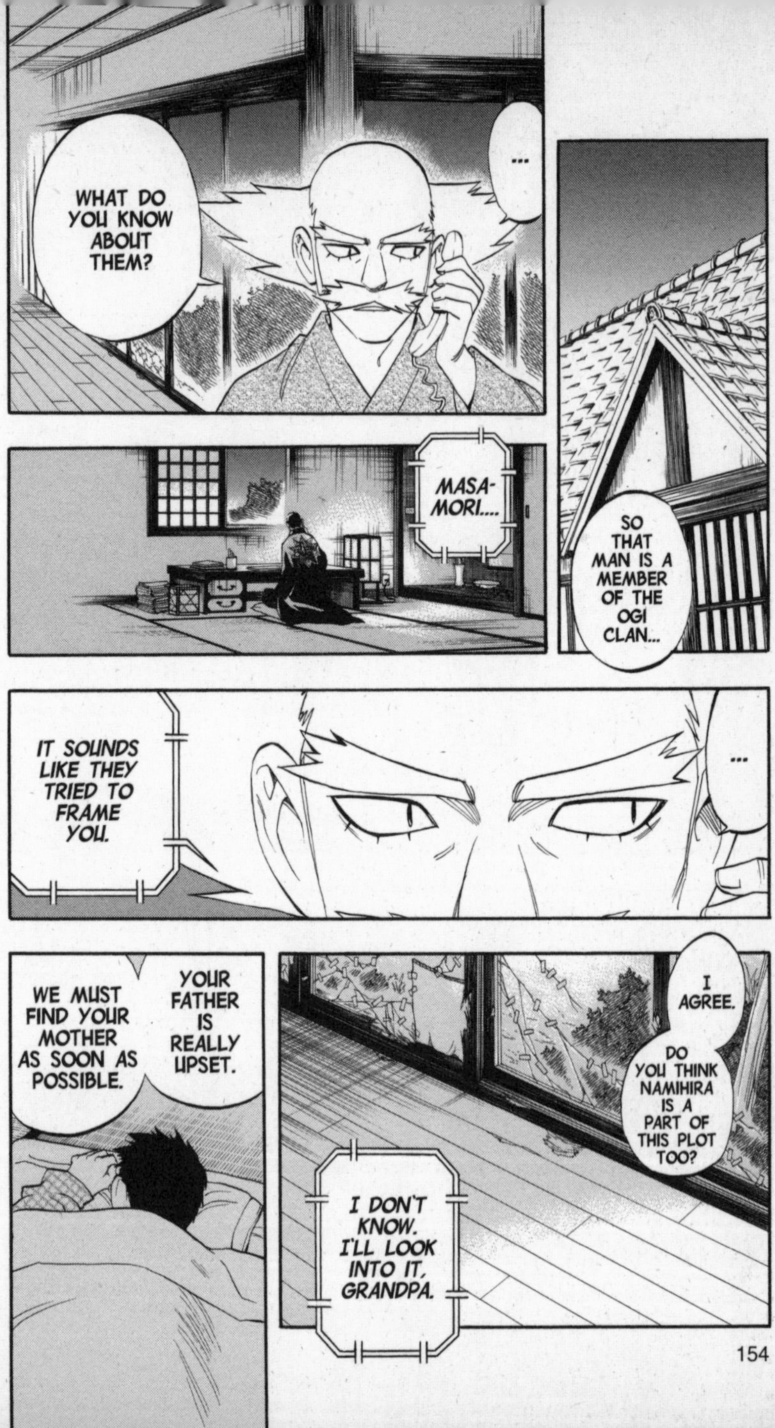
SO THAT MAN IS A MEMBER OF THE OGI CLAN...
...
WHAT DO YOU KNOW ABOUT THEM?
MASA-MORI....
...
IT SOUNDS LIKE THEY TRIED TO FRAME YOU.
I AGREE.
DO YOU THINK NAMIHIRA IS A PART OF THIS PLOT TOO?
I DON'T KNOW. I'LL LOOK INTO IT, GRANDPA.
YOUR FATHER IS REALLY UPSET.
WE MUST FIND YOUR MOTHER AS SOON AS POSSIBLE.

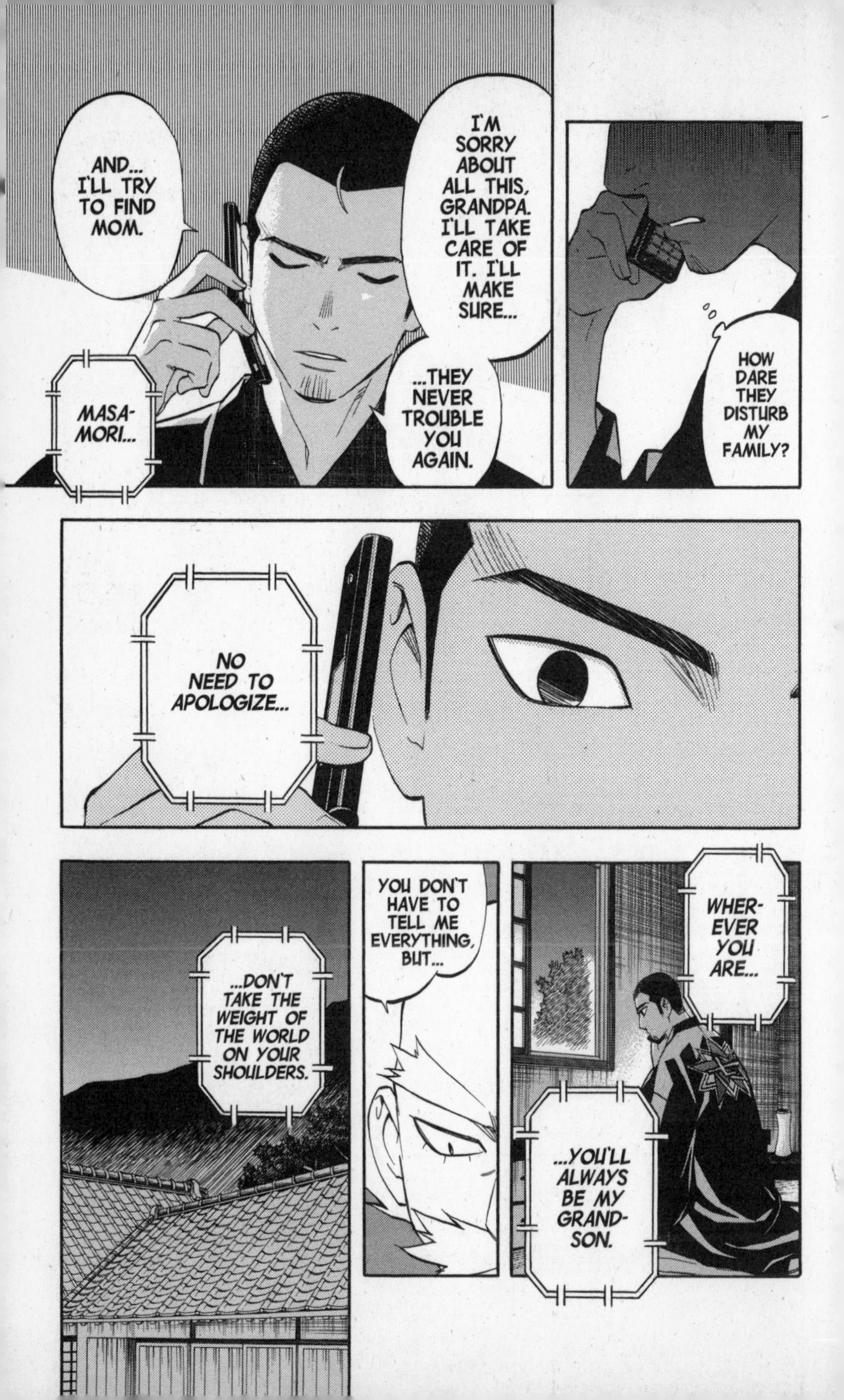
HOW DARE THEY DISTURB MY FAMILY?
I'M SORRY ABOUT ALL THIS, GRANDPA. I'LL TAKE CARE OF IT. I'LL MAKE SURE...
...THEY NEVER TROUBLE YOU AGAIN.
AND... I'LL TRY TO FIND MOM.
MASAMORI...
NO NEED TO APOLOGIZE...
WHEREVER YOU ARE...
...YOU'LL ALWAYS BE MY GRANDSON.
YOU DON'T HAVE TO TELL ME EVERYTHING, BUT...
...DON'T TAKE THE WEIGHT OF THE WORLD ON YOUR SHOULDERS.

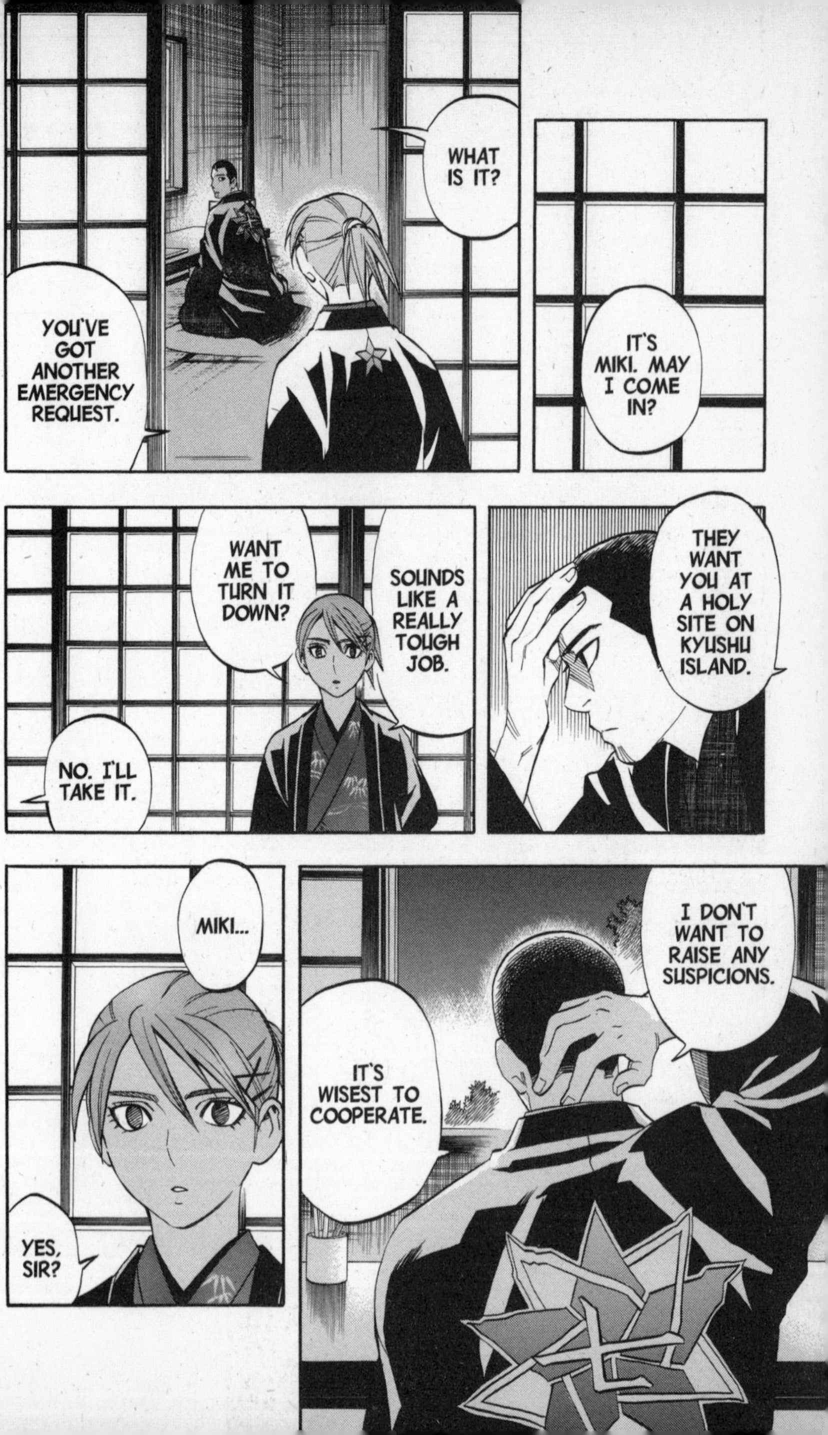
IT'S MIKI. MAY I COME IN?
WHAT IS IT?
YOU'VE GOT ANOTHER EMERGENCY REQUEST.
THEY WANT YOU AT A HOLY SITE ON KYUSHU ISLAND.
SOUNDS LIKE A REALLY TOUGH JOB.
WANT ME TO TURN IT DOWN?
NO. I'LL TAKE IT.
I DON'T WANT TO RAISE ANY SUSPICIONS.
IT'S WISEST TO COOPERATE.
MIKI...
YES, SIR?

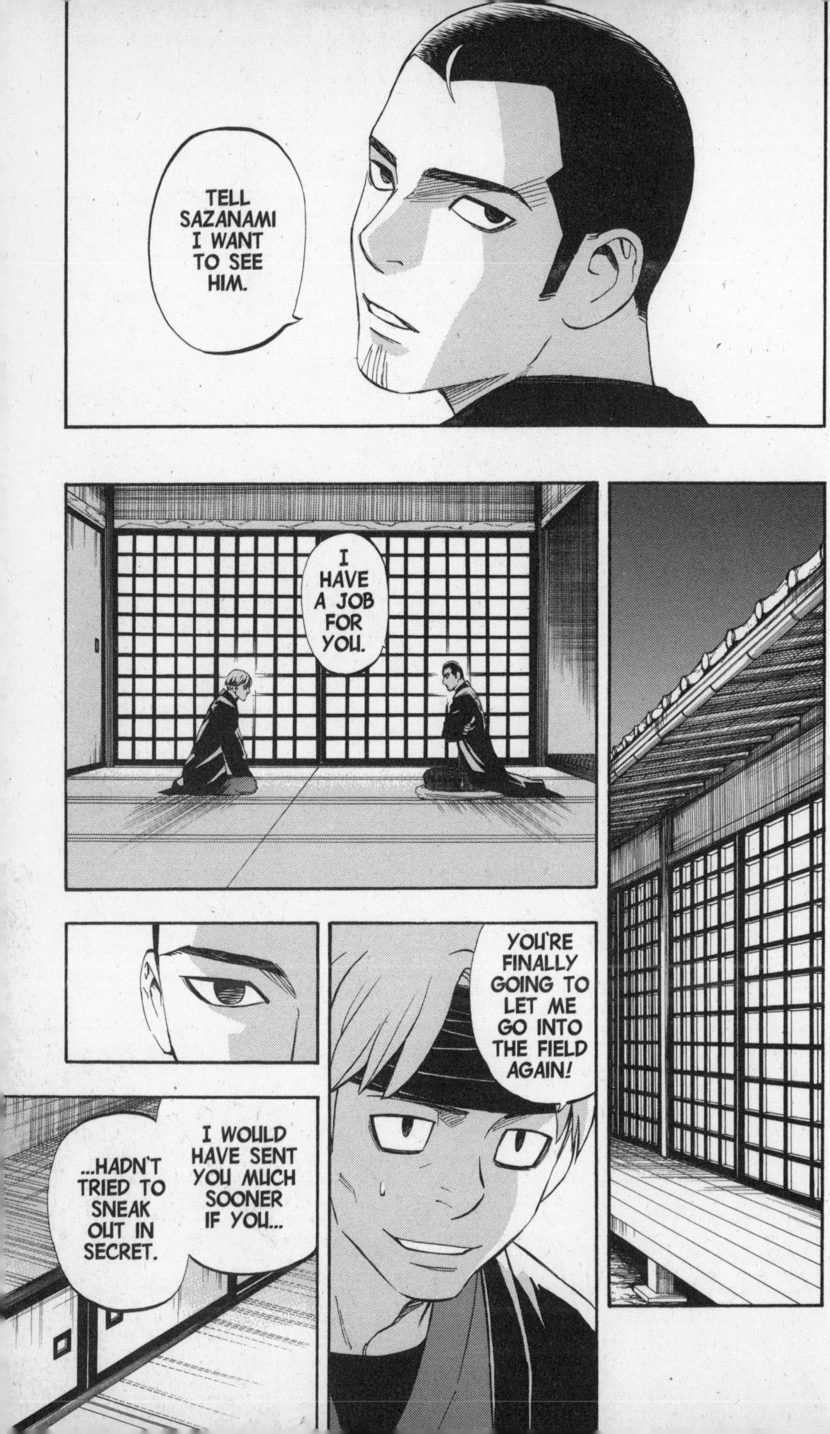
TELL SAZANAMI I WANT TO SEE HIM.
I HAVE A JOB FOR YOU.
YOU'RE FINALLY GOING TO LET ME GO INTO THE FIELD AGAIN!
I WOULD HAVE SENT YOU MUCH SOONER IF YOU...
...HADN'T TRIED TO SNEAK OUT IN SECRET.

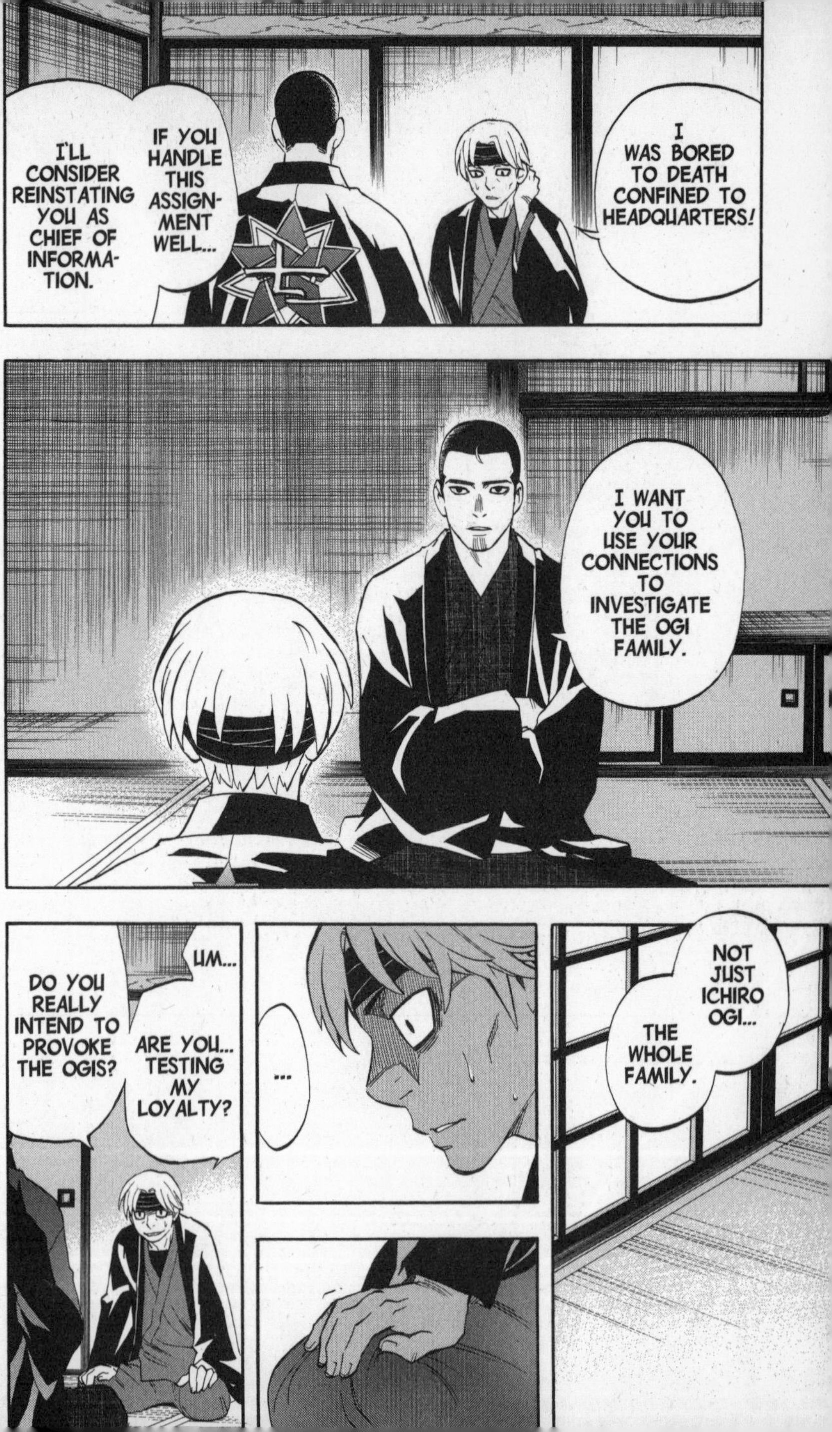
I WAS BORED TO DEATH CONFINED TO HEADQUARTERS!
IF YOU HANDLE THIS ASSIGNMENT WELL...
I'LL CONSIDER REINSTATING YOU AS CHIEF OF INFORMATION.
I WANT YOU TO USE YOUR CONNECTIONS TO INVESTIGATE THE OGI FAMILY.
NOT JUST ICHIRO OGI...
THE WHOLE FAMILY.
...
UM...
ARE YOU... TESTING MY LOYALTY?
DO YOU REALLY INTEND TO PROVOKE THE OGIS?

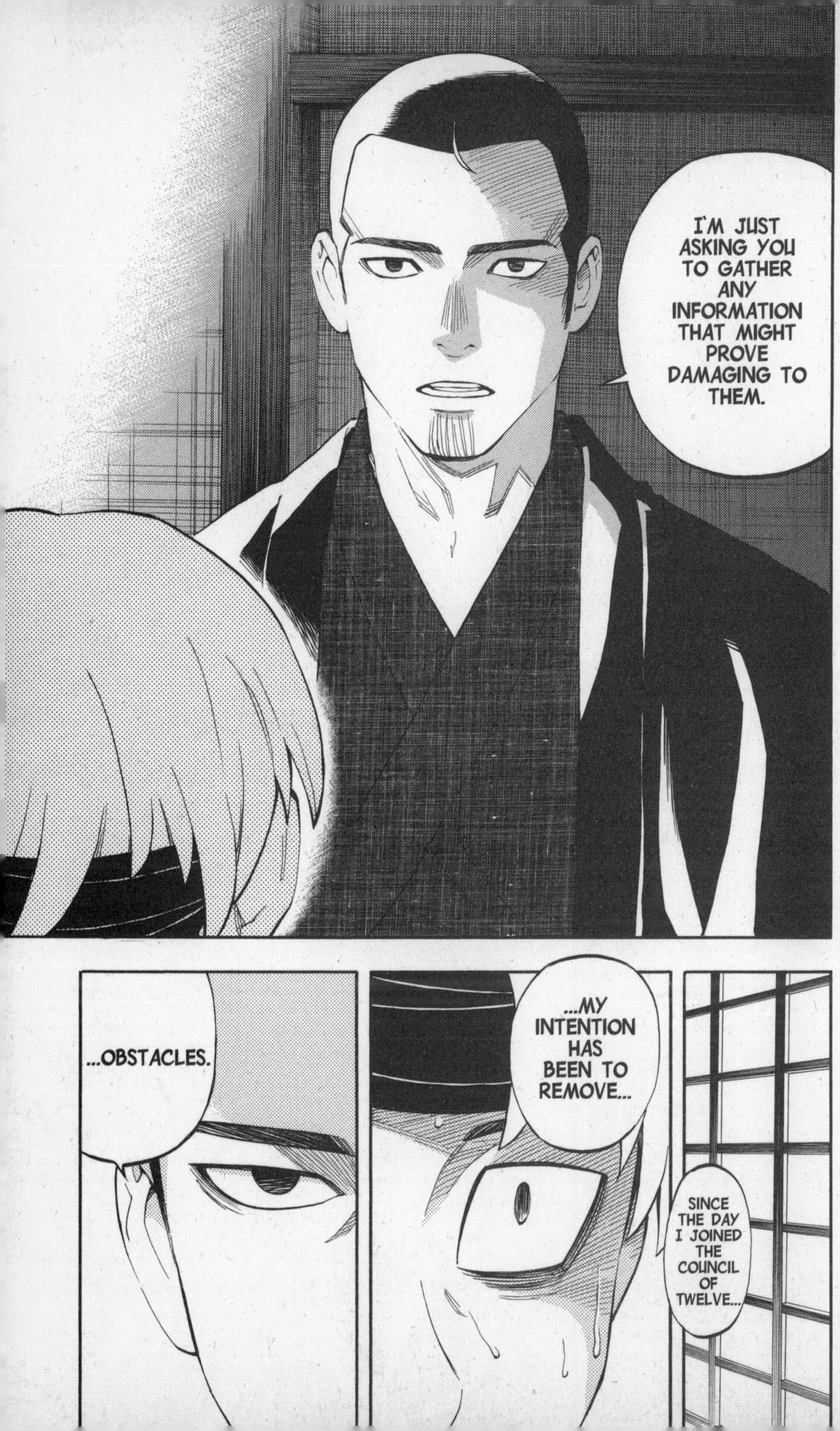
I'M JUST ASKING YOU TO GATHER ANY INFORMATION THAT MIGHT PROVE DAMAGING TO THEM.
SINCE THE DAY I JOINED THE COUNCIL OF TWELVE...
...MY INTENTION HAS BEEN TO REMOVE...
...OBSTACLES.

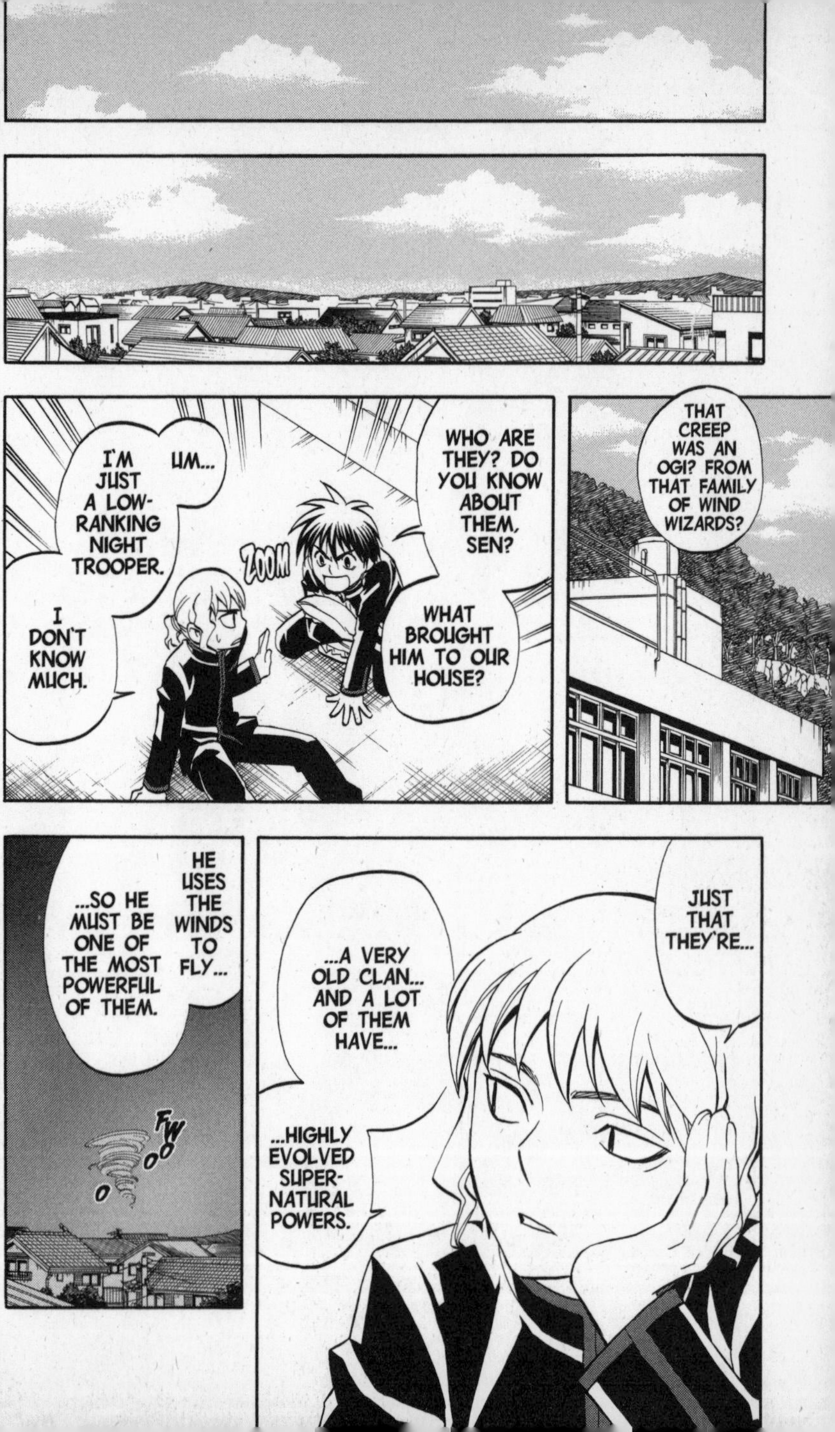
THAT CREEP WAS AN OGI? FROM THAT FAMILY OF WIND WIZARDS?
WHO ARE THEY? DO YOU KNOW ABOUT THEM, SEN?
WHAT BROUGHT HIM TO OUR HOUSE?
ZOOM
UM...
I'M JUST A LOW-RANKING NIGHT TROOPER.
I DON'T KNOW MUCH.
JUST THAT THEY'RE...
...A VERY OLD CLAN... AND A LOT OF THEM HAVE...
...HIGHLY EVOLVED SUPER-NATURAL POWERS.
HE USES THE WINDS TO FLY...
...SO HE MUST BE ONE OF THE MOST POWERFUL OF THEM.
FWOOOO

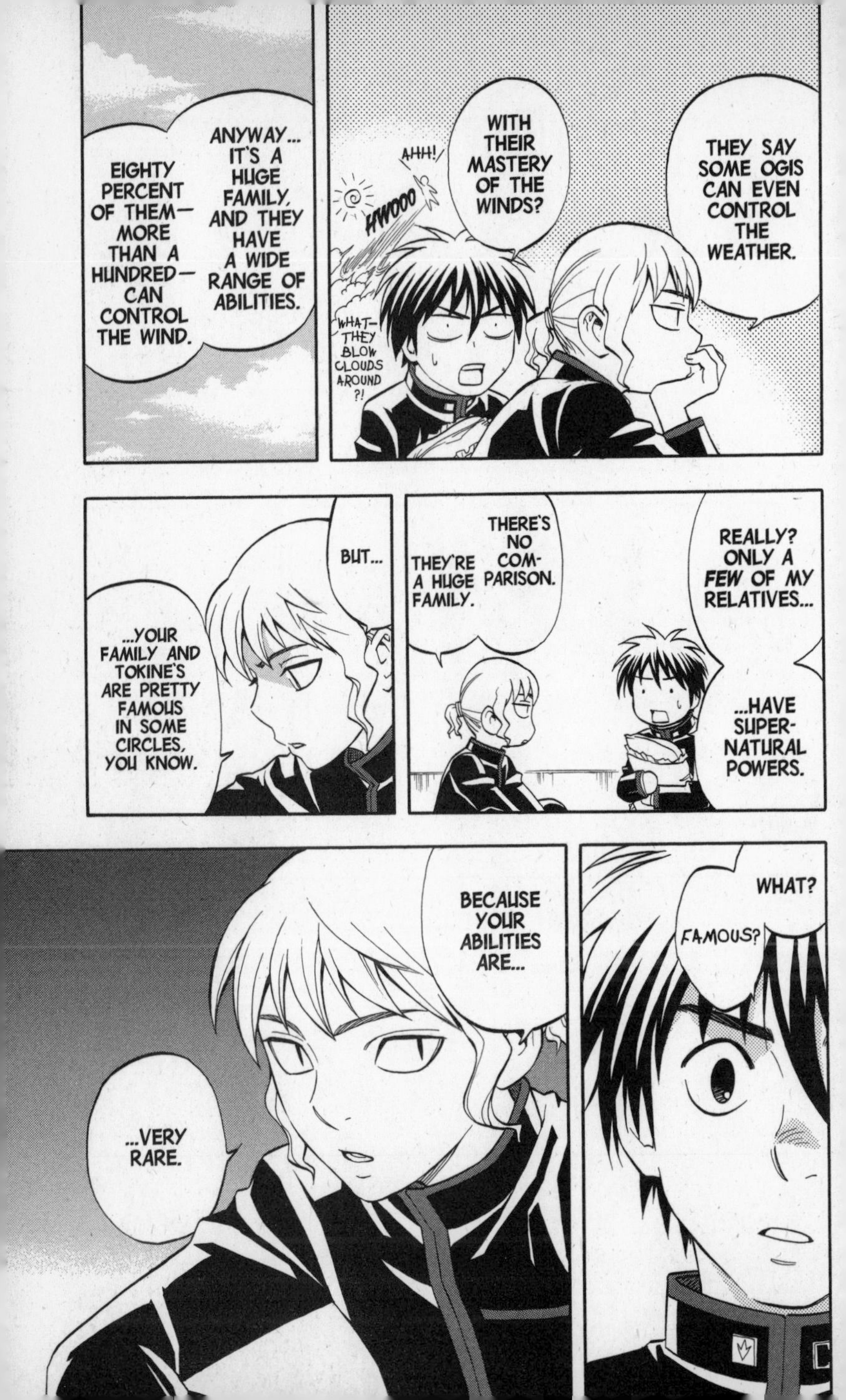
THEY SAY SOME OGIS CAN EVEN CONTROL THE WEATHER.
WITH THEIR MASTERY OF THE WINDS?
AHH!
HWOOO
WHAT—THEY BLOW CLOUDS AROUND?!
ANYWAY... IT'S A HUGE FAMILY, AND THEY HAVE A WIDE RANGE OF ABILITIES.
EIGHTY PERCENT OF THEM—MORE THAN A HUNDRED—CAN CONTROL THE WIND.
REALLY? ONLY A *FEW* OF MY RELATIVES...
...HAVE SUPER-NATURAL POWERS.
THERE'S NO COM-PARISON.
THEY'RE A HUGE FAMILY.
BUT...
...YOUR FAMILY AND TOKINE'S ARE PRETTY FAMOUS IN SOME CIRCLES, YOU KNOW.
WHAT?
FAMOUS?
BECAUSE YOUR ABILITIES ARE...
...VERY RARE.

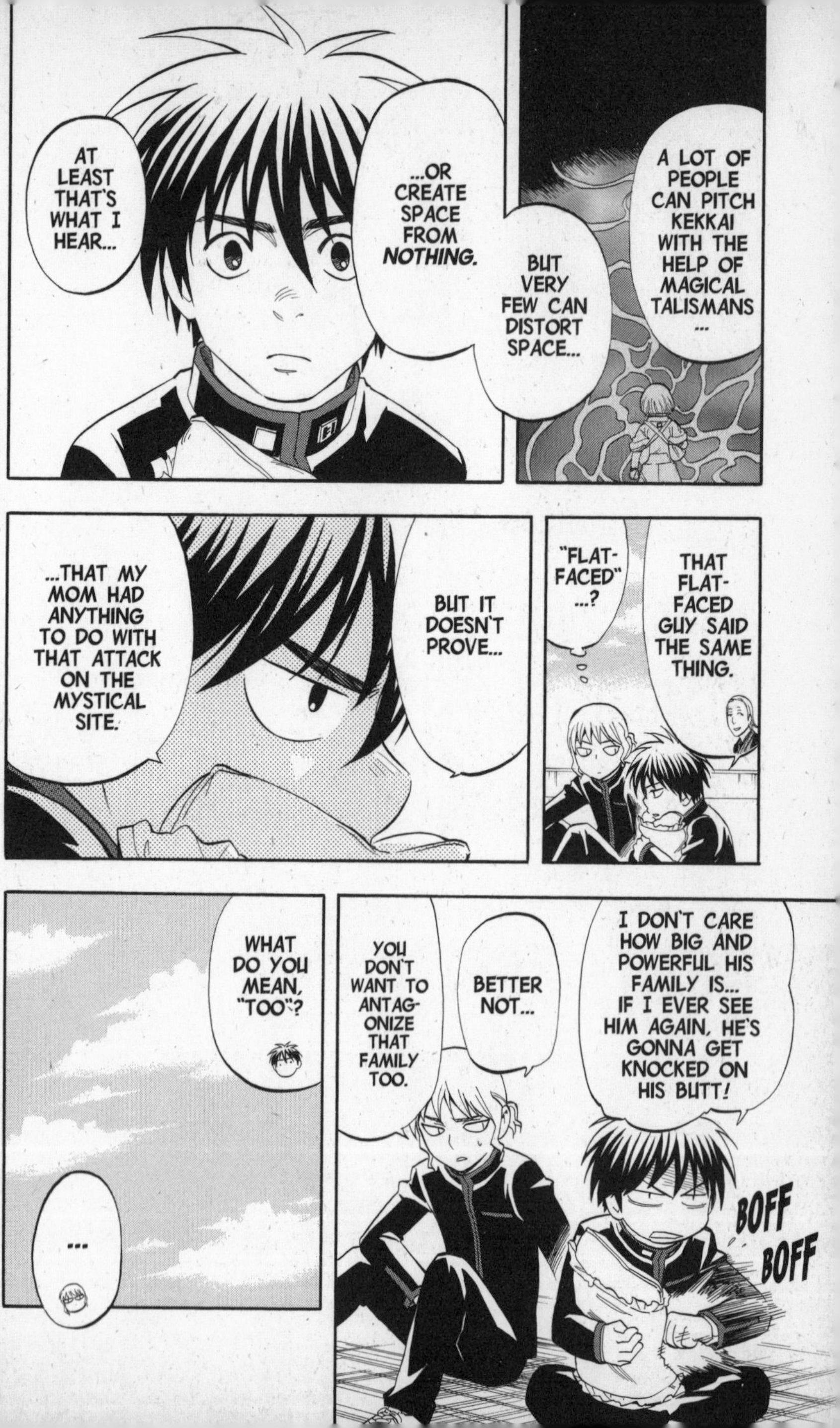
A LOT OF PEOPLE CAN PITCH KEKKAI WITH THE HELP OF MAGICAL TALISMANS...
BUT VERY FEW CAN DISTORT SPACE...
...OR CREATE SPACE FROM *NOTHING.*
AT LEAST THAT'S WHAT I HEAR...
THAT FLAT-FACED GUY SAID THE SAME THING.
"FLAT-FACED"...?
BUT IT DOESN'T PROVE...
...THAT MY MOM HAD ANYTHING TO DO WITH THAT ATTACK ON THE MYSTICAL SITE.
I DON'T CARE HOW BIG AND POWERFUL HIS FAMILY IS... IF I EVER SEE HIM AGAIN, HE'S GONNA GET KNOCKED ON HIS BUTT!
BETTER NOT...
YOU DON'T WANT TO ANTAGONIZE THAT FAMILY TOO.
BOFF BOFF
WHAT DO YOU MEAN, "TOO"?
...

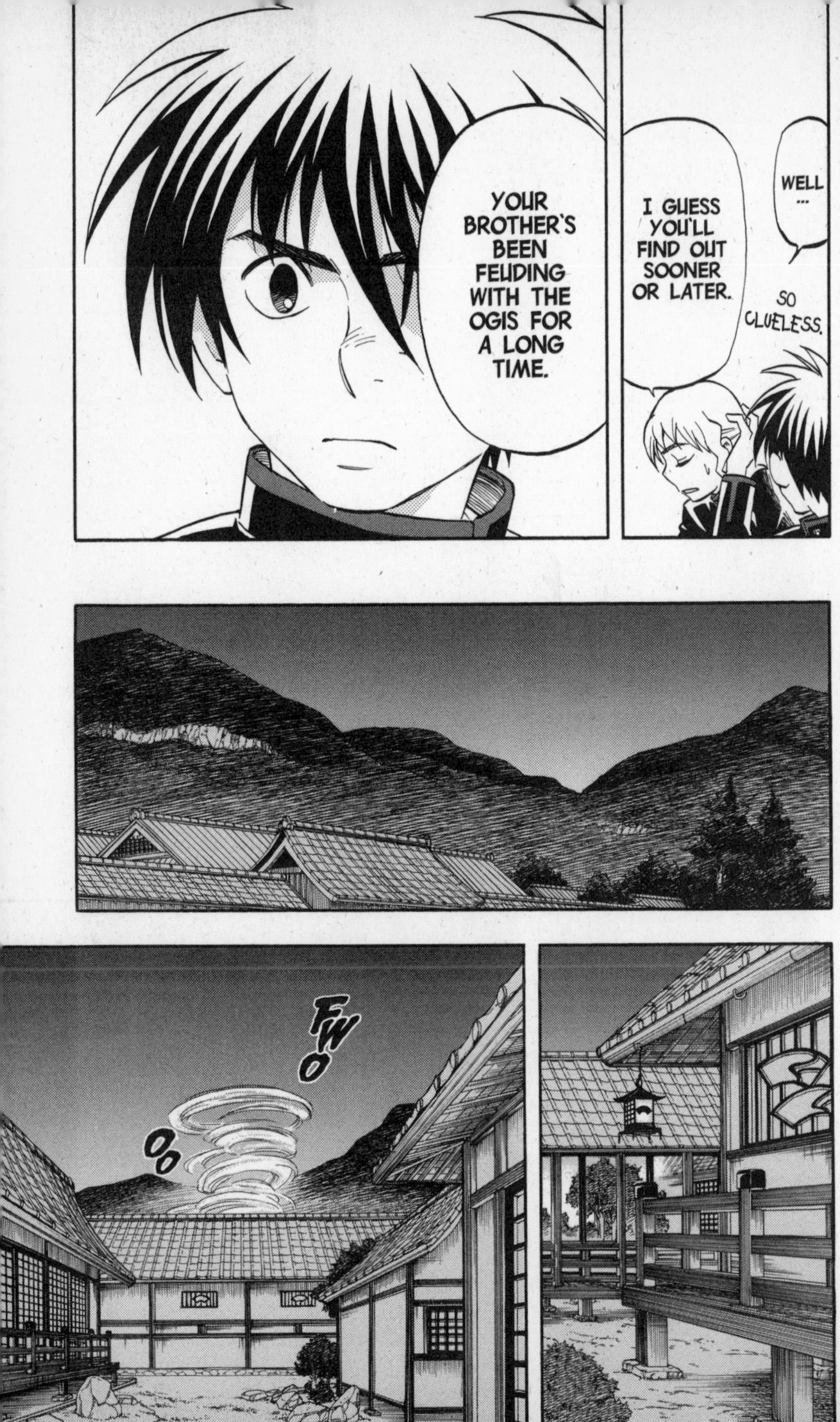
WELL ...
I GUESS YOU'LL FIND OUT SOONER OR LATER.
SO CLUELESS.
YOUR BROTHER'S BEEN FEUDING WITH THE OGIS FOR A LONG TIME.
FWOO

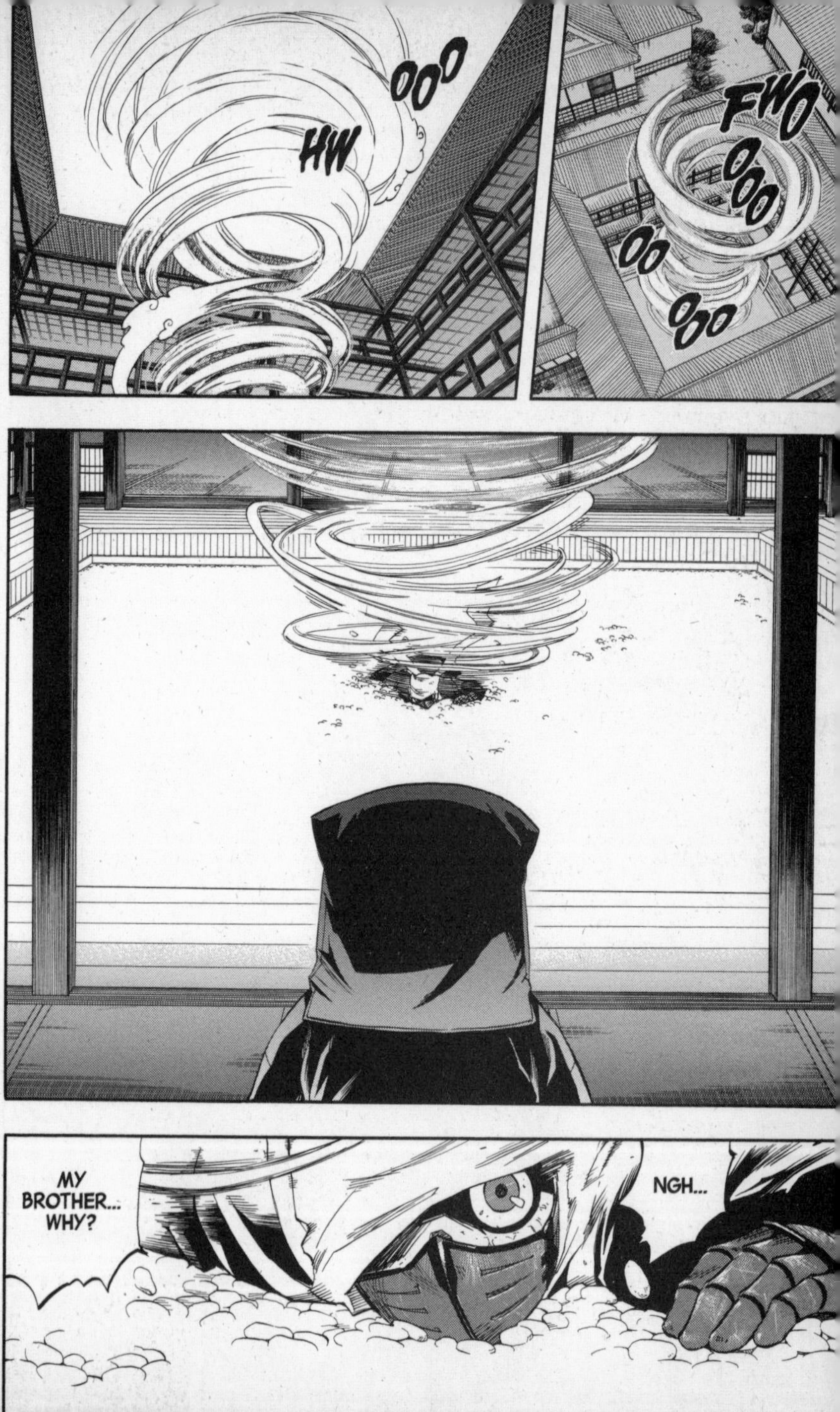
FWO
OOO
OO
OOO
HW
OOO
NGH...
MY BROTHER... WHY?

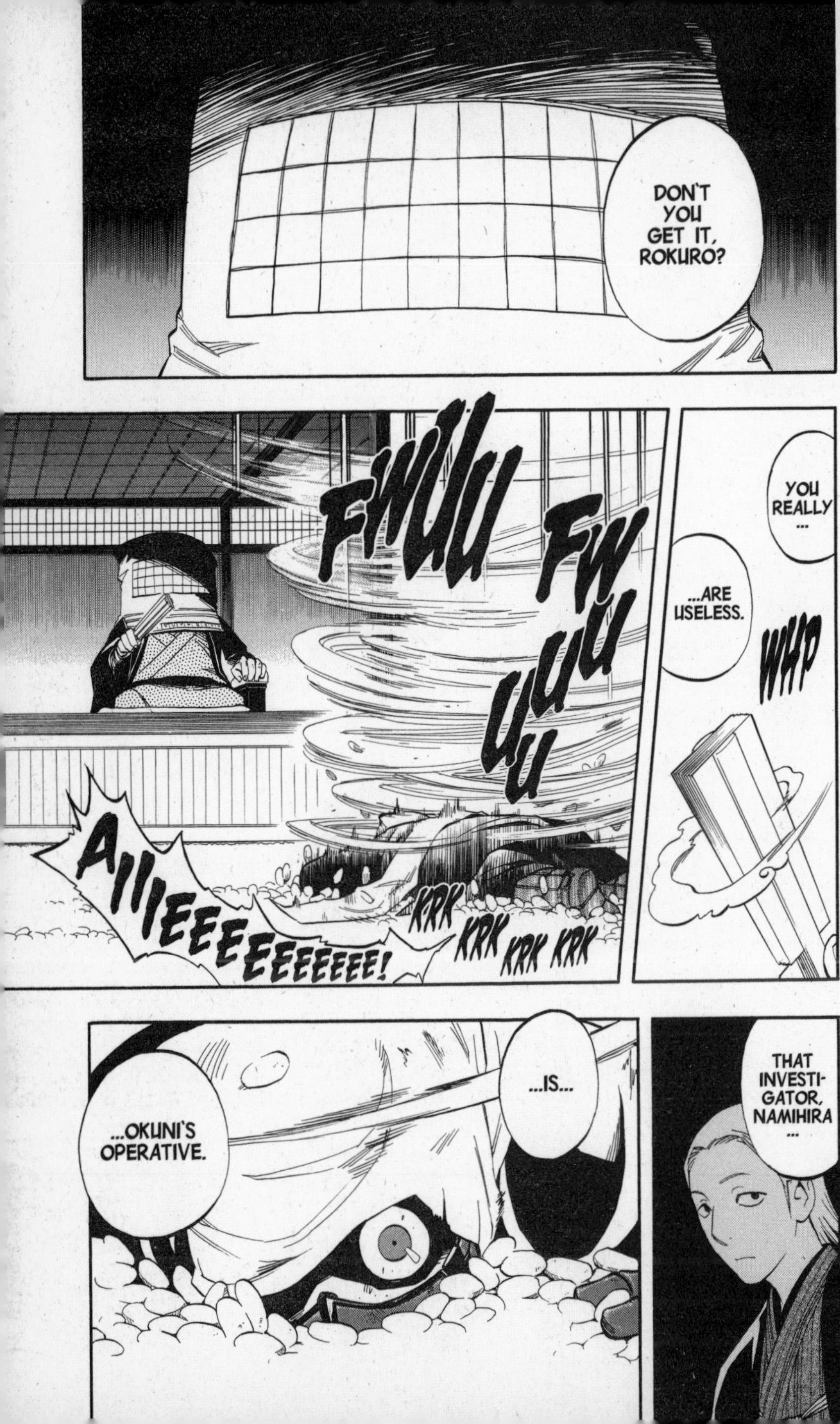
DON'T YOU GET IT, ROKURO?
YOU REALLY ...
...ARE USELESS.
WHP
FWUU
FWUUUUUU
AIIIEEEEEEEEEEE!
KRK KRK KRK KRK
THAT INVESTIGATOR, NAMIHIRA ...
...IS...
...OKUNI'S OPERATIVE.

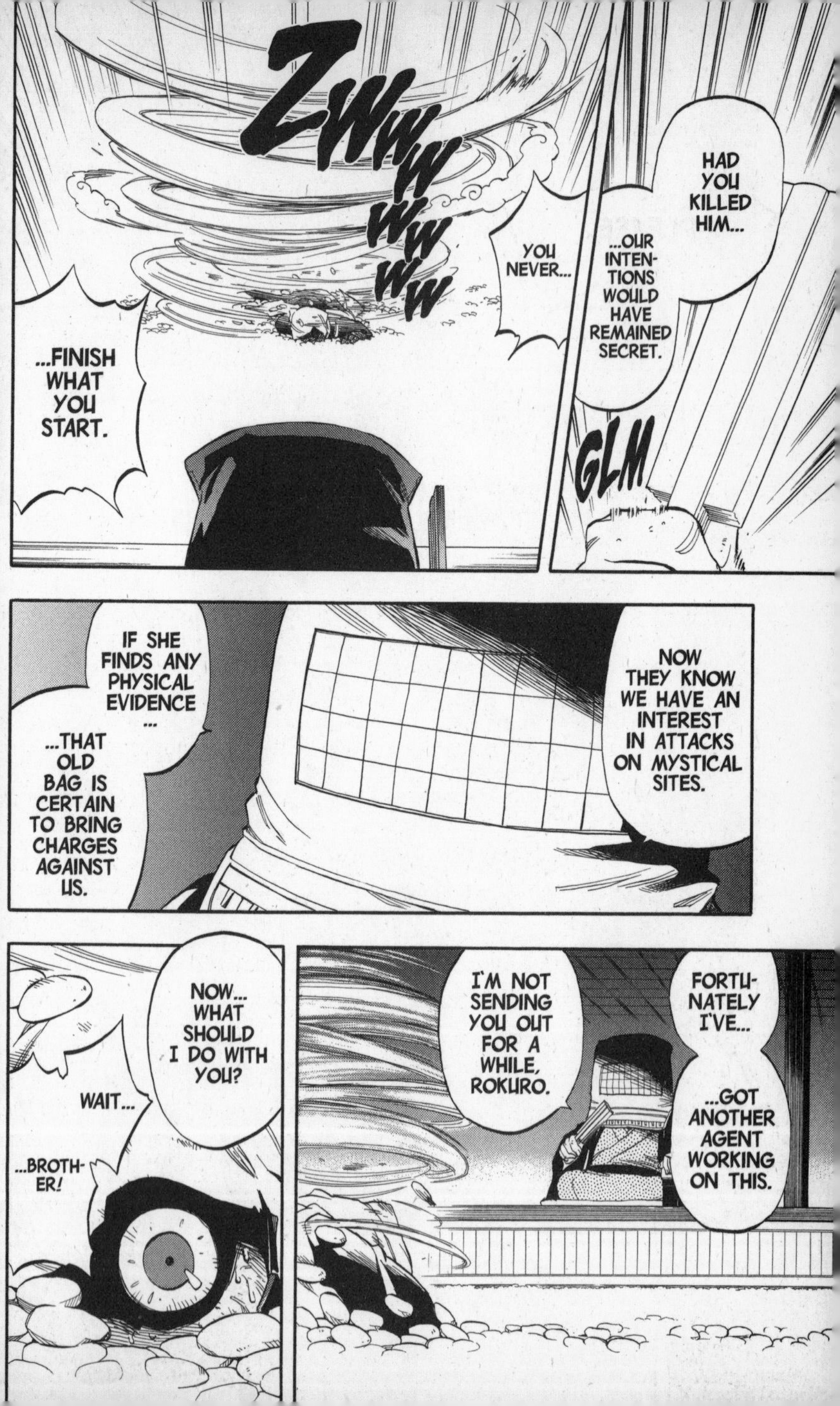
HAD YOU KILLED HIM...
...OUR INTEN-TIONS WOULD HAVE REMAINED SECRET.
GLM
ZWWWWWWWW
YOU NEVER...
...FINISH WHAT YOU START.
NOW THEY KNOW WE HAVE AN INTEREST IN ATTACKS ON MYSTICAL SITES.
IF SHE FINDS ANY PHYSICAL EVIDENCE...
...THAT OLD BAG IS CERTAIN TO BRING CHARGES AGAINST US.
FORTU-NATELY I'VE...
...GOT ANOTHER AGENT WORKING ON THIS.
I'M NOT SENDING YOU OUT FOR A WHILE, ROKURO.
NOW... WHAT SHOULD I DO WITH YOU?
WAIT...
...BROTH-ER!

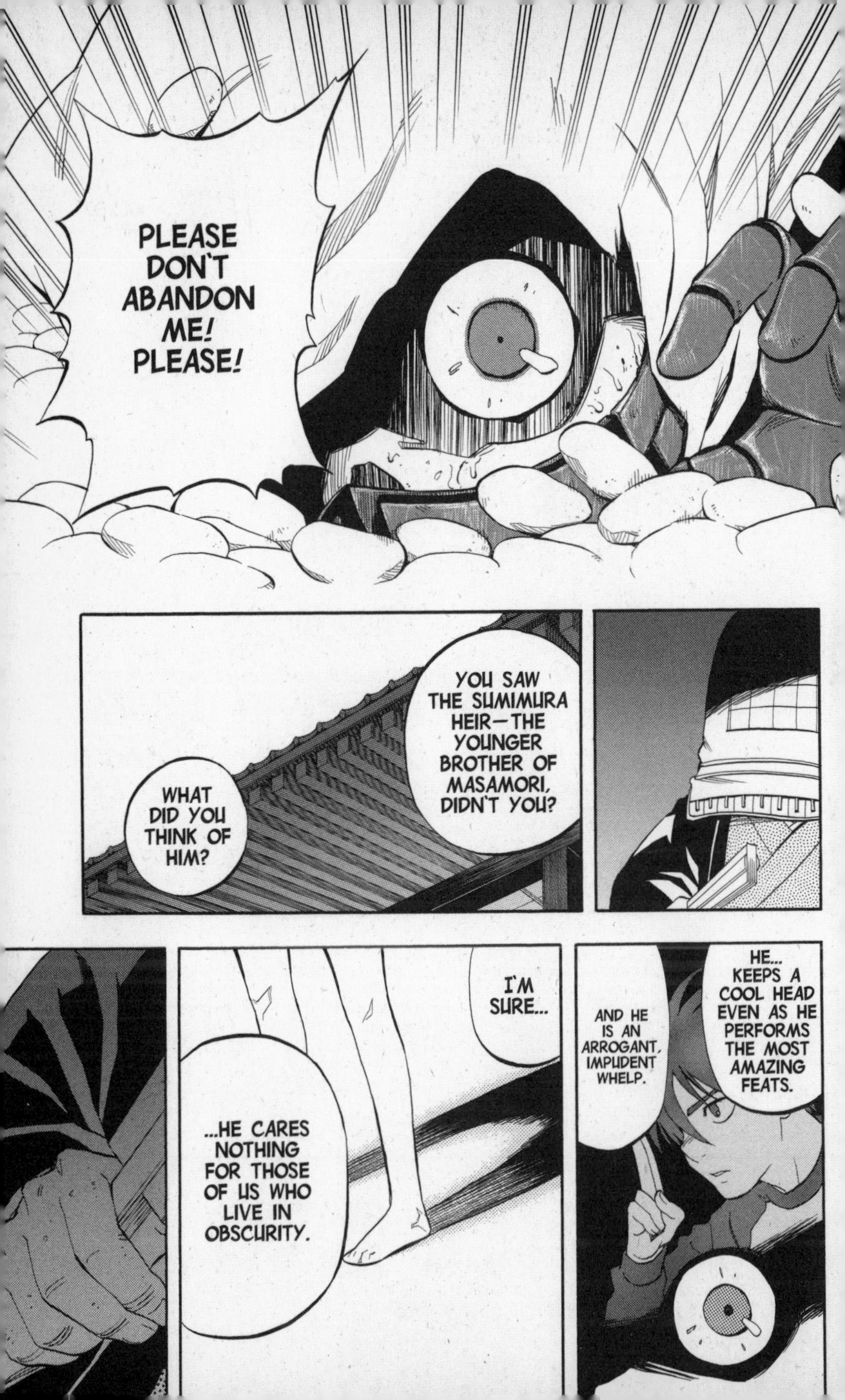
PLEASE DON'T ABANDON ME! PLEASE!
YOU SAW THE SUMIMURA HEIR—THE YOUNGER BROTHER OF MASAMORI, DIDN'T YOU?
WHAT DID YOU THINK OF HIM?
HE... KEEPS A COOL HEAD EVEN AS HE PERFORMS THE MOST AMAZING FEATS.
AND HE IS AN ARROGANT, IMPUDENT WHELP.
I'M SURE...
...HE CARES NOTHING FOR THOSE OF US WHO LIVE IN OBSCURITY.

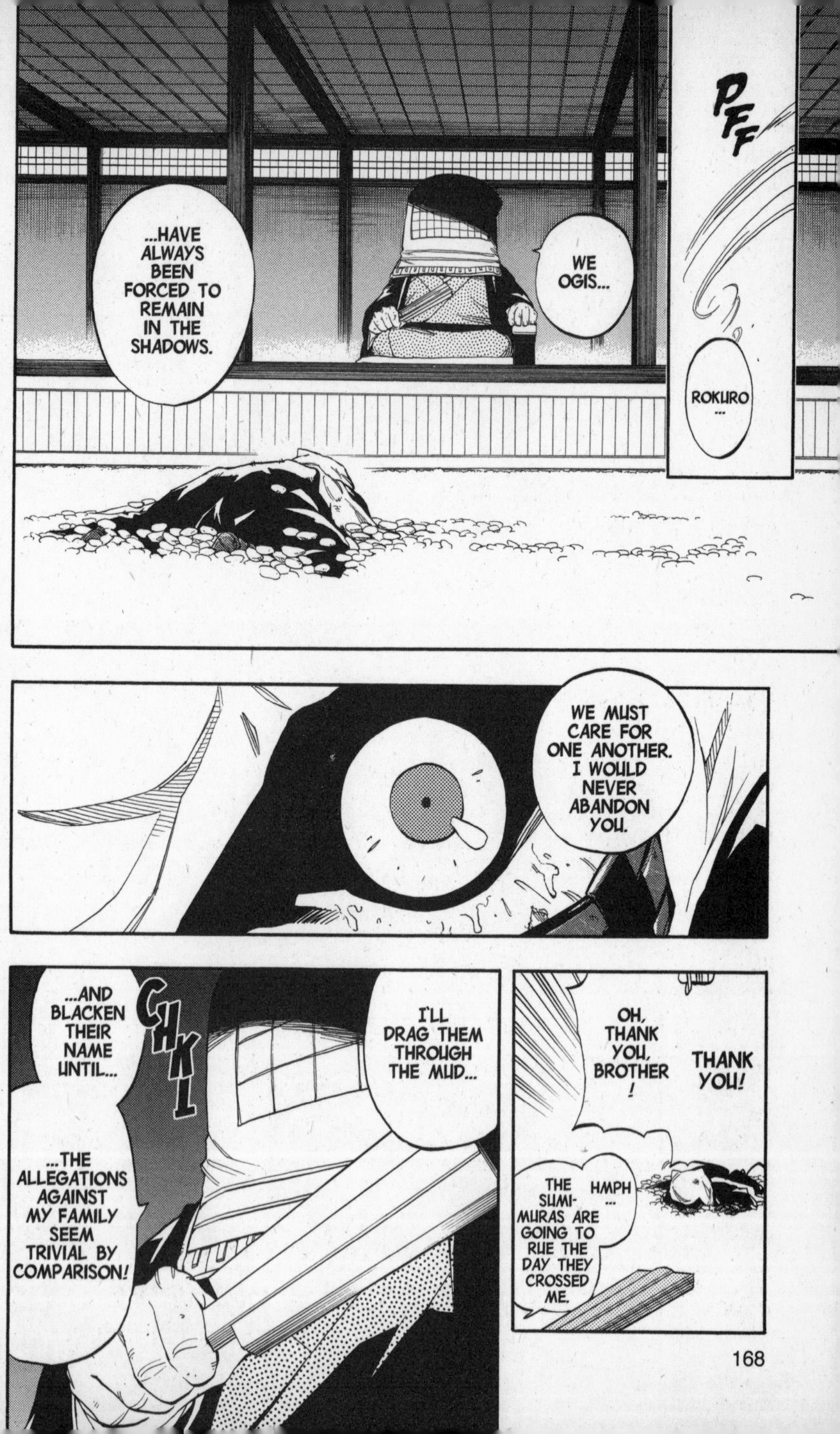
PFF
ROKURO...
WE OGIS...
...HAVE ALWAYS BEEN FORCED TO REMAIN IN THE SHADOWS.
WE MUST CARE FOR ONE ANOTHER. I WOULD NEVER ABANDON YOU.
THANK YOU!
OH, THANK YOU, BROTHER!
HMPH...
THE SUMIMURAS ARE GOING TO RUE THE DAY THEY CROSSED ME.
I'LL DRAG THEM THROUGH THE MUD...
CHKI
...AND BLACKEN THEIR NAME UNTIL...
...THE ALLEGATIONS AGAINST MY FAMILY SEEM TRIVIAL BY COMPARISON!

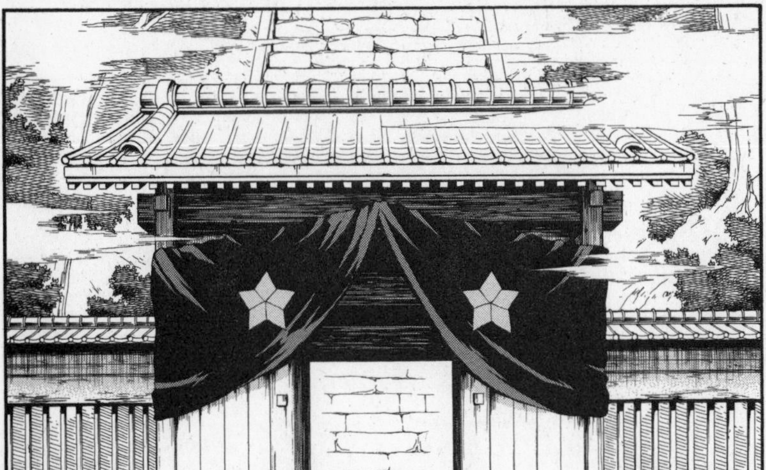
CHAPTER 184:
Deity Slayer

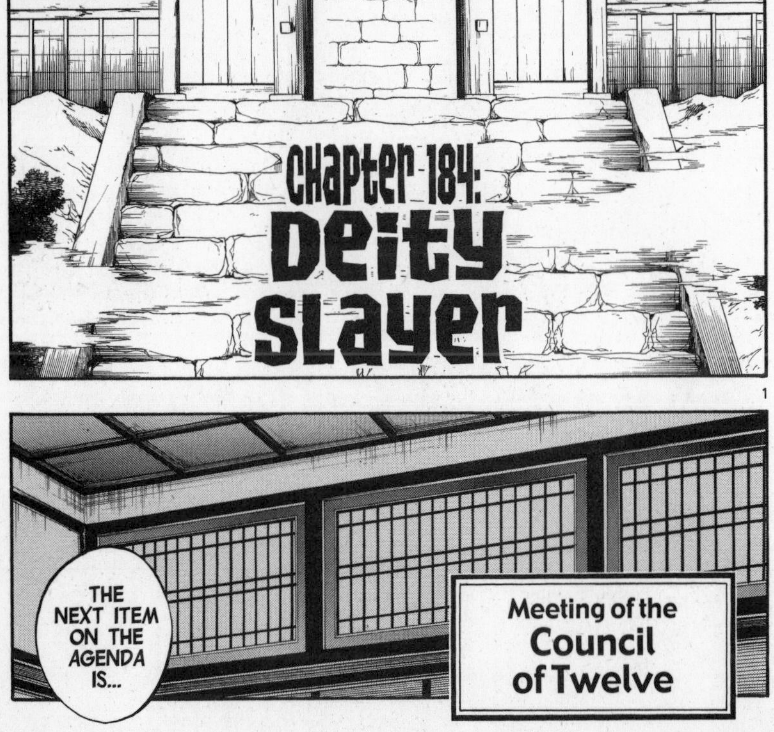
Meeting of the Council of Twelve
THE NEXT ITEM ON THE AGENDA IS...

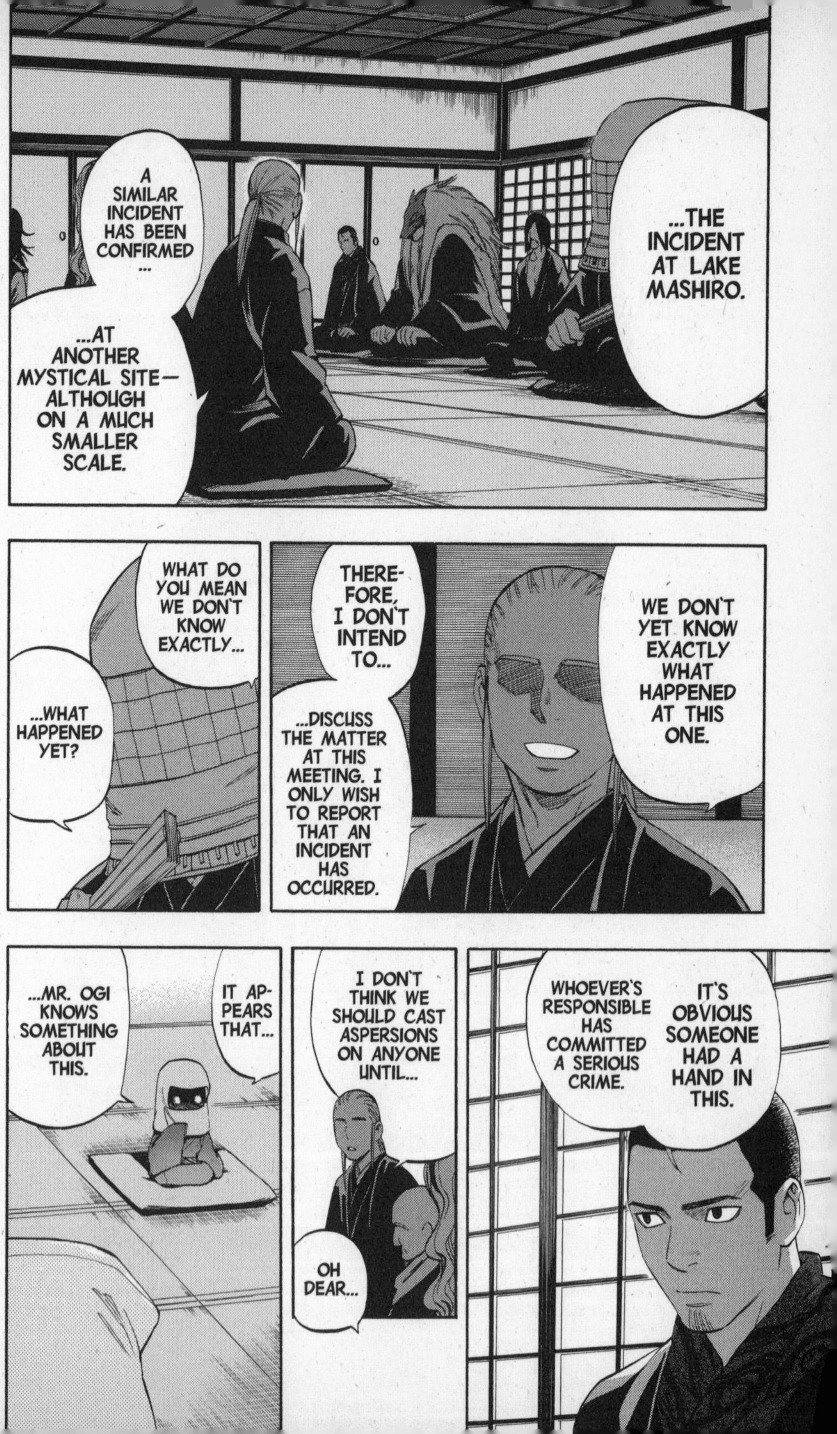
...THE INCIDENT AT LAKE MASHIRO.
A SIMILAR INCIDENT HAS BEEN CONFIRMED ...
...AT ANOTHER MYSTICAL SITE—ALTHOUGH ON A MUCH SMALLER SCALE.
WE DON'T YET KNOW EXACTLY WHAT HAPPENED AT THIS ONE.
THERE-FORE, I DON'T INTEND TO...
...DISCUSS THE MATTER AT THIS MEETING. I ONLY WISH TO REPORT THAT AN INCIDENT HAS OCCURRED.
WHAT DO YOU MEAN WE DON'T KNOW EXACTLY...
...WHAT HAPPENED YET?
IT'S OBVIOUS SOMEONE HAD A HAND IN THIS.
WHOEVER'S RESPONSIBLE HAS COMMITTED A SERIOUS CRIME.
I DON'T THINK WE SHOULD CAST ASPERSIONS ON ANYONE UNTIL...
OH DEAR...
IT AP-PEARS THAT...
...MR. OGI KNOWS SOMETHING ABOUT THIS.

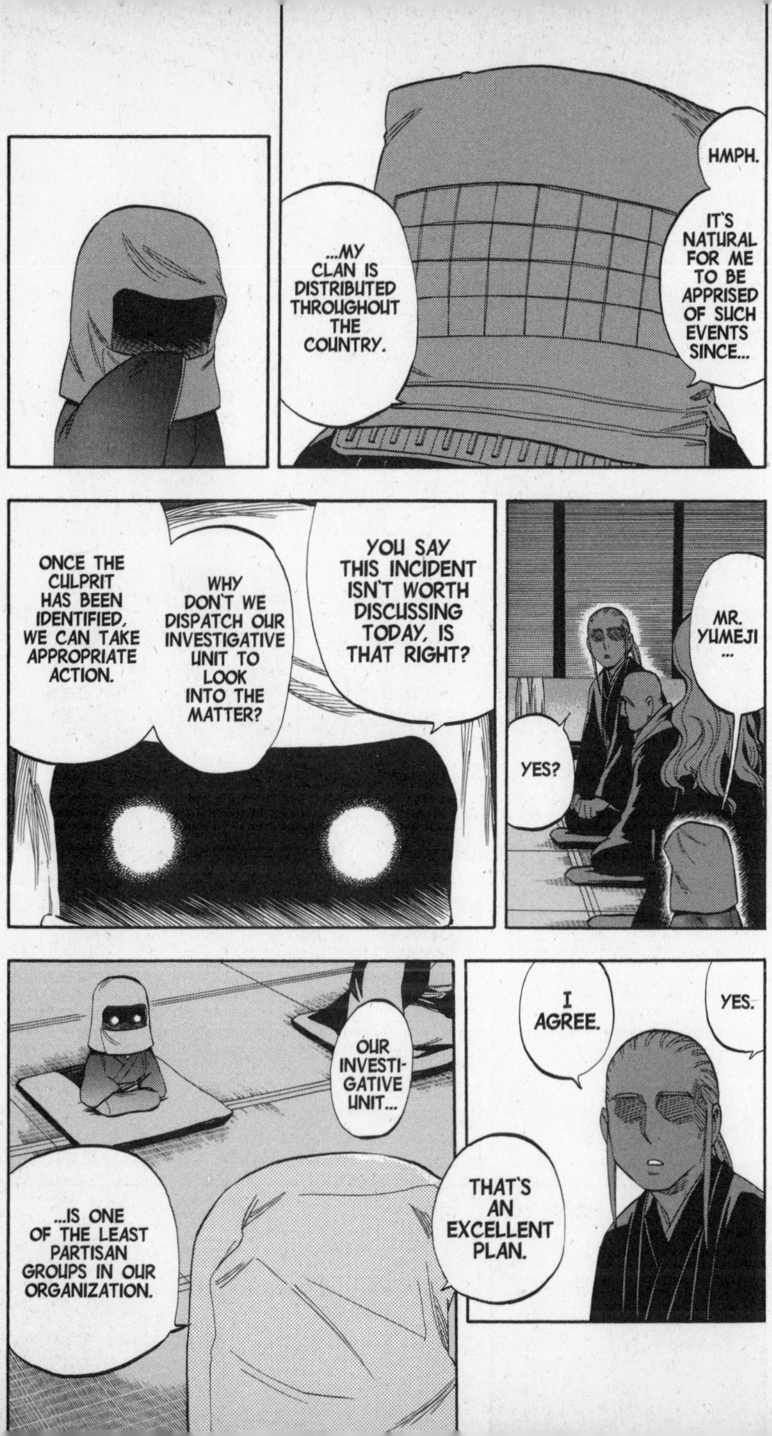
HMPH.
IT'S NATURAL FOR ME TO BE APPRISED OF SUCH EVENTS SINCE...
...MY CLAN IS DISTRIBUTED THROUGHOUT THE COUNTRY.
MR. YUMEJI ...
YES?
YOU SAY THIS INCIDENT ISN'T WORTH DISCUSSING TODAY, IS THAT RIGHT?
WHY DON'T WE DISPATCH OUR INVESTIGATIVE UNIT TO LOOK INTO THE MATTER?
ONCE THE CULPRIT HAS BEEN IDENTIFIED, WE CAN TAKE APPROPRIATE ACTION.
YES.
I AGREE.
THAT'S AN EXCELLENT PLAN.
OUR INVESTI-GATIVE UNIT...
...IS ONE OF THE LEAST PARTISAN GROUPS IN OUR ORGANIZATION.

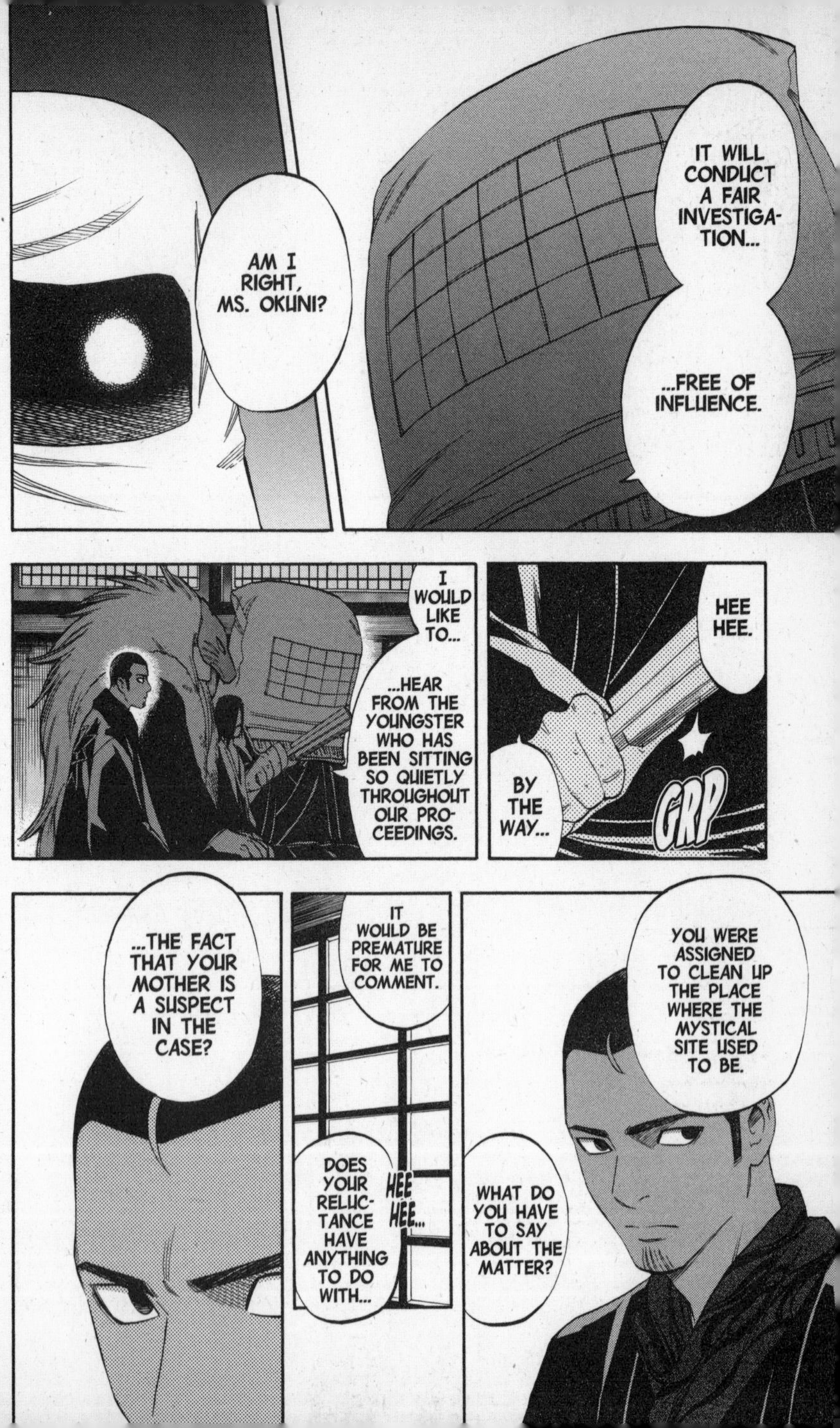
IT WILL CONDUCT A FAIR INVESTIGATION...
...FREE OF INFLUENCE.
AM I RIGHT, MS. OKUNI?
HEE HEE.
GRP
BY THE WAY...
I WOULD LIKE TO...
...HEAR FROM THE YOUNGSTER WHO HAS BEEN SITTING SO QUIETLY THROUGHOUT OUR PROCEEDINGS.
YOU WERE ASSIGNED TO CLEAN UP THE PLACE WHERE THE MYSTICAL SITE USED TO BE.
WHAT DO YOU HAVE TO SAY ABOUT THE MATTER?
IT WOULD BE PREMATURE FOR ME TO COMMENT.
HEE HEE...
DOES YOUR RELUCTANCE HAVE ANYTHING TO DO WITH...
...THE FACT THAT YOUR MOTHER IS A SUSPECT IN THE CASE?

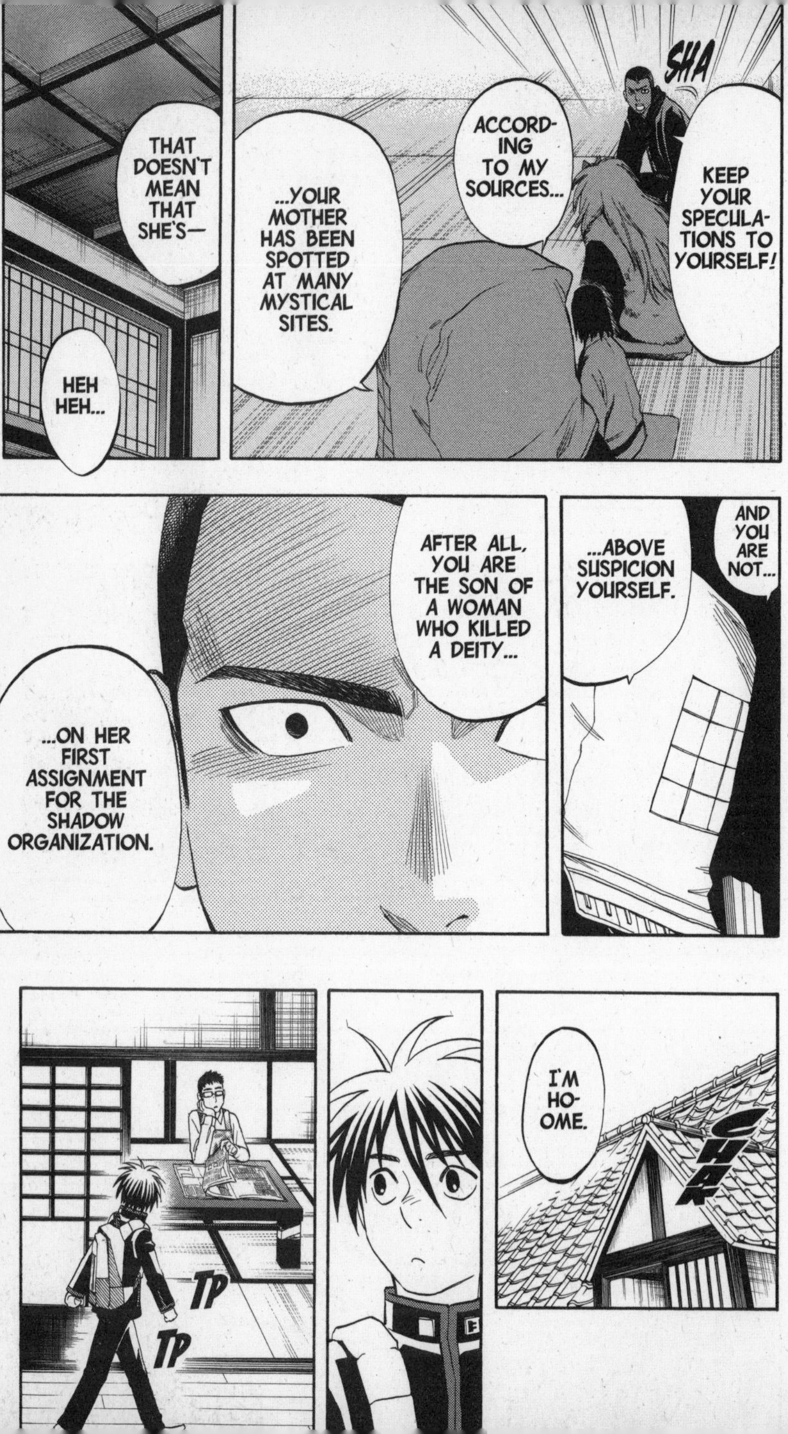
SHA
KEEP YOUR SPECULATIONS TO YOURSELF!
ACCORDING TO MY SOURCES...
...YOUR MOTHER HAS BEEN SPOTTED AT MANY MYSTICAL SITES.
THAT DOESN'T MEAN THAT SHE'S—
HEH HEH...
AND YOU ARE NOT...
...ABOVE SUSPICION YOURSELF.
AFTER ALL, YOU ARE THE SON OF A WOMAN WHO KILLED A DEITY...
...ON HER FIRST ASSIGNMENT FOR THE SHADOW ORGANIZATION.
I'M HO-OME.
CHAK
TP
TP

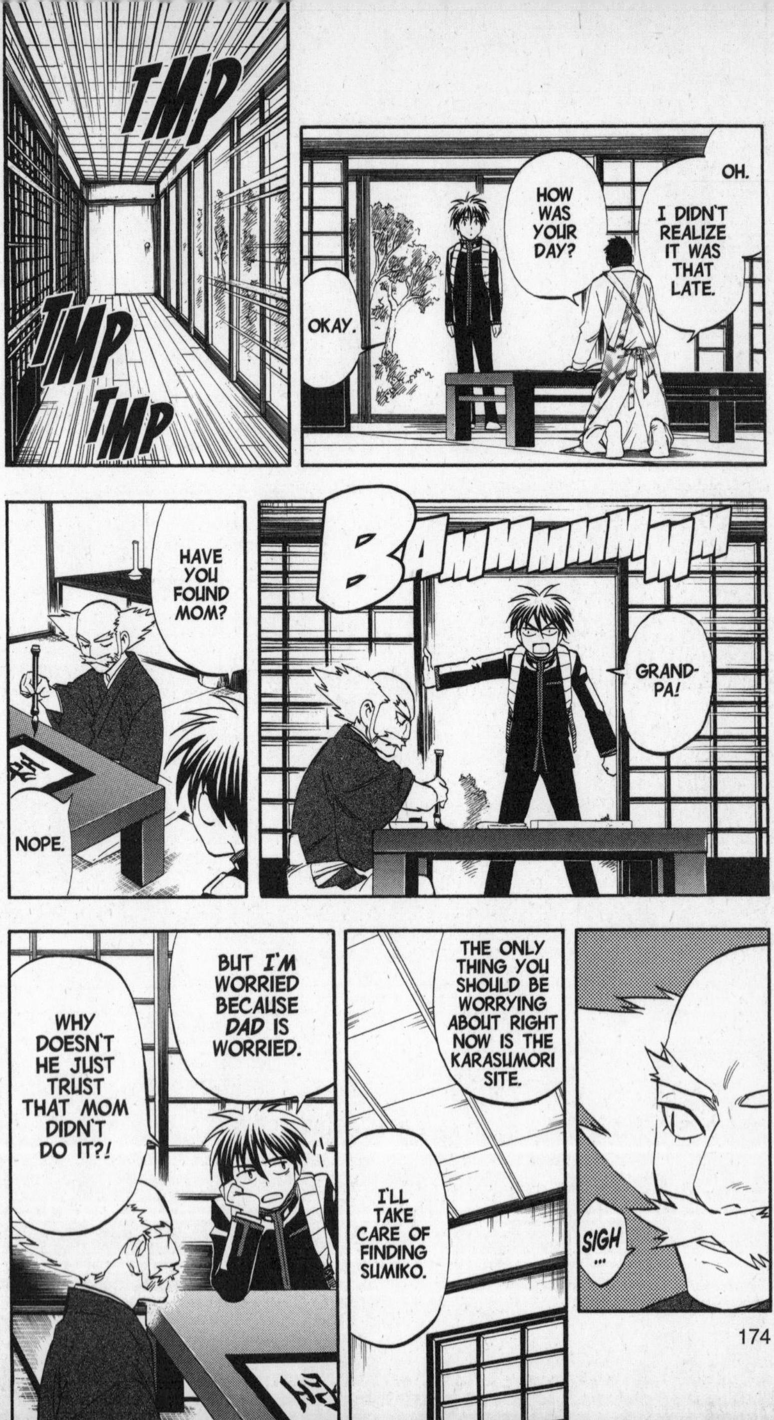
OH.
I DIDN'T REALIZE IT WAS THAT LATE.
HOW WAS YOUR DAY?
OKAY.
TMP
TMP
TMP
BAMMMMMMM
GRAND-PA!
HAVE YOU FOUND MOM?
NOPE.
SIGH...
THE ONLY THING YOU SHOULD BE WORRYING ABOUT RIGHT NOW IS THE KARASUMORI SITE.
I'LL TAKE CARE OF FINDING SUMIKO.
BUT *I'M* WORRIED BECAUSE *DAD* IS WORRIED.
WHY DOESN'T HE JUST TRUST THAT MOM DIDN'T DO IT?!

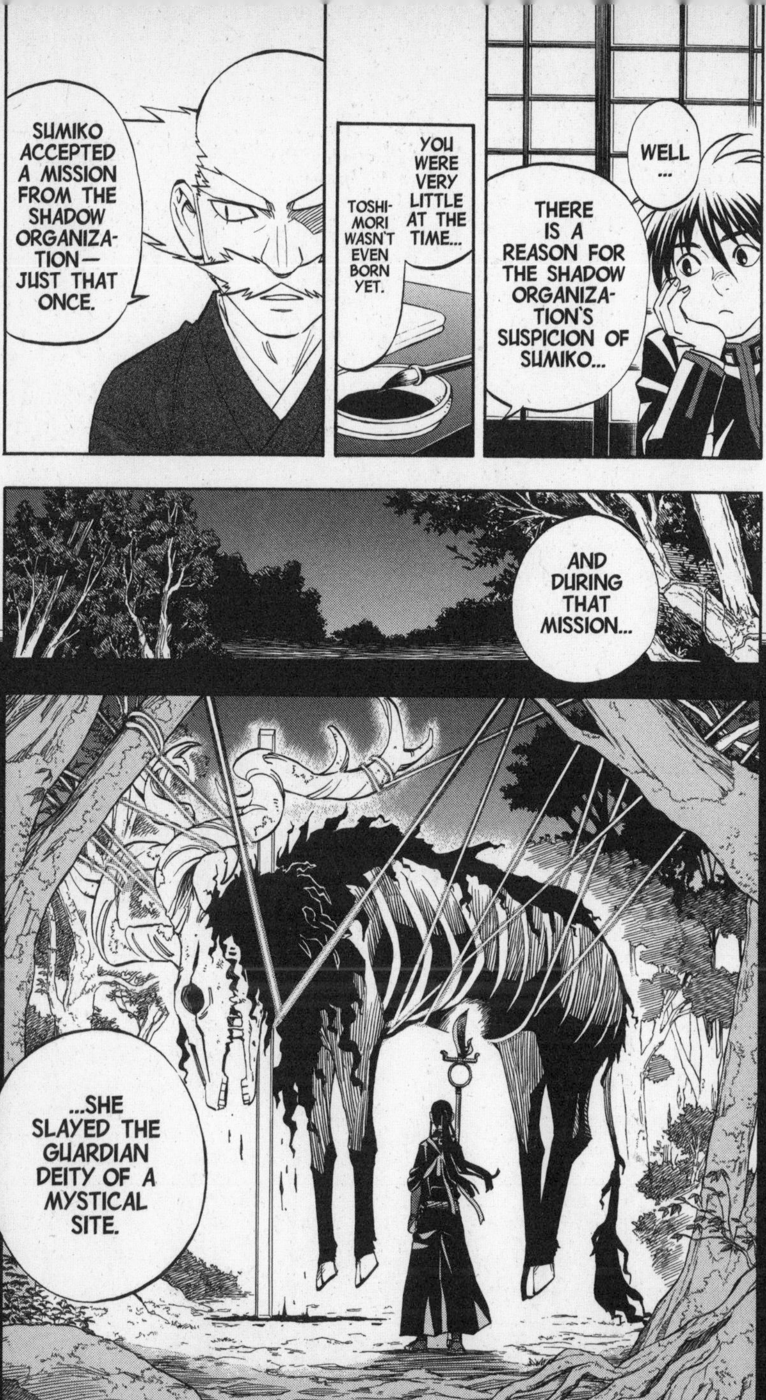
WELL ...
THERE IS A REASON FOR THE SHADOW ORGANIZATION'S SUSPICION OF SUMIKO...
YOU WERE VERY LITTLE AT THE TIME...
TOSHIMORI WASN'T EVEN BORN YET.
SUMIKO ACCEPTED A MISSION FROM THE SHADOW ORGANIZATION—JUST THAT ONCE.
AND DURING THAT MISSION...
...SHE SLAYED THE GUARDIAN DEITY OF A MYSTICAL SITE.

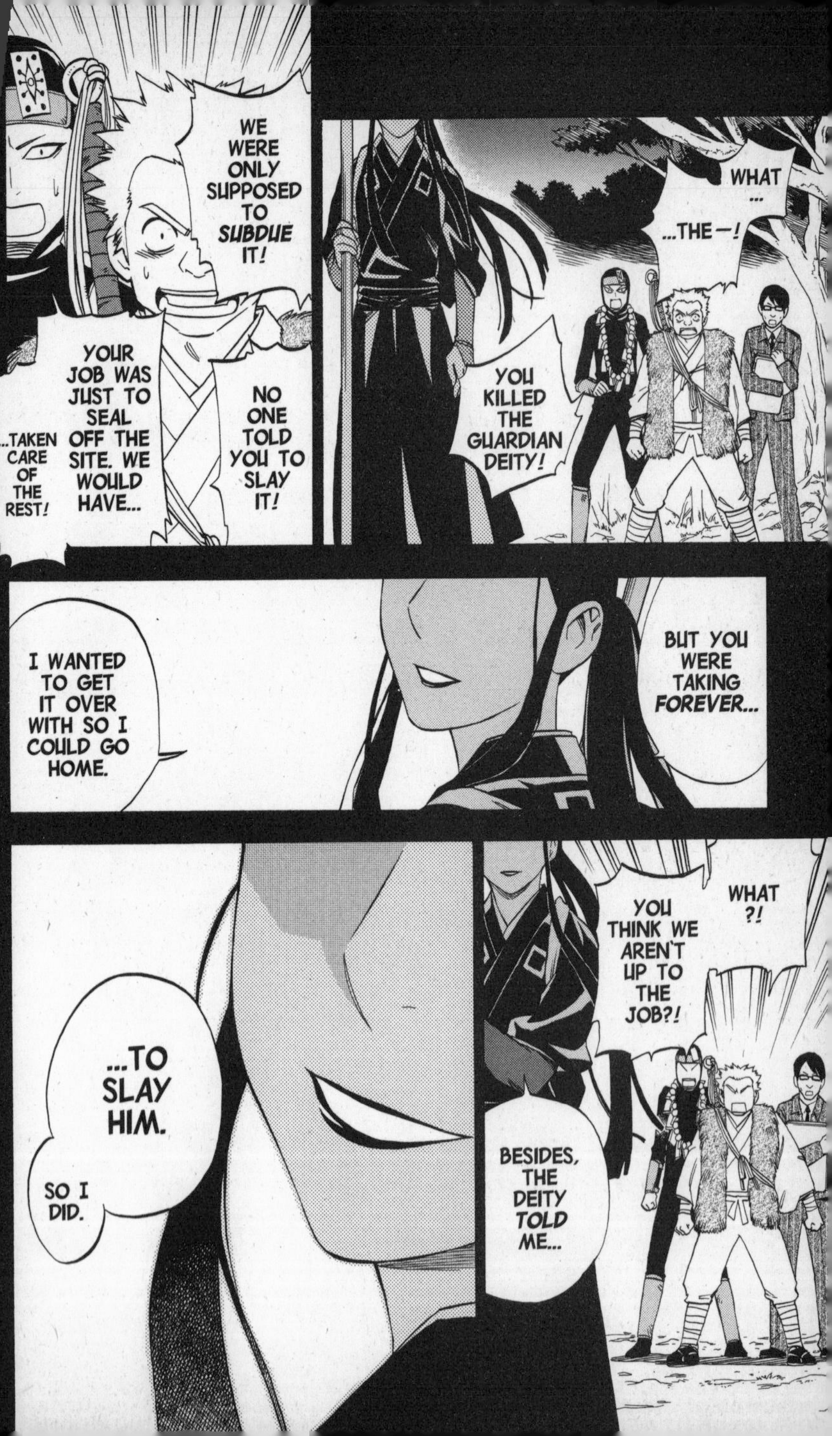
WHAT... ...THE—!
YOU KILLED THE GUARDIAN DEITY!
WE WERE ONLY SUPPOSED TO *SUBDUE* IT!
NO ONE TOLD YOU TO SLAY IT!
YOUR JOB WAS JUST TO SEAL OFF THE SITE. WE WOULD HAVE...
...TAKEN CARE OF THE REST!
BUT YOU WERE TAKING *FOREVER*...
I WANTED TO GET IT OVER WITH SO I COULD GO HOME.
WHAT?!
YOU THINK WE AREN'T UP TO THE JOB?!
BESIDES, THE DEITY *TOLD* ME...
...TO SLAY HIM.
SO I DID.

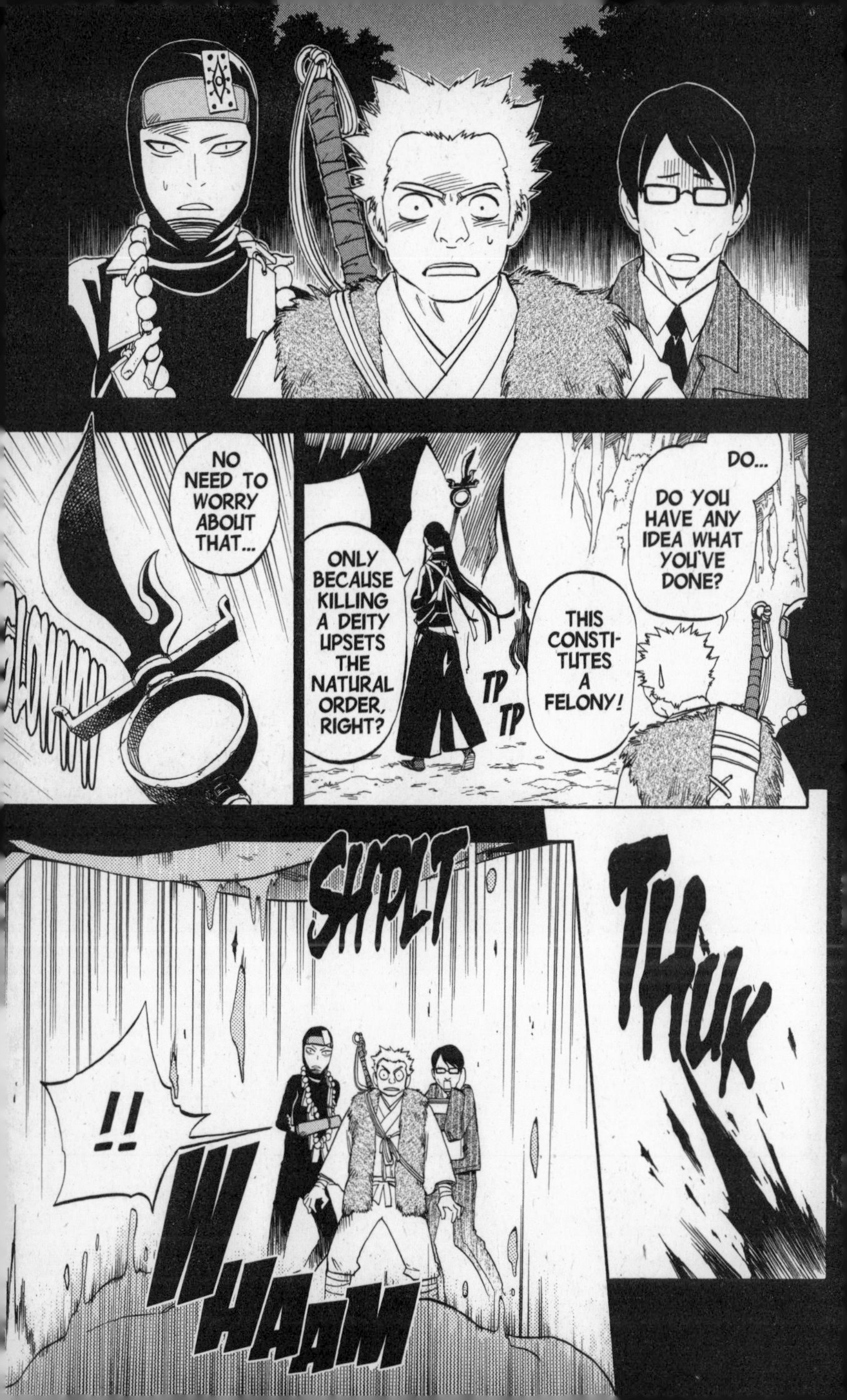
DO...
DO YOU HAVE ANY IDEA WHAT YOU'VE DONE?
THIS CONSTITUTES A FELONY!
TP TP
ONLY BECAUSE KILLING A DEITY UPSETS THE NATURAL ORDER, RIGHT?
NO NEED TO WORRY ABOUT THAT...
THUK
SHPLT
!!
WHAAM

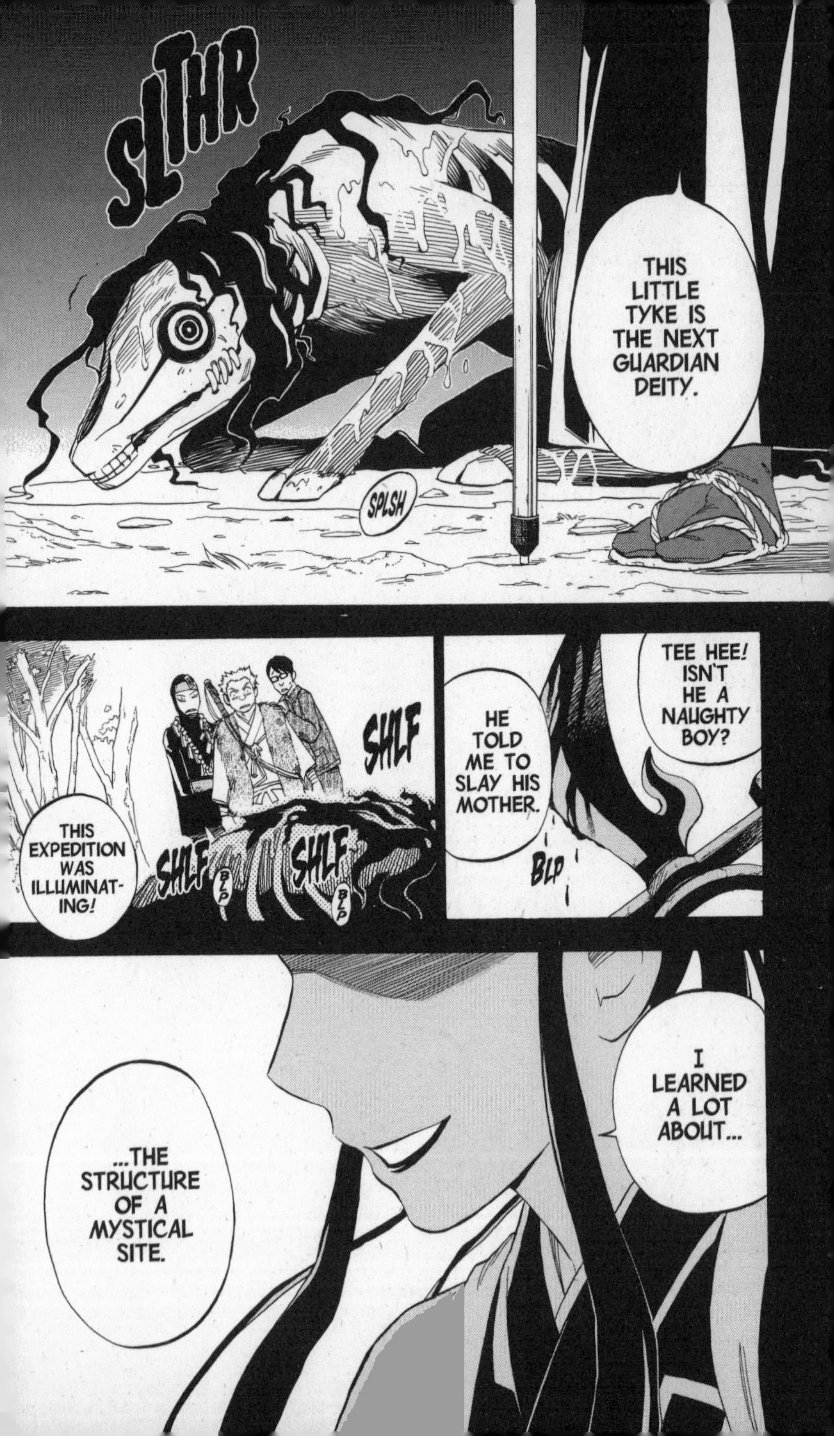
THIS LITTLE TYKE IS THE NEXT GUARDIAN DEITY.
SLITHR
SPLSH
TEE HEE! ISN'T HE A NAUGHTY BOY?
HE TOLD ME TO SLAY HIS MOTHER.
BLP
SHLF
THIS EXPEDITION WAS ILLUMINAT-ING!
SHLF
BLP
SHLF
BLP
I LEARNED A LOT ABOUT...
...THE STRUCTURE OF A MYSTICAL SITE.

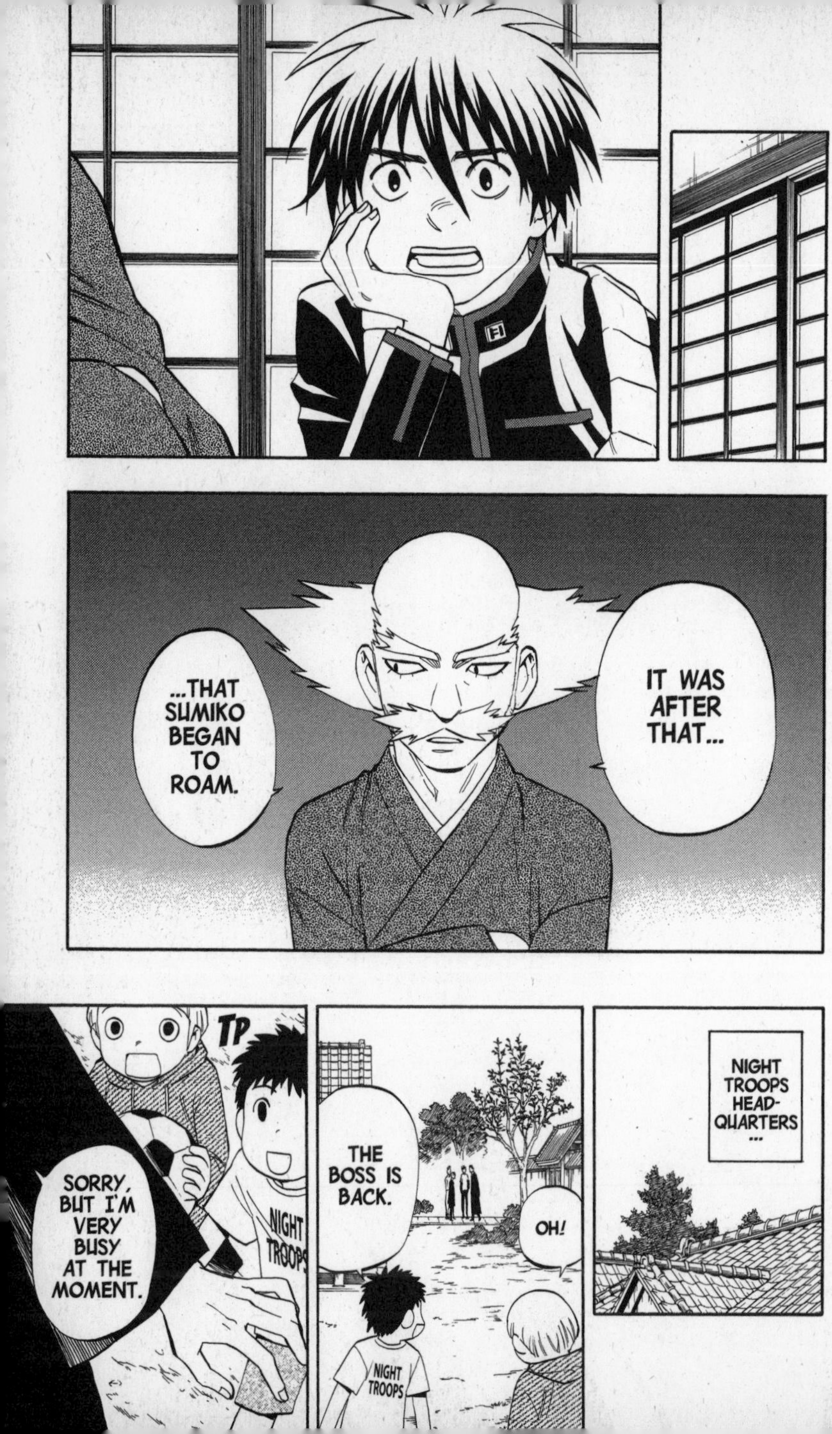
IT WAS AFTER THAT...
...THAT SUMIKO BEGAN TO ROAM.
NIGHT TROOPS HEAD-QUARTERS ...
OH!
THE BOSS IS BACK.
NIGHT TROOPS
TP
NIGHT TROOPS
SORRY, BUT I'M VERY BUSY AT THE MOMENT.

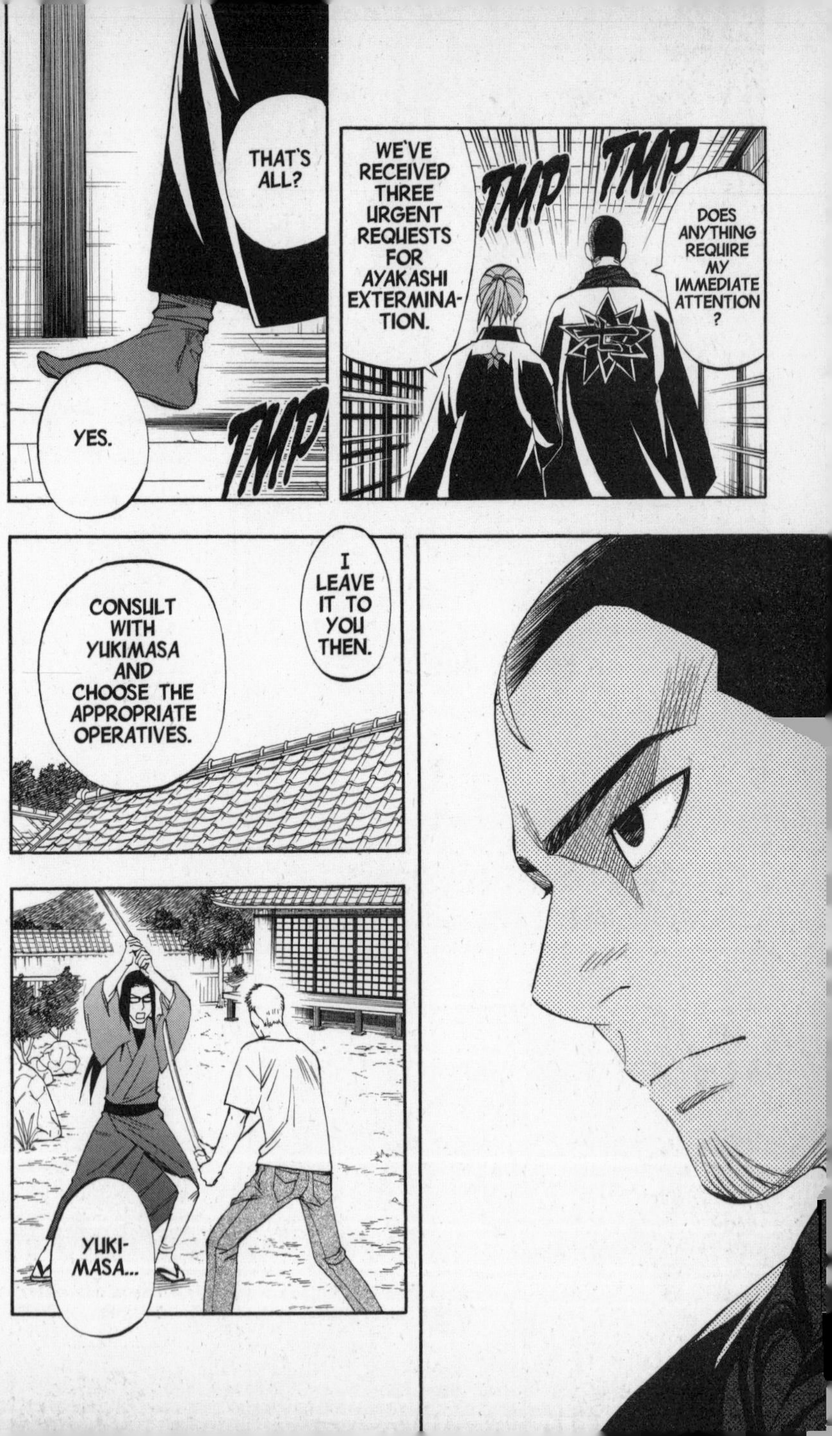
TMP TMP
DOES ANYTHING REQUIRE MY IMMEDIATE ATTENTION?
WE'VE RECEIVED THREE URGENT REQUESTS FOR AYAKASHI EXTERMINATION.
THAT'S ALL?
YES.
TMP
I LEAVE IT TO YOU THEN.
CONSULT WITH YUKIMASA AND CHOOSE THE APPROPRIATE OPERATIVES.
YUKIMASA...

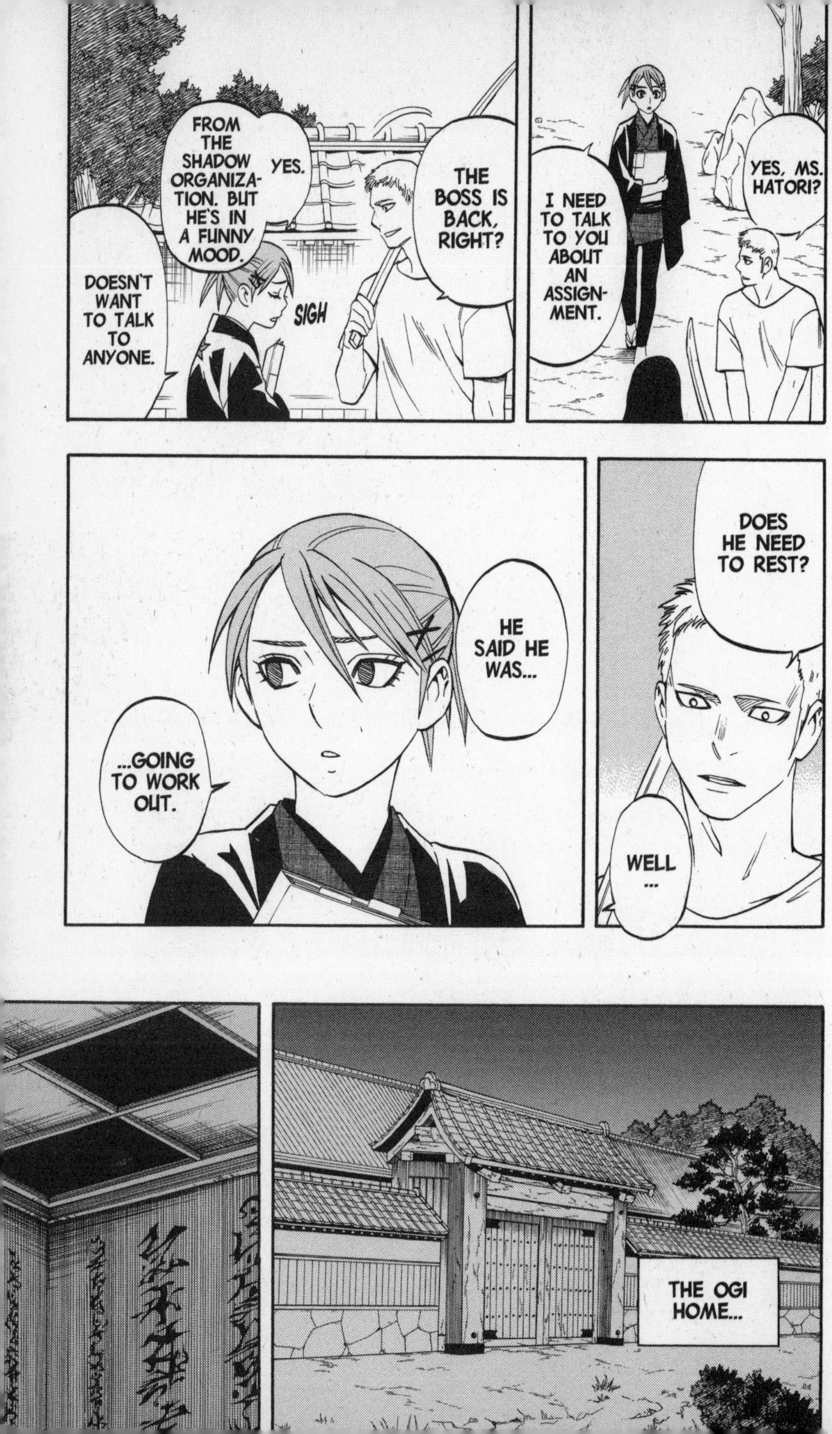
YES, MS. HATORI?
I NEED TO TALK TO YOU ABOUT AN ASSIGNMENT.
THE BOSS IS BACK, RIGHT?
YES.
FROM THE SHADOW ORGANIZATION. BUT HE'S IN A FUNNY MOOD.
SIGH
DOESN'T WANT TO TALK TO ANYONE.
DOES HE NEED TO REST?
WELL...
HE SAID HE WAS...
...GOING TO WORK OUT.
THE OGI HOME...

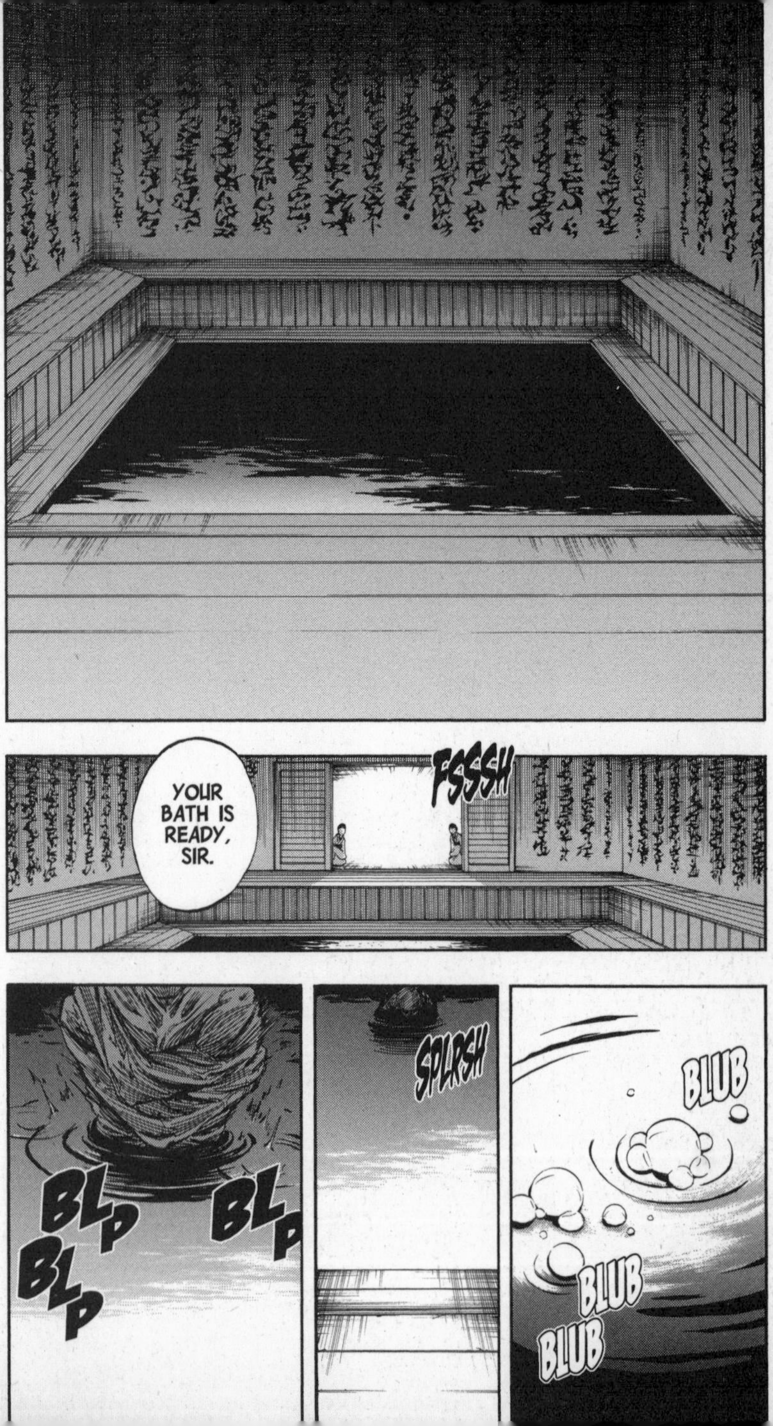
FSSSH
YOUR BATH IS READY, SIR.
BLUB
BLUB
BLUB
SPLASH
BLP
BLP
BLP

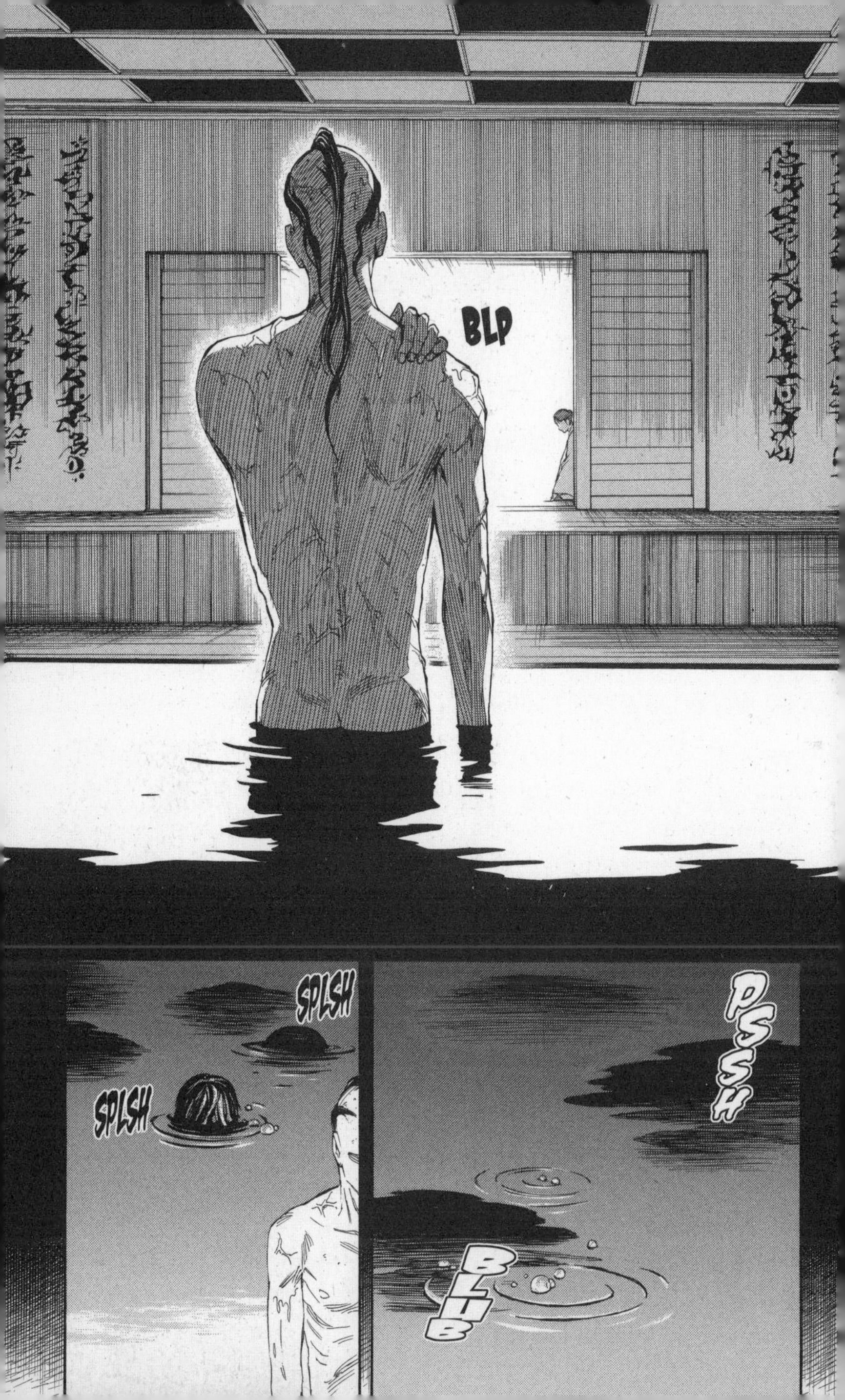
BLP
PSSH
BLUB
SPLSH
SPLSH

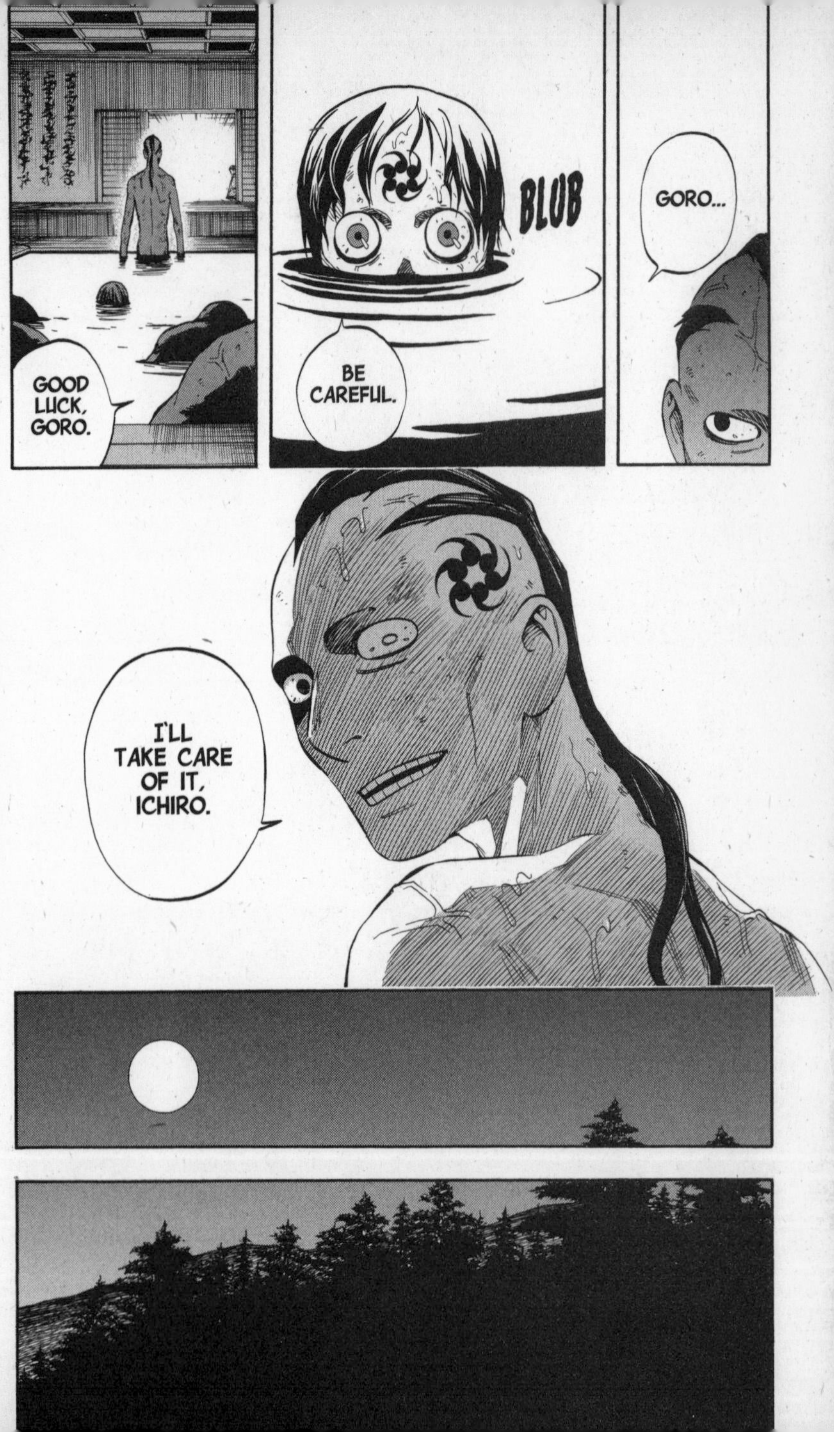
GORO...
BLUB
BE CAREFUL.
GOOD LUCK, GORO.
I'LL TAKE CARE OF IT, ICHIRO.

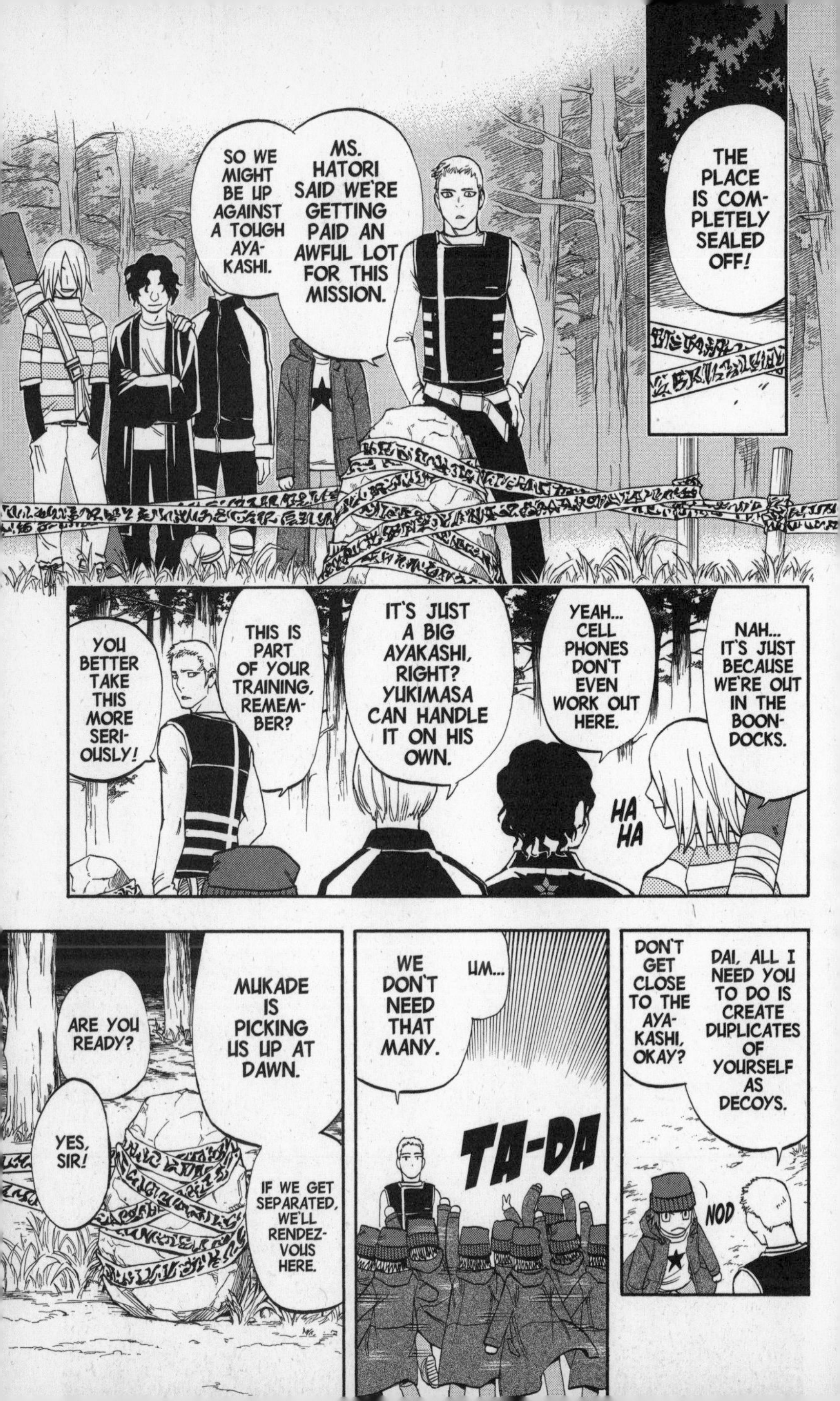
THE PLACE IS COMPLETELY SEALED OFF!
MS. HATORI SAID WE'RE GETTING PAID AN AWFUL LOT FOR THIS MISSION.
SO WE MIGHT BE UP AGAINST A TOUGH AYAKASHI.
NAH... IT'S JUST BECAUSE WE'RE OUT IN THE BOONDOCKS.
YEAH... CELL PHONES DON'T EVEN WORK OUT HERE.
HA HA
IT'S JUST A BIG AYAKASHI, RIGHT? YUKIMASA CAN HANDLE IT ON HIS OWN.
THIS IS PART OF YOUR TRAINING, REMEMBER?
YOU BETTER TAKE THIS MORE SERIOUSLY!
DAI, ALL I NEED YOU TO DO IS CREATE DUPLICATES OF YOURSELF AS DECOYS.
DON'T GET CLOSE TO THE AYAKASHI, OKAY?
NOD
UM...
WE DON'T NEED THAT MANY.
TA-DA
MUKADE IS PICKING US UP AT DAWN.
IF WE GET SEPARATED, WE'LL RENDEZVOUS HERE.
ARE YOU READY?
YES, SIR!

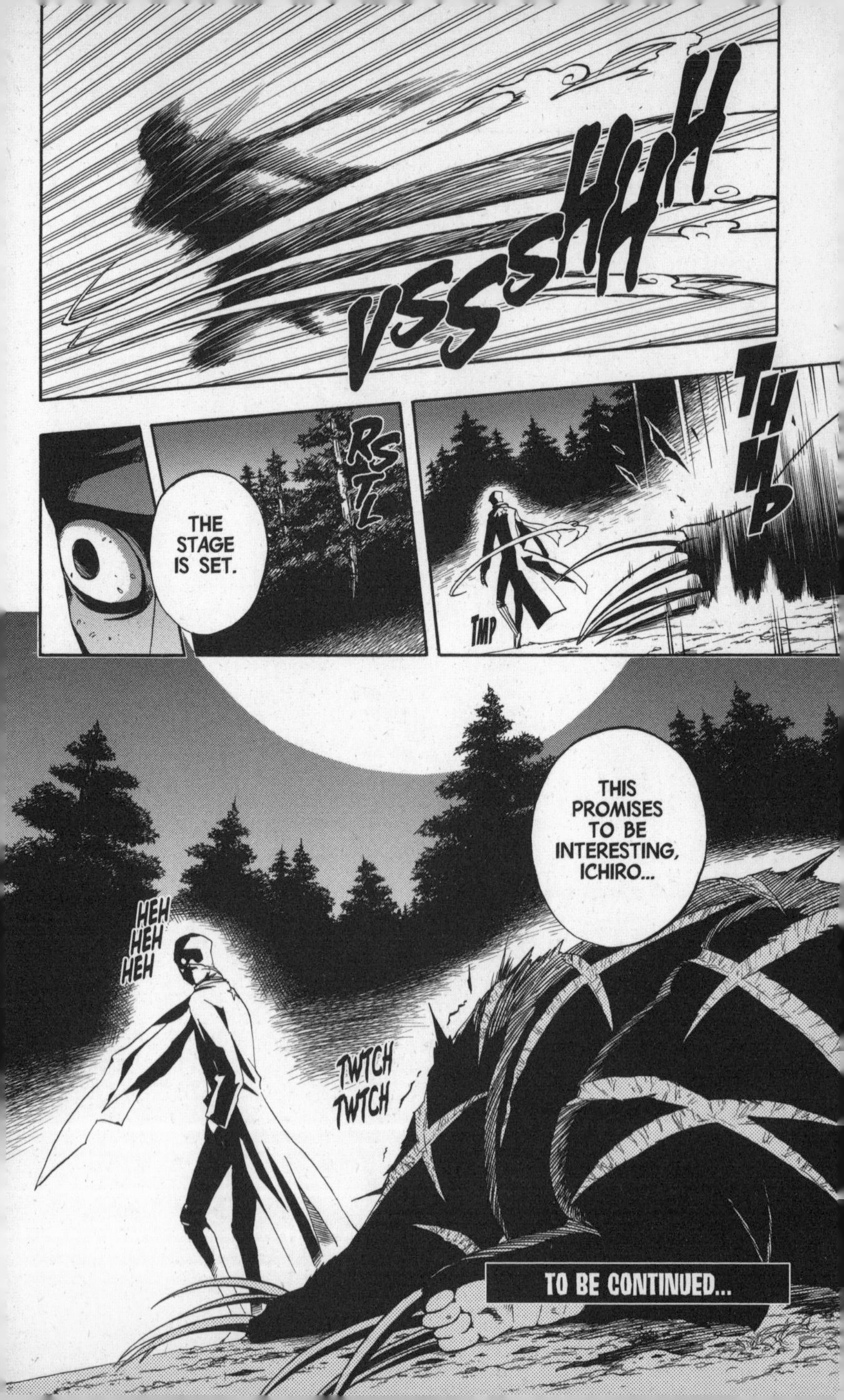
VSSSHHHH
THMP
TMP
RSTL
THE STAGE IS SET.
THIS PROMISES TO BE INTERESTING, ICHIRO...
HEH HEH HEH
TWTCH TWTCH
TO BE CONTINUED...

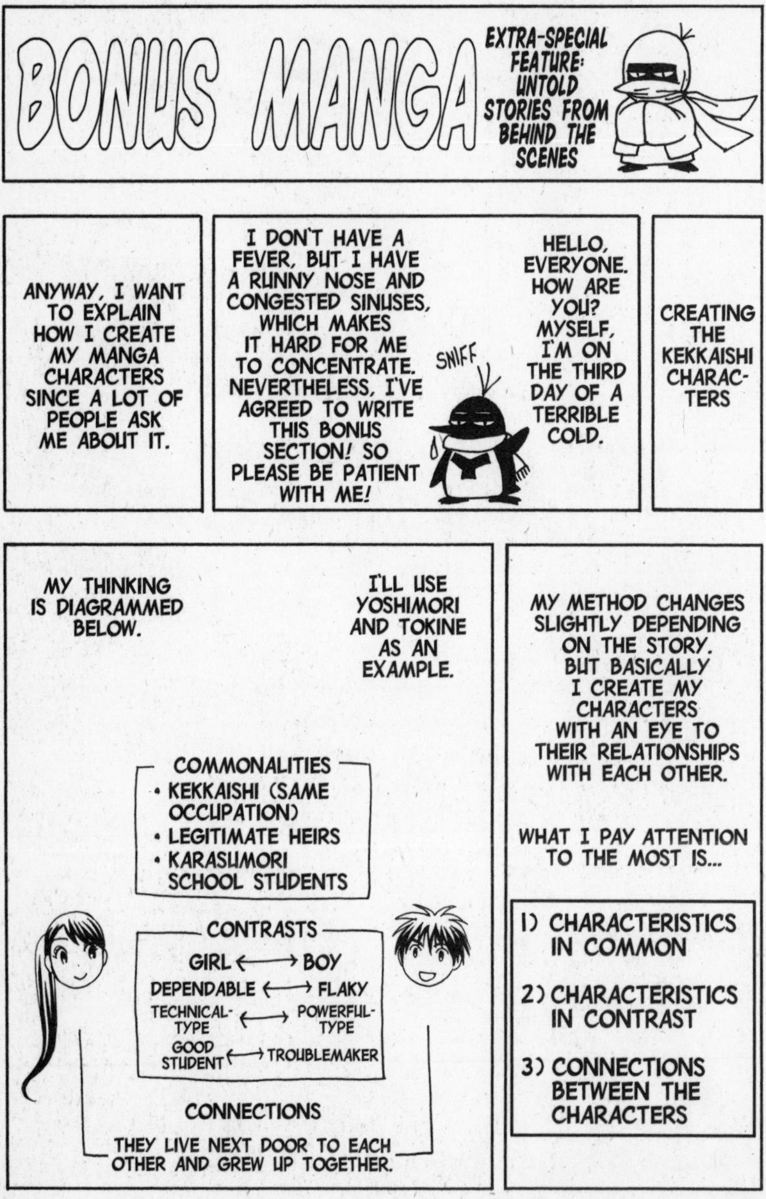
BONUS MANGA
EXTRA-SPECIAL FEATURE: UNTOLD STORIES FROM BEHIND THE SCENES
CREATING THE KEKKAISHI CHARACTERS
HELLO, EVERYONE. HOW ARE YOU? MYSELF, I'M ON THE THIRD DAY OF A TERRIBLE COLD.
I DON'T HAVE A FEVER, BUT I HAVE A RUNNY NOSE AND CONGESTED SINUSES, WHICH MAKES IT HARD FOR ME TO CONCENTRATE. NEVERTHELESS, I'VE AGREED TO WRITE THIS BONUS SECTION! SO PLEASE BE PATIENT WITH ME!
SNIFF
ANYWAY, I WANT TO EXPLAIN HOW I CREATE MY MANGA CHARACTERS SINCE A LOT OF PEOPLE ASK ME ABOUT IT.
MY METHOD CHANGES SLIGHTLY DEPENDING ON THE STORY. BUT BASICALLY I CREATE MY CHARACTERS WITH AN EYE TO THEIR RELATIONSHIPS WITH EACH OTHER.
WHAT I PAY ATTENTION TO THE MOST IS...
1) CHARACTERISTICS IN COMMON
2) CHARACTERISTICS IN CONTRAST
3) CONNECTIONS BETWEEN THE CHARACTERS
I'LL USE YOSHIMORI AND TOKINE AS AN EXAMPLE.
MY THINKING IS DIAGRAMMED BELOW.
COMMONALITIES
• KEKKAISHI (SAME OCCUPATION)
• LEGITIMATE HEIRS
• KARASUMORI SCHOOL STUDENTS
CONTRASTS
GIRL ⟷ BOY
DEPENDABLE ⟷ FLAKY
TECHNICAL-TYPE ⟷ POWERFUL-TYPE
GOOD STUDENT ⟷ TROUBLEMAKER
CONNECTIONS
THEY LIVE NEXT DOOR TO EACH OTHER AND GREW UP TOGETHER.

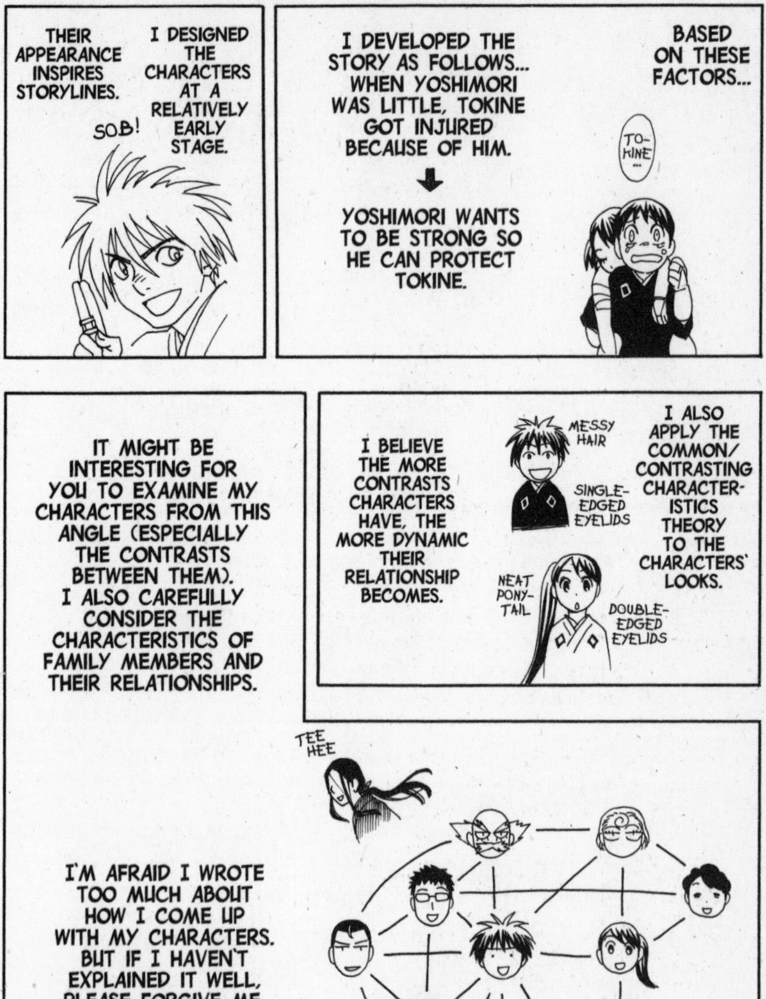
BASED ON THESE FACTORS...
I DEVELOPED THE STORY AS FOLLOWS... WHEN YOSHIMORI WAS LITTLE, TOKINE GOT INJURED BECAUSE OF HIM.
YOSHIMORI WANTS TO BE STRONG SO HE CAN PROTECT TOKINE.
TO-KINE...
I DESIGNED THE CHARACTERS AT A RELATIVELY EARLY STAGE.
THEIR APPEARANCE INSPIRES STORYLINES.
SOB!
I ALSO APPLY THE COMMON/CONTRASTING CHARACTER-ISTICS THEORY TO THE CHARACTERS' LOOKS.
MESSY HAIR
SINGLE-EDGED EYELIDS
I BELIEVE THE MORE CONTRASTS CHARACTERS HAVE, THE MORE DYNAMIC THEIR RELATIONSHIP BECOMES.
NEAT PONY-TAIL
DOUBLE-EDGED EYELIDS
IT MIGHT BE INTERESTING FOR YOU TO EXAMINE MY CHARACTERS FROM THIS ANGLE (ESPECIALLY THE CONTRASTS BETWEEN THEM). I ALSO CAREFULLY CONSIDER THE CHARACTERISTICS OF FAMILY MEMBERS AND THEIR RELATIONSHIPS.
TEE HEE
I'M AFRAID I WROTE TOO MUCH ABOUT HOW I COME UP WITH MY CHARACTERS. BUT IF I HAVEN'T EXPLAINED IT WELL, PLEASE FORGIVE ME, BECAUSE I HAVE A BAD COLD.

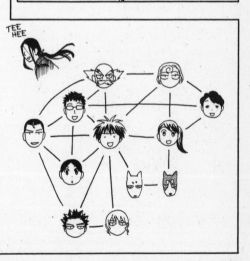

MESSAGE FROM YELLOW TANABE

When I was in elementary school, I spent my summer vacations catching insects in the countryside. (I had nothing else to do.) In my prime, I could catch dragonflies in midair with a graceful swoop of my net—or deftly capture swallowtail butterflies in my bare hands.

Even now, if I see an insect buzzing around a room, my hunting instinct kicks in. I have a hard time suppressing the urge to go after it...

KEKKAISHI

VOLUME 19

SHONEN SUNDAY EDITION

STORY AND ART BY YELLOW TANABE

Translation/Yuko Sawada
Touch-up Art & Lettering/Stephen Dutro
Cover Design & Graphic Layout/Julie Behn
Editor/Annette Roman

VP, Production/Alvin Lu
VP, Publishing Licensing/Rika Inouye
VP, Sales & Product Marketing/Gonzalo Ferreyra
VP, Creative/Linda Espinosa
Publisher/Hyoe Narita

KEKKAISHI 19 by Yellow TANABE © 2008 Yellow TANABE
All rights reserved. Original Japanese edition published in 2008 by
Shogakukan Inc., Tokyo.

The rights of the author(s) of the work(s) in this publication to be
so identified have been asserted in accordance with the Copyright,
Designs and Patents Act 1988. A CIP catalogue record for this book is
available from the British Library.

The stories, characters and incidents mentioned in this publication are
entirely fictional.

Printed in the U.S.A.

Published by VIZ Media, LLC
P.O. Box 77010
San Francisco, CA 94107

10 9 8 7 6 5 4 3 2 1
First printing, November 2009

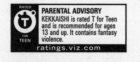

PARENTAL ADVISORY
KEKKAISHI is rated T for Teen
and is recommended for ages
13 and up. It contains fantasy
violence.
ratings.viz.com

www.viz.com

WWW.SHONENSUNDAY.COM

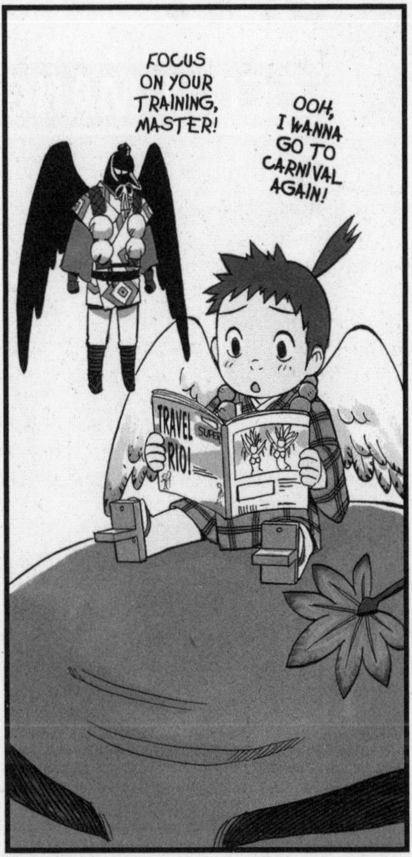
OOH, I WANNA GO TO CARNIVAL AGAIN!
FOCUS ON YOUR TRAINING, MASTER!
TRAVEL SUPER RIO!